Mavis Gates

THE COMPLETE GUIDE TO PATTERN-MAKING

THE COMPLETE GUIDE TO PATTERN-MAKING

by Dr. Barbara K. Nordquist

ᛞ DRAKE PUBLISHERS INC   NEW YORK

Published in 1974 by
Drake Publishers Inc.
381 Park Avenue South
New York, New York 10016

© Barbara K. Nordquist, 1973

Library of Congress Cataloging In Publication Data

Nordquist, Barbara.
   The complete guide to pattern-making.

   1. Dressmaking—Pattern design. 2. Children's clothing—
Pattern design. I. Title.
TT520.N66 646.4'04 73-18041
ISBN 0-87749-595-5

Printed in the United States of America

TO MY PARENTS, PETER AND ALICE ALTPETER, MY HUSBAND, MYRON, AND MY STUDENTS

All have been a part of my life, my growth, and my happiness.

TABLE OF CONTENTS

CHAPTER I   DESIGNING PATTERNS   11

CHAPTER II   PLACEMENT OF GRAIN MARKINGS   15

CHAPTER III   USE OF PATTERN-MAKING EQUIPMENT   17

CHAPTER IV   THE BODICE FRONT   21

                               The Process of Bodice Front Pattern-Making by the Flat-Pattern Method. The Eight Basic Steps   21

                               Manipulation to Two Darts   44

                               Manipulation to Three Darts   46

                               Manipulation to Waist Tucks   48

                               Cowl Neck   50

                               Cowl Neck with Dart   52

                               Yoke in Bodice   54

                               Adding Fullness   56

                               Lowered Neckline with Fullness Added   58

                               Fullness Added Under Bust   60

                               Traditional Princess Line—Darts into Seams   62

                               Princess Variation—Darts into Seams   64

                               Asymmetrical Bodice Front   66

                               Bodice Front Pleats   68

                               Bodice Front and Back—Lowered Shoulder   70

CHAPTER V	THE BODICE BACK	73

    Traditional Princess Line—Bodice Back—Darts into Seams   78

    Bodice Back Pleats   80

CHAPTER VI	THE SLEEVE	83

    Sleeve with Short Top Pleat   88

    Shirtwaist Sleeve   89

    Bell Sleeve   92

    Bishop Sleeve   94

    Sleeve with Short Bottom Puff   96

    Sleeve with Full Puff   97

    Sleeve with Short Top Puff   98

    Lantern Sleeve   99

    Petal Sleeve   100

    Two-Piece Sleeve   102

    Elizabethan Sleeve   104

    Epaulet Sleeve   107

    Kimono Sleeve   110

    Dolman Sleeve   112

    Kimono Sleeve with Gusset   114

    Raglan Sleeve   117

    Cap Sleeve   120

CHAPTER VII	FACINGS AND BUTTON EXTENSIONS	123

    Button Extension, Front Facing   124

    Neck and Armhole Facings for Bodice Front and Back   125

    Neck and Armhole Facings for Bodice Front and Back with Lowered Neckline   126

    Sleeve Facing   127

CHAPTER VIII	SKIRTS	129

    Skirt with Three Darts   137

    Four-Gore or A-Line Skirt   139

	Peg-Top Skirt 141
	Peg-Top Skirt—Alternate Method 143
	Six-Gore Skirt 145
	Six-Gore Skirt with Flare 147
	Six-Gore Skirt and Flare and Gathers 150
	Twelve-Gore Trumpet Skirt 152
	Full-Circle Skirt 155
	Pleated Skirt 157
CHAPTER IX	ONE-PIECE GARMENTS 167
	Sheath Dress 167
	Princess-Line Back 170
	Princess-Line Front 172
CHAPTER X	COLLARS 175
	Full Roll and Peter Pan Collars 175
	Five Variations on the Basic Collar 178
	Sailor Collar 180
	Turtle-Neck Collar 182
	Ruffle Collar 183
	Mandarin Collar 184
	Shawl Collar 185
	Shawl Collar with Center Front Closing 187
	Shawl Collar Variations 189
CHAPTER XI	OUTER GARMENTS 191
	Narrow Cape 191
	Jacket 194
	Jacket Sleeve 196
	Coat 197
	Coat Sleeve 200
CHAPTER XII	PANTS 201
	Hip-Hugger Pants 202
	Flared or Bell-Bottom Pants 203

    Western-Style Slacks 205
    Pants with Yoke at Hip 207
    Slacks with Front Pleats and Cuffs 209
    Pants with Leg Fullness 211
    Points of Leg Flare for Pants 213
    Jumpsuit Pants 214

CHAPTER XIII   PUTTING IT ALL TOGETHER: THE COMPLETED GARMENT 217

CHAPTER XIV   MAKING A PERSONALIZED SLOPER 223

CHAPTER XV   VARIOUS LADIES' SHAPES 231

CHAPTER XVI   PERSONALIZED SLOPER FOR SLACKS 235

CHAPTER XVII   CHILDREN'S GARMENTS 239
    Child's Dress with Smocking 241
    Child's Pinafore with Front and Back Yokes 243
    Child's Dress with Puffed Sleeve and Gathered Skirt 246
    Child's Shirt or Blouse Without Shoulder Seams 248
    Child's Trapeze Dress 250
    Child's Traditional Shirt 252
    Child's Apron with Flare from Shoulder 255
    Child's Coat 258
    Child's Trousers 262

APPENDIX I   WOMEN'S SLOPERS—QUARTER-SCALE 263

APPENDIX II   WOMEN'S SLOPERS—HALF-SCALE 267

APPENDIX III   CHILDREN'S SLOPERS—FULL-SCALE

CHAPTER I

DESIGNING PATTERNS

To understand the process of making patterns for fashion designs one must bear in mind that fabric is two-dimensional and that the human figure is three-dimensional. The problem of the pattern-maker, therefore, is to convert the fabric from two to three dimensions. The easiest way to do this, as early civilizations discovered, is to drape the fabric on the body and to secure it with tucks, pins, or cords. The Greeks wore a *chiton,* which was simply a draped cloth secured at the shoulder with *fibulae* (pins) and at the bust, waist, and/or hips by girdles (cords or belts).

An exquisite example of the body-draping technique in use today is the Indian sari, which consists of a six-yard length of cloth, draped around the body, secured by pleats and folds, and tucked into the waist slip. An obvious disadvantage of this method of converting two dimensions to three is the lack of freedom of movement. Can you imagine trying to play tennis, to paint, or to garden in a sari? More versatile techniques of adapting two-dimensional fabric to the three-dimensional human body had to be developed.

Quite early in man's history the cutting and sewing of fabric to give shape, or a third dimension, was devised. A famous statue of the Minoan snake goddess (ca. 1700-1550 B.C.) shows a lady with a tight-fitting bodice and a skirt with ruffles which apparently were cut and sewn to a shaped skirt. The Aztecs of Mexico, with the aid of needle and thread found ready-made in the stems of the cactus plant, also produced shaped garments.

The styles and shapes of garments in ancient cultures often stayed the same for centuries. In the fast-moving society of today, styles can, and do, change two or even three times a year. The designer constantly searches for new solutions to the old problem—how to make the two-dimensional fabric fit the three-dimensional figure in an exciting, different way.

To solve this problem, three systems of pattern-making have evolved: draping, drafting, and flat pattern.

Draping

Draping (in modern usage) is a method of pattern-making whereby the designer uses a padded, adjustable dress form. Fabric is draped on the form in the desired shape. From the draped design the pattern is made.

When draping the designer may use the dress fabric or, more commonly, he may use a similar weight of muslin. The draping technique allows for considerable freedom of expression and variations in taste and is probably the most creative method of making patterns. However, it should be noted that this method of pattern-making often wastes material. The designer must use more fabric than for the same garment made by another method.

Drafting

Drafting consists of making patterns by using measurements. The first task in designing by drafting is to measure the figure. These measurements are then used to develop a basic pattern according to specific relationships among these measurements. The drafter commonly uses a guidebook to aid in this process.

Because precise drafting is tedious work, this method of making patterns is more often used for mass-produced garments or for shops specializing in a limited number of designs. Once the pattern is drafted, it will be used many times to produce the design desired.

Some use of drafting is necessary with any of the techniques. The draper or flat-pattern worker finds drafting an efficient way to make collars and closures for example.

Flat Pattern

Flat pattern makes use of a standard sloper or basic pattern graded to a marketable size. In the United States, common sizes are: Misses 8, 10, 12, 14, 16; Junior 7, 9, 11, 13; Children's 2, 4, 6, 8, 10, and so forth.

If you sew, you have probably already discovered that pattern companies' sizes vary. You may know which one makes a pattern most closely fitted to your figure.

When you purchase clothes, you know which size to look for and in which designation (Misses, Children's, Junior). If you have discovered that certain manufacturers' clothes fit you better than any others, you may have wondered why.

The reason for the better fit, whether in a pattern or a manufactured garment, is that the particular manufacturer happens to use a basic pattern which resembles your figure. From this basic sloper all his clothes are developed.

The first task in designing your own pattern by the flat-pattern method is to develop a basic pattern, or sloper, to fit your figure as perfectly as possible. From this sloper you can make most of the designs used today.

The pattern-making method described in this book is primarily the flat-pattern method. It is the easiest method for a beginner and has the advantage that nearly any design can be made from a flat-pattern sloper. Some designs will require the use of drafting techniques as well. However, this is simple drafting and only a few measurements are required.

Once you are familiar with the pattern-making method followed in this text you should be able to work out the relationships between sizes and styles. You should

13 DESIGNING PATTERNS

also be able to adapt drafted additions to the flat pattern by thinking through what you are trying to accomplish. For example, when making gussets, certain collar styles, and capes, you are given measurements to follow. After you have completed these patterns as described in the text, it should be simple for you to develop your own variations following the principles you have mastered.

The method of pattern-making followed in this text has an important advantage: it releases you from dependence upon the text once you have gone through each basic procedure. To be really useful and fun pattern-making must be easy and free-flowing. It must allow you to express yourself after you have learned the fundamentals. The method followed in this book will permit just that.

The proper procedure to follow is to make each of the patterns in this book in the order given. Use the half-scale or quarter-scale slopers provided in the appendices at the back of the book and go through each pattern step by step. Follow the steps given with each pattern.

Once you have made all the patterns in half-scale or quarter-scale, develop a sloper for yourself or the person for whom you wish to make full-size garments. See Chapter XIV for making a dress sloper and Chapter XVI for making a pants sloper.

One additional word of advice. When you are presented with a new fashion design and are in a quandry about how to make it, get out your half-scale patterns and start to work with those. By following the basic principles described in the book, you should have no difficulty working out the new design. It will then be immediately apparent whether or not you have successfully duplicated the new fashion design.

CHAPTER **II**

PLACEMENT OF GRAIN MARKING

The placement of grain markings on the patterns has been, for the most part, omitted in this book. This is not because it need not be done, but because it is part of the designer's decision in determining the final look of the garment.

What Is Grain?

In placing grain markings, the designer must first be aware of what causes grain in a garment.

In all woven fabric, the filling yarns are placed at right angles to the warp yarns. (*Warp yarns* are those parallel to the selvage; they are the lengthwise yarns on the loom. *Filling yarns* are the crosswise yarns on the loom.)

Imagine a piece of cloth stretched over a horizontal rod with a filling yarn exactly following the length of the rod. With the cloth in this position, the warp yarns will all hang perpendicular to the floor. If you pull the cloth so that the filling yarn follows the rod only part way and the remainder drapes off the end of the rod, the warp yarns will no longer hang perpendicular to the floor. What happens? Unless the fabric is extremely stiff, the warp yarns will try to readjust to fall perpendicular to the floor. This causes folds in the cloth. The reason this occurs, of course, is because of gravity. The force of gravity pulls the warp threads perpendicular to the floor.

The point to remember is that this happens when fabric is placed on the human figure as well. The pull of gravity can cause wrinkles or drag lines if not planned for; folds or drapes if planned for.

Straight grain in the warp direction should be placed where you wish the garment to hang straight, without folds.

The filling or crosswise direction has more give or stretch. It molds easily around the figure without the stiffness the warp threads would produce when placed crosswise around the body. The filling or crosswise direction is called *crosswise straight grain* in most commercial patterns.

Anything not straight grain (warp or filling) is called *bias*. True bias is the 45° angle between warp and filling straight grain. Bias is used where you desire stretching and draping characteristics.

Fabrics Without Grain

Nonwoven or felted cloth has no grain and therefore does not present these problems. The same is true of most leathers.

Knits

Knits should be treated the same as woven fabrics. Although there is no filling yarn at right angles to a warp, the filling knit construction basically consists of a yarn following back and forth across the cloth interlocking loops. This creates a definite, visible line which, if placed off-grain, will affect the appearance of the garment. A warp knit likewise has a construction pattern which creates visible lines. These lines will create a poor finished appearance if placed off-grain and will tend to hang in folds, although less definitely so than in woven goods.

Grain Placement

To provide a few general guidelines for placing grain, the following typical placements are presented. Do not feel bound by these rules, however, as individual creations often lead to original techniques which are acceptable.

Most *bodices* have the straight grain down the center front and center back. This allows the warp threads to hang perpendicular to the floor and creates no wrinkles in the center front and center back area.

Skirts likewise usually have straight grain down the center front and center back. In gored skirts the straight grain is usually down the center of the panel.

Sleeves usually have straight grain down the center of the sleeve to the elbow.

Collars usually have straight grain over the shoulder so that the center back is bias and will give. On large collars such as a sailor collar, the straight grain is typically in the center back.

For a *cowl* neck, place the straight grain at a 45° angle to the center front. This will create the soft folds characteristic of the true bias in the neck area.

Finally, before placing grain—think: What will this accomplish? Where should the garment fold and where should it hang straight? Place the grain with these objectives well in mind.

CHAPTER **III**

USE OF PATTERN-MAKING EQUIPMENT

The pattern-making equipment shown here can be purchased at most fabric stores, at well-supplied stationery shops, or at department stores. The *Dietzgen curve,* shown here, can be copied in heavy cardboard if you cannot buy a plastic one. It is used to draw curves at the neck and armhole. The curve can be moved along the edge being drawn to obtain a greater or lesser curve as desired (see Fig. 3-1).

A see-through *plastic ruler* will be helpful for drawing design lines and for adding seam allowances.

The *L-square* and *T-square* are useful for measuring between points, and in marking long distances, especially on skirts (see Fig. 3-2).

The *curve stick* is especially useful in drawing princess lines and in drawing side seams of skirts (see Figs. 3-3, 3-4, 3-5).

These tools can make your pattern-making job much easier and more accurate.

THE COMPLETE GUIDE TO PATTERN-MAKING 18

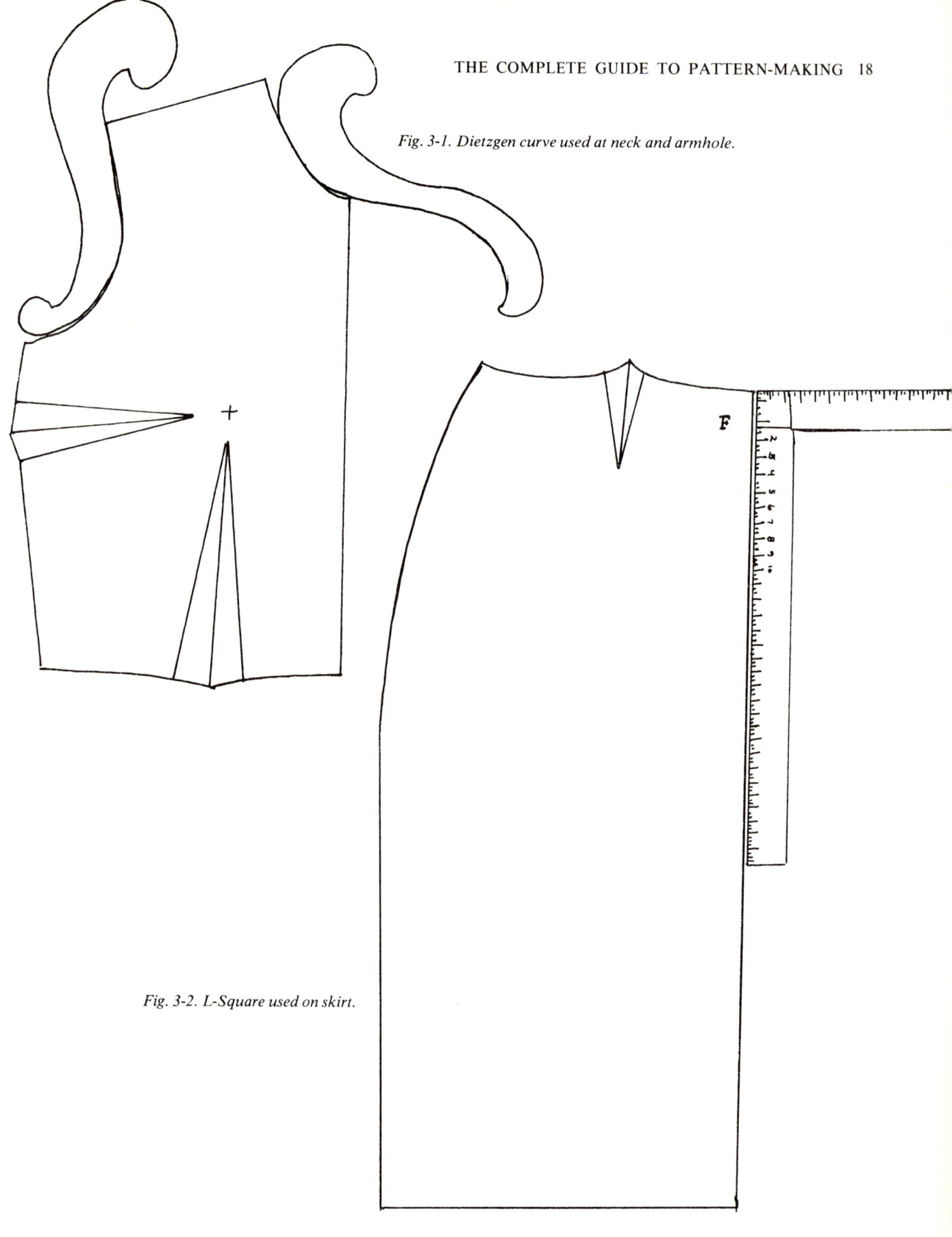

Fig. 3-1. Dietzgen curve used at neck and armhole.

Fig. 3-2. L-Square used on skirt.

Fig. 3-3. Curve stick used on bodice.

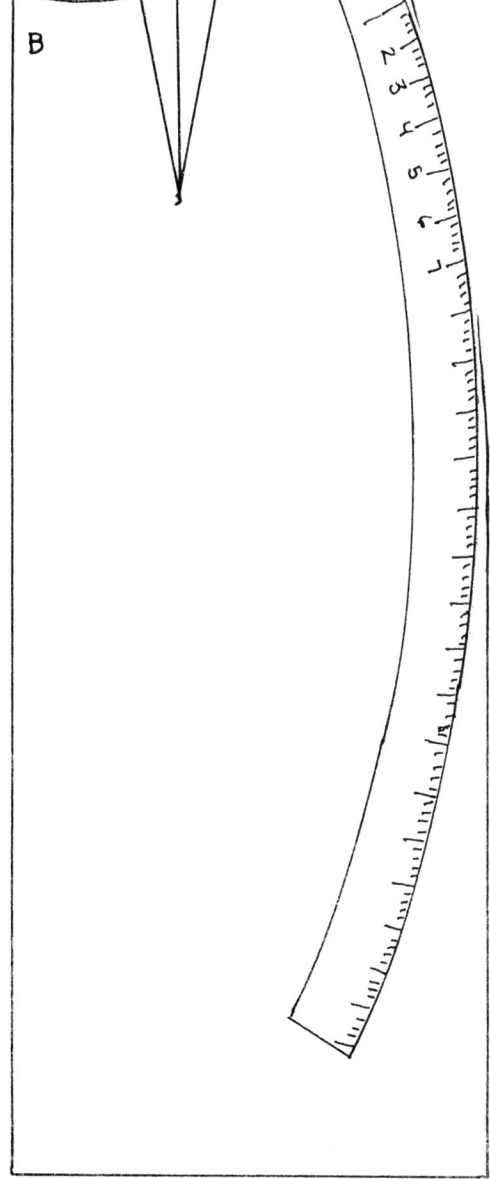

THE COMPLETE GUIDE TO PATTERN-MAKING

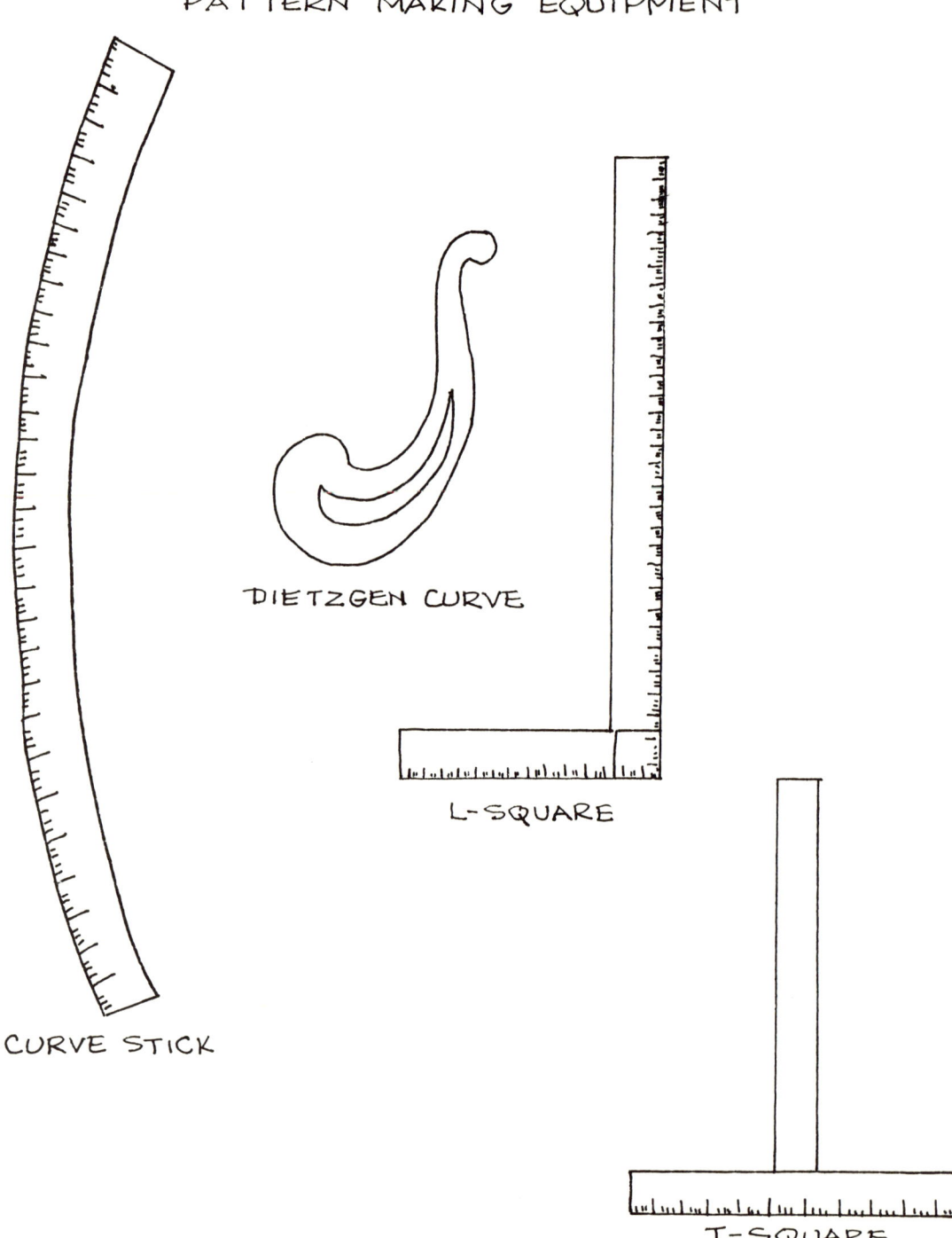

Fig. 3-5. *Curve stick, Dietzgen curve, L-square, and T-square.*

CHAPTER **IV**

THE BODICE FRONT

We start with the bodice front. It is potentially the most interesting and certainly the most difficult of the parts of the costume to change.

The basic bodice front sloper has two darts leading to the bust: one from the waist and one from the side seam. It you draw a line through the center of each, they will cross at the bust point. This point should correspond exactly with the point of the bust of the individual for whom the garment is being made. As you work with the bodice patterns, you will need to know the location of this point. It has been marked on the half-scale and quarter-scale slopers.

The curve of the bust is of major importance in the bodice front. The adaptation of the fabric to the third dimension is determined largely by the size and shape of the bust. The size of the darts vary according to the bust curve, as the darts are the mechanism for transforming the two-dimensions into three.

Of secondary consideration in the bodice front is the curve of the waist. If it is small in relation to the bust, the dart must be increased in width to give a greater curve to the fabric.

Further discussion of variations in shape and size of the waist and bust will be discussed in the section on making the full-size sloper. The pattern you will work with in the half-size and quarter-size examples is for the normal figure.

THE PROCESS OF BODICE FRONT PATTERN/MAKING BY THE FLAT-PATTERN METHOD

The Eight Basic Steps

There are eight basic steps that must be learned to make bodice front patterns successfully by the flat-pattern method. All of the steps are essential. You should become so familiar with them that you perform them automatically.

THE COMPLETE GUIDE TO PATTERN-MAKING 22

Some of the steps are also used for the bodice back, sleeve, and skirt. Master the bodice front first, and then go on to the others.

The ninth step is used when making patterns in full size. It may be omitted when working with the quarter- and half-scale patterns.

Begin your study by working sequentially through each step in the illustrations before you attempt any variations. It is very important to master the eight basic steps at the outset as they form the foundation for all other patterns.

STEP 1: Trace sloper.

The sloper is the basic pattern without seams. It should be traced on paper. (Half-scale and quarter-scale slopers for women are found in Appendices II and III.)

Use a medium-weight, good-quality paper to trace the sloper. Construction paper or 20-l. typing paper are suitable materials.

Trace all the sloper pieces needed for the design being made. Trace in the darts and bust point. (The bust point was established when the sloper was made by drawing through the center of each dart. The point where the lines cross is the bust point.)

Cut pattern pieces out on traced lines. (see Fig. 4-1).

STEP 2: Draw in new design lines.

At this stage you become a designer. Where do you want the new dart to be? Where do you want a new seam

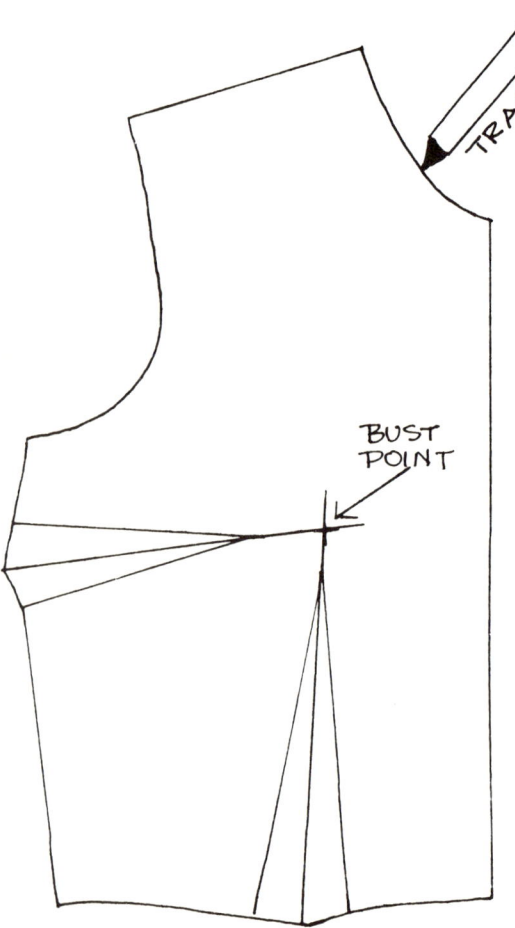

Fig. 4-1. Step 1: Trace sloper.

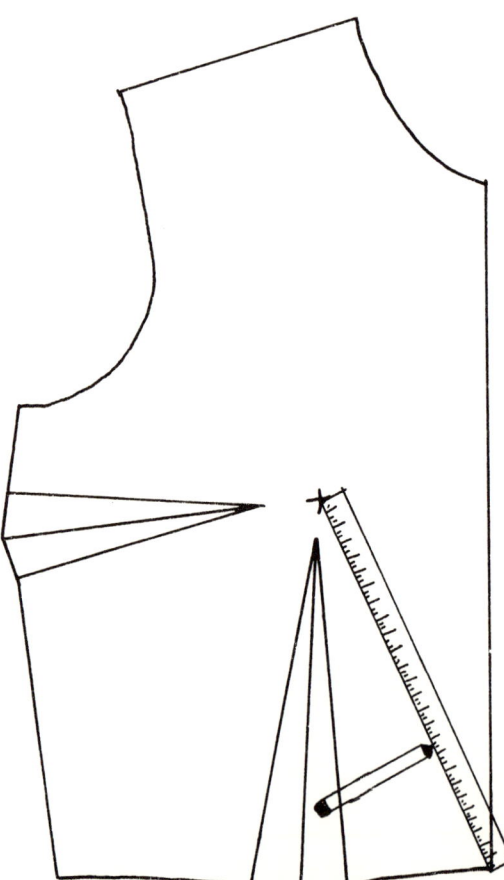

Fig. 4-2. Step 2: Draw in new design lines.

23 THE BODICE FRONT

line? You should have your design well in mind, for here is where you draw it onto your sloper.

For this first pattern, make one new dart out of the two old ones. The side and waist darts will be replaced by a dart from the center front waist.

Make a dot at the center front of the waistline. Use a ruler and connect the bust point and the center front waist point. The line must be drawn all the way to the bust point (see Figs. 4-2, 4-3).

STEP 3: Cross-notch.

Cross-notches are made over new design lines to aid in stitching the seams together.

When you have cut on the new line(s) and the pattern is separated, these notches will indicate what lines must meet when stitching.

Draw two short lines close together and at right angles to the new design line. If you have several seams, mark one with a one-line notch, one with a two-line notch, and one with a three-line notch (see Fig. 4-4).

STEP 4: Fold out darts.

Before proceeding with the new design, the original darts on the sloper must be folded out. This means that they are folded together just as they would be when sewing them.

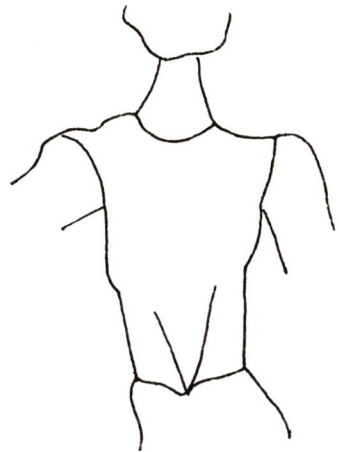

Fig. 4-3. Center front waist dart.

Fig. 4-4. Step 3: Cross-notch.

Fig. 4-5. Step 4a: Fold out darts.

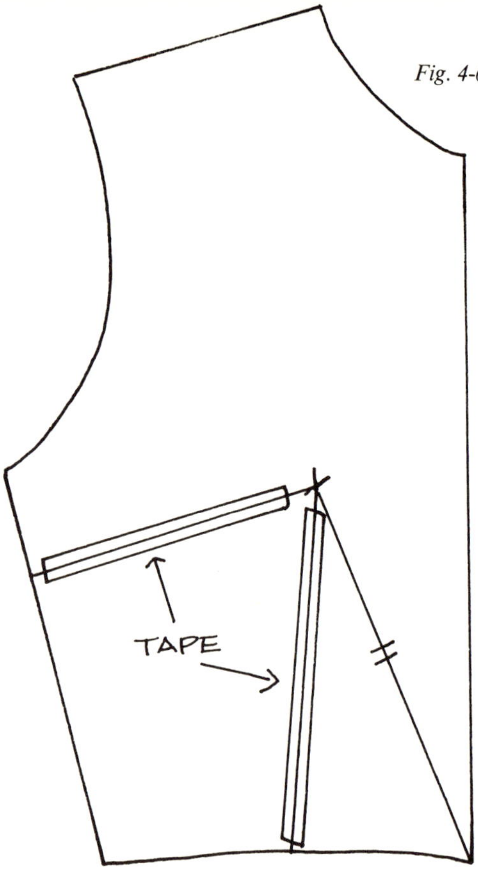

Fig. 4-6. Step 4b: Fold out darts.

THE COMPLETE GUIDE TO PATTERN-MAKING 24

Cut on one side of each dart to the bust point. Leave 1/16" of paper at the bust point so that the pattern will not fall apart. Keep the pattern on the work surface to avoid tearing it apart. If you should accidentally tear it apart, mend it with a tiny piece of cellophane tape at the bust point (see Fig. 4-5).

Lap the cut side of the dart over to the other stitching line, starting at the bust point and continuing to the seam. Tape down.

The folded-out pattern will be curved and will not lie flat on the work surface. Do not attempt to flatten it out (see Fig. 4-6).

STEP 5: Cut on new design lines.

Cut on the new design line from seam to bust point. The pattern opens to lie flat, thus creating the new dart where it was cut.

No adjustment is necessary at this point. The flat pattern will still be the same size as the original. You simply combined two darts into one; the pattern adjusted automatically.

This is the key to the simplified flat-pattern technique. If the pattern was flat when you began and if it is again flat after you have folded out the darts and cut the new line, it remains the same size. Only the position of the darts has changed (see Fig. 4-7).

STEP 6: Add paper.

Place a piece of tissue paper or other paper of similar weight under the new open dart. Allow enough paper beyond the pattern edge for the new dart end line. Tape the pattern to the tissue along the cut edges of the new dart or glue it to the paper (see Fig. 4-8).

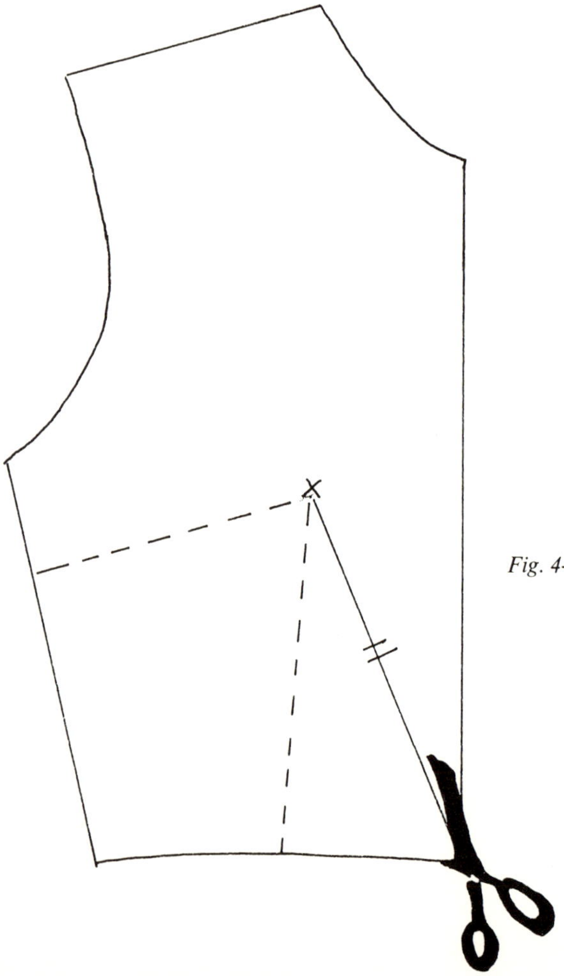

Fig. 4-7. Step 5: Cut on new design lines.

25 THE BODICE FRONT

STEP 7: Re-draw new dart.

First, draw a center line in the new dart opening. To do this, measure the distance between the cut edges near the seam end of the dart. Draw a dot at the halfway point of the measurement. With a ruler, draw a line connecting the bust point with the dot. This line is the center or fold line for the dart.

In most bodices, darts do not extend all the way to the bust point. Instead, the tip of the dart stops ½″ to 1″ short of the bust point. This gives an extra bit of ease over the bust and creates a better-appearing bodice.

So that you can understand why the bust dart must be shortened, let us review Step 4. When the darts in the bodice front were folded out, they were extended beyond their tips to the bust point. This was necessary to cut a flat pattern. However, in this procedure, some ease space over the bust was lost. In Step 7 the ease is returned.

Establish the tip of the dart ½″ to 1″ from the bust on the center fold line. With a ruler draw in the new dart by connecting this point with the seam ends of the dart (see Fig. 4-9).

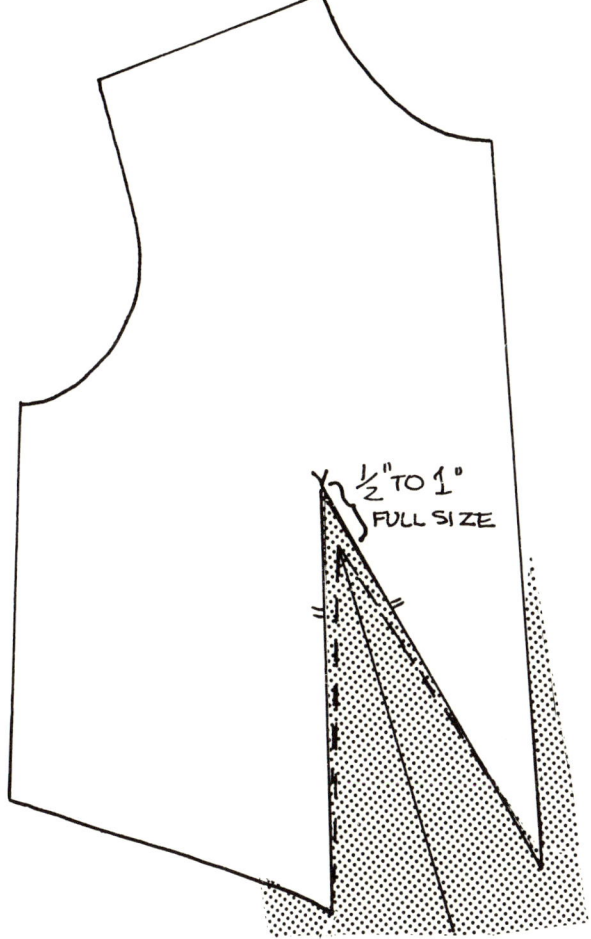

Fig. 4-9. Step 7: Re-draw new dart.

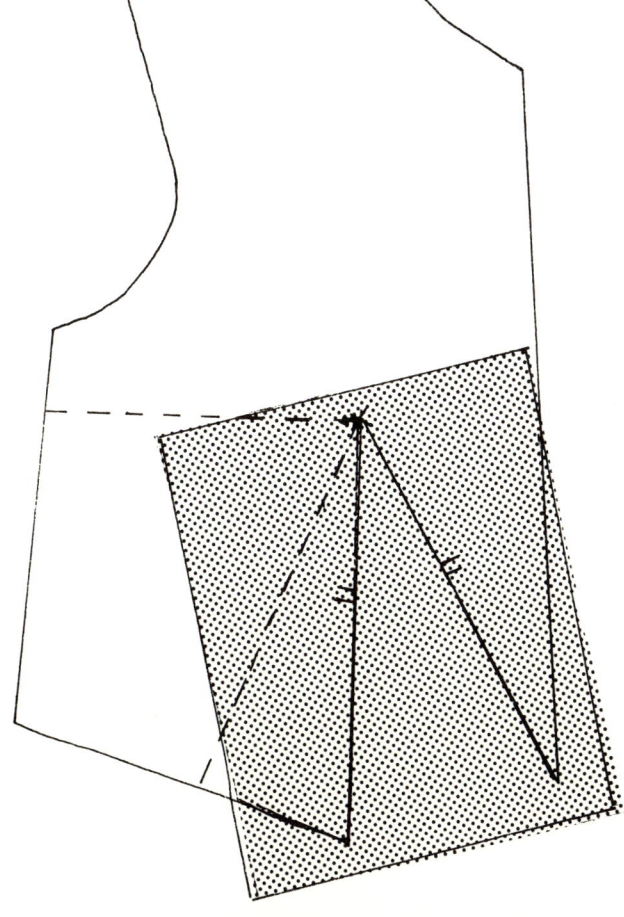

Fig. 4-8. Step 6: Add paper.

THE COMPLETE GUIDE TO PATTERN-MAKING 26

STEP 8: Finish dart ends.

Bring the cross-notches together, and fold out the dart (see Fig. 4-10).

At this point, you must make another design decision. The dart can be folded toward or away from the center front. A side dart can be folded up or down. How do you decide which way?

Pattern guides and sewing books use the following rules of thumb. Fold side darts down and waist and shoulder darts toward center front. This rule is based on the artistic concept that the person looking at the garment should not see the stitching on a dart. For instance, if a waist dart is folded toward the center front, a slight shadow will be cast on the side section. There is ever so slight a roll on the top of the dart caused by the bulk of the dart lying under the fold. The side section is flat and receives the shadow cast from this raised portion. Try out this effect by stitching darts and folding them first toward the center front, then away from center front. You will see that the stitching line is more visible when the darts are folded away from the center front (see Figs. 4-11, 4-12).

While the rationale of hiding the stitching line is a sound basis for the general rule in most cases, there are instances where the problem is more complicated. In the following example, the dart is folded toward the center front, and the paper ends are trimmed off flush with the center front line (see Fig. 4-13).

Unless there is a center front seam to which you can stitch the edges of the dart, you will have a flap or end loose. While this might be a good design, it is not a good construction (see Fig. 4-13).

Fold the dart toward the side seam, and trim the ends flush with the waistline edge. Now you can stitch the dart into the waistline seam (see Fig. 4-14).

Each time you get to Step 8, try folding your darts, tucks or pleats in the two directions possible. You will then be able to make your design decision on a rational basis, taking into account both artistic and practical considerations.

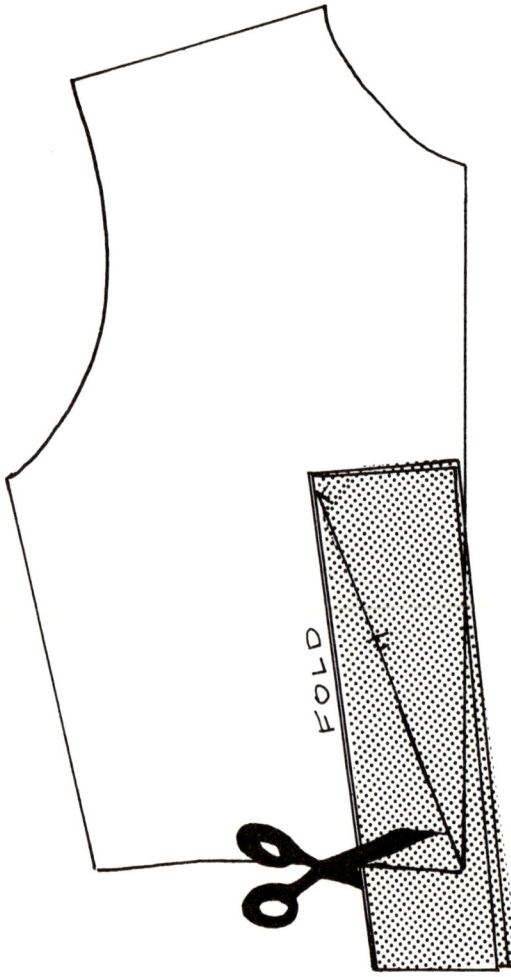

Fig. 4-10. Step 8: Finish dart ends.

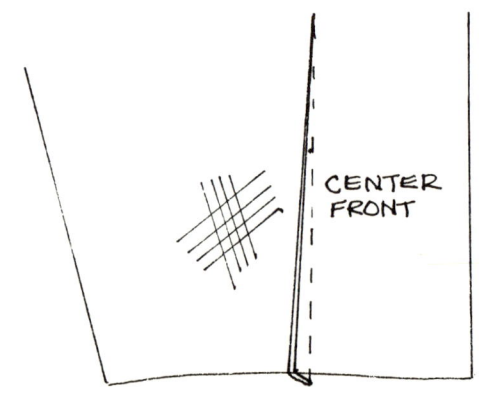

Fig. 4-11. Step 8b: Dart folded toward side seam.

27 THE BODICE FRONT

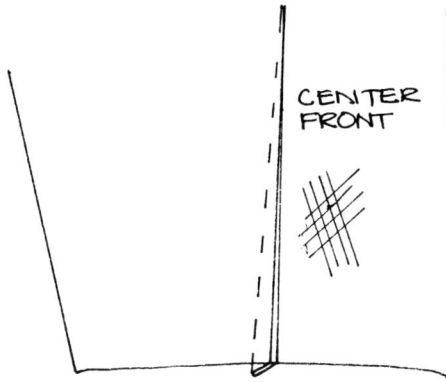

Fig. 4-12. Step 8b: Dart folded toward center front.

Fig. 4-13. Step 8: Cut end of dart folded toward center front.

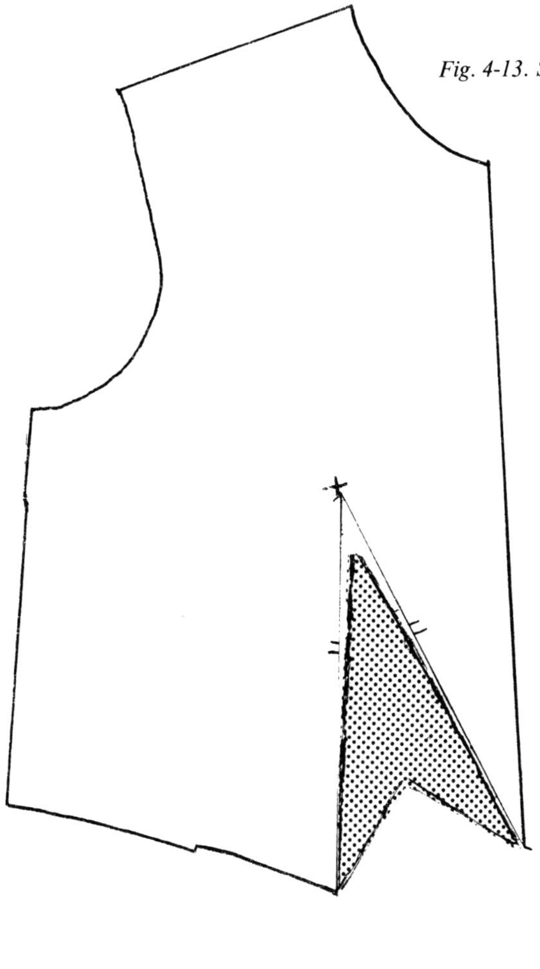

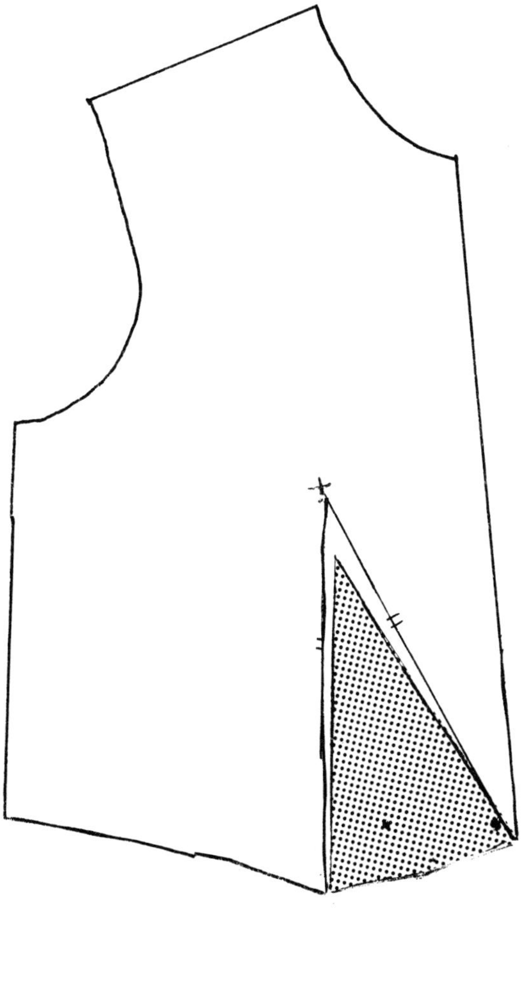

Fig. 4-14. Step 8: Cut end of dart folded toward side seam.

STEP 9: Trace pattern adding seam allowances, grain markings, and other instructive information.

When you work in full-size with a pattern that you intend to cut from fabric, you must complete Step 9. Otherwise it may be omitted. In this step, you trace the newly designed pattern onto the tissue paper to be used to cut out the fabric.

To trace the pattern, place the new pattern you have developed on a flat, smooth surface. If you have a surface into which you can stick pins (such as cork or cardboard) or one to which you can attach tape, use it to help hold the pattern still. Place the tracing paper over the pattern, and pin or tape it down at the edges. (Be certain you have ironed the tissue lightly if it has creases or wrinkles.) Use the designer's tools—the L-square, T-square, yard stick, curve stick, and Dietzgen curve—to help you draw lines. A small, see-through plastic ruler is also helpful in adding seam allowances (see illustration and explanation on pages 17-20).

Seam allowances on commercial patterns are usually ⅝" wide. This is a sufficient amount for seams that will be trimmed, graded, enclosed, or otherwise altered after seaming. Seams which may be altered in fitting, such as side, center front, center back, shoulder, waist seams, and bust seams in princess styles, should be made 1" or wider. The extra fabric gives a better hang to the garment after it is made up and also allows for adjustment should the wearer change size in the future. Hand-made, couturier, and commercial garments of superior quality also have wide seams. Now even some of the commercial patterns use wider seams in their more expensive designer patterns.

For children's garments, ½" seams are usually ample, especially if you are making a French seam. If you are making a flat-fell seam (e.g., for pants), ⅝" is usually necessary for an adequate working width.

Grain markings have been discussed (page 15). These are marked on the pattern with an arrow. The arrow indicates the direction of the lengthwise or warp straight grain, or it may be specifically stated for crosswise or filling grain, which is perpendicular to the selvage.

Other markings to be included are: center front or center back on fold, if applicable; notches for joining pieces; placement of pockets and flaps; pleat and tuck folding direction.

29 THE BODICE FRONT

Trace the pattern, using a soft lead pencil or a good-quality pen. Add the seam allowances and the pattern markings. Trace all the pieces necessary to complete the design (see Figs. 4-15, 4-16).

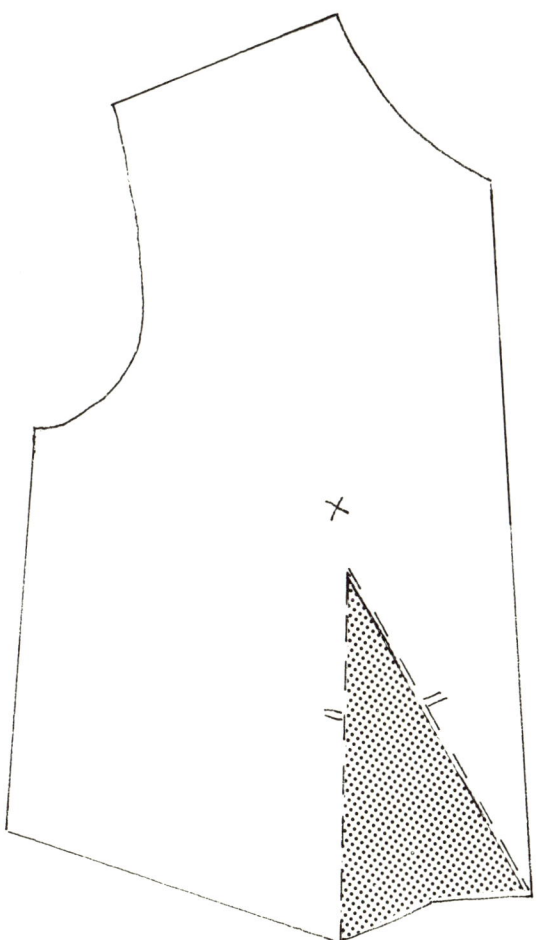

Fig. 4-15. Step 9a: Trace completed pattern.

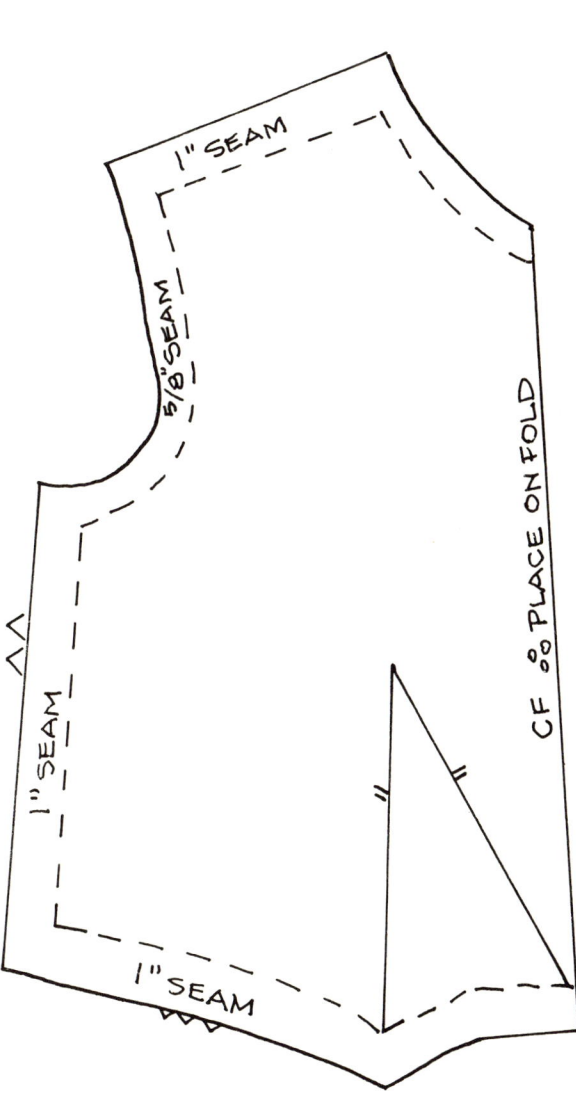

Fig 4-16. Step 9b: Add seam allowances and markings.

THE COMPLETE GUIDE TO PATTERN-MAKING 30

If you have mastered the first variation, develop a bodice front with the dart moved to the center front location by following the nine steps (see Fig. 4-17).

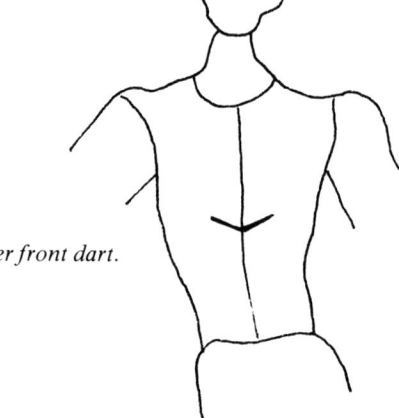

Fig. 4-17. Center front dart.

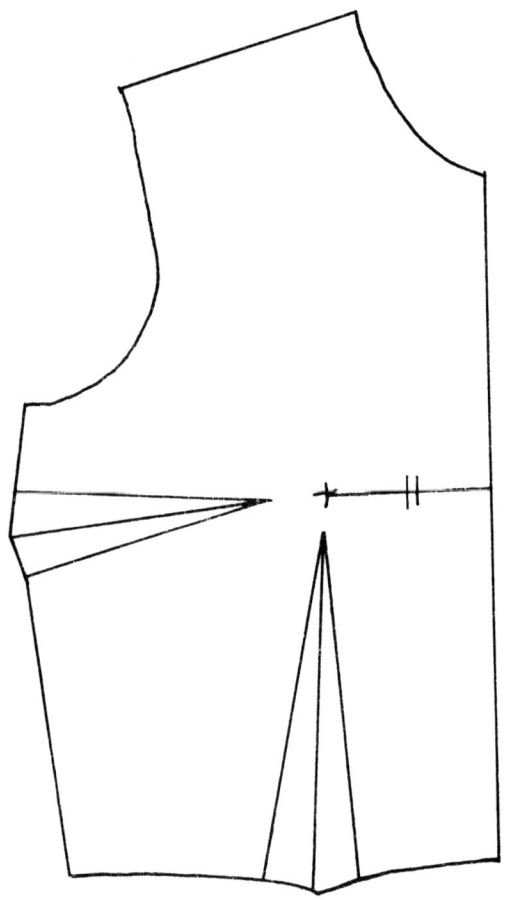

Fig. 4-18. Center front dart, Steps 1, 2, 3.

STEP 1: Trace sloper (bodice front only).

STEP 2: Draw in new design line, center front dart; draw all the way to bust point.

STEP 3: Cross-notch (see Fig. 4-18).

STEP 4: Fold out darts.

STEP 5: Cut on new design lines.

STEP 6: Add paper (see Fig. 4-19).

STEP 7: Re-draw dart in bodice front.

STEP 8: Fold out new dart; cut ends (see Fig. 4-20).

STEP 9: Trace, adding seam allowances, markings, etc., this step can now be omitted from practice problems.

A note is required about the center front dart location. This dart position would most commonly be used in a sun-top dress, strapless gown, or bathing-suit design. The dart appears to be much smaller than the original two which have been combined to make it. However, it is not. The illusion of size is created by the fact that you are working with a circular shape. As you go out from the center of the circle the distance or radius increases but the angle does not (see Fig. 4-21).

A center front neck dart creates an inverted V shape in the bodice front neck to bust area (see Fig. 4-22).

31 THE BODICE FRONT

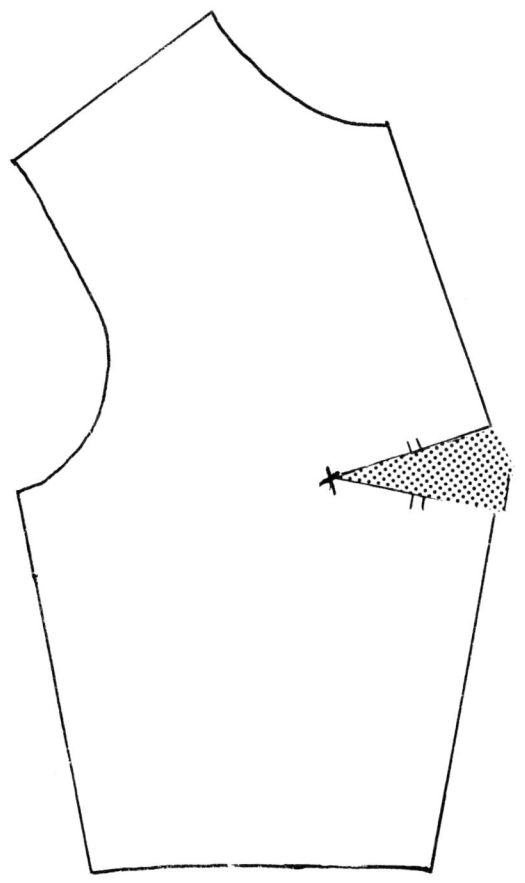

Fig. 4-19. Center front dart, Steps 4, 5, 6.

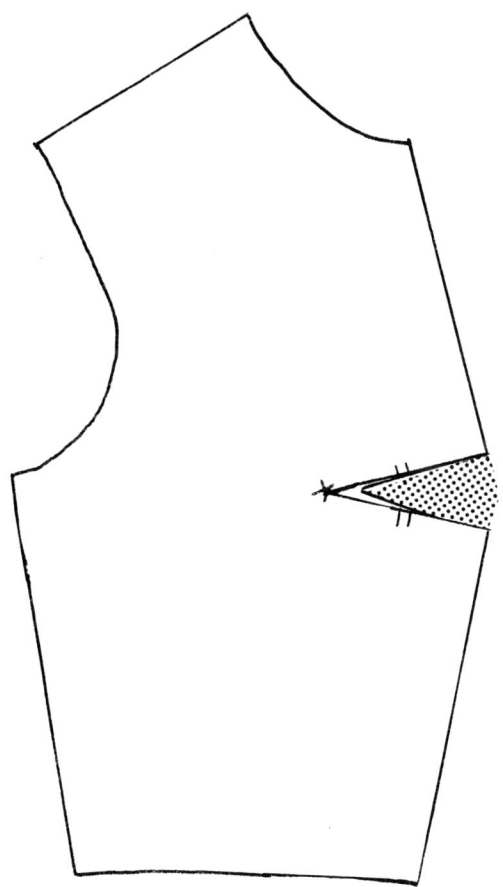

Fig. 4-20. Center front dart, Steps 7, 8.

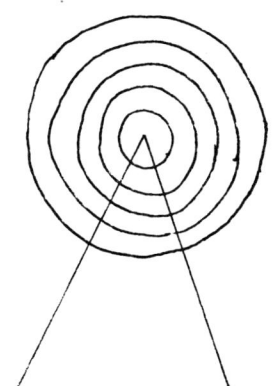

Fig. 4-21. Dart as radius of a circle.

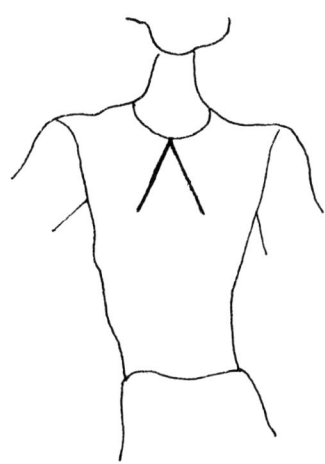

Fig. 4-22. Center front neck dart.

THE COMPLETE GUIDE TO PATTERN-MAKING

STEP 1: Trace sloper (bodice front only).

STEP 2: Draw in new design line, center front neck dart; draw all the way to the bust point.

STEP 3: Cross-notch (see Fig. 4-23).

STEP 4: Fold out darts.

STEP 5: Cut on new design line.

STEP 6: Add paper (see Fig. 4-24).

STEP 7: Re-draw dart in bodice front.

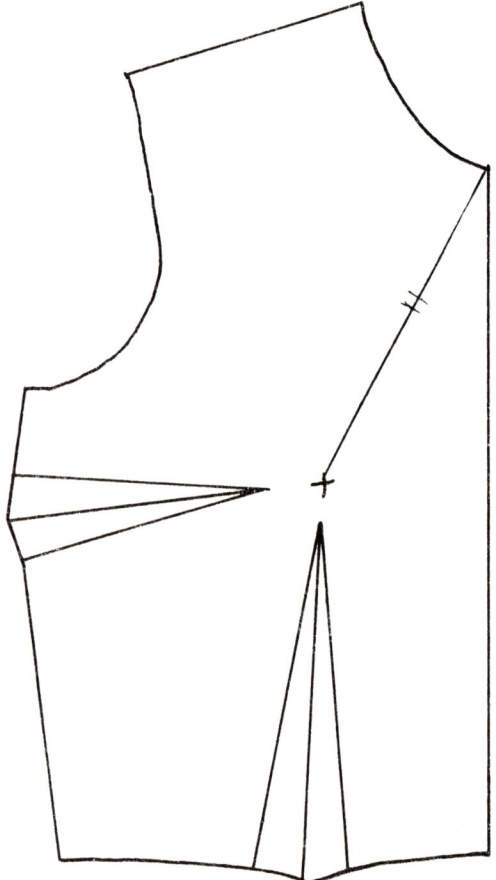

Fig. 4-23. Center front neck dart, Steps 1, 2, 3.

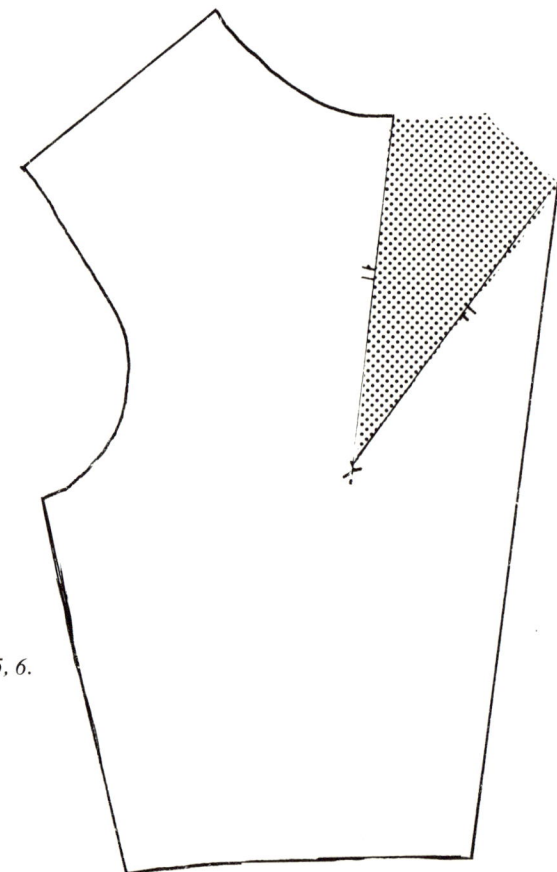

Fig. 4-24. Center front neck dart, Steps 4, 5, 6.

33 THE BODICE FRONT

STEP 8: Fold out new dart; cut ends (Fig. 4-25).

The neck edge at the shoulder dart placement creates nearly parallel lines in the garment top. This can divide the figure into three parts which causes an illusion of decreased figure size (see Fig. 4-26).

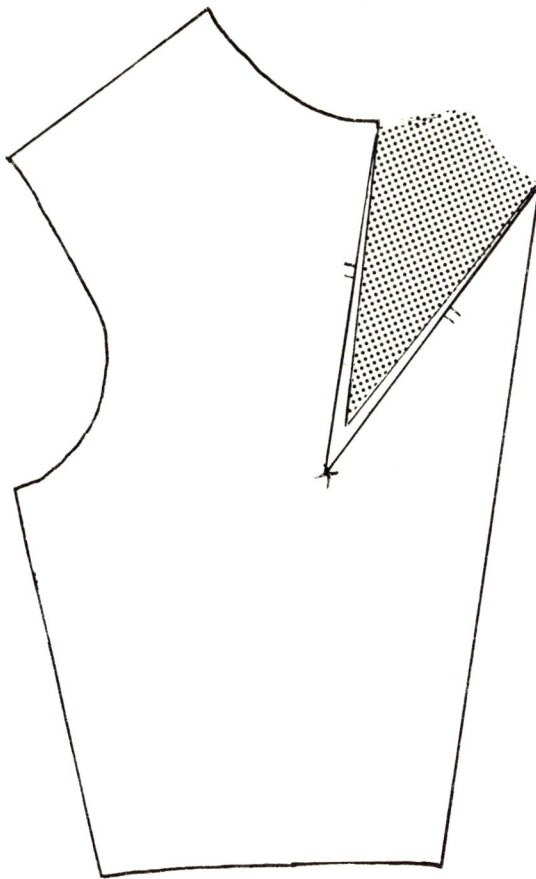

Fig. 4-25. Center front neck dart, Steps 7,8.

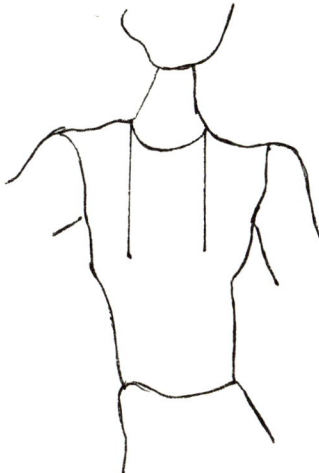

Fig. 4-26. Neck edge at shoulder dart.

THE COMPLETE GUIDE TO PATTERN-MAKING 34

STEP 1: Trace sloper (bodice front only).

STEP 2: Draw in new design line, neck edge at shoulder dart; draw the line all the way to the bust point.

STEP 3: Cross-notch (see Fig. 4-27).

STEP 4: Fold out darts.

STEP 5: Cut on new design line.

STEP 6: Add paper (see Fig. 4-28).

STEP 7: Re-draw dart in bodice front.

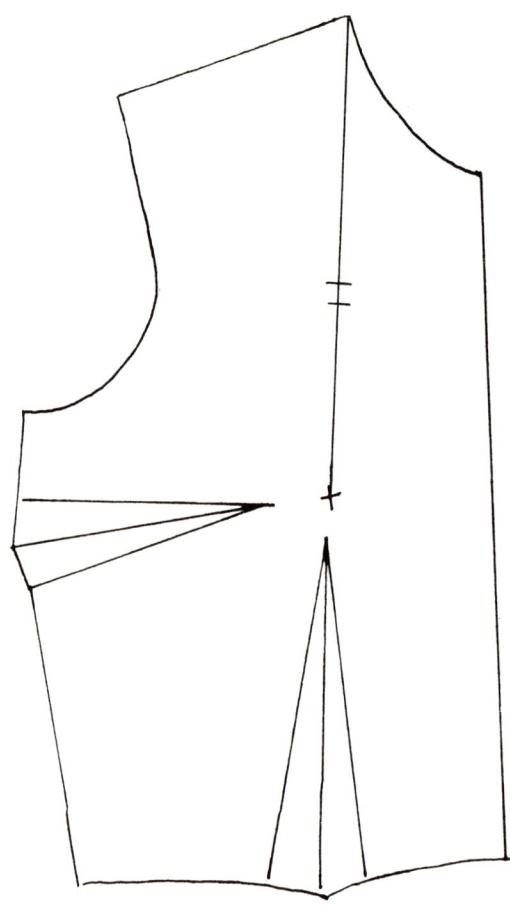

Fig. 4-27. Neck edge at shoulder dart, Steps 1, 2, 3.

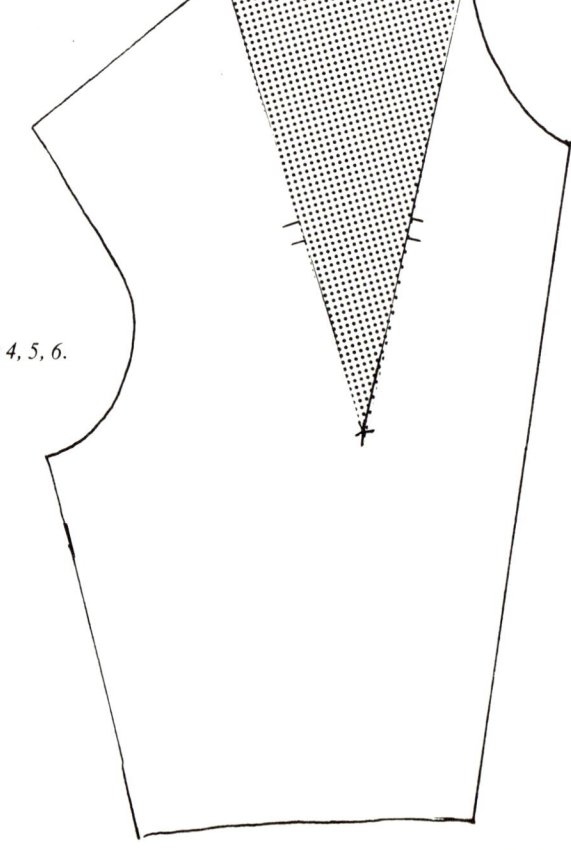

Fig. 4-28. Neck edge at shoulder dart, Steps 4, 5, 6.

35 THE BODICE FRONT

STEP 8: Fold out new dart; cut ends (see Fig. 4-29).

When the dart is moved to the shoulder edge, it is often converted into a tuck. A tuck is sewn only 2" down, rather than all the way to the bust point. This dart placement is flattering for a full-busted figure (see Fig. 4-30).

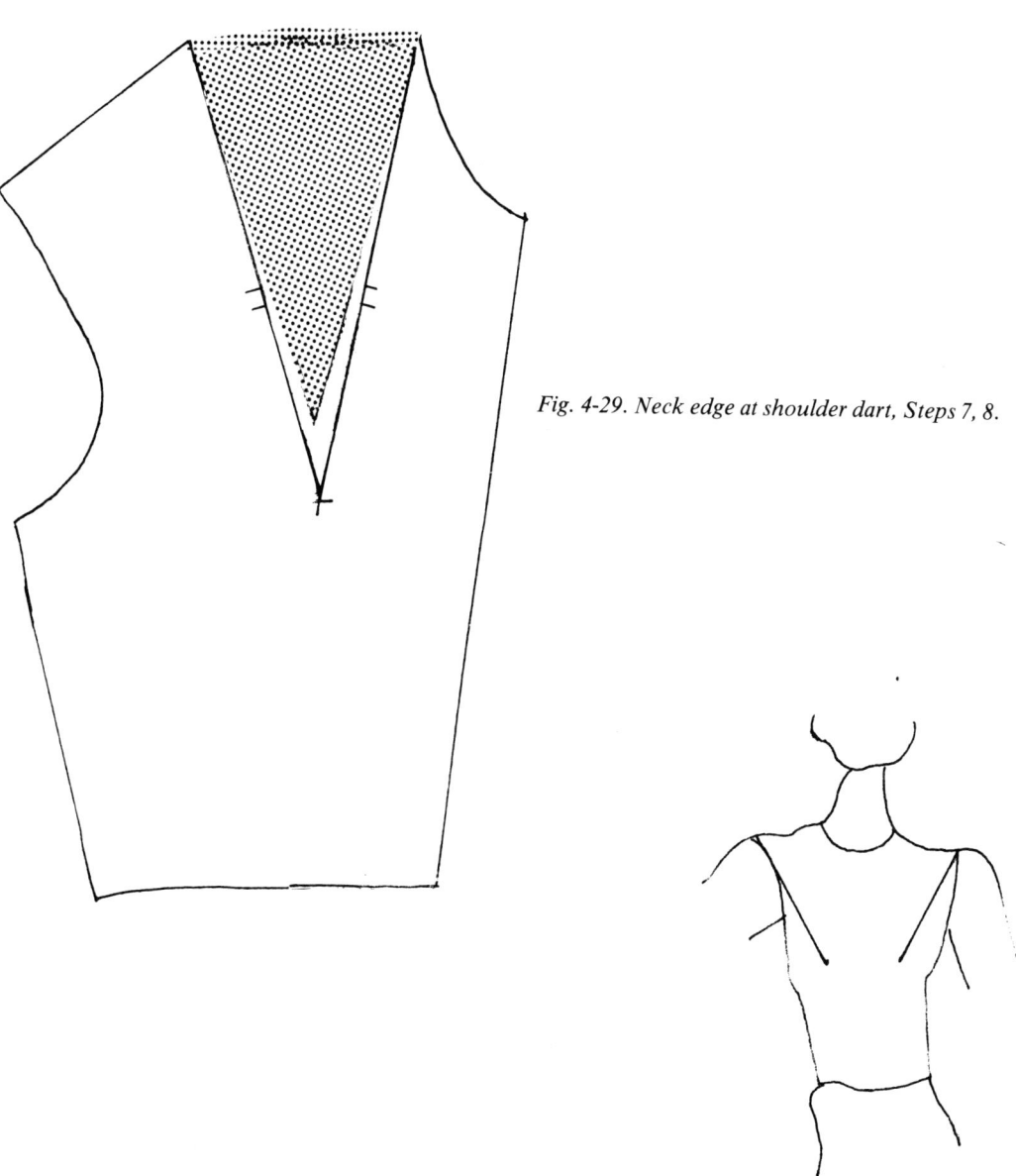

Fig. 4-29. Neck edge at shoulder dart, Steps 7, 8.

Fig. 4-30. Shoulder edge dart or tuck.

THE COMPLETE GUIDE TO PATTERN-MAKING 36

STEP 1: Trace sloper (bodice front only)

STEP 2: Draw in new design line, shoulder, armhole edge to bust point; draw the line all the way to the bust point.

STEP 3: Cross-notch (see Fig. 4-31).

STEP 4: Fold out darts.

STEP 5: Cut on new design line.

STEP 6: Add paper (see Fig. 4-32).

STEP 7: Re-draw dart in bodice front.

STEP 8: Fold out new dart; cut ends (see Fig. 4-33).

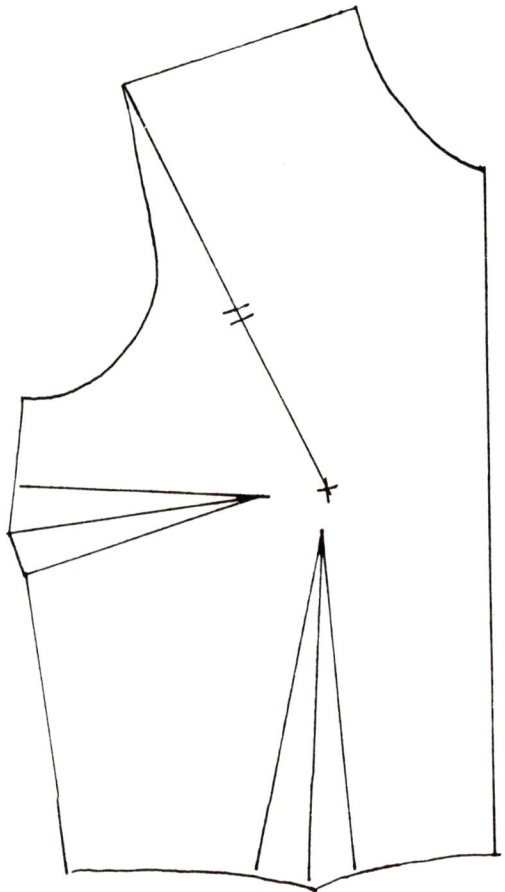

Fig. 4-31. Shoulder edge dart or tuck, Steps 1, 2, 3.

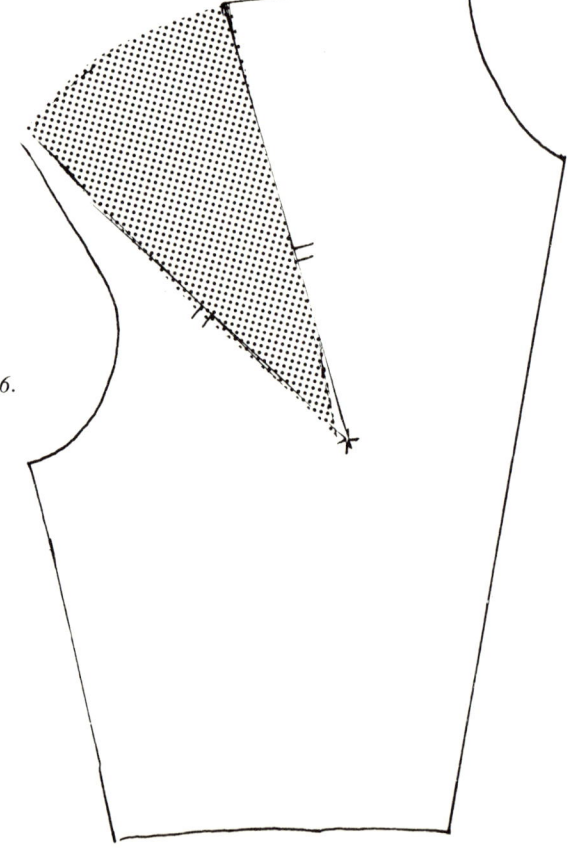

Fig. 4-32. Shoulder edge dart or tuck, Steps 4, 5, 6.

37 THE BODICE FRONT

A bust dart location uses the original position and converts the two darts into one (see Fig. 4-34).

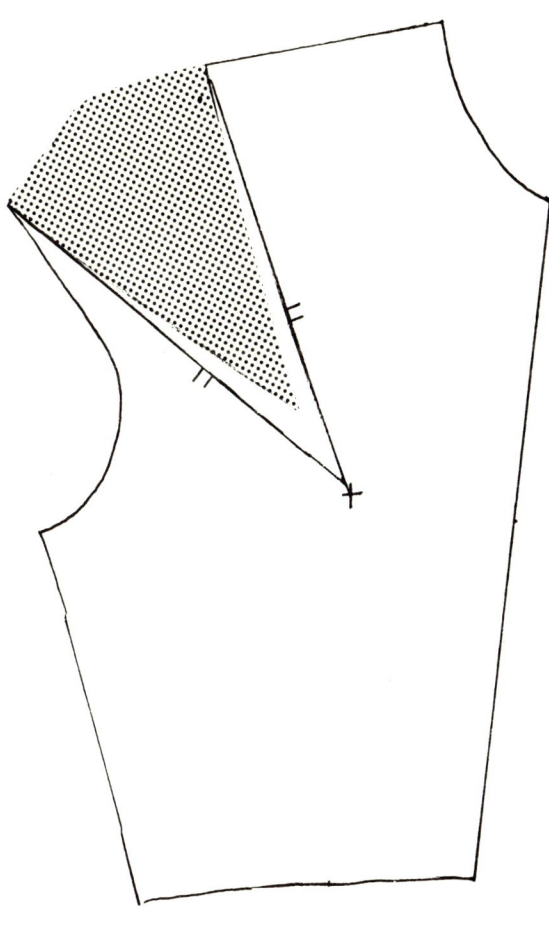

Fig. 4-33. Shoulder edge dart or tuck, Steps 7, 8.

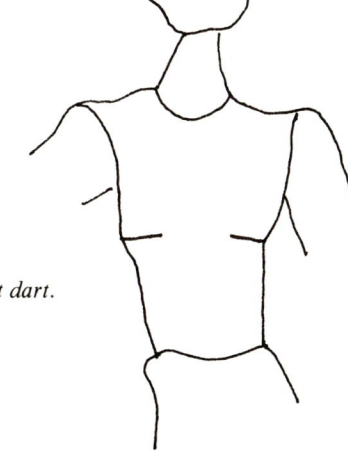

Fig. 4-34. Bust dart.

THE COMPLETE GUIDE TO PATTERN-MAKING 38

STEP 1: Trace sloper (bodice front only).

STEP 2: Draw in new design line, original bust dart location, draw the line all the way to the bust point.

STEP 3: Cross-notch (see Fig. 4-35).

STEP 4: Fold out darts.

STEP 5: Cut on new design line.

STEP 6: Add paper (see Fig. 4-36).

STEP 7: Re-draw dart in bodice front.

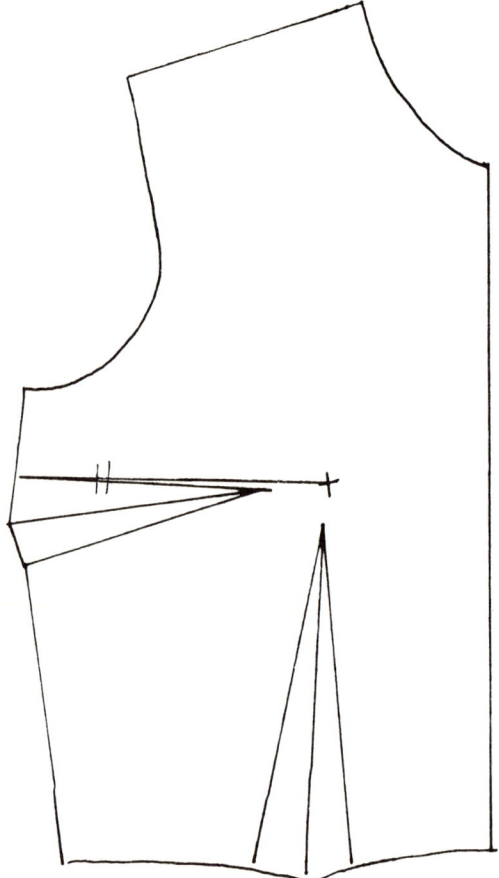

Fig. 4-35. Bust dart, Steps 1, 2, 3.

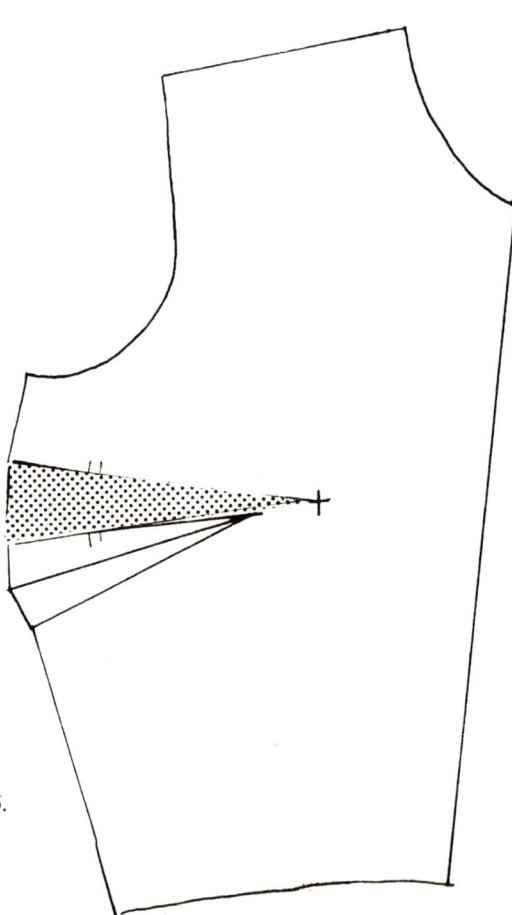

Fig. 4-36. Bust dart, Steps 4, 5, 6.

39 THE BODICE FRONT

STEP 8: Fold out new dart; cut ends (see Fig. 4-37).

The French dart location is 1½" (full-size) above the waist on the side seam. This is a most attractive dart location as it creates a diagonal line to cut the figure, thus creating a more narrow illusion (see Fig. 4-38).

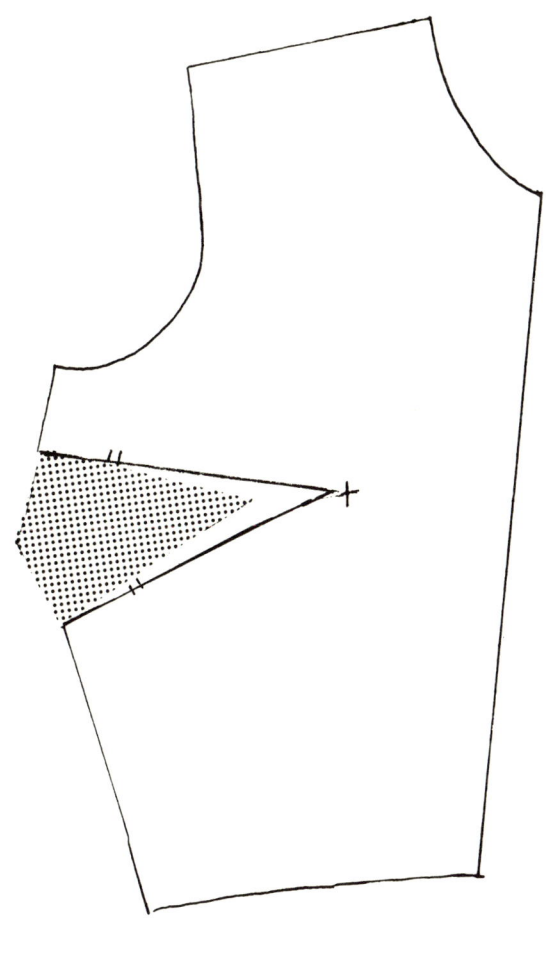

Fig. 4-37. Bust dart, Steps 7, 8.

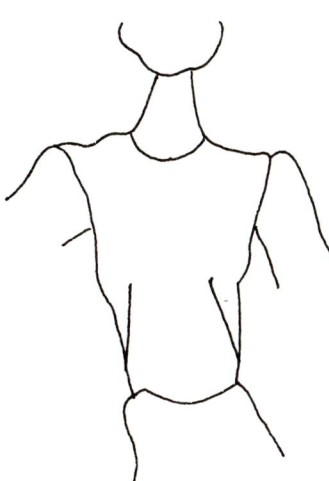

Fig. 4-38. French dart.

THE COMPLETE GUIDE TO PATTERN-MAKING 40

STEP 1: Trace sloper (bodice front only).

STEP 2: Draw in new design line, 1½" (full-size) above waist on side seam to bust point; draw the line all the way to the bust point.

STEP 3: Cross-notch (see Fig. 4-39).

STEP 4: Fold out darts.

STEP 5: Cut on new design line.

STEP 6: Add paper (see Fig. 4-40).

STEP 7: Re-draw dart in bodice front.

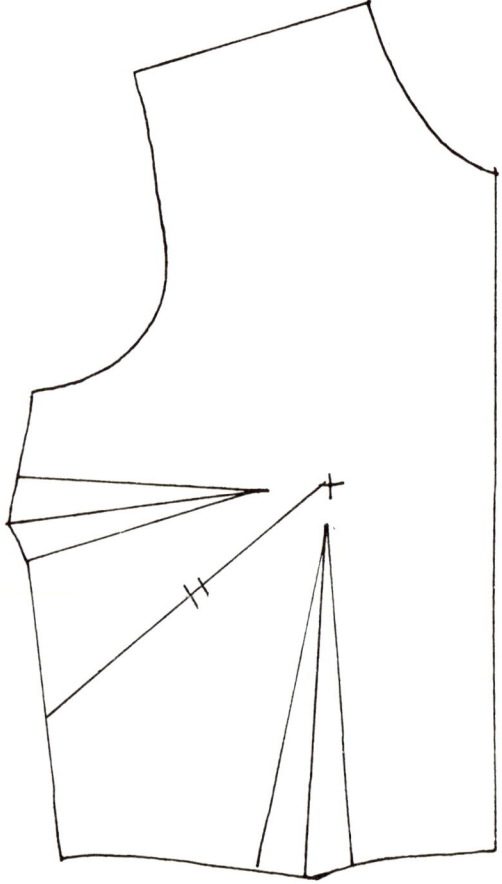

Fig. 4-39. French dart, Steps 1, 2, 3.

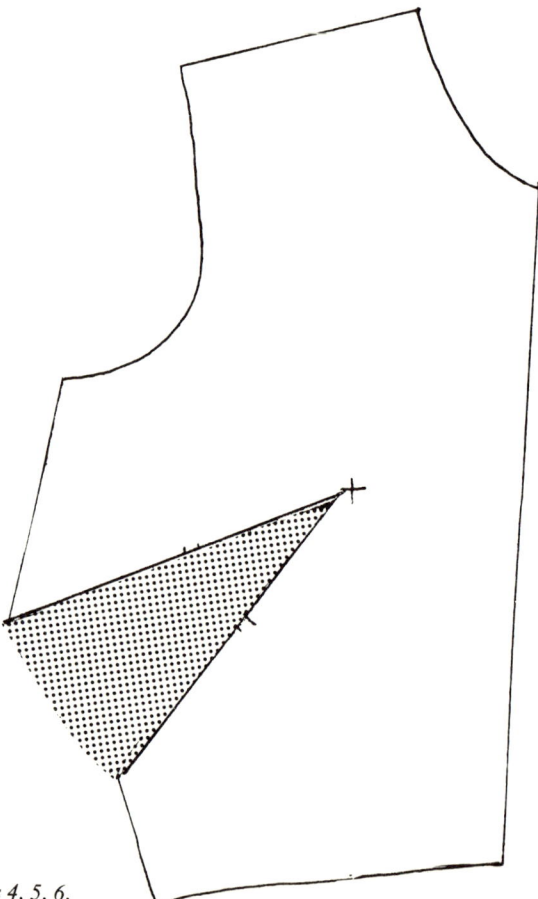

Fig. 4-40. French dart, Steps 4, 5, 6.

41 THE BODICE FRONT

STEP 8: Fold out new dart; cut ends (see Fig. 4-41).

A final example of creating one new dart from the basic two uses the original waist dart location. The bust dart is added to the waist dart, and the increased size compensates (see Fig. 4-42).

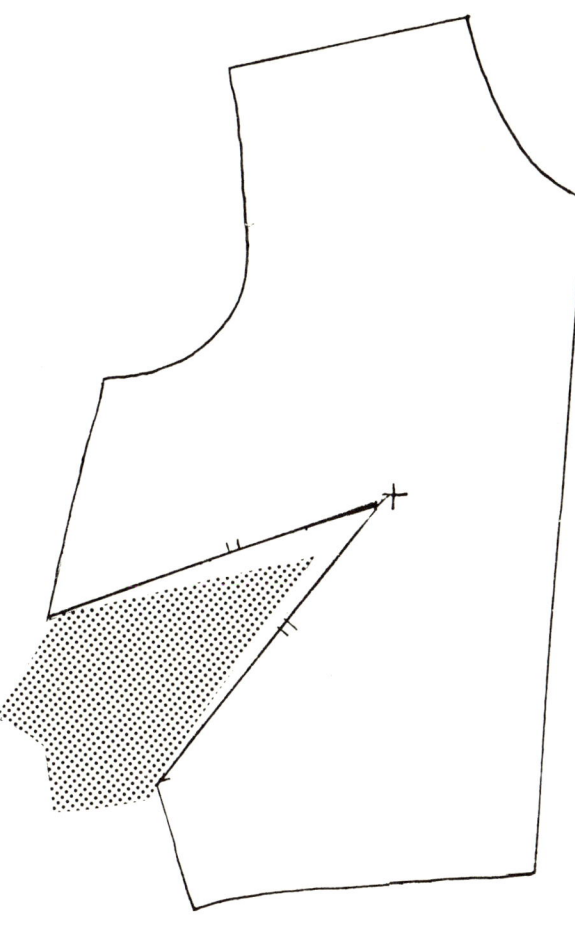

Fig. 4-41. French dart, Steps 7, 8.

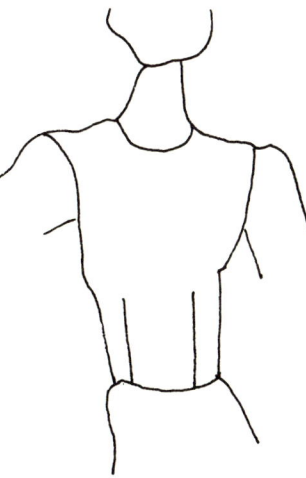

Fig. 4-42. Waist dart.

THE COMPLETE GUIDE TO PATTERN-MAKING 42

STEP 1: Trace sloper (bodice front only).

STEP 2: Draw in new design line, original waist dart location to bust point; draw the line all the way to the point of bust.

STEP 3: Cross-notch (see Fig. 4-43).

STEP 4: Fold out darts.

STEP 5: Cut on new design line.

STEP 6: Add paper (see Fig. 4-44).

STEP 7: Re-draw dart in bodice front.

STEP 8: Fold out new darts; cut ends (see Fig. 4-45).

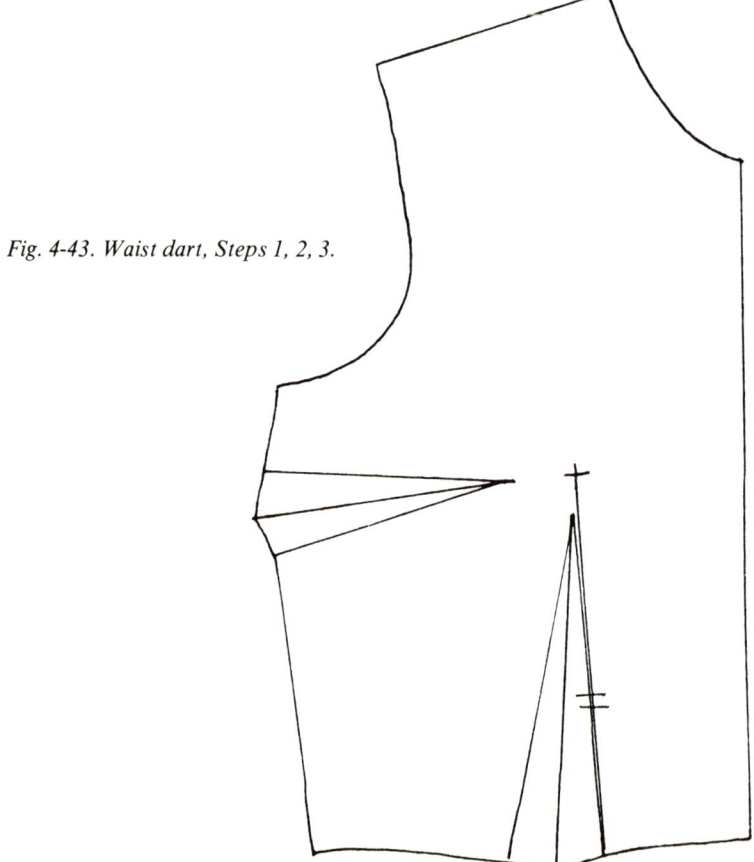

Fig. 4-43. Waist dart, Steps 1, 2, 3.

43 THE BODICE FRONT

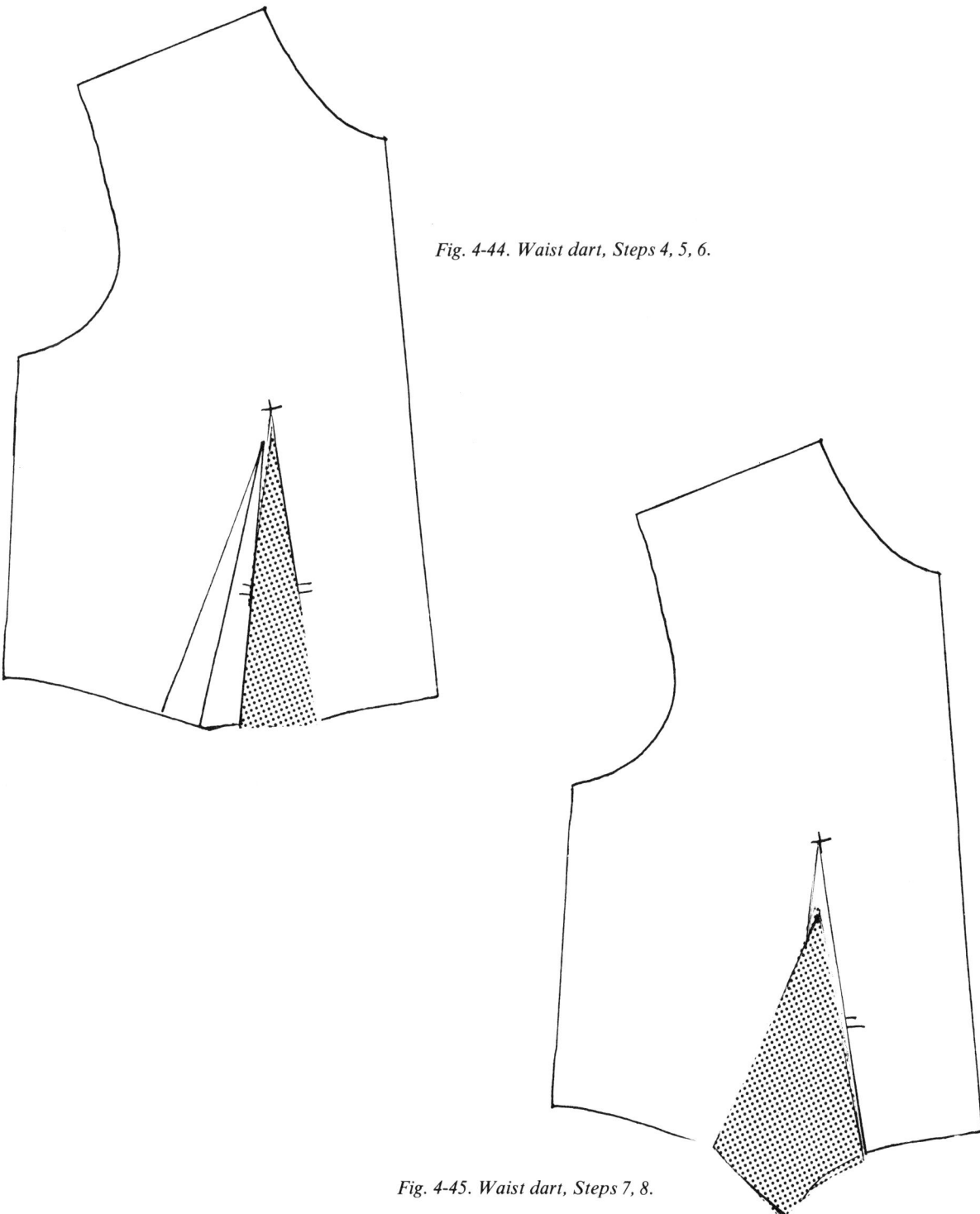

Fig. 4-44. Waist dart, Steps 4, 5, 6.

Fig. 4-45. Waist dart, Steps 7, 8.

THE COMPLETE GUIDE TO PATTERN-MAKING

Manipulation to two Darts

In this example two new darts are created from the original two. Many locations could have been chosen, but the one illustrated gives a diamond shape in the center of the completed bodice which is attractive either in a plain fabric or a stripe. The two new darts can be unequal in size or exactly equal. The latter is more usual (see Fig. 4-46).

STEP 1: Trace sloper (bodice front only).

STEP 2: Draw in new design lines, center front neck to bust point, and center front waist to bust point; draw the lines all the way to the bust point.

STEP 3: Cross-notch each dart (see Fig. 4-47).

STEP 4: Fold out darts.

STEP 5: Cut on new design lines.

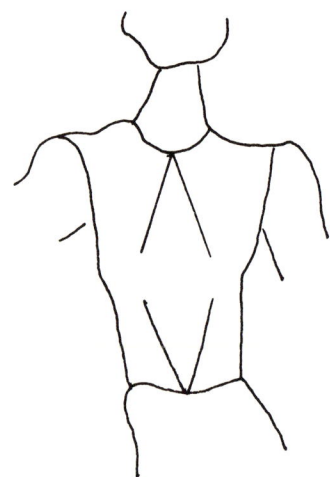

Fig. 4-46. Two darts.

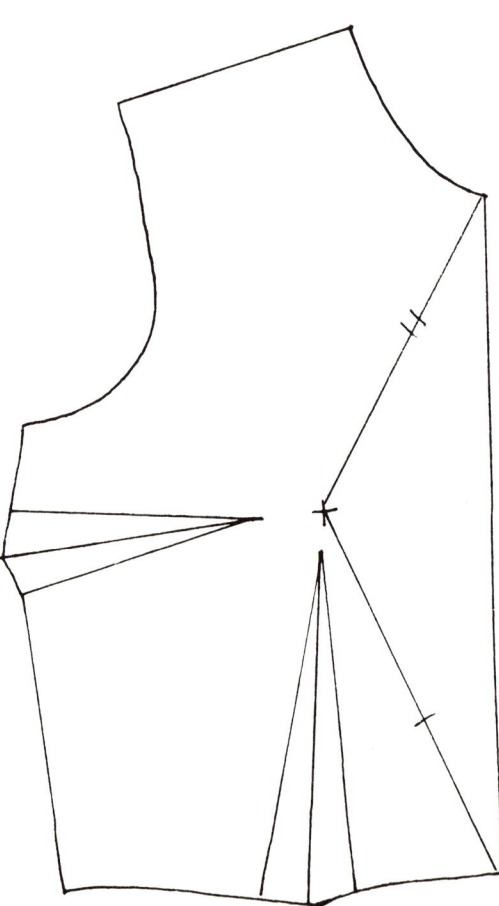

Fig. 4-47. Two darts, Steps 1, 2, 3.

45 THE BODICE FRONT

STEP 6: Add paper to each dart (see Fig. 4-48).

STEP 7: Re-draw darts in bodice front.

STEP 8: Fold out new darts; cut ends (see Fig. 4-49).

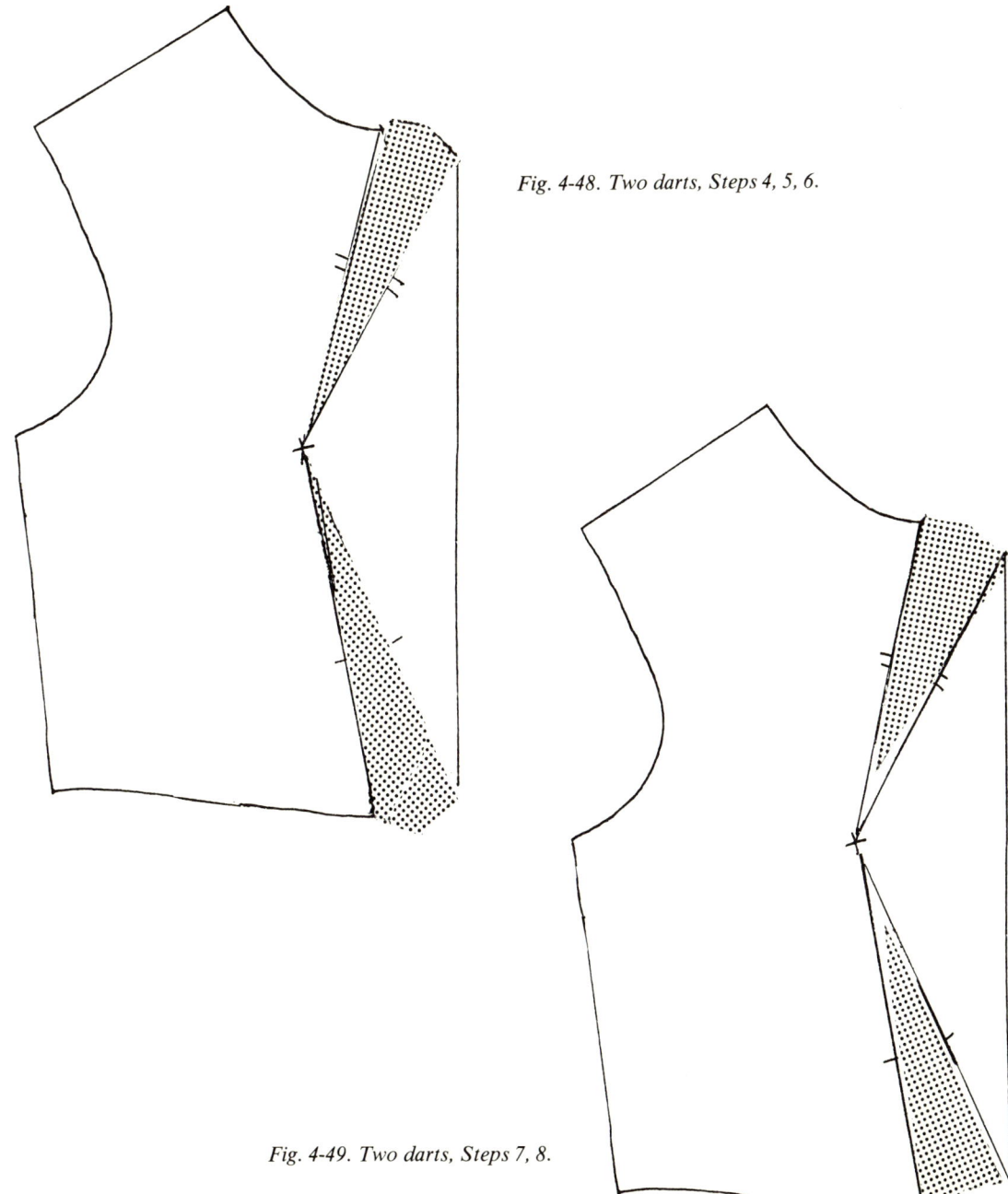

Fig. 4-48. Two darts, Steps 4, 5, 6.

Fig. 4-49. Two darts, Steps 7, 8.

THE COMPLETE GUIDE TO PATTERN-MAKING

Manipulation to three Darts

Three darts can be created from the original two. In this example, the waist location has been chosen, though other locations are, of course, possible. The darts illustrated are drawn one on each side of the original waist dart and one over the original waist dart. The new darts on either side of the original waist dart do not head toward the bust point but rather straight up. You must cut to the bust point to release fullness. Thhs is shown by the dotted lines (see Fig. 4-50).

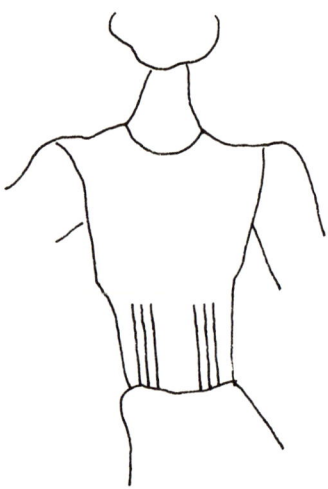

Fig. 4-50. Three darts.

STEP 1: Trace sloper (bodice front only).

STEP 2: Draw in new design lines, one waist dart on each side of original waist dart and one on top of original waist dart.

STEP 3: Cross-notch each dart (see Fig. 4-51).

STEP 4: Fold out darts.

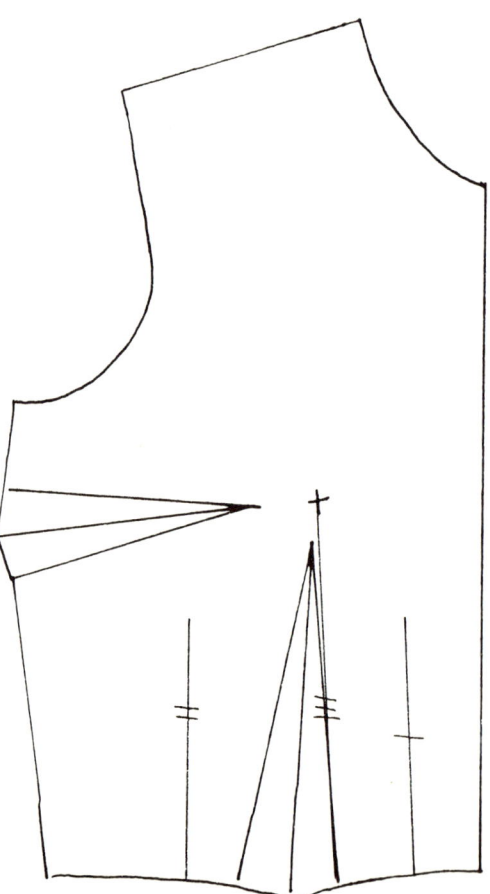

Fig. 4-51. Three darts, Steps 1, 2, 3.

47 THE BODICE FRONT

STEP 5: Cut on new design lines.

STEP 6: Add paper to each dart (see Fig. 4-52).

STEP 7: Re-draw all three darts.

STEP 8: Fold out new darts; cut ends (see Fig. 4-53).

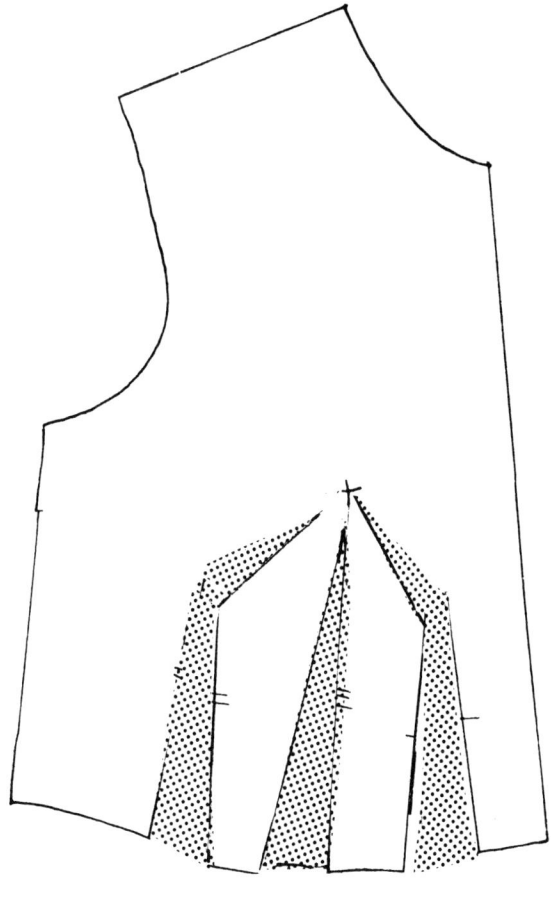

Fig. 4-52. Three darts, Steps 4, 5, 6.

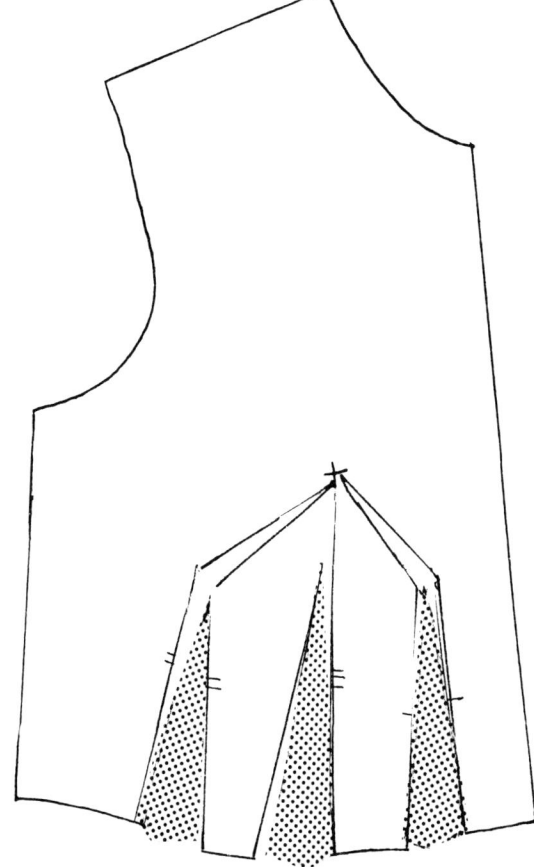

Fig. 4-53. Three darts, Steps 7, 8.

THE COMPLETE GUIDE TO PATTERN-MAKING 48

Manipulation to Waist Tucks

Waist tucks are made in the same way as the shoulder tucks. The fullness will be above the waist, in the midriff area in this design (see Fig. 4-54).

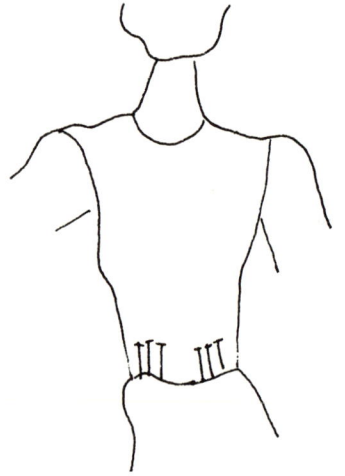

Fig. 4-54. Waist tucks.

STEP 1: Trace sloper (bodice front only).

STEP 2: Draw in new design lines, waist tucks, parallel lines at waist each 2″ long; center line is on one side of original waist dart line.

STEP 3: Cross-notch (see Fig. 4-55).

STEP 4: Fold out darts.

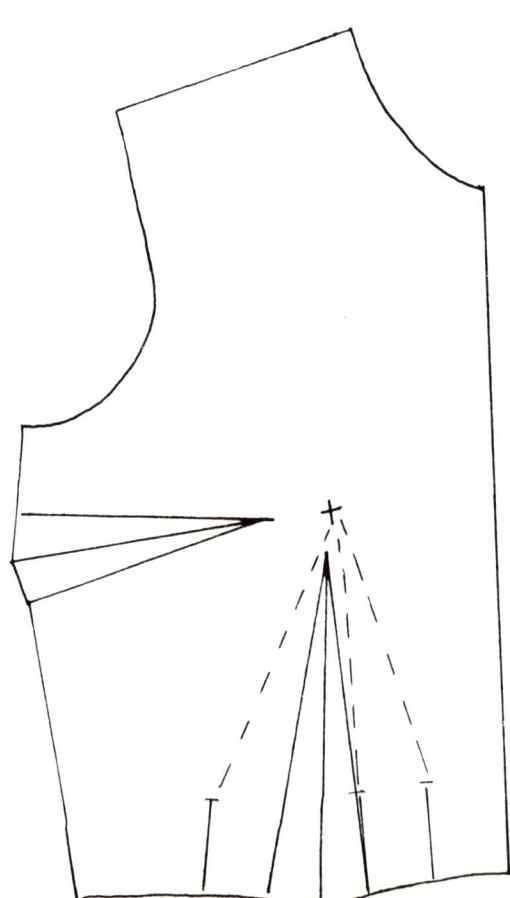

Fig. 4-55. Waist tucks, Steps 1, 2, 3.

49 THE BODICE FRONT

STEP 5: Cut on new design lines; cut all the way to the bust point, following dotted lines.

STEP 6: Add paper (see Fig. 4-56).

STEP 7: Redraw tucks, ending 2" above waist.

STEP 8: Fold out tucks; cut ends (see Fig. 4-57).

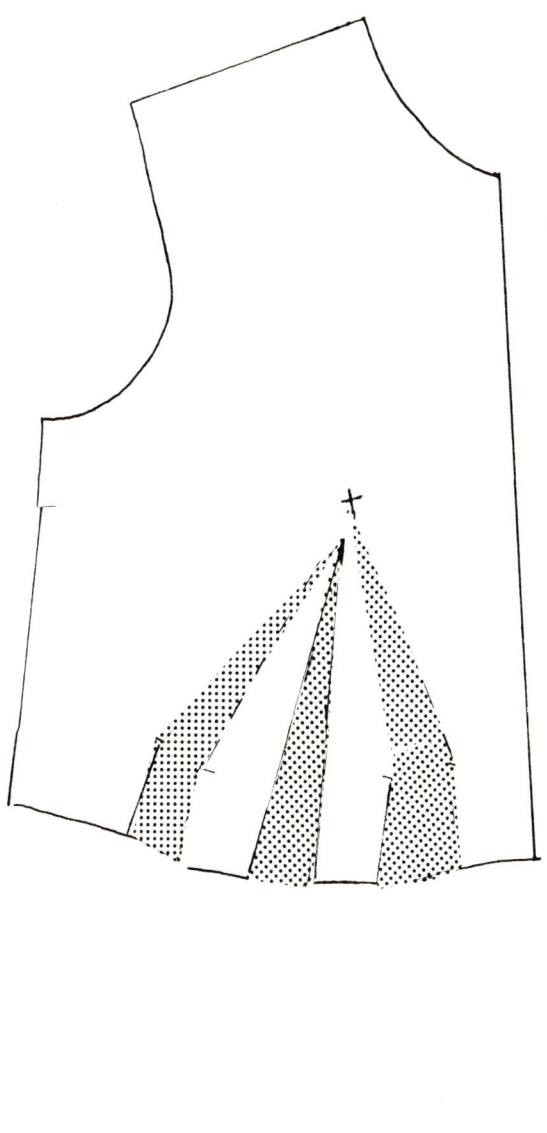

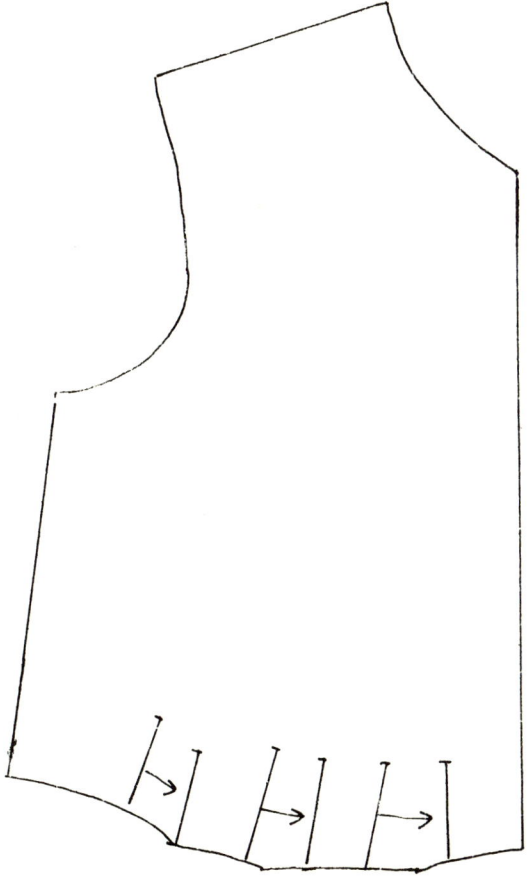

Fig. 4-56. Waist tucks, Steps 4, 5, 6.

Fig. 4-57. Waist tucks, Steps 7, 8.

Cowl Neck

The cowl neckline has soft folds at a squared-off neckline. The self-facing often conceals metal weights which help hold down the folds. The darts are transferred to the neck edge. The paper added creates a right angle at center front and shoulder at neck. There are no darts in the completed pattern (see Fig. 4-58).

STEP 1: Trace sloper (bodice front only).

STEP 2: Draw in new design line, center front neck to bust point.

STEP 3: Fold out darts (see Fig. 4-59).

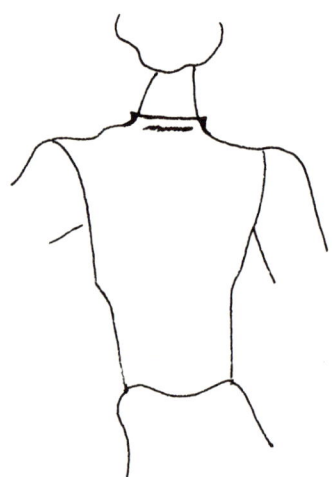

Fig. 4-58. Cowl neck.

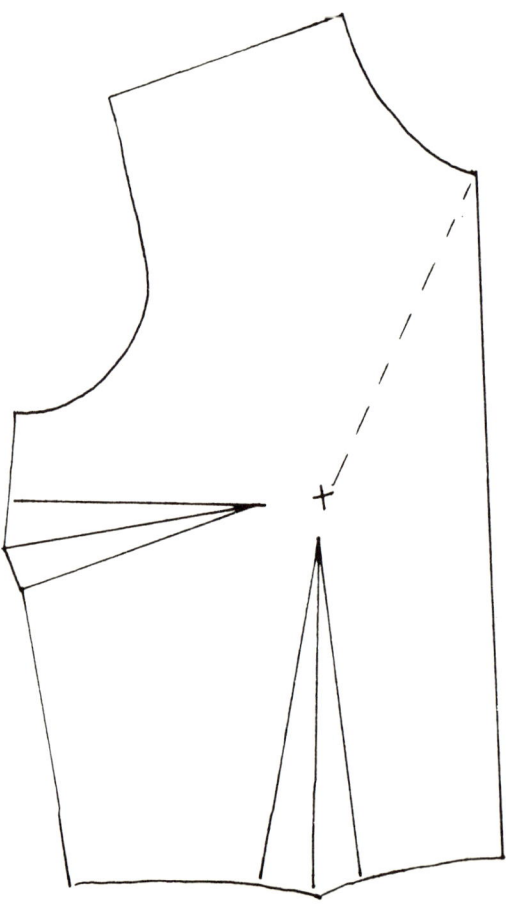

Fig. 4-59. Cowl neck, Steps 1, 2, 3.

51 THE BODICE FRONT

STEP 4: Cut on new design line.

STEP 5: Add paper; place center front on one edge of piece of paper; place neck edge at shoulder on edge at 90° angle to front edge; this is the amount of paper necessary to add for the cowl neck.

STEP 6: Add facing; facing is usually 2″ wide, and the left edge is angled so that when it is folded down it will fit smoothly over the shoulder seam (see Fig. 4-60).

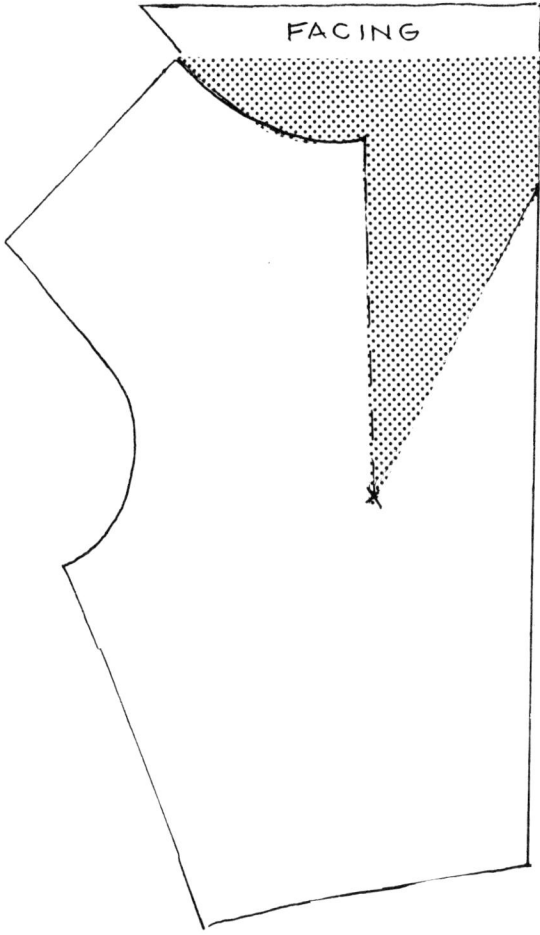

Fig. 4-60. Cowl neck, Steps 4, 5, 6.

Cowl Neck with Dart

An alternate version for the cowl neck gives less fullness at the neck by leaving one dart intact and transferring the other to the neck edge for soft folds at the neck (see Fig. 4-61).

STEP 1: Trace sloper (bodice front only).

STEP 2: Draw in new design line, center front neck to bust point.

STEP 3: Fold out one dart only (see Fig. 4-62).

STEP 4: Cut on new design line.

STEP 5: Add paper; place center front on one edge of piece of paper; place neck edge at shoulder on edge at 90° angle to front edge; this is the amount of paper necessary to add for the cowl neck.

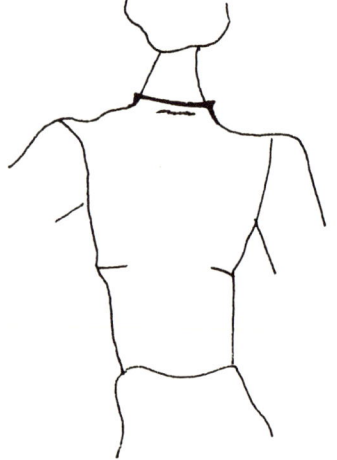

Fig. 4-61. Cowl neck with dart.

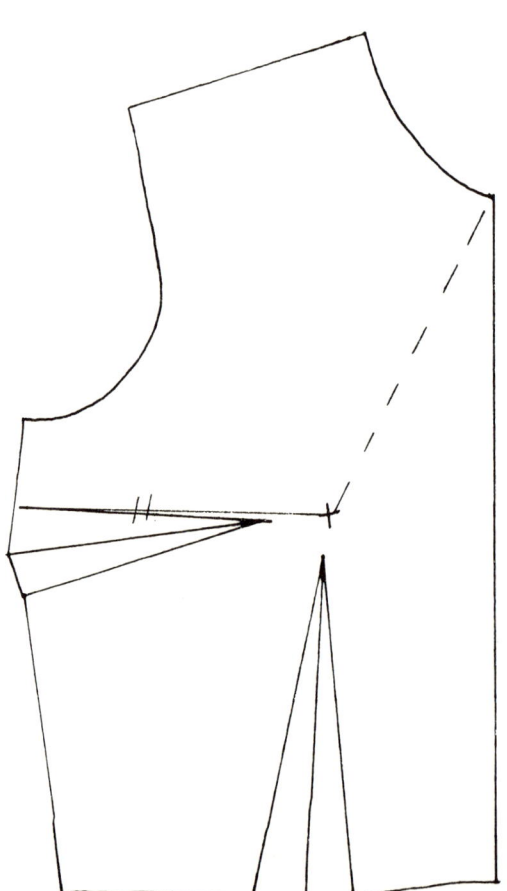

Fig. 4-62. Cowl neck with dart, Steps 1, 2, 3.

STEP 6: Add facing; facing is usually 2″ wide, and the left edge is angled so that when it is folded down it will fit smoothly over the shoulder seam (see Fig. 4-63).

> **NOTE:** In this design, the remaining dart can be moved to any location, following the basic procedures.

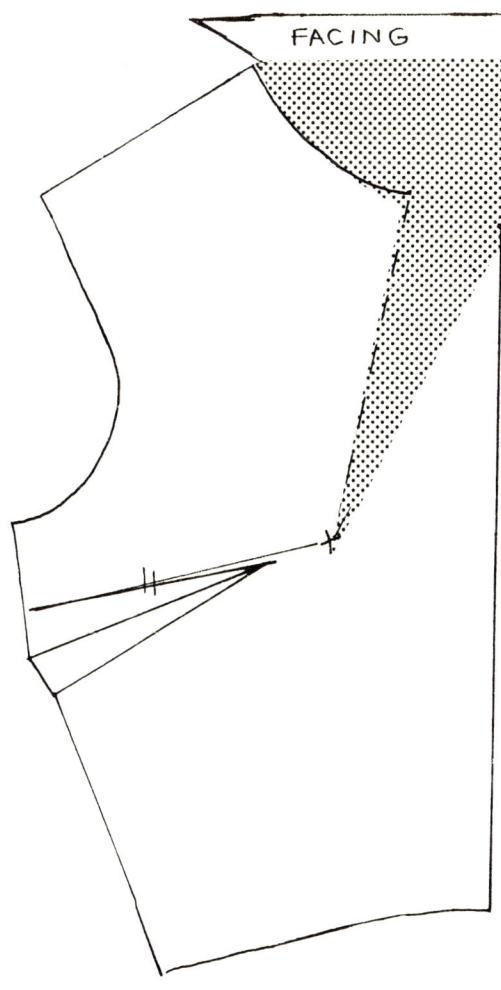

Fig. 4-63. Cowl neck with dart, Steps 4, 5, 6.

THE COMPLETE GUIDE TO PATTERN-MAKING 54

Yoke in Bodice

To create a yoke in the bodice, draw in the desired shape in the location selected. In the example illustrated, a curved yoke is drawn in the upper part of the bodice. The darts are changed to waist gathers, and an extension drawn onto the lower bodice front in order to accommodate stitching the yoke onto the bodice. To do this, you would face the yoke and top-stitch it onto the lower bodice front (see Fig. 4-64).

STEP 1: Trace sloper (bodice front only).

STEP 2: Draw in new design line; draw curved yoke in bodice front as illustrated.

STEP 3: Cross-notch (see Fig. 4-65).

STEP 4: Fold out darts.

STEP 5: Cut on new design line for yoke; cut over original waist dart line to changed darts into waist gathers.

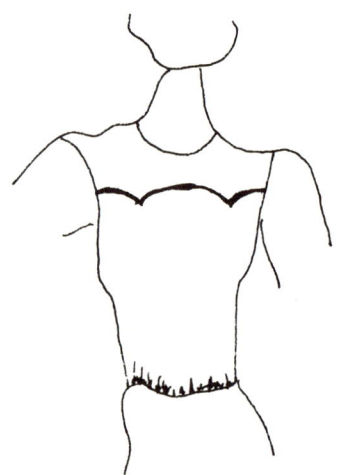

Fig. 4-64. Yoke in bodice.

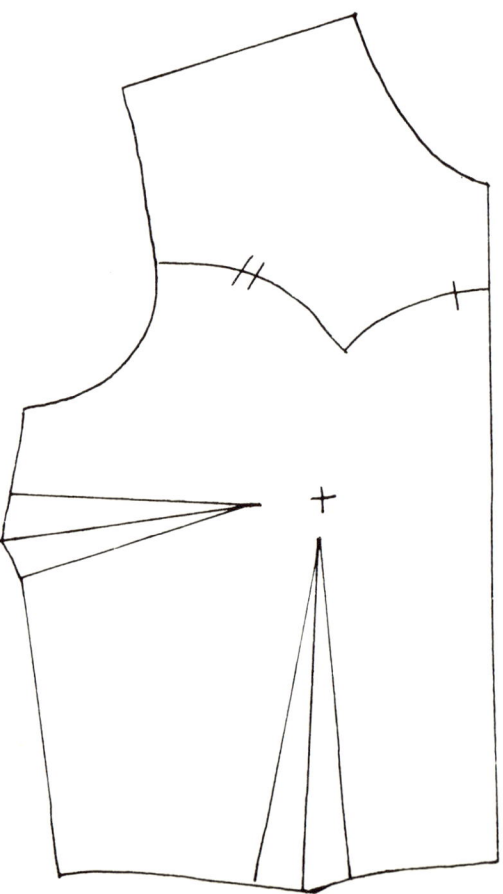

Fig. 4-65. Yoke in bodice, Steps 1, 2, 3.

55 THE BODICE FRONT

STEP 6: Add paper to waist dart area; add extension to top of lower bodice section as extension for stitching yoke section to lower section (see Fig. 4-66).

STEP 7: Indicate waist dart is to be gathers by labeling with word "gather" and using arrows on either side of dart area.

STEP 8: Cut end of paper using Dietzgen curve to obtain a smooth line (see Fig. 4-67).

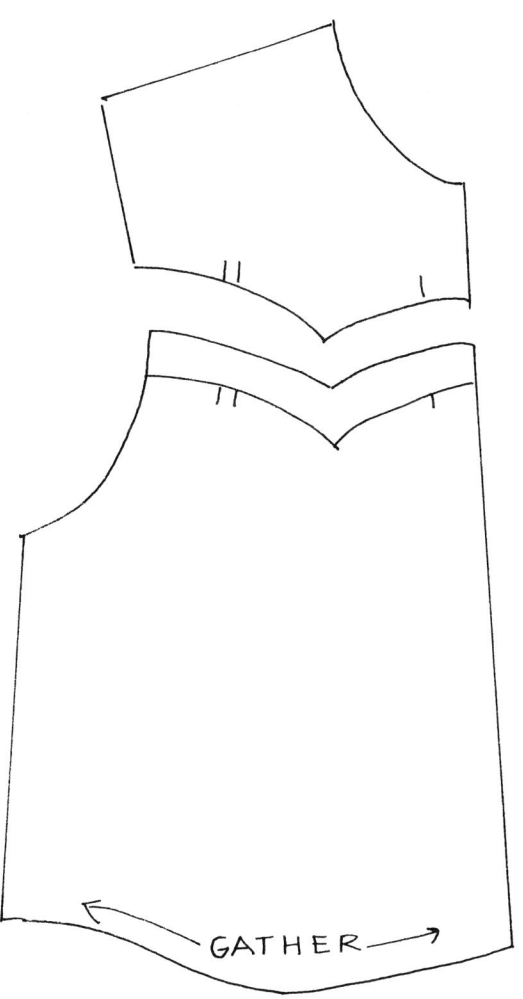

Fig. 4-67. Yoke in bodice, Steps 7, 8.

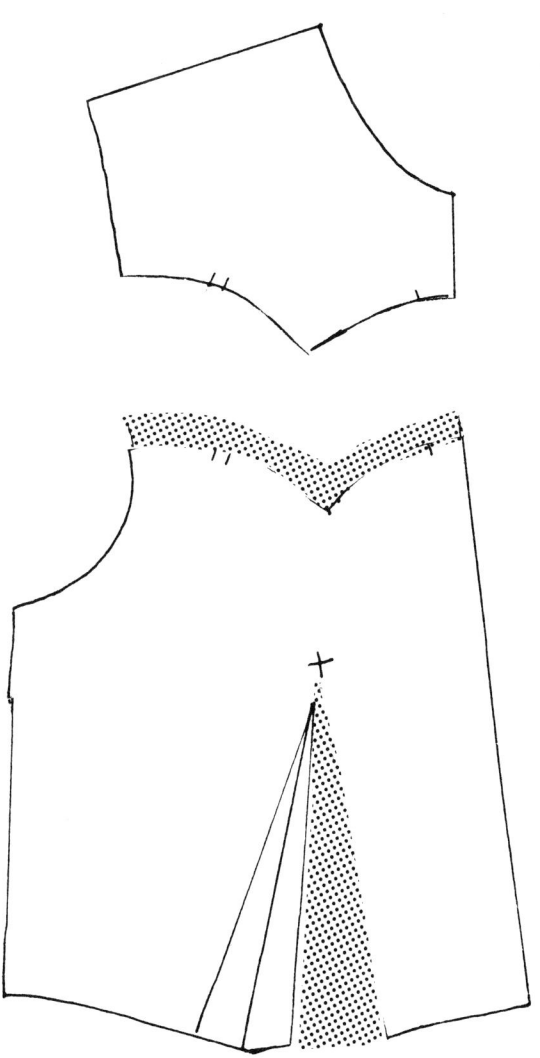

Fig. 4-66. Yoke in bodice, Steps 4, 5, 6.

THE COMPLETE GUIDE TO PATTERN-MAKING

Adding Fullness

Often the designer wishes to do more with the bodice front than just move darts and/or change them into tucks and gathers. Adding fullness is one such techniques. To make the pattern lie flat you must always cut all the way to an edge. In releasing dart fullness it was necessary to cut to the point of the bust. When fullness is added, one cut must be made through the bust point and the remainder must go to an edge of the pattern.

The first example adds fullness at the lower or waist edge (see Fig. 4-68).

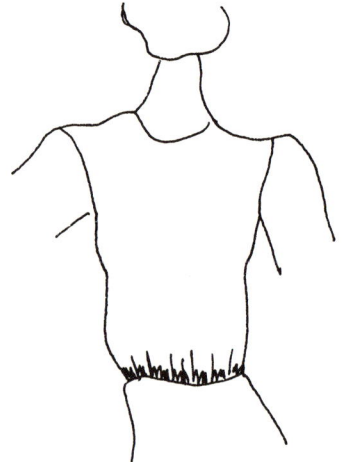

STEP 1: Trace sloper (bodice front only).

STEP 2: Draw in new design lines; waist gathers extend from lower or waist edge to shoulder and/or neck edge; draw lines from waist to shoulder and neck edges; one line ends at bust point to release dart fullness.

STEP 3: Fold out darts (see Fig. 4-69).

STEP 4: Cut on new design lines; cut all the way to the edges but not through shoulder and neck edges.

Fig. 4-68. Waist gathers.

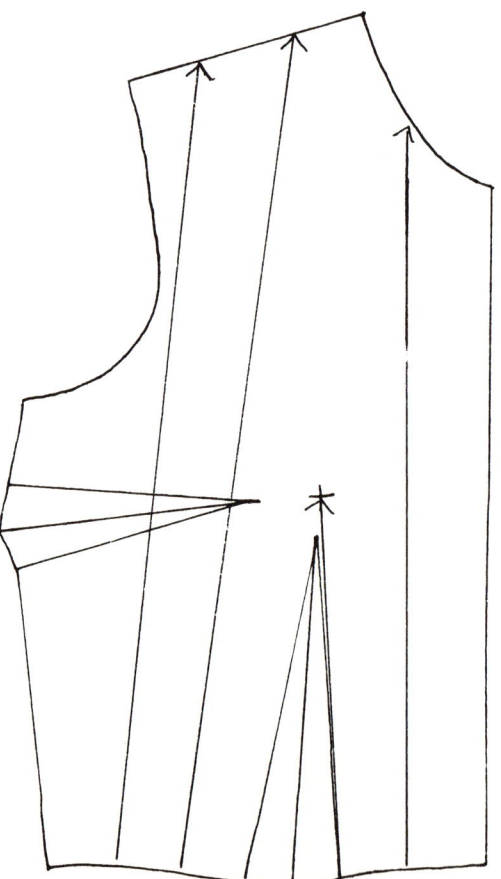

Fig. 4-69. Waist gathers, Steps 1, 2.

57 THE BODICE FRONT

STEP 5: Spread desired amount, and add paper; gathers usually are from two to three times the original width; measure original waist and spread so that resulting measurement is two to three times the original (see Fig. 4-70).

STEP 6: Indicate that lower edge is to be gathered by writing word "gather" and drawing arrows on either side of word.

STEP 7: Draw and cut waist edge, using curve stick or Dietzgen curve to help you obtain a smooth line (see Fig. 4-7).

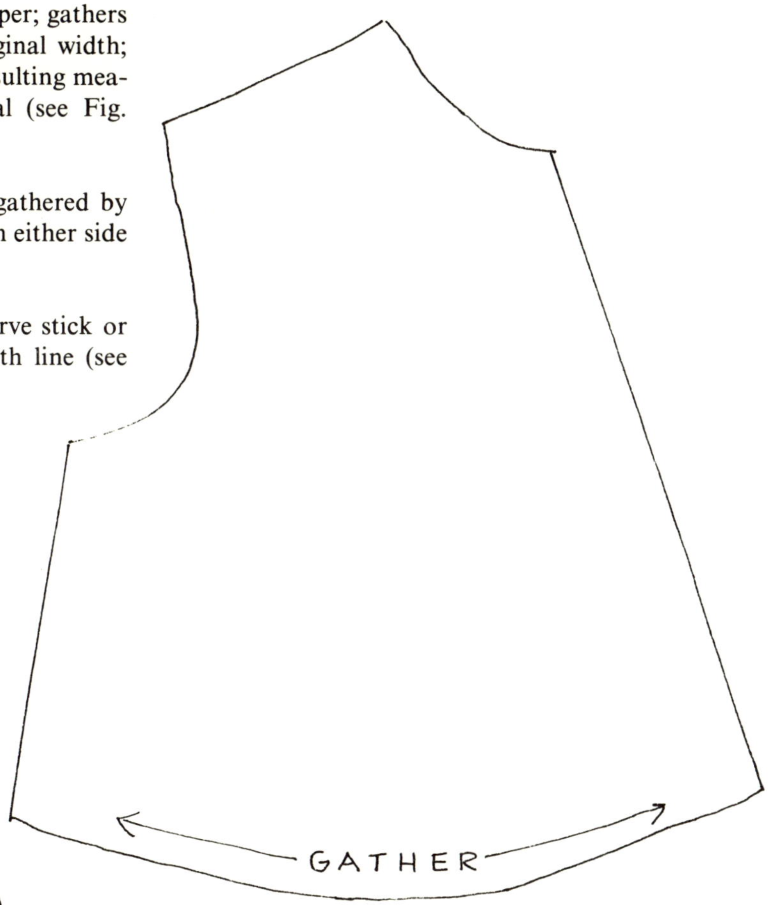

Fig. 4-70. Waist gathers, Steps 3, 4, 5.

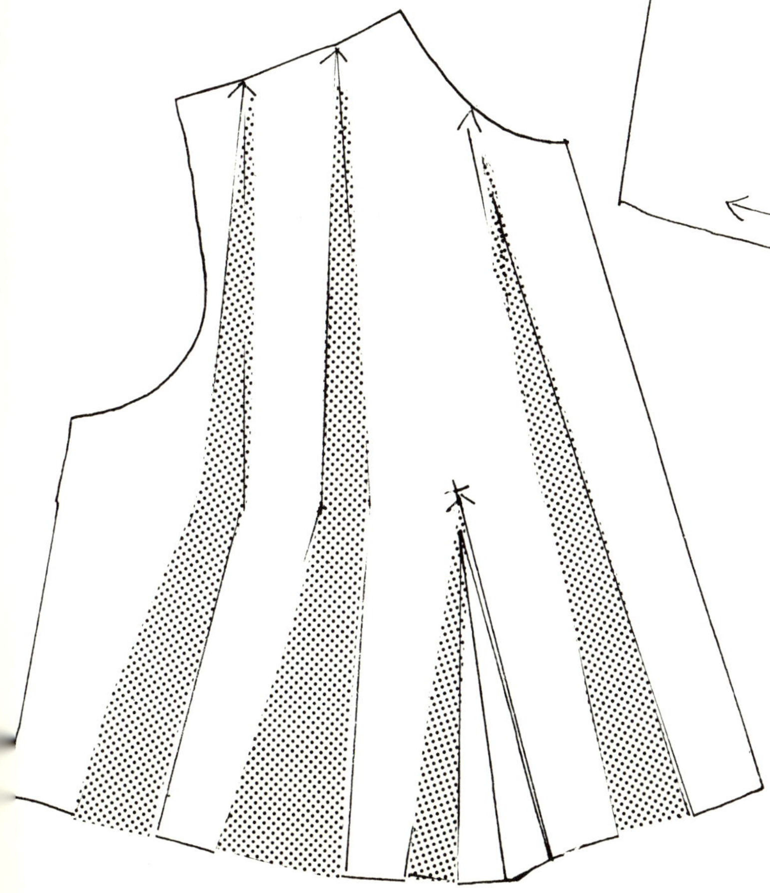

Fig. 4-71. Waist gathers, Steps 6, 7.

THE COMPLETE GUIDE TO PATTERN-MAKING 58

Lowered Neckline with Fullness Added

When a lowered neckline is desired, the portion of the sloper not needed in the new design must be cut away first. Other changes are made thereafter. In this example, gathers are added at the neck edge, as for a peasant blouse (see Fig. 4-72).

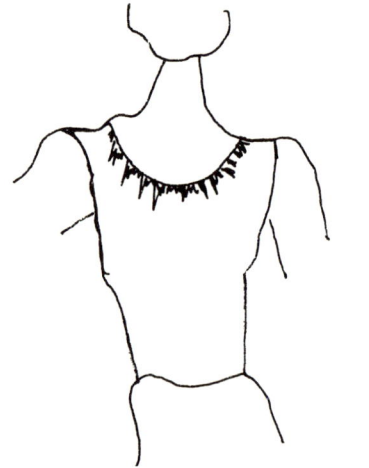

STEP 1: Trace sloper (bodice front only).

STEP 2: Draw in new design lines; draw in lowered neckline in position desired; cut away neckline area on line as drawn in (see Fig. 4-73).

STEP 3: Draw in new design lines for fullness; draw lines from neck curve to waist; one line must be drawn through the bust point (see Fig. 4-74).

STEP 4: Fold out darts.

Fig. 4-72. Lowered neckline, fullness added.

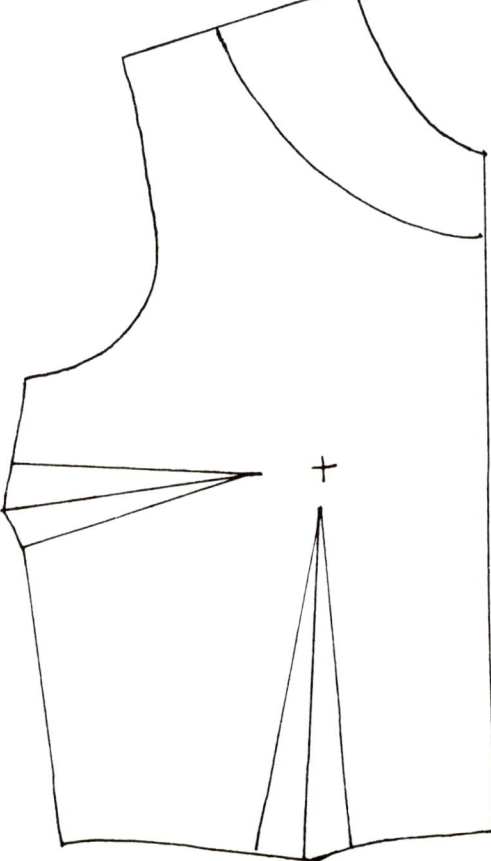

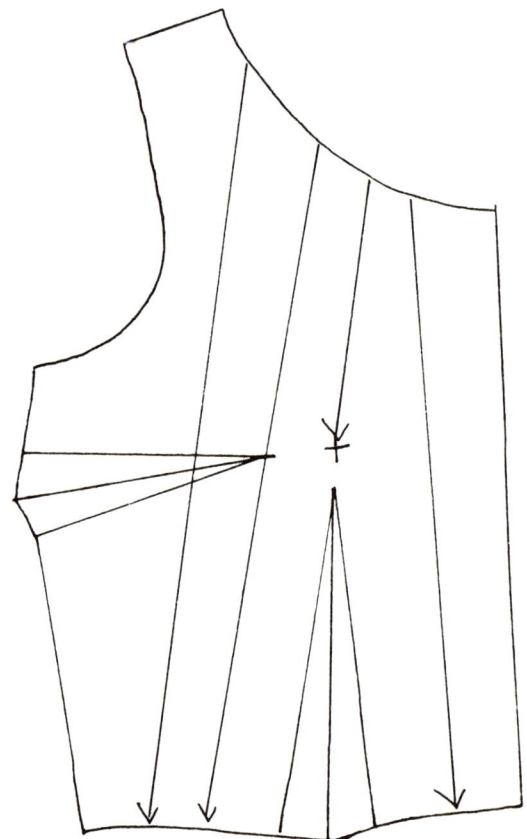

Fig. 4-74. Lowered neckline, fullness added, Step 3.

Fig. 4-73. Lowered neckline, fullness added, Steps 1, 2.

59 THE BODICE FRONT

STEP 5: Cut on new design lines; cut all the way to waist seam but not through it; mend any tears with cellophane tape.

STEP 6: Spread and add paper; twice the original width is usually plenty to give fullness at the lowered neck edge (see Fig. 4-75).

STEP 7: Indicate that neck edge is to be gathered by writing word "gather" and drawing arrows on either side of word.

STEP 8: Draw and cut neck edge, using curve stick or Dietzgen curve to help you obtain a smooth line (see Fig. 4-76).

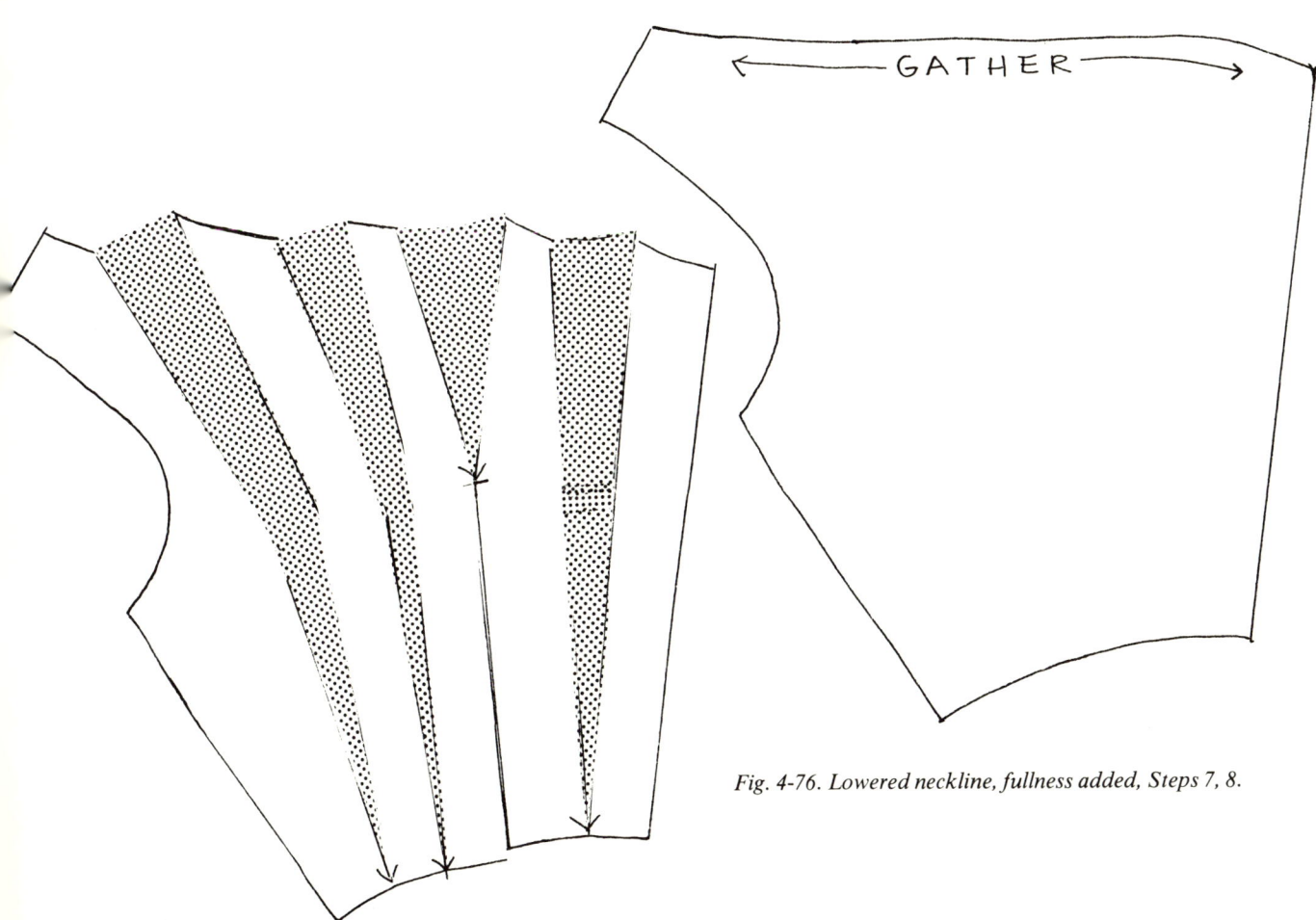

Fig. 4-76. Lowered neckline, fullness added, Steps 7, 8.

Fig. 4-75. Lowered neckline, fullness added, Steps 4, 5, 6.

Fullness Added Under Bust

Adding fullness under the bust creates an impression of a yoke in this area without actually separating the pattern pieces. The design adds emphasis to the bust area. Since fullness is added, one must choose a fabric that will lend itself to soft gathers (see Fig. 4-77).

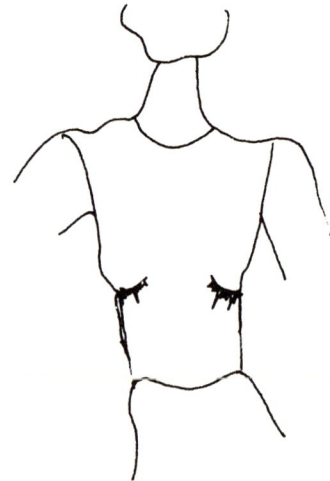

STEP 1: Trace sloper (bodice front only).

STEP 2: Draw in new design lines; draw curved false yoke line from side seam under bust dart to point of bust; draw arrows from this line to waistline to show cutting lines for gathers.

STEP 3: Cross-notch (see Fig. 4-78).

Fig. 4-77. Under bust fullness.

Fig. 4-78. Under bust fullness, Steps 1, 2, 3.

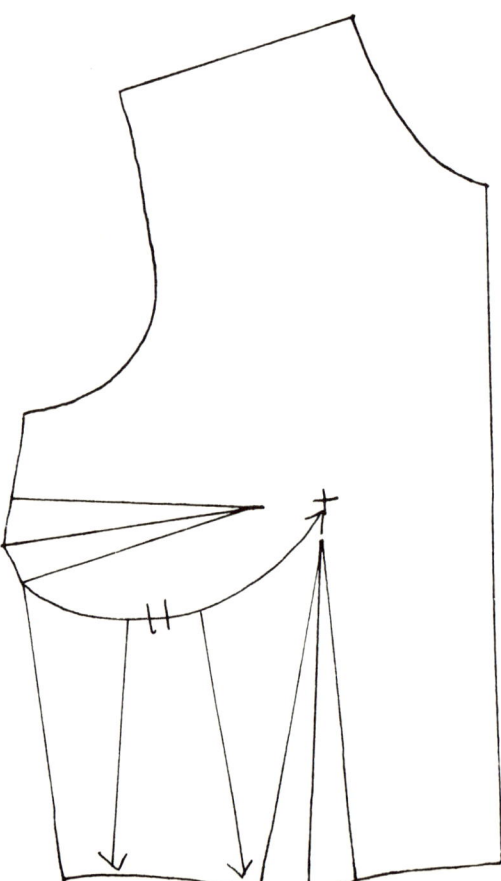

61 THE BODICE FRONT

STEP 4: Fold out darts.

STEP 5: Cut on new design lines; cut on curved line first, then on arrows from false yoke line to waistline.

STEP 6: Spread and add paper; twice the original distance is enough to spread (see Fig. 4-79).

STEP 7: Write word "gather" along curved false yoke line, and draw arrows on either side of word.

STEP 8: Draw and cut yoke line, creating a smooth line with the help of the curve stick or Dietzgen curve (see Fig. 4-80).

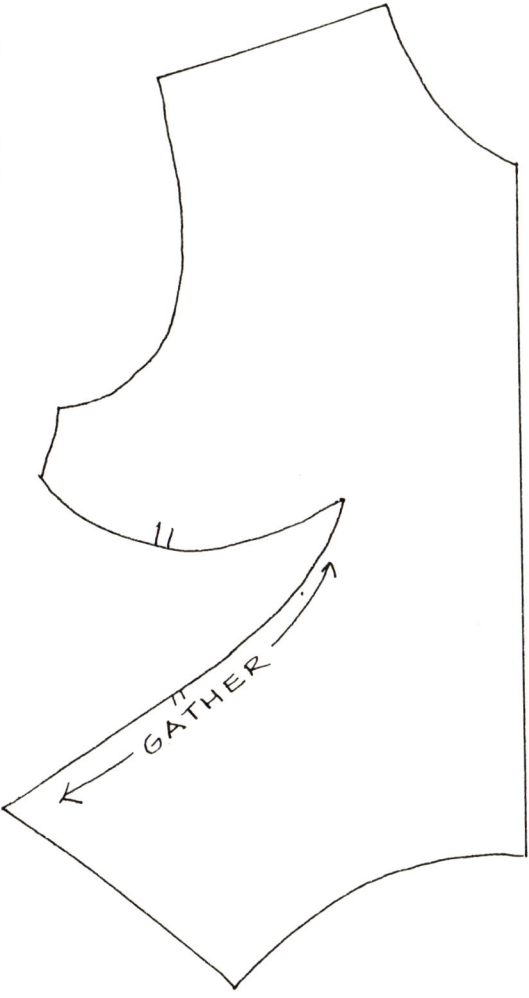

Fig. 4-80. Under bust fullness, Steps 7, 8.

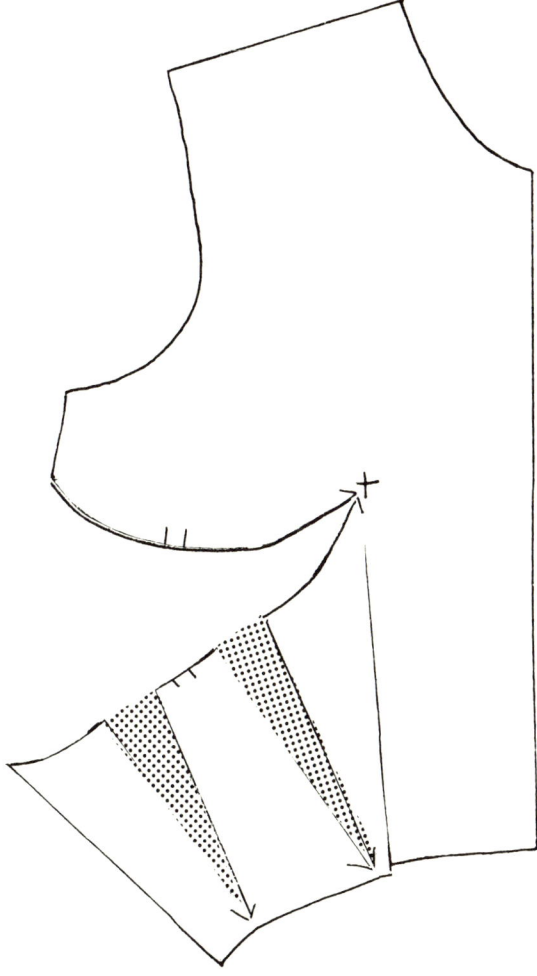

Fig. 4-79. Under bust fullness, Steps 4, 5, 6.

Traditional Princess Line—Darts into Seams

The designer can change darts into seams by following the basic steps. In the traditional princess line, a seam extends from the center of the shoulder through the point of the bust to the center of the waist seam. A small amount of ease is added over the bust to compensate for the ease lost when the darts were folded out to the bust point. One cannot re-draw the dart to replace the ease when the darts are changed into seams (see Fig. 4-81).

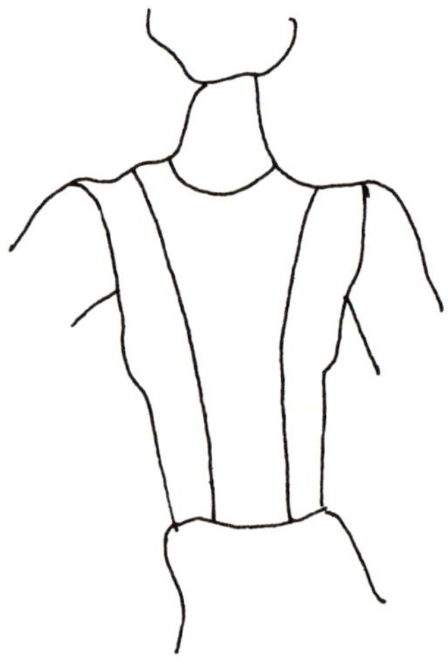

STEP 1: Trace sloper (bodice front only).

STEP 2: Draw in new design line; draw line from center of shoulder, through point of bust to center of waistline seam; use the curve stick to help you get a smooth line.

STEP 3: Cross-notch (see Fig. 4-82).

STEP 4: Fold out darts.

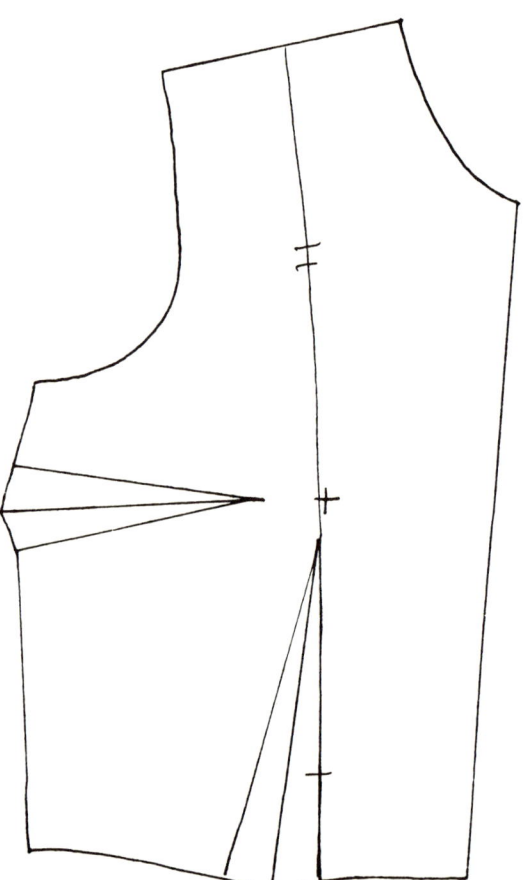

Fig. 4-81. Traditional princess line, darts into seams.

Fig. 4-82. Traditional princess line, Steps 1, 2, 3.

63 THE BODICE FRONT

STEP 5: Cut on new design line.

STEP 6: Add small amount of ease over bust by attaching paper with glue or cellophane tape; ⅛" is enough to replace the ease lost when you folded out the darts to the bust point (see Fig. 4-83).

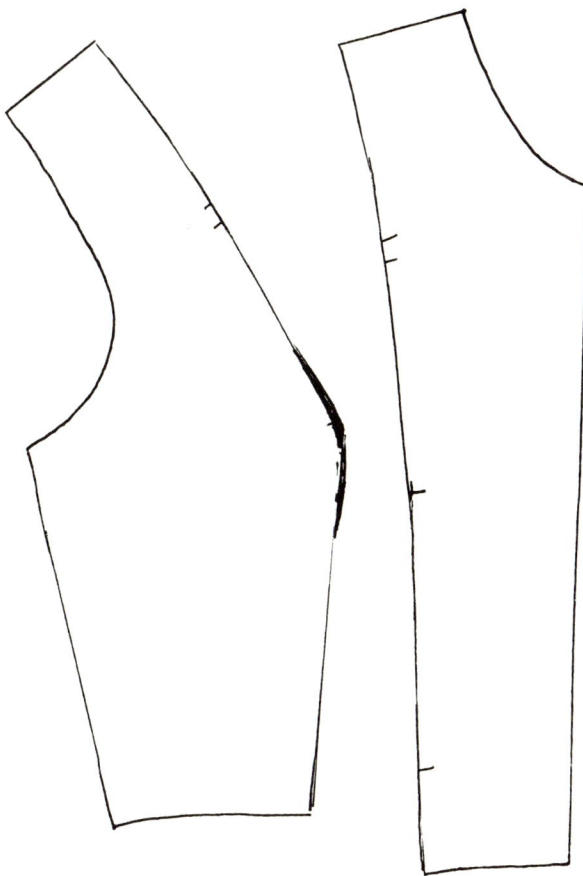

Fig. 4-83. Traditional princess line, Steps 4, 5, 6.

THE COMPLETE GUIDE TO PATTERN-MAKING 64

Princess Variation—Darts into Seams

Variations in the princess line can be made by changing the point from which the lines are drawn. For this example, the line begins in the center of the armhole instead of from the center of the shoulder seam. The line continues through the point of the bust to the center of the waistline (see Fig. 4-84).

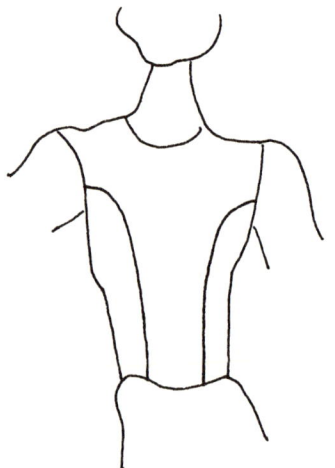

STEP 1: Trace sloper (bodice front only).

STEP 2: Draw in new design line; draw line from center of armhole through point of bust to center of waistline.

STEP 3: Cross-notch (see Fig. 4-85).

STEP 4: Fold out darts.

Fig. 4-84. Princess variation.

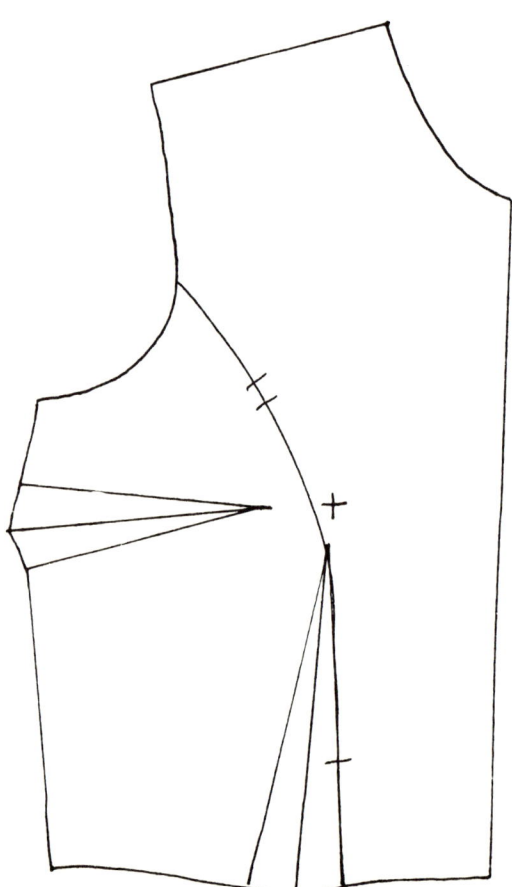

Fig. 4-85. Princess variation, Steps 1, 2, 3.

65 THE BODICE FRONT

STEP 5: Cut on new design line.

STEP 6: Add small amount of ease over bust by attaching paper with glue or cellophane tape to this area; 1/8" is enough to replace the ease lost when the darts were folded out to the bust point (see Fig. 4-86).

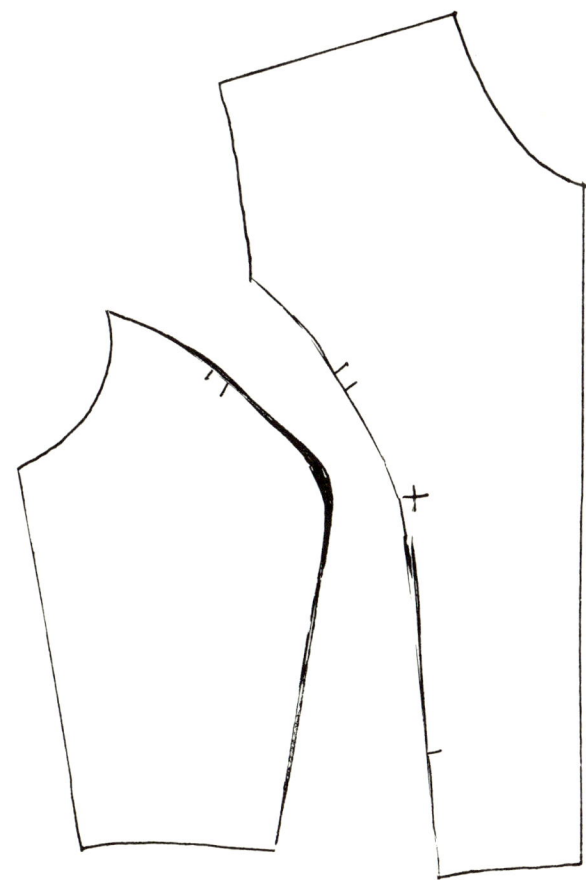

Fig. 4-86. Princess variation, Steps 4, 5, 6.

THE COMPLETE GUIDE TO PATTERN-MAKING 66

Asymmetrical Bodice Front

The asymmetrical bodice front requires the use of the whole bodice front. Since the two sides are not the same, one must work with the whole pattern. The technique is the same for any asymmetrical design. This illustration changes darts into seams by passing them through the bust points (see Fig. 4-87).

STEP 1: Trace sloper; trace two bodice fronts, drawing the darts on the right side of one, the left side of the other so you will have a complete bodice front.

Tape the bodice fronts together down center front.

STEP 2: Draw in new design lines; for this design the lines are drawn from under the left armhole to center neck, from under left bust dart to top of right armhole, and from the lower left waist edge to the center of the right armhole; the second line passes through the left bust point, and the third line passes through the right bust point; use the curve stick to help you get smooth lines.

Label sections "a," "b," "c," "d," (see Fig. 4-88).

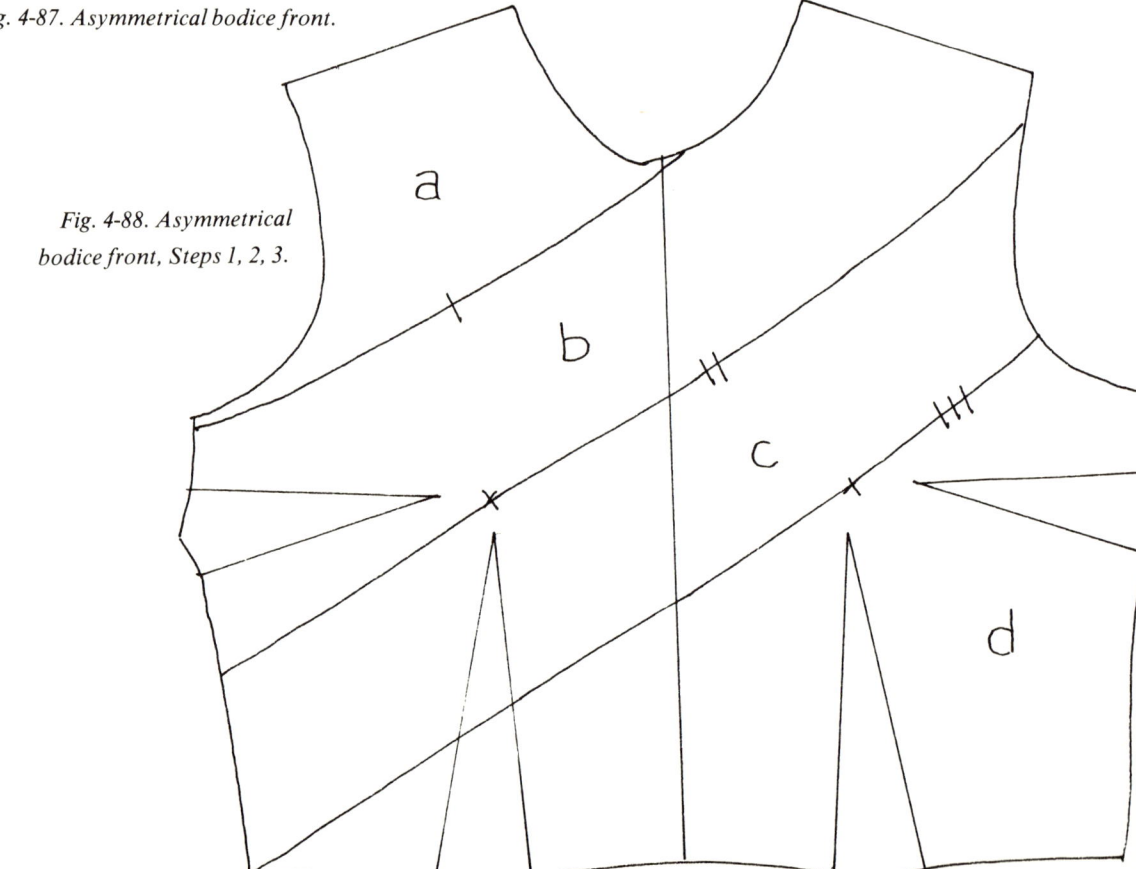

Fig. 4-87. Asymmetrical bodice front.

Fig. 4-88. Asymmetrical bodice front, Steps 1, 2, 3.

67 THE BODICE FRONT

STEP 3: Cross-notch (see Fig. 4-112).

STEP 4: Fold out darts.

STEP 5: Cut on new design lines.

STEP 6: Add ease over bust, both right and left; attach paper to bust point, leaving 1/8" for ease (see Fig. 4-89).

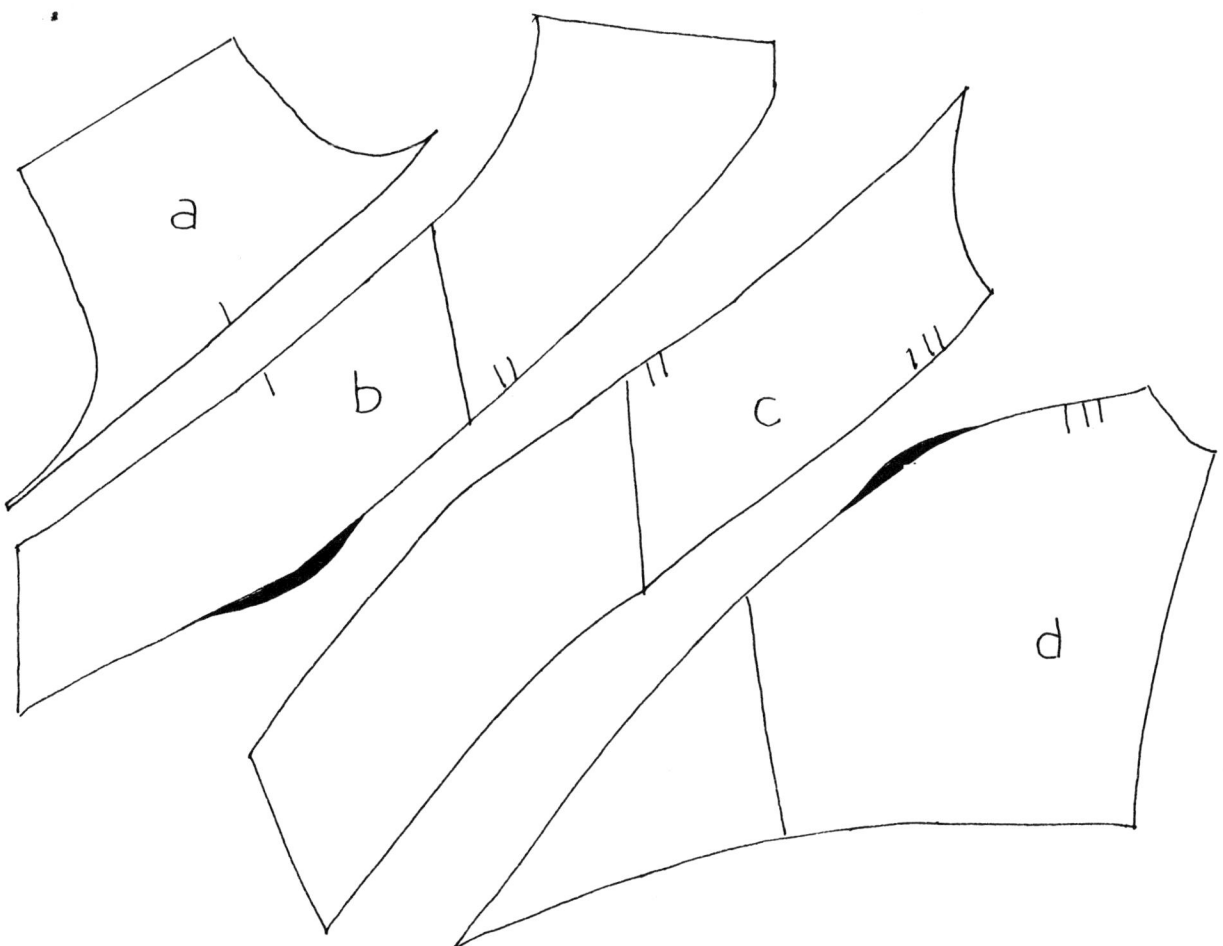

Fig. 4-89. Asymmetrical bodice front, Steps 4, 5, 6.

THE COMPLETE GUIDE TO PATTERN-MAKING 68

Bodice Front Pleats

Bodice front pleats can be an attractive addition to the bodice area. The number and size of pleats must be decided before work begins. For this example, the waist dart has been moved to the bust dart location. Three knife pleats are added to the bodice front (see Fig. 4-90).

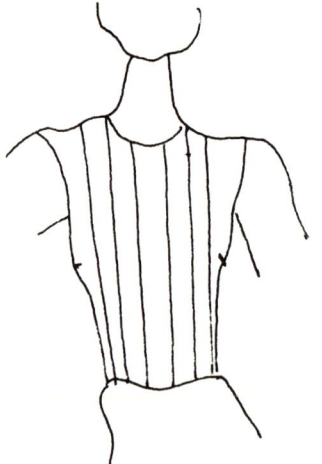

Fig. 4-90. Bodice front pleats.

STEP 1: Trace sloper (bodice back only).

STEP 2: Draw in new design lines; draw in new dart location at bust dart area; complete the steps required to move this dart before continuing with pleats.

Draw in three pleat lines; space pleats evenly remembering that the center front space between pleats will be twice as wide as the space between the other pleats as drawn here (see Figs. 4-91, 4-92).

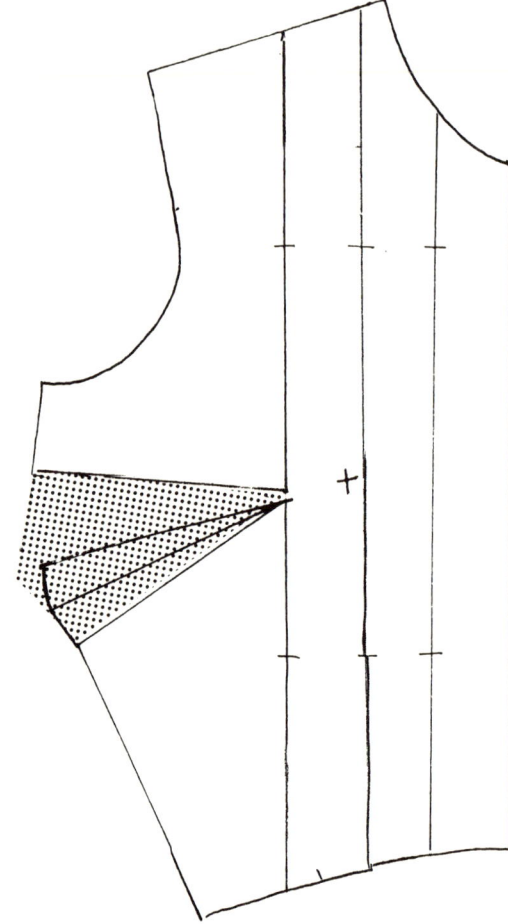

Fig. 4-92. Bodice front pleats, Steps 2, 3.

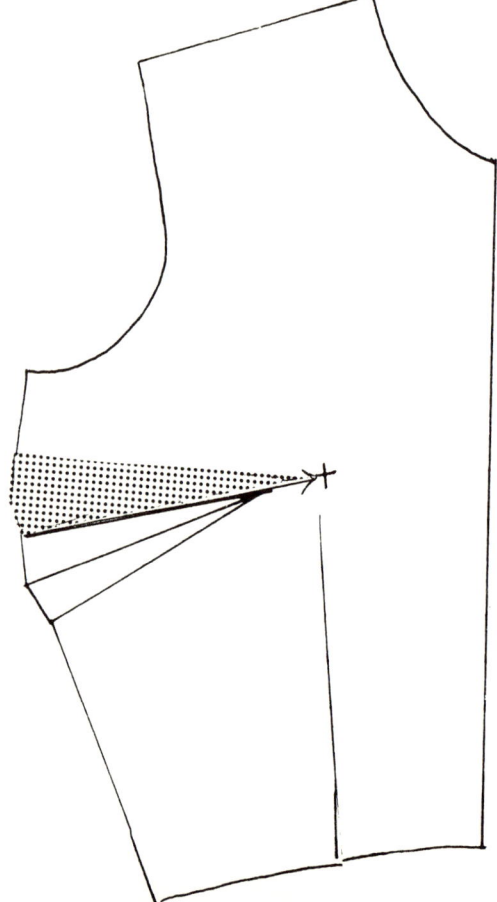

Fig. 4-91. Bodice front pleats, Steps 1, 2.

69 THE BODICE FRONT

STEP 3: Cross-notch (see Fig. 4-92).

STEP 4: Cut on new design lines.

STEP 5: Spread and add paper; knife pleats fall under one side of pleat; they must go in and out, and therefore twice as much area must be left as desired for the depth of the finished pleat.

In this example, ½″ has been added, which would give a ¼″ deep pleat when folded and stitched (see Fig. 4-93).

STEP 6: Fold out new pleats, and cut top and lower edges; draw arrows to indicate direction pleat is to be folded (see Fig. 4-94).

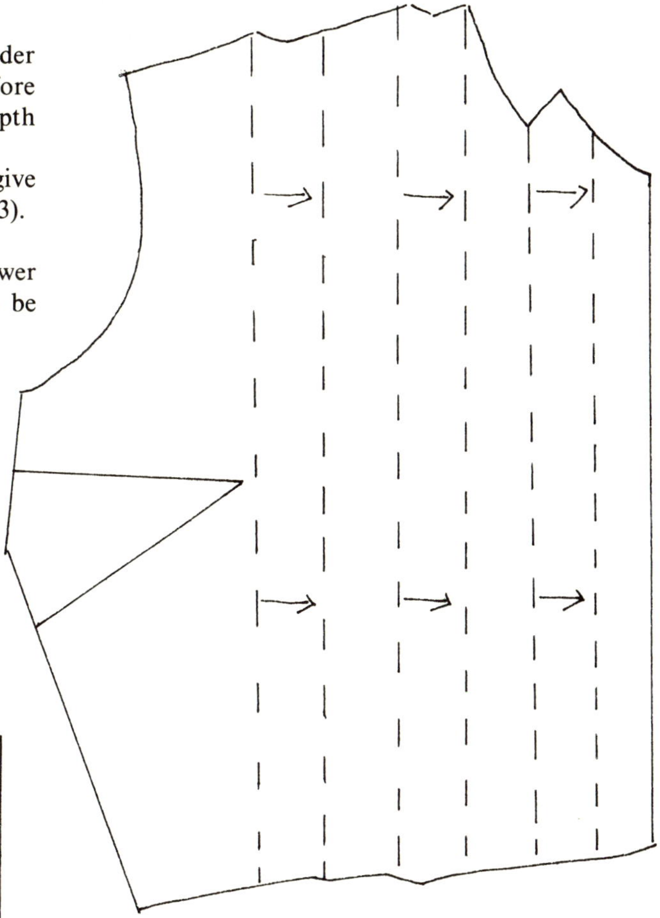

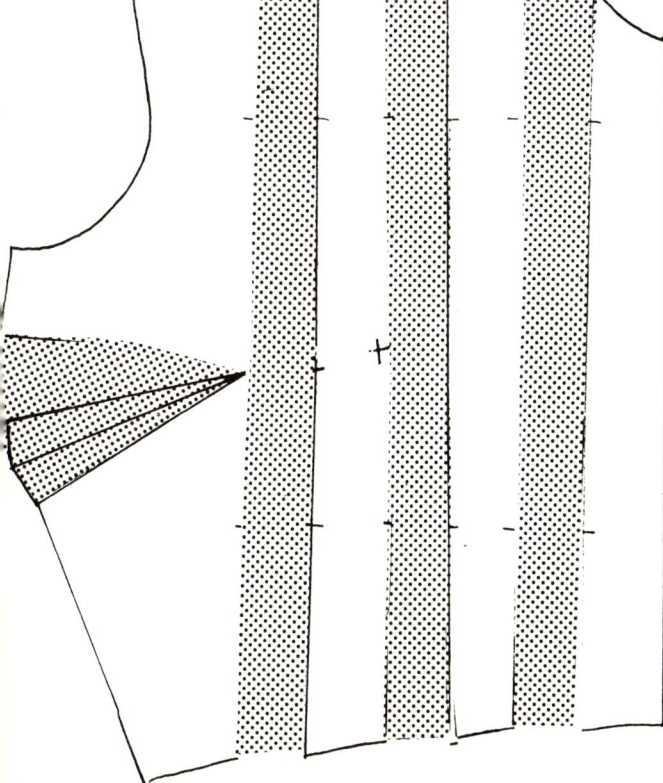

Fig. 4-93. Bodice front pleats, Steps 4, 5.

Fig. 4-94. Bodice front pleats, Step 6.

THE COMPLETE GUIDE TO PATTERN-MAKING 70

Bodice Front and Back—Lowered Shoulder

When there is a change in the position of the shoulder seam, the designer must work with both the bodice front and bodice back. The bodice back shoulder dart must be moved to the neck edge in order to match the shoulder seam. The bodice front darts can be changed in any manner desired following the completion of the shoulder seam change. In this example, the darts have been changed into a tuck at the new lowered shoulder line (see Fig. 4-95).

STEP 1: Trace sloper (bodice front and back required).

STEP 2: Draw in new design lines; first, move bodice back shoulder dart to neck edge, following the basic steps for moving darts; next, attach the shoulder seams with tape; draw in lowered shoulder line on bodice front (see Fig. 4-96).

STEP 3: Cross-notch (see Fig. 4-96).

STEP 4: Draw new design line for bodice front dart location; cross-notch this dart tuck line (see Fig. 4-96).

STEP 5: Cut on new design line (see Fig. 4-97).

STEP 6: Fold out darts in bodice front (see Fig. 4-97).

STEP 7: Cut on new dart line.

STEP 8: Add paper.

STEP 9: Fold out new dart tuck; cut ends (see Fig. 4-97).

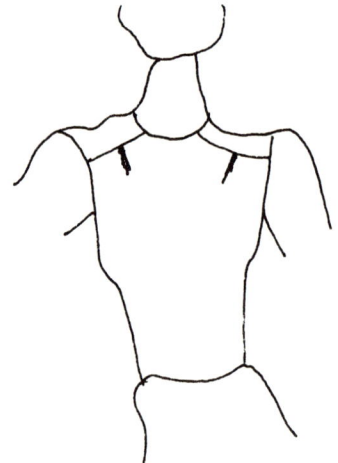

Fig. 4-95. Bodice front and back with lowered shoulder.

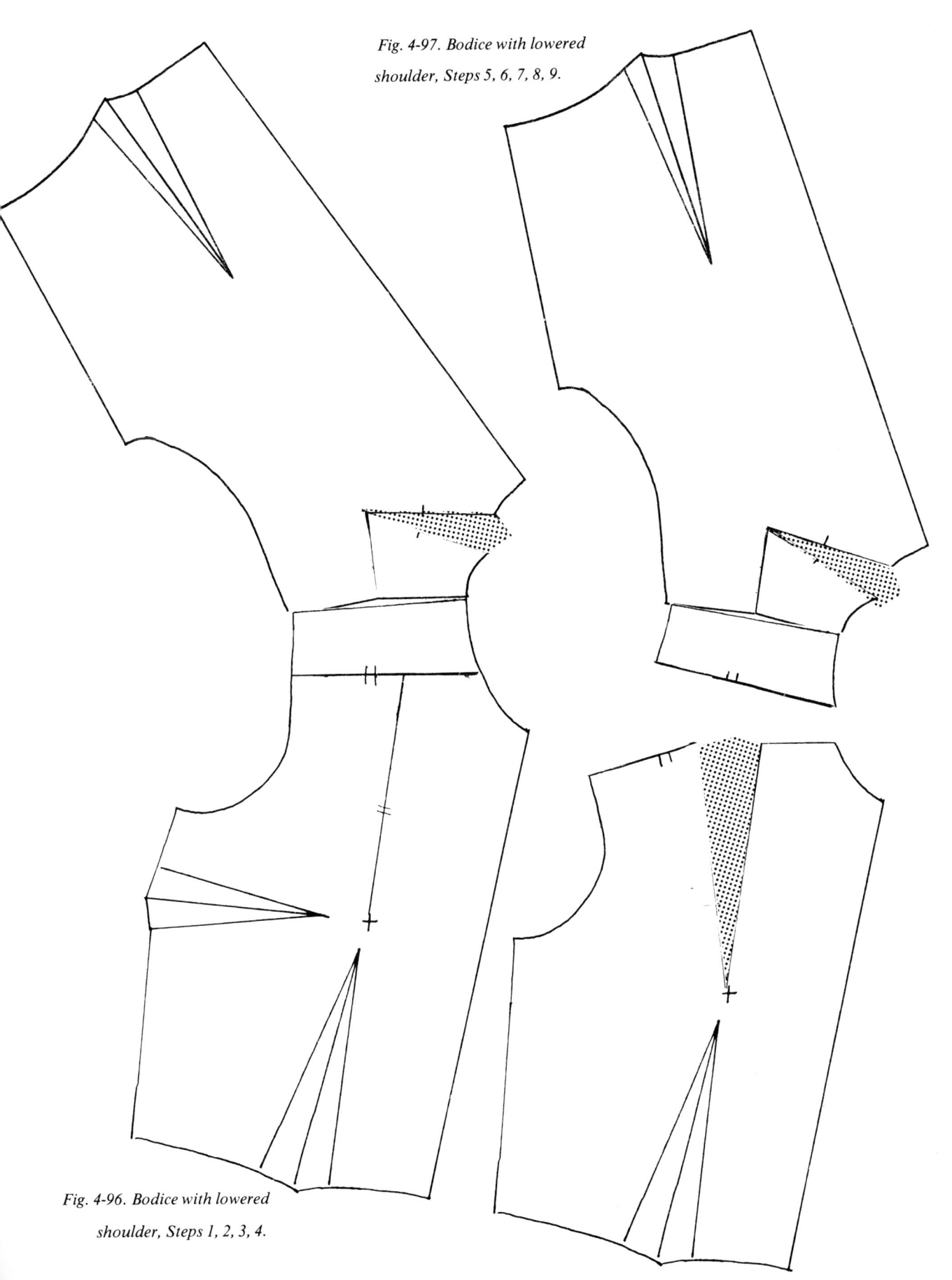

Fig. 4-97. Bodice with lowered shoulder, Steps 5, 6, 7, 8, 9.

Fig. 4-96. Bodice with lowered shoulder, Steps 1, 2, 3, 4.

CHAPTER V

THE BODICE BACK

The bodice back sloper has two darts, one at the shoulder and one at the waist.

The two darts make the third dimension in the area of the two back curves at the shoulder and the waist. These two curves are separate and distinct, and so the two back darts can never be combined into one as was done on the bodice front.

The shoulder dart can be moved to the neck edge, can be changed into a seam, or can be eased into the bodice front at the shoulder. Never omit it entirely. The fabric needs to be curved at this point to cover the shoulder curve.

The waist dart will be small or large depending upon the waist curve. If the waist is small in relation to the back width, the dart will be large at the lower edge to add more curve to the fabric. If the waist is large in comparison with the back width measurement, the dart will be small at the lower edge.

All back slopers have ease across the back shoulder width to allow for the forward swinging of the arms, which creates strain on the jack of the bodice. (We do not often swing our raised arms back, except in certain sporting activities.)

The basic steps for the bodice back are as follows:

STEP 1: Trace sloper.

Use a medium-weight, good-quality paper to trace the sloper. Trace all the pieces needed for the design being made. Trace in both the darts (see Fig. 5-1).

THE COMPLETE GUIDE TO PATTERN-MAKING 74

STEP 2: Draw in new design lines.

The bodice back does not usually receive as much attention as the bodice front. The design lines coordinate with those of the bodice front. The waist dart can be moved, divided, changed into tucks or gathers, or omitted, as in the princess style. The shoulder dart can be moved to the neck edge or eased at the shoulder. It can be omitted only when it is changed into a seam in the princess style. The neck can be lowered or raised slightly.

In this example, the shoulder dart is moved from the shoulder edge to the neck edge (see Fig. 5-2).

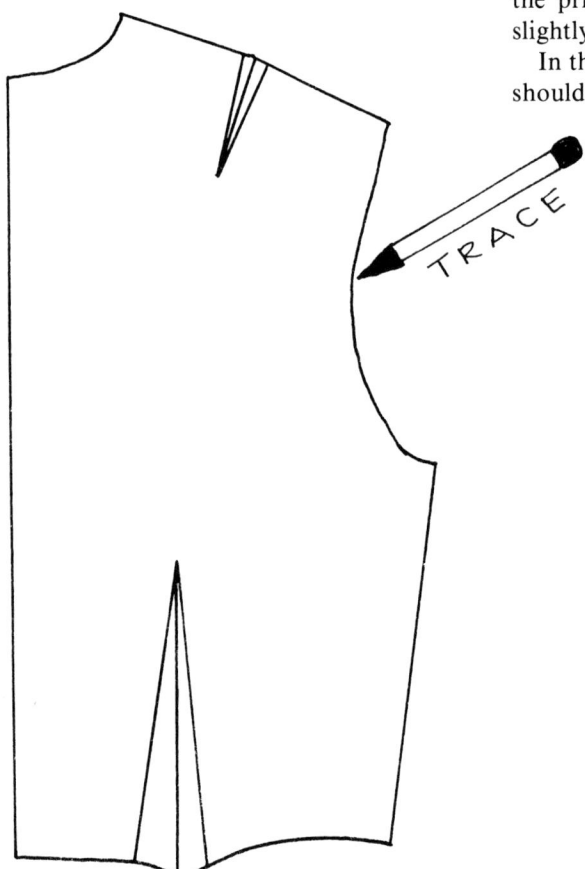

Fig. 5-1. Step 1: Bodice back sloper, trace sloper.

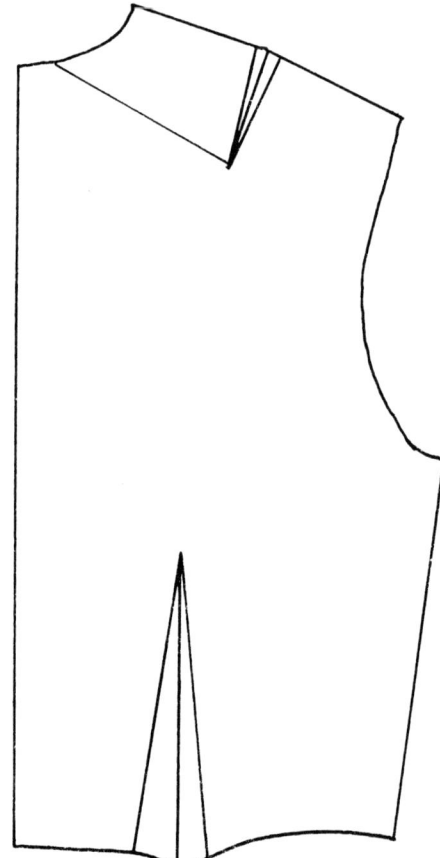

Fig. 5-2. Step 2: Draw in new design lines.

75 THE BODICE BACK

STEP 3: Cross-notch.

Cross-notch over the new design line to aid in stitching the fabric together after the pattern is completed (see Fig. 5-3).

STEP 4: Fold out dart(s).

Fold out the dart(s) you have decided to move or change by cutting on one side of the dart to the point and lapping this side of the dart over to the other side of the dart. Tape it down to produce a curved area, which will not lie flat on the working surface (see Fig. 5-4).

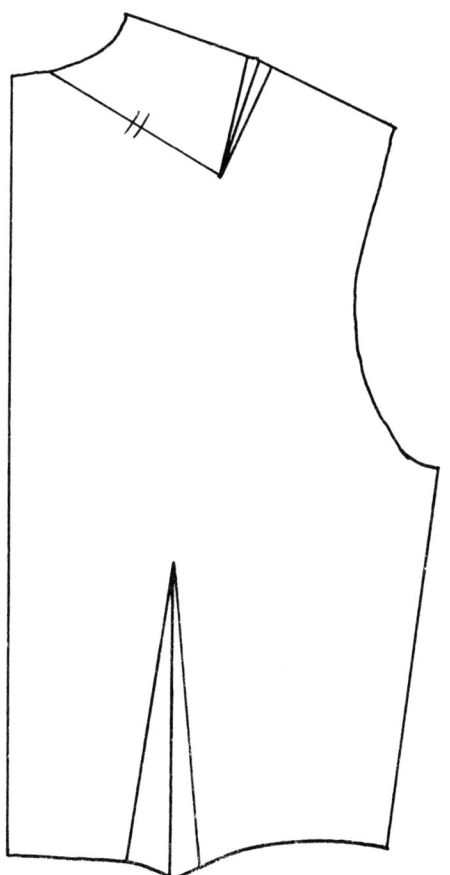

Fig. 5-3. Step 3: Cross-notch.

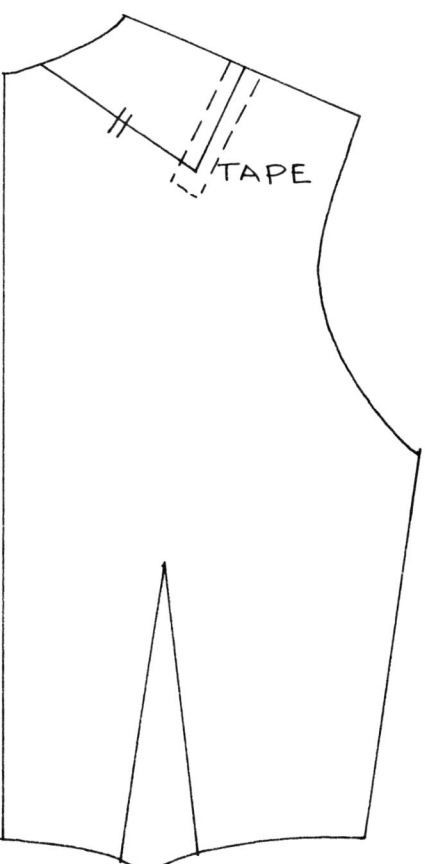

Fig. 5-4. Step 4: Fold out dart.

THE COMPLETE GUIDE TO PATTERN-MAKING

STEP 5: Cut on new design lines.

Cut on the new design line. The pattern will open to lie flat and create the new dart. There is no adjustment necessary. The pattern will be the right size while it lies flat on the working surface (see Fig. 5-5).

STEP 6: Add paper.

Add tissue paper to the open space created after you have cut on the new design line. Glue or tape the pattern to the tissue (see Fig. 5-6).

STEP 7: Fold out new dart(s), tuck(s), pleat(s), etc., to cut ends.

Draw in the center line for the new darts or tucks. Bring the cross-notches together, and fold out the dart on the new design line.

Fold the dart toward the center back. Cut the ends (see Fig. 5-7).

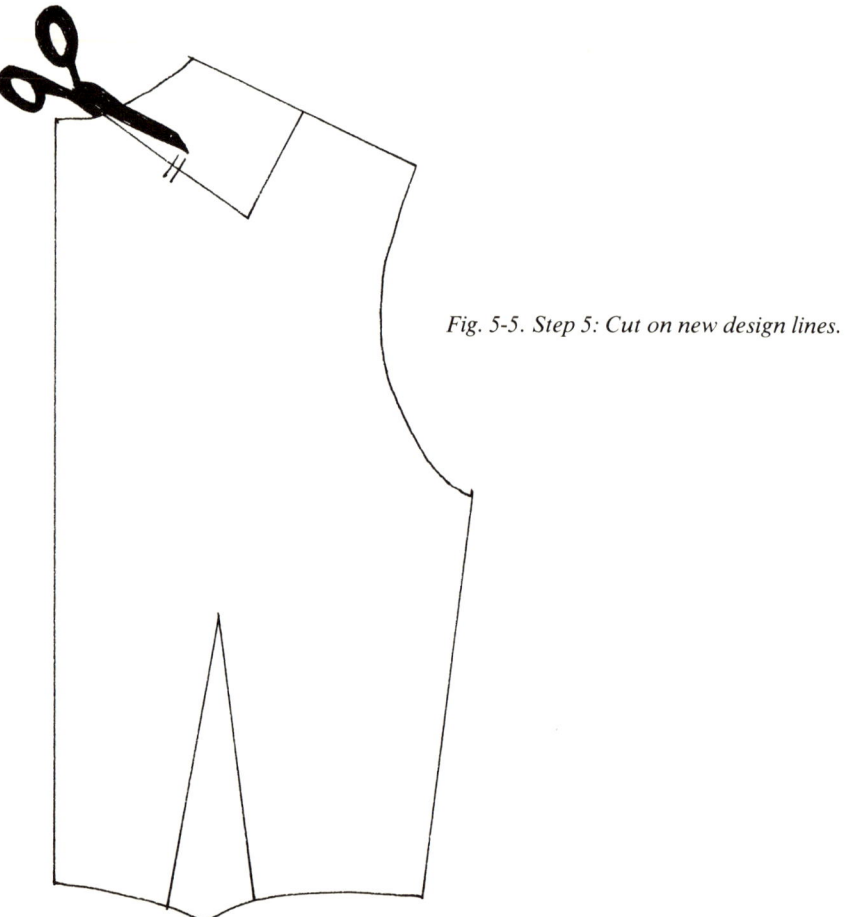

Fig. 5-5. Step 5: Cut on new design lines.

77 THE BODICE BACK

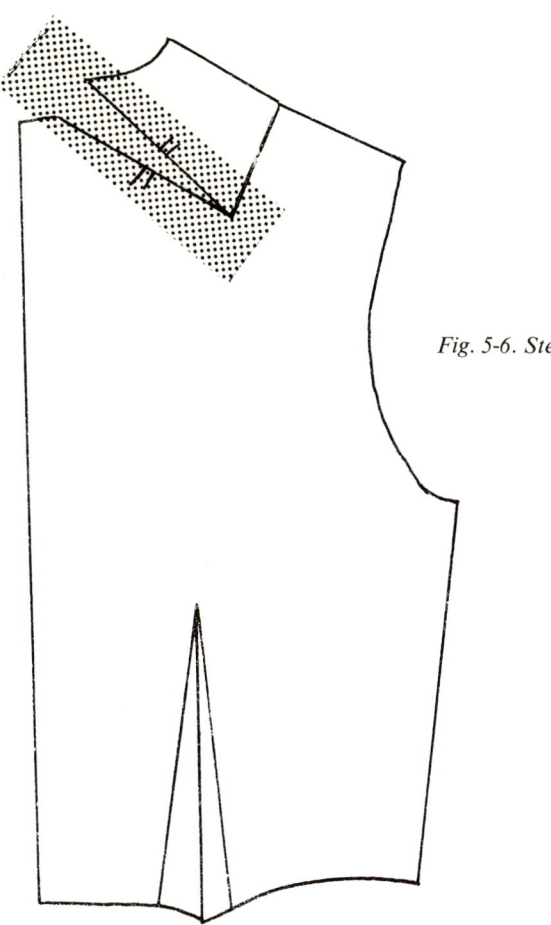

Fig. 5-6. Step 6: Add paper.

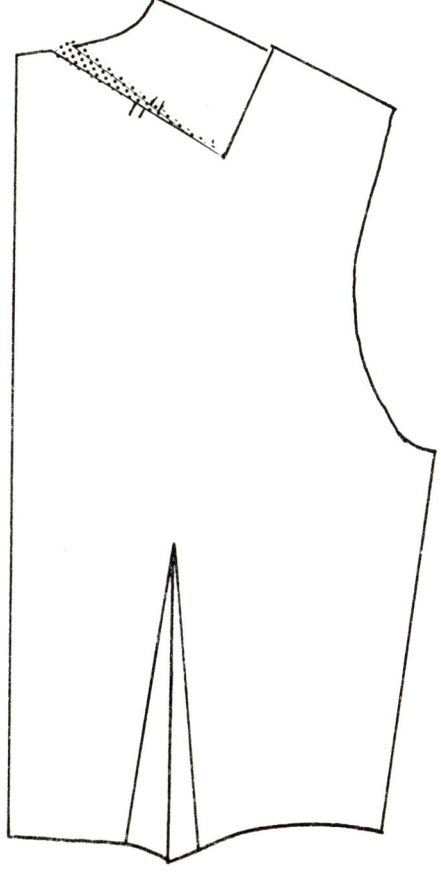

Fig. 5-7. Step 7: Fold out new dart.

Traditional Princess Line—Bodice Back—Darts into Seams

The traditional princess line back is cut to match the front, the seam extending from the center of the shoulder through the point of the back waist dart to the lower edge of the waist dart. The darts are changed into seams. It is not necessary to add ease in the bodice back. The two distinct curves of the back do not present the same problem as to the bust area in the bodice front (see Fig. 5-8).

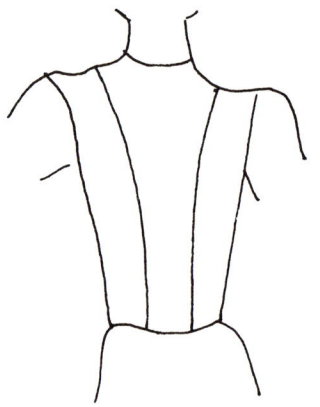

Fig. 5-8. Traditional princess line, bodice back.

STEP 1: Trace sloper (bodice back only).

STEP 2: Draw in new design line; draw line from center of shoulder (to correspond with line on bodice front) through point of shoulder dart to tip of waist dart, through lower edge of waist dart; use the curve stick to help you get a smooth line.

STEP 3: Cross-notch (see Fig. 5-9).

STEP 4: Fold out darts.

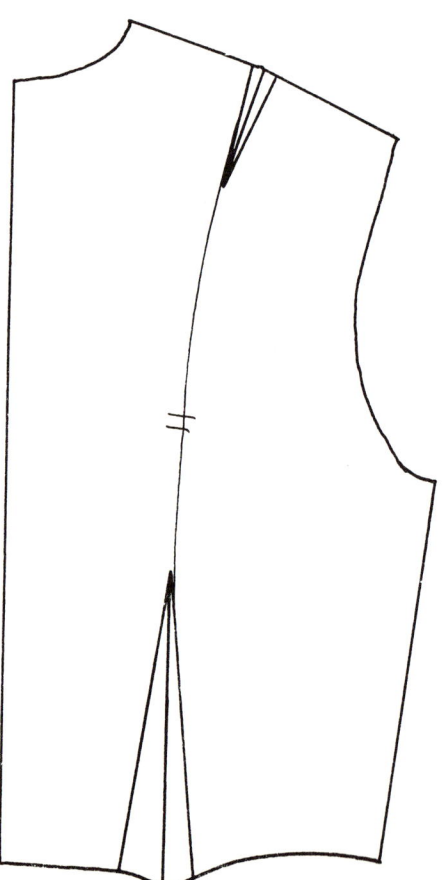

Fig. 5-9. Bodice back princess line, Steps 1, 2, 3.

79 THE BODICE BACK

STEP 5: Cut on new design line; no further steps are necessary for princess-style bodice back, as there is no ease to add and no darts to re-draw (see Fig. 5-10).

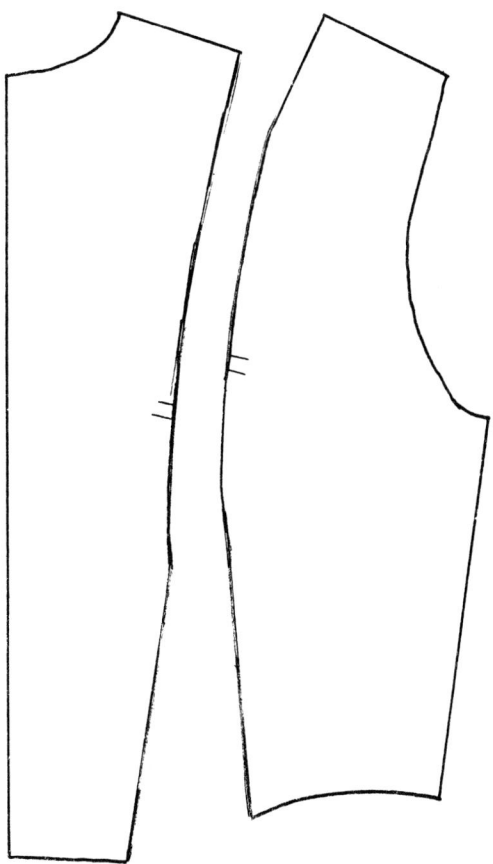

Fig. 5-10. Bodice back princess line, Steps 4, 5.

THE COMPLETE GUIDE TO PATTERN-MAKING 80

Bodice Back Pleats

Pleats can be added to the bodice back to make an attractive variation. To eliminate the back waist dart we have moved it to the side seam. The arrow indicates the cutting direction necessary to complete this step. The shoulder dart can be eased to eliminate one additional design line. Add pleats in the same manner as for the bodice front (see Fig. 5-11).

STEP 1: Trace sloper (bodice back only).

STEP 2: Draw in new design lines; draw lines for pleats, spacing them so that the finished bodice back will be divided into sections of logical width; draw arrow at side seam from waist line to armhole; this line is used to move waist dart to side seam.

Draw in yoke line (see Fig. 5-12).

STEP 3: Cross-notch pleat lines (see Fig. 5-12).

Fig. 5-11. Bodice back pleats.

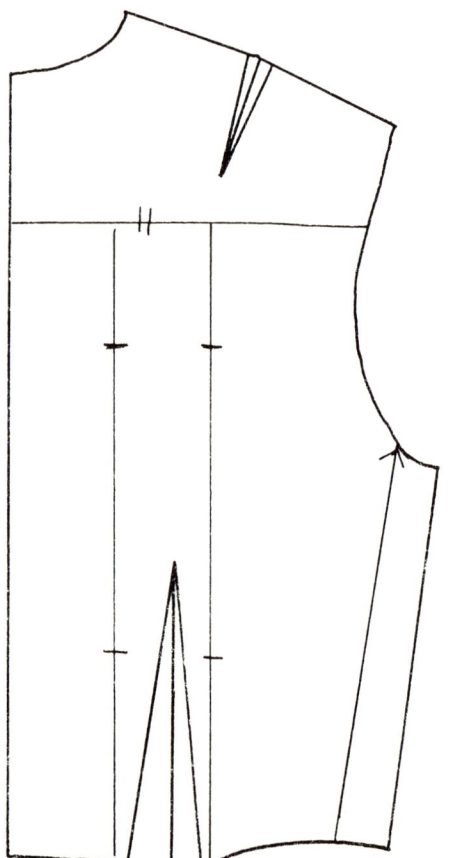

Fig. 5-12. Bodice back pleats, Steps 1, 2, 3.

81 THE BODICE BACK

STEP 4: Move waist dart to side seam; cut on arrow drawn at side seam; do not cut through the armhole.

Lap one side of the dart over the other and tape it down; draw lines through back dart to indicate it has now been moved (see Fig. 5-13).

STEP 5: Cut on yoke line, separating two pieces of bodice back.

STEP 6: Cut on pleat lines.

STEP 7: Separtate and add paper the width desired for knife pleats; ¾" finished knife pleats (see Fig. 5-13).

STEP 8: Fold out pleats; cut ends; indicate with arrows direction pleats are to be folded.

STEP 9: Cross out dart lines on yoke; write in "ease" over this area to indicate this will be eased onto bodice front shoulder (see Fig. 5-14).

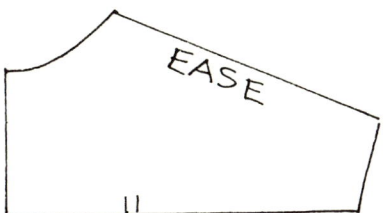

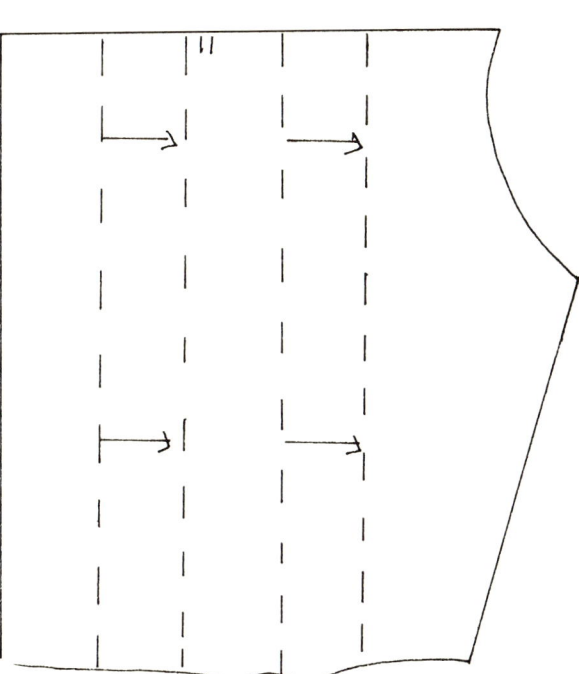

Fig. 5-14. Bodice back pleats, Steps 8, 9.

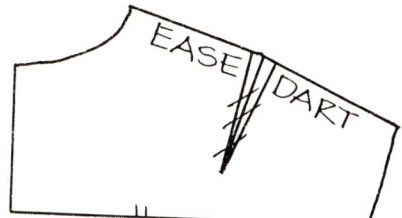

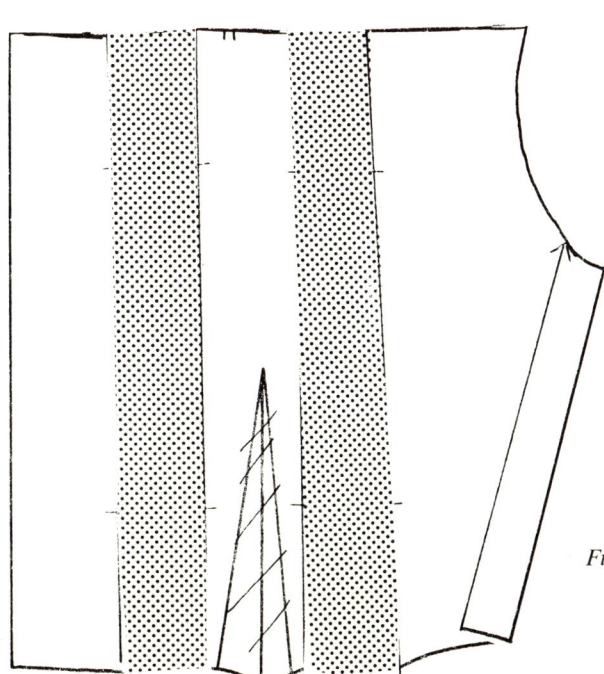

Fig. 5-13. Bodice back pleats, Steps 4, 5, 6, 7.

CHAPTER VI

THE SLEEVE

The basic sleeve has a curved top and a dart at the elbow. These features allow for the creation of the third dimension.

The arm curves from elbow to hand when one is standing still. Notice that when you hang your arm down at your side, it does not hang straight down but curves forward at the elbow. The elbow darts allow for this natural curvature.

The curve at the top of the sleeve—the *cap*—allows the sleeve to fit over the upper portion of the arm. The amount of curve in the cap will allow for variations in the width of the upper arm, *e.g.,* a larger upper arm will require a greater width and cap height than a smaller one.

The elbow dart can be transferred to the wrist edge, creating a fullness at the lower edge. When there is fullness here, there is enough room for the arm to move freely without straining the seam.

When the elbow dart is transferred to the cap of the sleeve, it creates a curved side seam. This will compensate for the curve necessary to allow the arm free movement.

The basic steps for the sleeve are as follows:

STEP 1: Trace sloper.
Use a medium-weight, good-quality paper to trace the sloper. Trace in the dart (see Fig. 6-1).

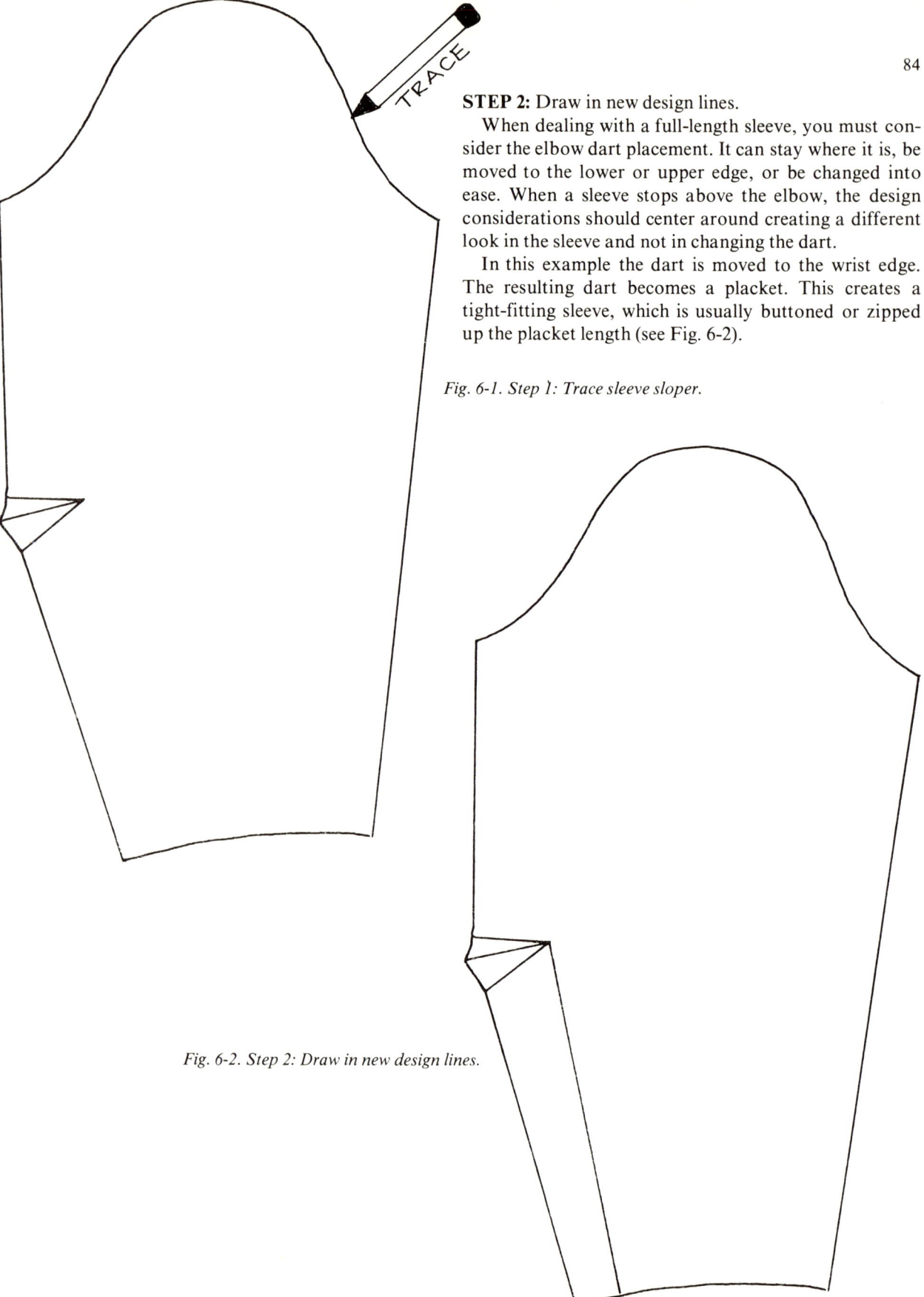

STEP 2: Draw in new design lines.

When dealing with a full-length sleeve, you must consider the elbow dart placement. It can stay where it is, be moved to the lower or upper edge, or be changed into ease. When a sleeve stops above the elbow, the design considerations should center around creating a different look in the sleeve and not in changing the dart.

In this example the dart is moved to the wrist edge. The resulting dart becomes a placket. This creates a tight-fitting sleeve, which is usually buttoned or zipped up the placket length (see Fig. 6-2).

Fig. 6-1. Step 1: Trace sleeve sloper.

Fig. 6-2. Step 2: Draw in new design lines.

85 THE SLEEVE

STEP 3: Cross-notch.

Cross-notch on the new design lines to aid in stitching the fabric together after the pattern is completed (see Fig. 6-3).

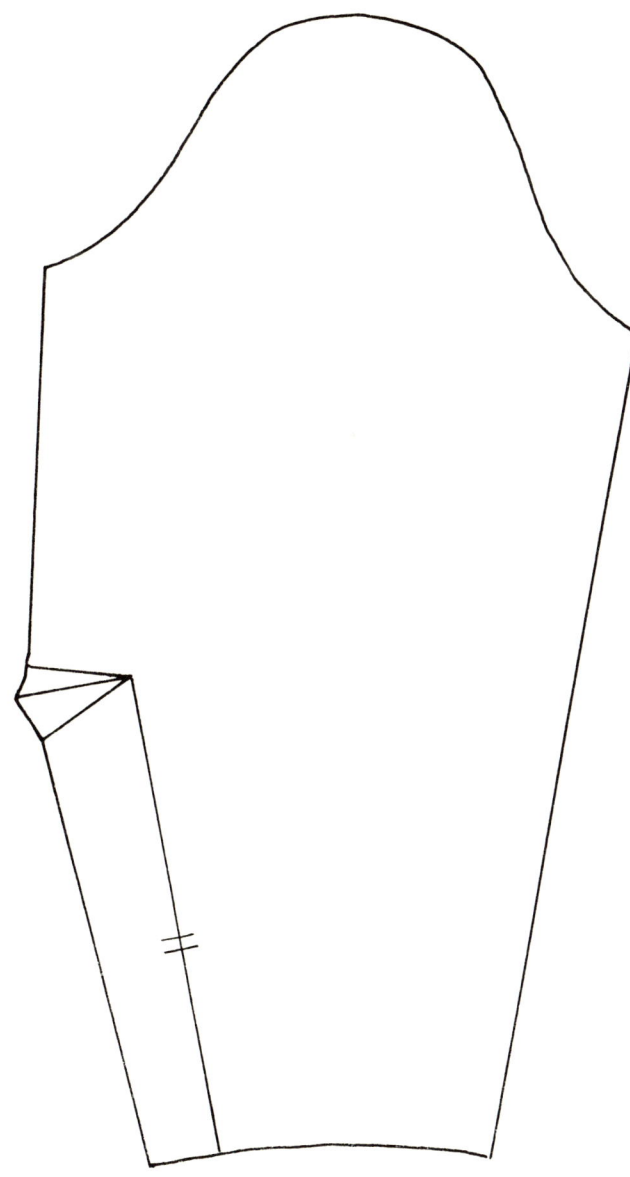

Fig. 6-3. Step 3: Cross-notch.

THE COMPLETE GUIDE TO PATTERN-MAKING 86

STEP 4: Fold out dart.

If you are working with the full-length sleeve, fold out the elbow dart. Cut on one side of the dart to the point. Lap one side of the dart over the other, and tape it down. The folded-out pattern will now be curved and will not lie flat on the working surface (see Fig. 6-4).

STEP 5: Cut on new design lines.

Cut on the new design lines. The pattern will open to lie flat and create the new dart area. There is no adjustment necessary. The pattern will be the right size while it lies flat on the working surface (see Fig. 6-5).

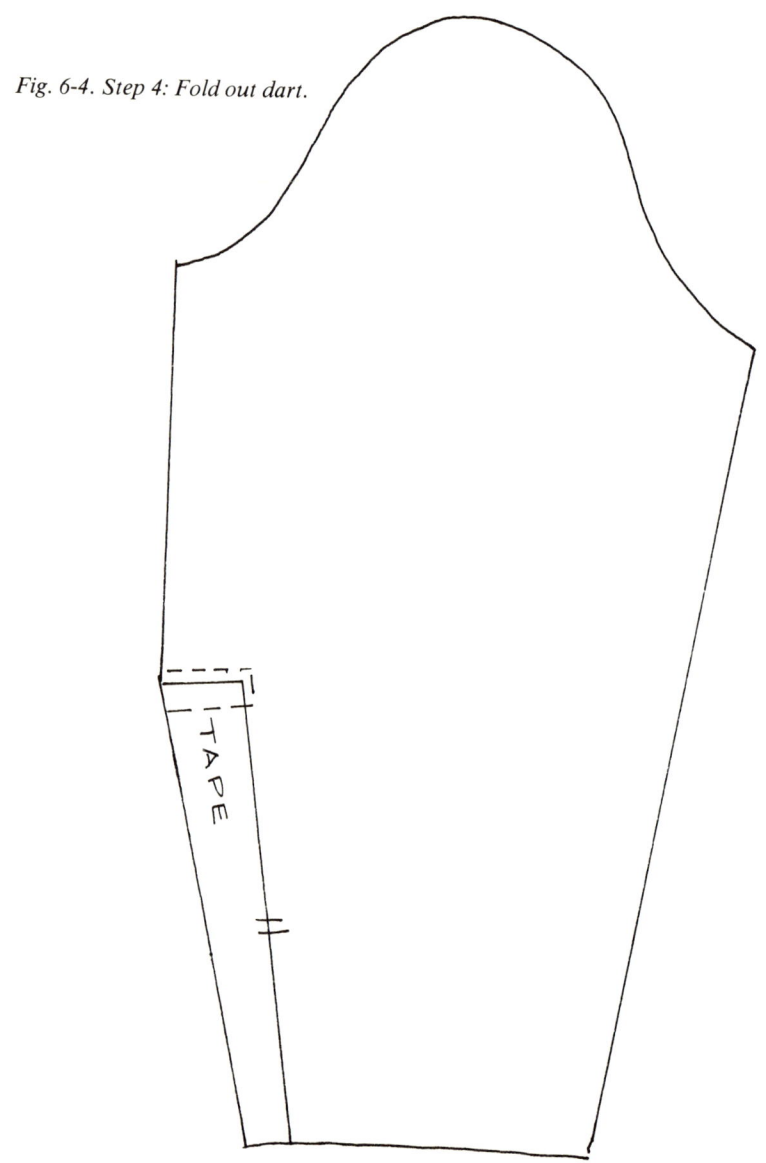

Fig. 6-4. Step 4: Fold out dart.

87 THE SLEEVE

STEP 6: Add paper.

Add tissue paper to the open space created when you cut on the new design line. Where there is a new dart, you must fold it out and cut the end as you did for the darts on the bodice front and back. When you design gathers, you must create a good curve at the edges with the aid of the Dietzgen curve and curve stick (see Fig. 6-6).

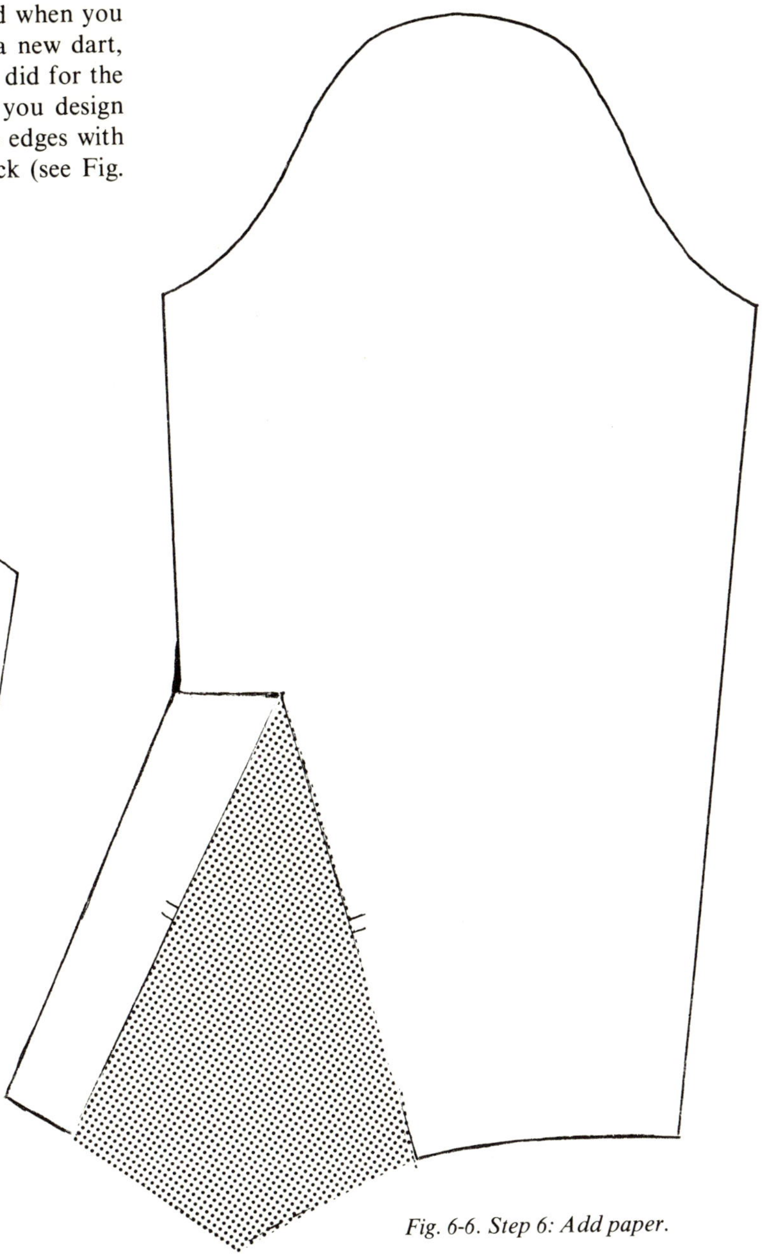

Fig. 6-6. Step 6: Add paper.

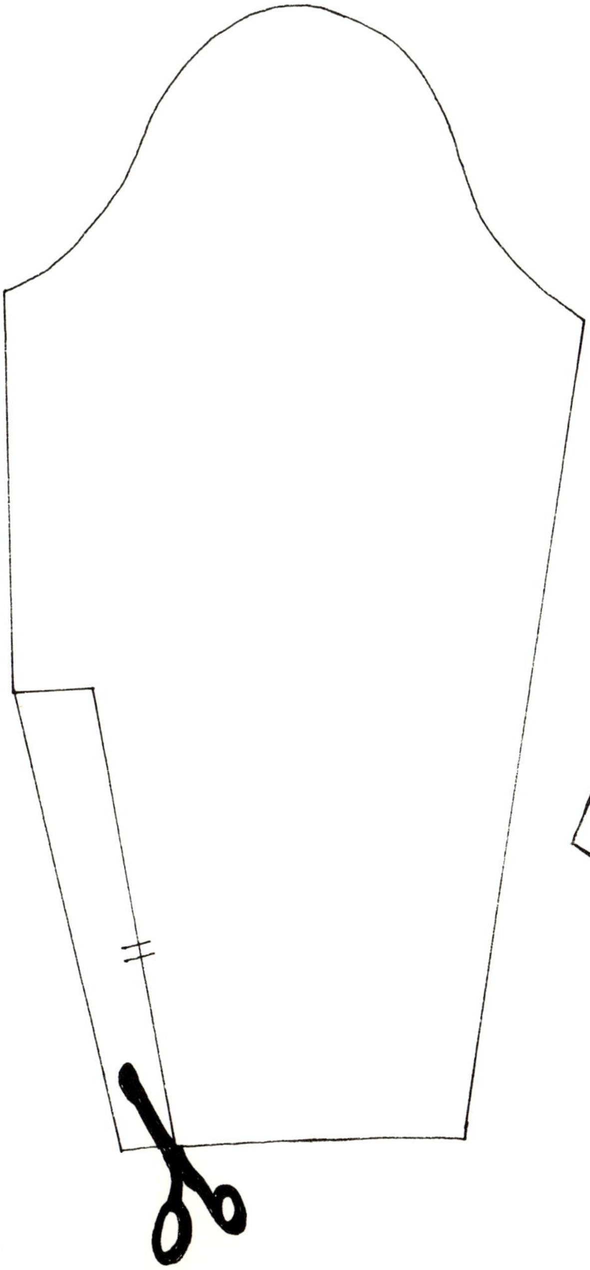

Fig. 6-5. Step 5: Cut on new design lines.

THE COMPLETE GUIDE TO PATTERN-MAKING 88

Sleeve with Short Top Pleat

The sleeve with short top pleat is so named because it is shown as a short sleeve with a pleat at the cap. This method can be used on a three-quarter or full-length sleeve sloper. The fullness is added only to the cap area. It does not extend into the body of the sleeve (see Fig. 6-7).

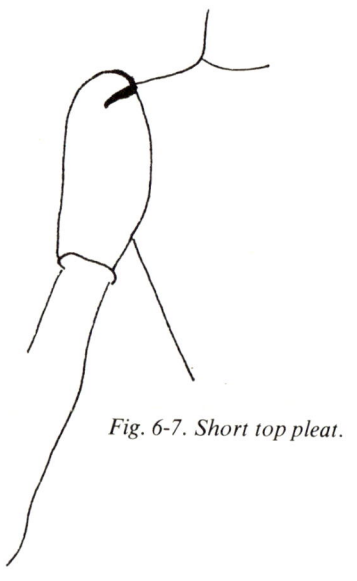

Fig. 6-7. Short top pleat.

STEP 1: Trace sloper (sleeve only). Cut off to short length.

STEP 2: Draw in new design lines; draw two parallel horizontal arrows in sleeve cap area.
Draw one vertical arrow from the center of the sleeve cap to the lower horizontal line (see Fig. 6-8).

STEP 3: Cut on new design lines; cut first on the vertical line; cut from this newly created edge to the sleeve cap edges, following the arrows (see Fig. 6-15).

STEP 4: Spread and add paper; the cap can be spread any amount, but, as you will notice as you work with the paper, when you get past a certain point, the shape of the cap will become bowed (see Fig. 6-9).

STEP 5: Smooth cap line with help of Dietzgen curve.

STEP 6: Fold out pleat thus drawn; and mark edges to show direction of fold. When pleat is folded out the cap should measure the same as the basic cap (see Fig. 6-9).

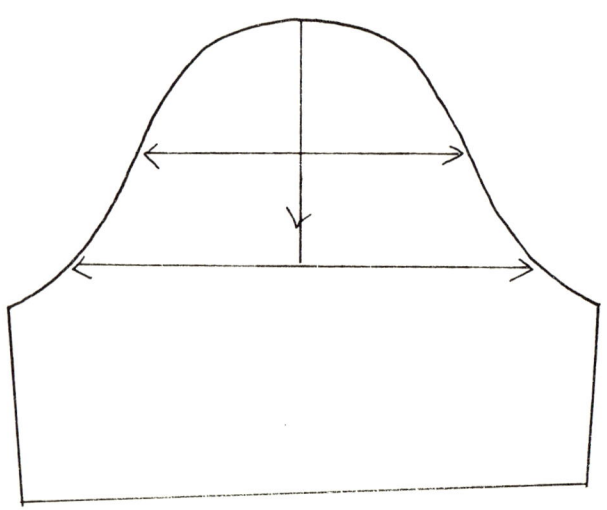

Fig. 6-8. Short top pleat, Steps 1, 2.

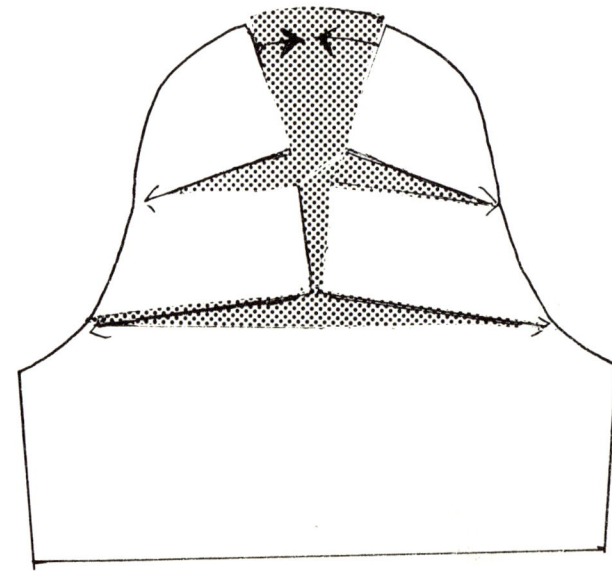

Fig. 6-9. Short top pleat, Steps 3, 4, 5, 6.

89 THE SLEEVE

Shirtwaist Sleeve

The shirtwaist sleeve is a straight sleeve with no elbow dart. Fullness is added at the wrist edge to allow for freedom of movement for the arm. The cuff is cut off from the lower edge of the sleeve and straightened. In the finished sleeve there is no dart but a placket opening for the hand (see Fig. 6-10).

STEP 1: Trace sloper (sleeve only).

STEP 2: Draw in new design lines; first measure up on each side seam the width of cuff desired; draw a curved line between these two points; draw a line from the tip of the dart to the wrist edge of the sleeve (see Fig. 6-11).

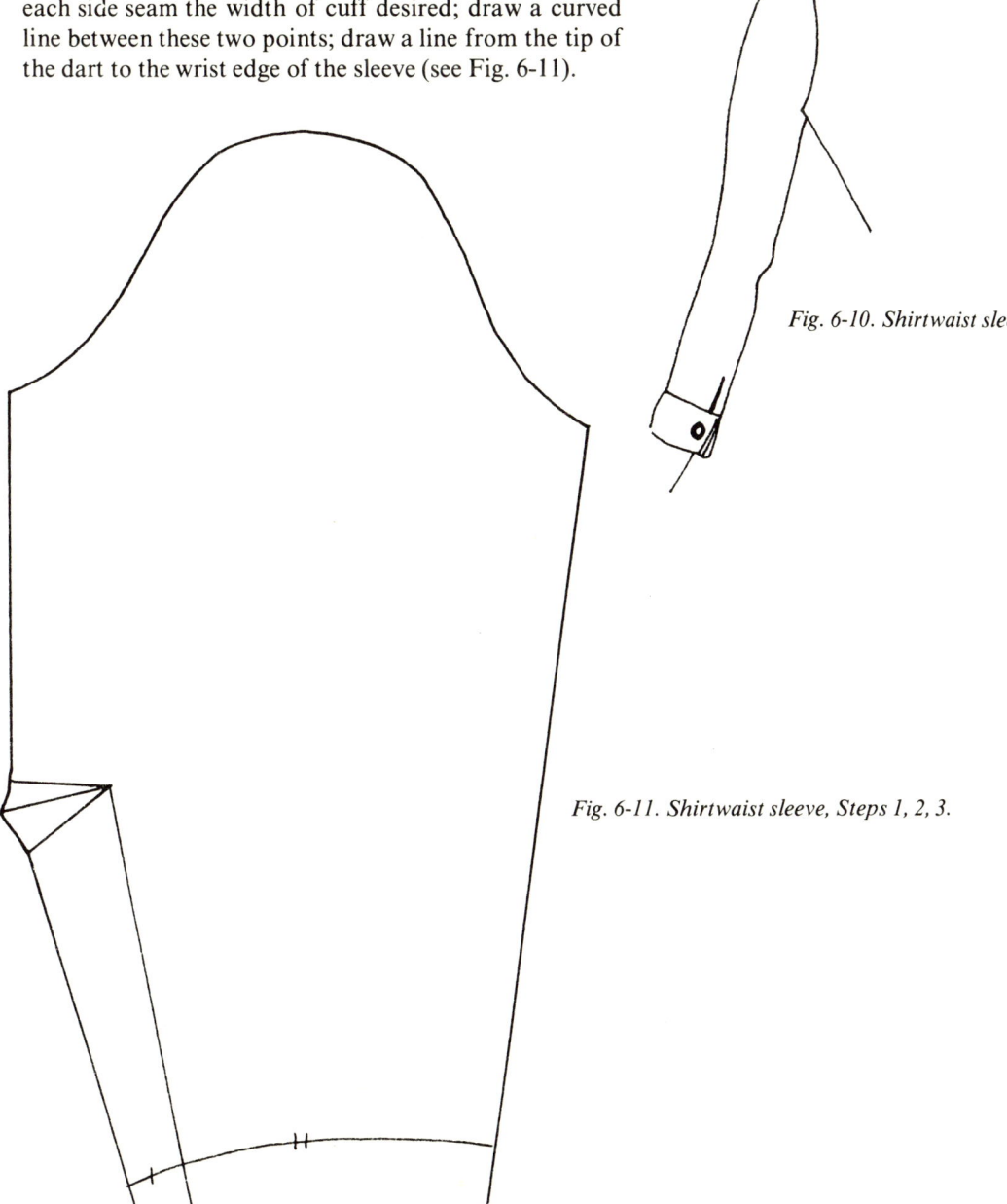

Fig. 6-10. Shirtwaist sleeve.

Fig. 6-11. Shirtwaist sleeve, Steps 1, 2, 3.

THE COMPLETE GUIDE TO PATTERN-MAKING 90

STEP 3: Cross-notch cuff marking.

STEP 4: Cut off cuff.

Cut up from lower sleeve edge to point of dart; cut on one side of dart to point of dart (see Fig. 6-12).

STEP 5: Straighten side seam of sleeve.

Close dart and open placket area until left side of sleeve is parallel with right side seam. Straighten lower edge of sleeve.

Measure right side seam length; make left side seam same length. Draw horizontal line across lower edge.

Area with lines will be cut off.

Transfer cross-notches to new seam line (see Fig. 6-12).

STEP 6: Draw in a placket line; write "gather" at lower sleeve edge.

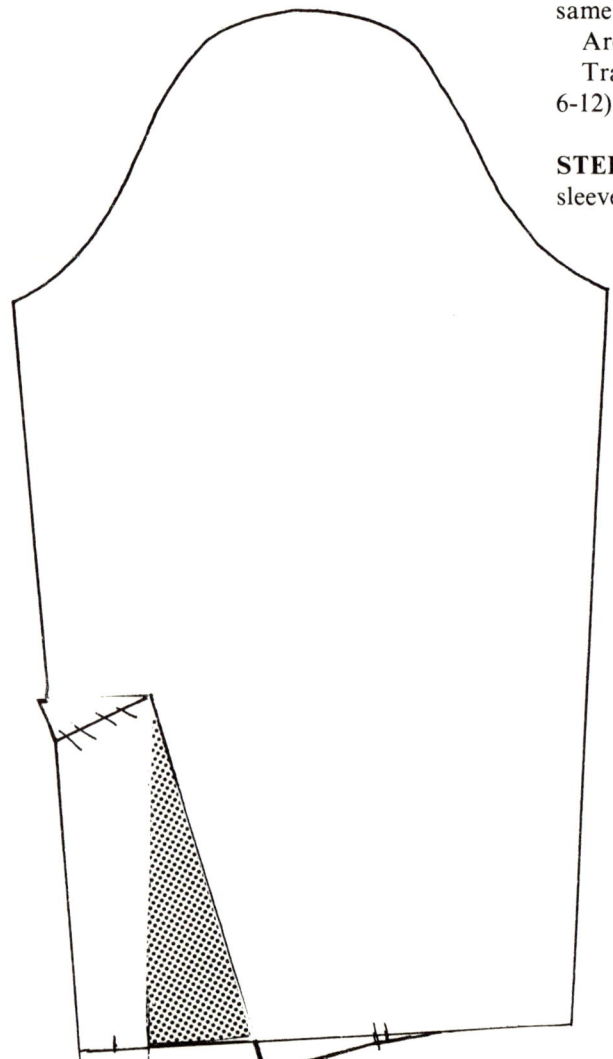

Fig. 6-12. Shirtwaist sleeve, Steps 4, 5.

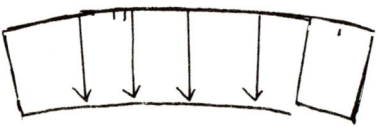

91 THE SLEEVE

STEP 7: Straighten cuff; cut through heavy line of cuff and move small section on left to the right side. This procedure shows the development of the cuff opening which will no longer be at the underarm.

Notches will now match with lower sleeve edge.

Slash from upper cuff edge to lower edge, not cutting through lower edge. Overlap top edge until piece is approximately straight.

In the future you may just cut a straight rectangular piece for the cuff; following this procedure once, however, will show you how the cuff is secured (see Fig. 6-1).

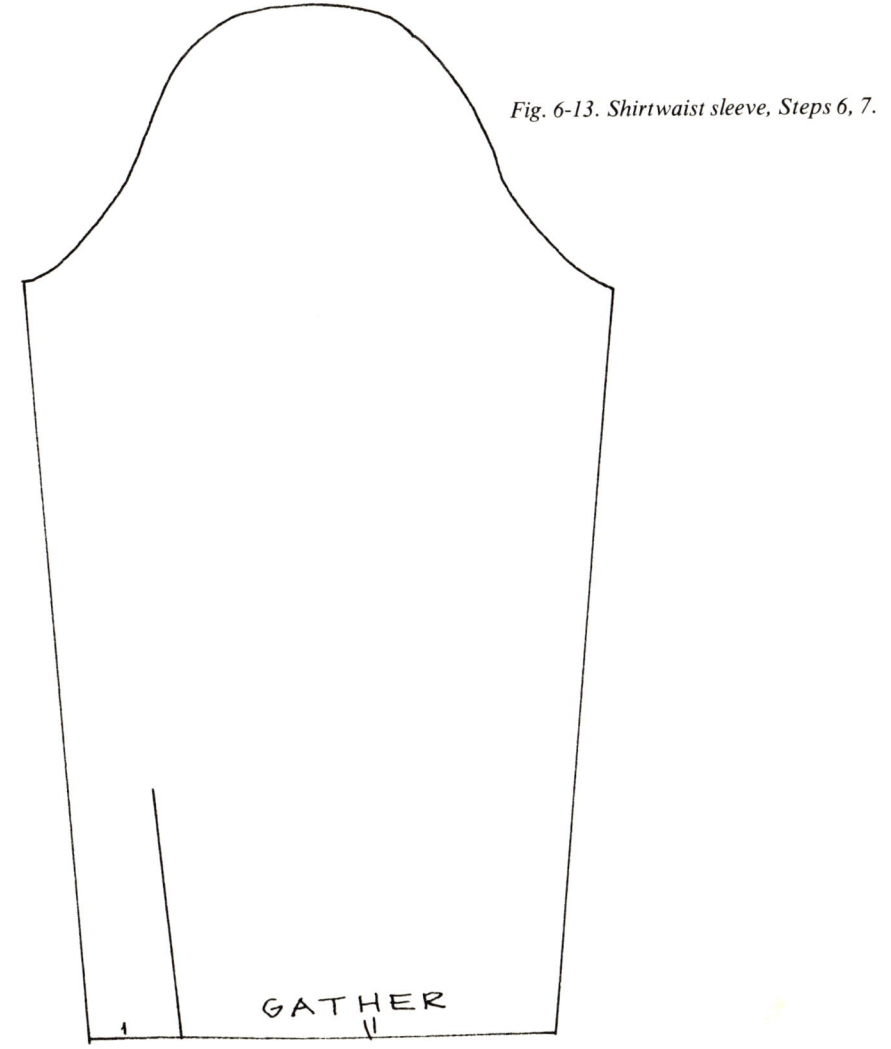

Fig. 6-13. Shirtwaist sleeve, Steps 6, 7.

Bell Sleeve

The bell sleeve hangs from the armhole with fullness at the lower edge. It has the appearance of a bell when worn (see Fig. 6-14).

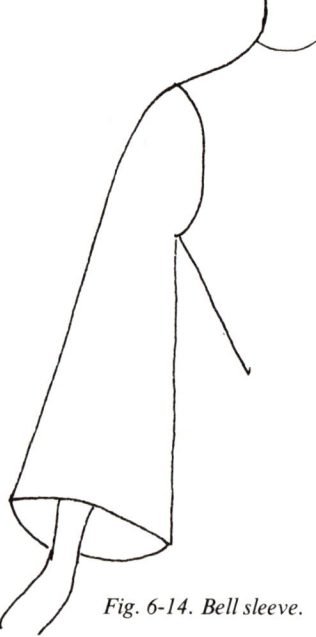

Fig. 6-14. Bell sleeve.

STEP 1: Trace sloper (sleeve only).

STEP 2: Draw in new design lines; draw lines from lower edge of sleeve to sleeve cap; draw one line from lower sleeve edge to point of elbow dart (see Fig. 6-15).

Fig. 6-15. Bell sleeve, Steps 1, 2.

93 THE SLEEVE

STEP 3: Cut from lower edge to cap edge, being careful not to cut through cap. Cut to point of dart; then cut along one side of dart to point of dart, not cutting through dart (see Fig. 6-16).

STEP 4: Spread.

First, straighten side seam by closing dart enough to allow seam to straighten. This will create a spread in the lower sleeve edge. Shorten left side seam to match right side seam of sleeve, and cut off excess as shown.

Next, spread lower edge of sleeve. The sleeve may be spread as much as desired, a soft fabric taking more fullness than a stiff one to create the bell effect (see Fig. 6-1).

STEP 5: Smooth lower edge with the help of the Dietzgen curve (see Fig. 6-16).

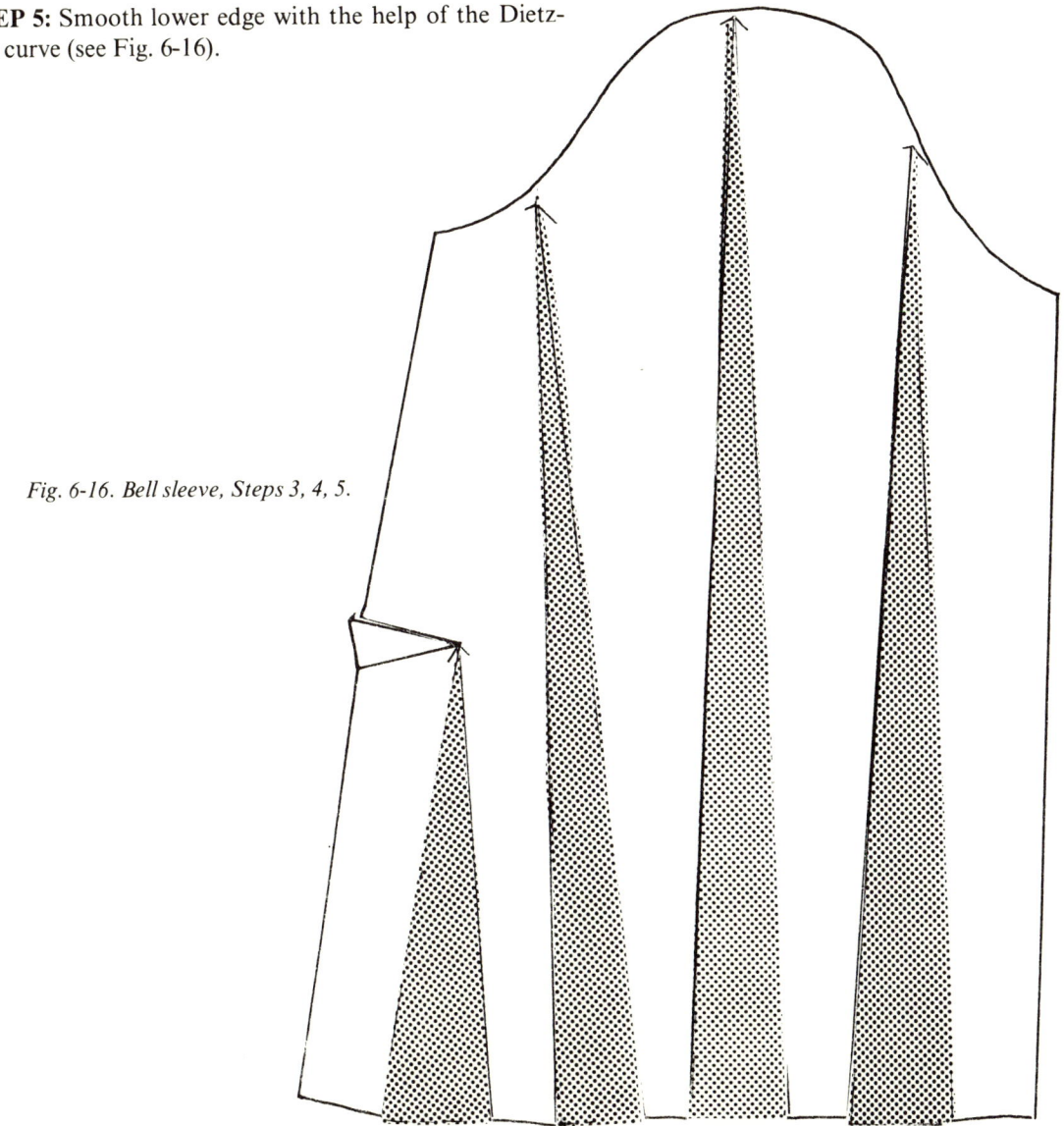

Fig. 6-16. Bell sleeve, Steps 3, 4, 5.

Bishop Sleeve

The bishop sleeve is full, like the bell sleeve, but is gathered onto a cuff. The lower edge of the sleeve falls over the cuff, especially on the top side and therefore an additional curve is added to the lower sleeve edge. The cuff is not cut from the lower edge of the sleeve as in the shirtwaist sleeve, because the sleeve blouses over the cuff. A placket is usually added to allow for a tighter-fitting cuff (see Fig. 6-17).

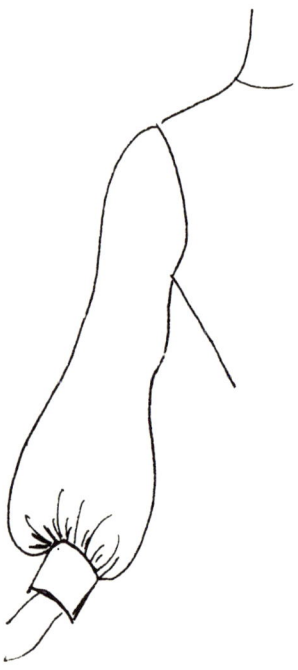

Fig. 6-17. Bishop sleeve.

STEP 1: Trace sloper (sleeve only).

STEP 2: Draw in new design lines; draw one line from lower sleeve edge to point of dart; draw several lines from lower sleeve edge to sleeve cap (see Fig. 6-18).

STEP 3: Cut on new design lines; cut to point of dart; cut along one edge of dart to point.
  Straighten side seam as on bell sleeve. Cut from lower edge to cap edge, not cutting through cap (see Fig. 6-1).

STEP 4: Spread. Again, one can spread any amount desired, remembering that a softer fabric will take more fullness than a stiff one (see Fig. 6-18).

STEP 5: Add curve at lower edge. Draw in curve at lower edge as shown. This will add an extra amount of blousing over the cuff.
  Draw in placket line (see Fig. 6-18).

STEP 6: The cuff may be any width, a 2½" to 3" cuff being average. The length of the cuff will be the length of the lower sleeve edge on the basic pattern (see Fig. 6-24).

STEP 7: Write "gather" at lower edge of completed sleeve (see Fig. 6-18).

95 THE SLEEVE

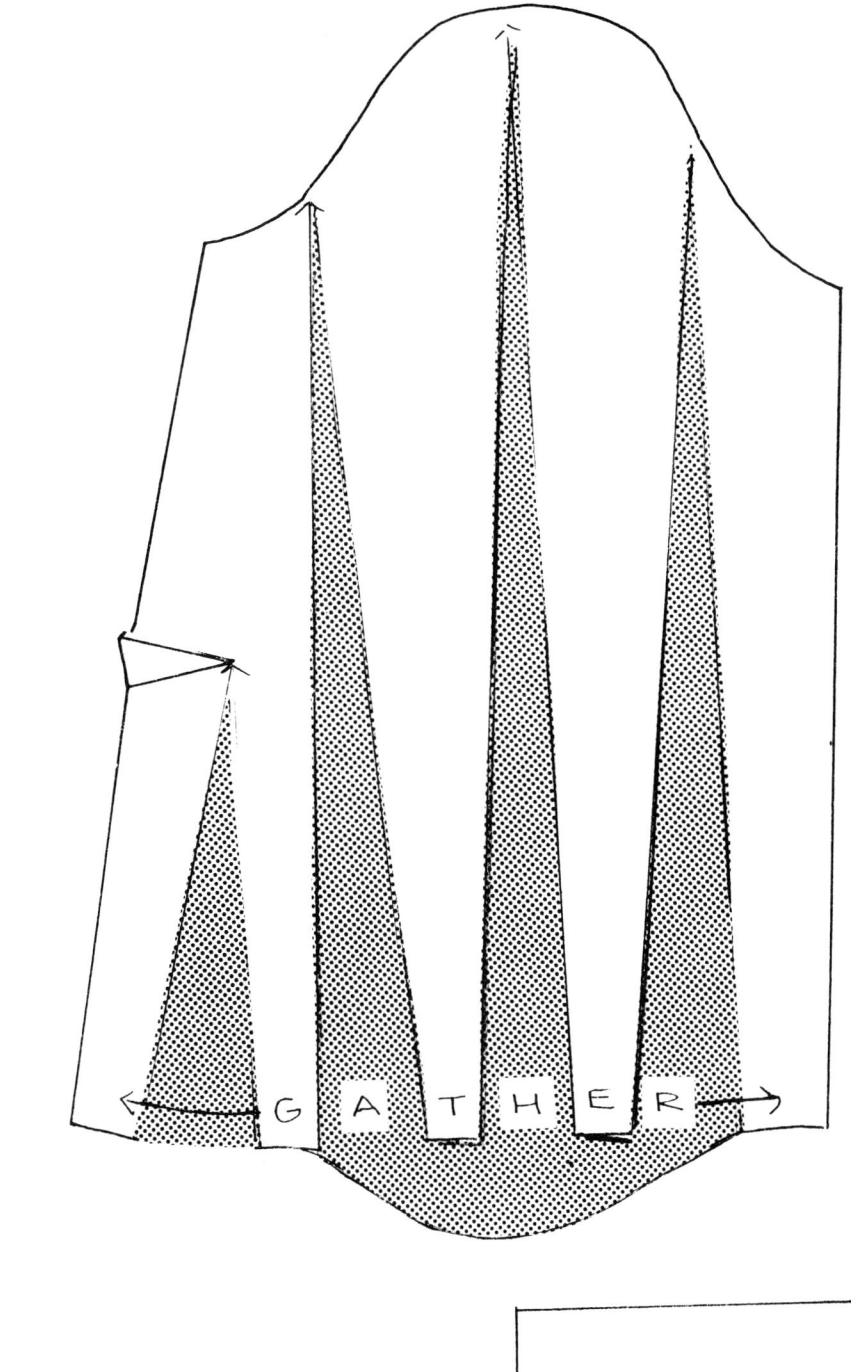

Fig. 6-18. Bishop sleeve, Steps 1, 2, 3, 4, 5, 6, 7.

THE COMPLETE GUIDE TO PATTERN-MAKING 96

Sleeve with Short Bottom Puff

Puffed sleeves have fullness added at either the bottom, top, or bottom and top. They may be long or short, but for the problems here they are shown short for convenience. The lower edges of puffed sleeves are usually bound with self-made bias (see Fig. 6-19).

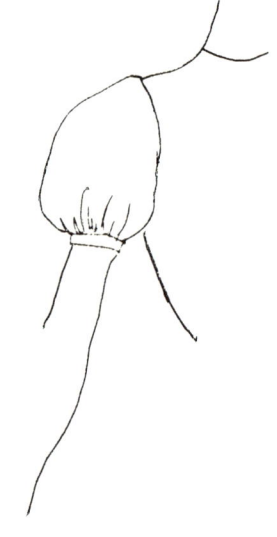

STEP 1: Trace sloper (sleeve only); shorten sleeve.

STEP 2: Draw in new design lines; draw lines from lower sleeve edge to cap; space these lines evenly across sleeve (see Fig. 6-20).

STEP 3: Cut on new design lines; cut from lower sleeve edge to cap edge, being careful not to cut through cap (see Fig. 6-21).

STEP 4: Spread, and add paper. Any amount of spread can be added; a soft fabric will take more fullness than a stiff one (see Fig. 6-21).

STEP 5: Smooth lower edge of sleeve with the help of the Dietzgen curve (see Fig. 6-21).

STEP 6: Write "gather" at lower sleeve edge (see Fig. 6-21).

Fig. 6-19. Short bottom puffed sleeve.

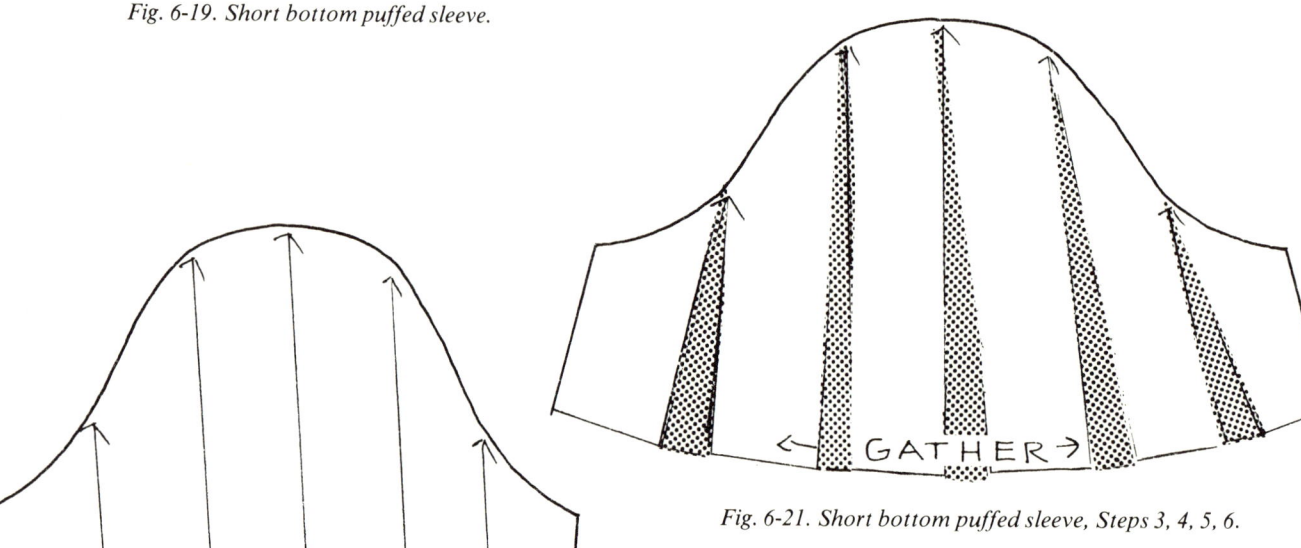

Fig. 6-21. Short bottom puffed sleeve, Steps 3, 4, 5, 6.

Fig. 6-20. Short bottom puffed sleeve, Steps 1, 2.

97 THE SLEEVE

Sleeve with Full Puff

The full puffed sleeve is gathered both at the cap edge and at the lower edge. This style of sleeve is used frequently in chidren's garments, and it looks best when made from a soft fabric (see Fig. 6-22).

STEP 1: Trace sloper (sleeve only); shorten sleeve.

STEP 2: Draw in new design lines; draw lines from top to bottom of sleeve; space lines evenly across sleeve (see Fig. 6-23).

STEP 3: Cut on new design lines; cut through sleeve from upper to lower edge (see Fig. 6-24).

STEP 4: Spread, add paper. A straight line on the tissue paper will help in making the lower sleeve edge straight when completed; spread evenly (see Fig. 6-24).

STEP 5: Smooth cap edge with the help of the Dietzgen curve.

STEP 6: Write "gather" on both cap edge and lower edge of sleeve (see Fig. 6-24).

Fig. 6-22. Full puffed sleeve.

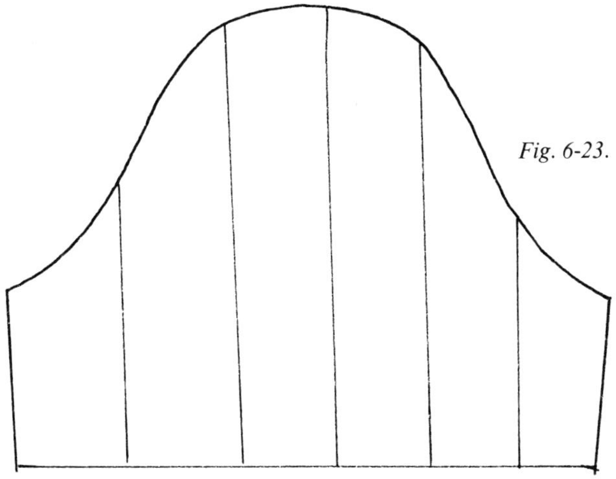

Fig. 6-23. Full puffed sleeve. Steps. 1, 2.

Fig. 6-24. Full puffed sleeve, Steps 3, 4, 5, 6.

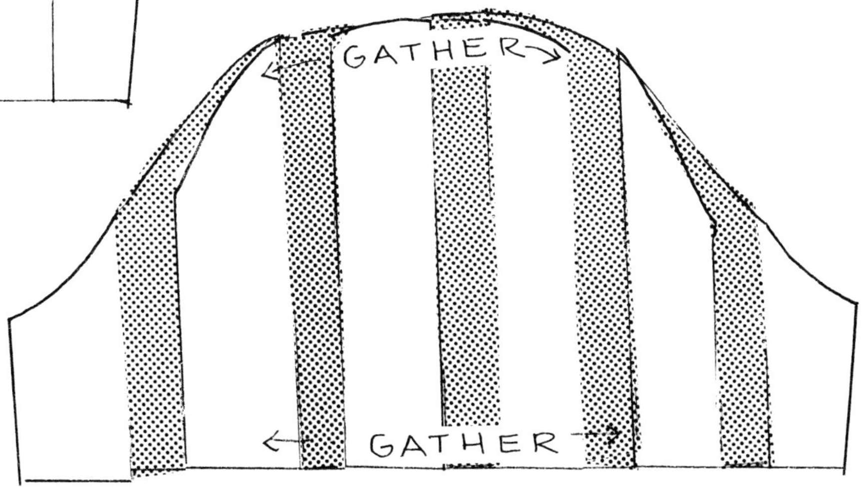

THE SLEEVE

Lantern Sleeve

The lantern sleeve is an interesting variation in either a short or three-quarter length. The completed sleeve resembles a Chinese lantern and can be an intriguing focal point for a garment (see Fig. 6-28).

STEP 1: Trace sloper (sleeve only); shorten sleeve.

STEP 2: Draw in new design lines; first, draw a horizontal line at the point you wish the widest part of the finished sleeve to be; in this example, the space below the cap has been divided in half; second, draw arrows from the horizontal line upward to the sleeve cap and downward to the lower sleeve edge. Space these lines evenly across the sleeve; the lines above and below the horizontal line must match (see Fig. 6-29).

STEP 3: Cross-notch horizontal line (see Fig. 6-29).

STEP 4: Cut on new design lines; first, cut sleeve apart on horizontal line; next, cut lower sleeve from the new upper edge to the lower edge, not cutting through lower edge.

Cut upper sleeve from its lower edge to cap edge, but do not cut through the cap (see Fig. 6-30).

STEP 5: Spread and add paper; spread each piece an equal amount; the amount you spread will depend upon how full you want the completed sleeve. Whatever amount you decide upon (½" to 1" is logical), spread each piece the same amount. If you do not do this, the completed sleeve will not stitch together correctly, and you will not have a smooth curve (see Fig. 6-30).

STEP 6: Smooth curves with the help of the curve stick or Dietzgen curve (see Fig. 6-30).

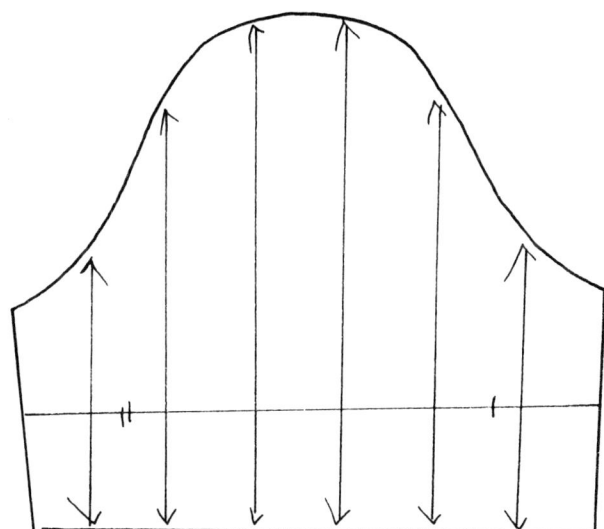

Fig. 6-29. Lantern sleeve, Steps 1, 2, 3.

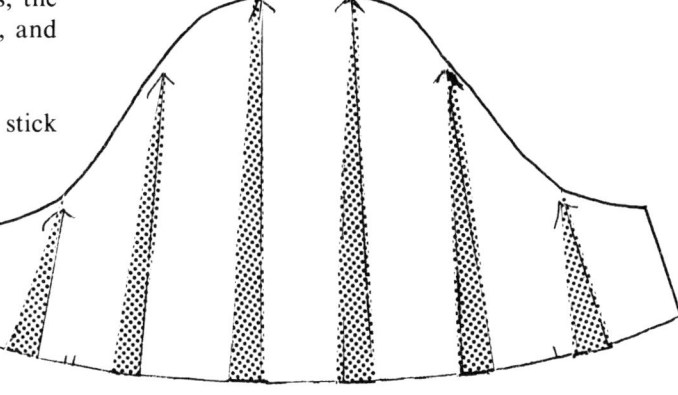

Fig. 6-30. Lantern sleeve, Steps 4, 5, 6.

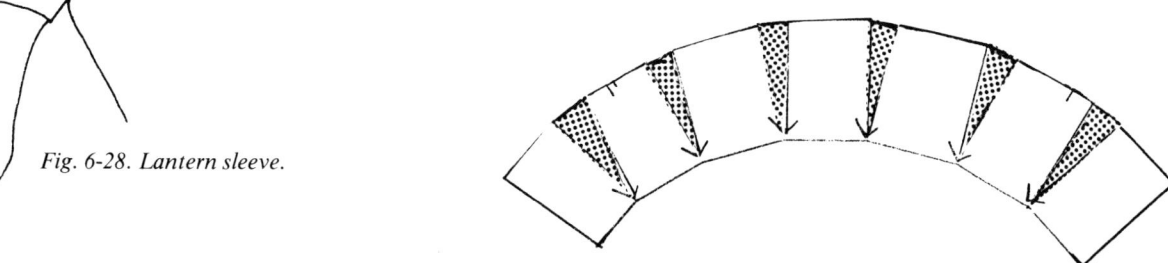

Fig. 6-28. Lantern sleeve.

Petal Sleeve

The petal sleeve looks something like a petal when completed and on the fiture. It is a comfortable sleeve because it does not bind at the lower edge and therefore is often recommended for children's garments. The sleeve is faced with self or contrasting fabric, and the raw edges at the cap sewn into the armhole of the bodice (see Fig. 6-31).

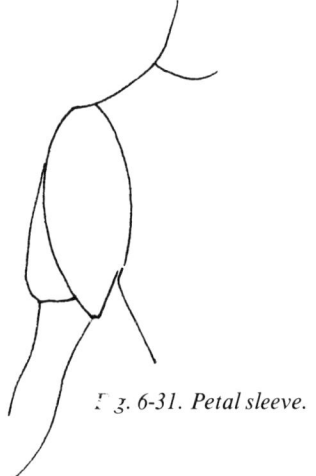

Fig. 6-31. Petal sleeve.

STEP 1: Trace sloper (two sleeves needed for this design); shorten sleeve.

STEP 2: Draw in new design lines; draw a curve from armhole to lower edge on left side of sleeve on left and right side of sleeve on right. These two curves should be identical in slope (see Fig. 6-32).

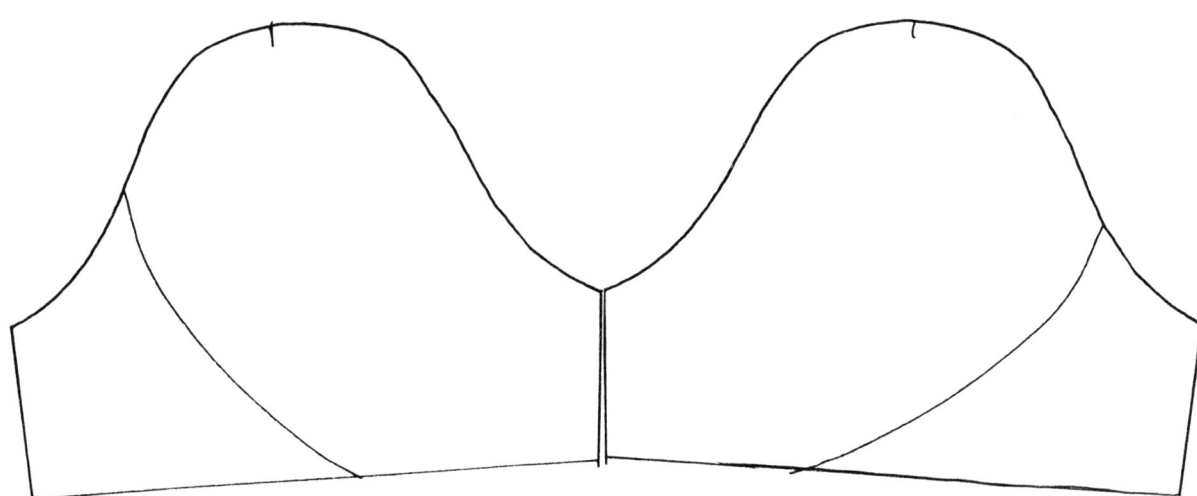

Fig. 6-32. Petal sleeve, Steps 1, 2.

101 THE SLEEVE

STEP 3: Cut side pieces away; place sleeve together at underarm, and tape or glue (see Fig. 6-33).

The sleeve is complete. To sew in the garment, bring center cap points together and stitch into bodice armhole.

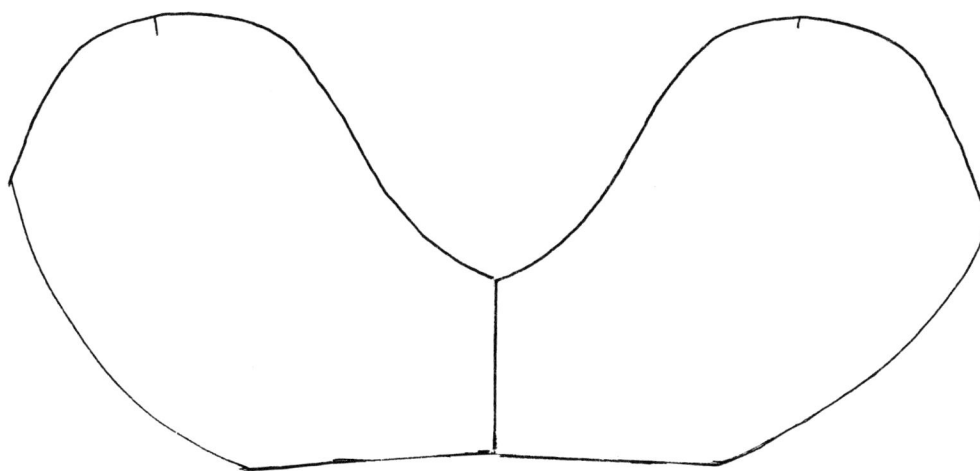

Fig. 6-33. Petal sleeve, Step 3.

THE COMPLETE GUIDE TO PATTERN-MAKING 102

Two-Piece Sleeve

The two-piece is used in tailored garments. The elbow dart is omitted, and the pattern curved to compensate (see Fig. 6-34).

STEP 1: Trace sloper (sleeve only).

STEP 2: Draw in new design lines; draw vertical lines from sleeve cap to lower edge approximately a quarter of the distance from the left side seam and a quarter of the distance from the right side seam (see Fig. 6-35).

STEP 3: Cross-notch.

Fig. 6-34. Two-piece sleeve

Fig. 6-35. Two-piece sleve, Steps 1, 2, 3.

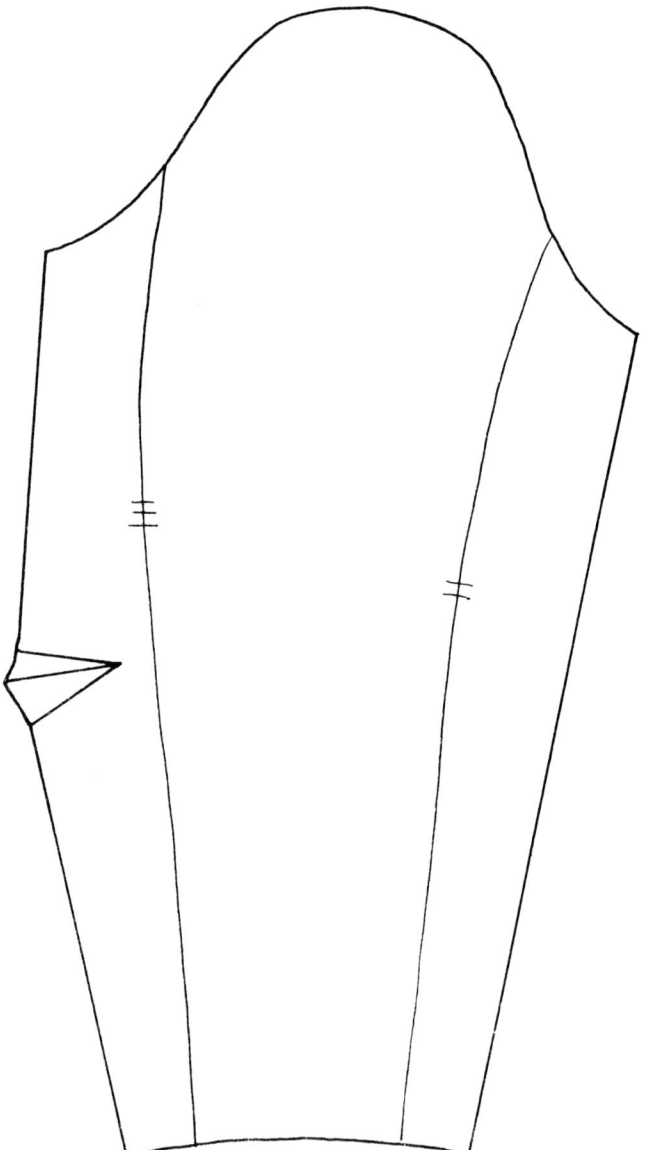

103 THE SLEEVE

STEP 4: Cut apart on new design lines (see Fig. 6-36).

STEP 5: Fold out dart, cutting beyond point to edge (see Fig. 6-36).

STEP 6: Place sleeve side sections together at underarm, and tape or glue (see Fig. 6-36).

STEP 7: Straighten curves if necessary.

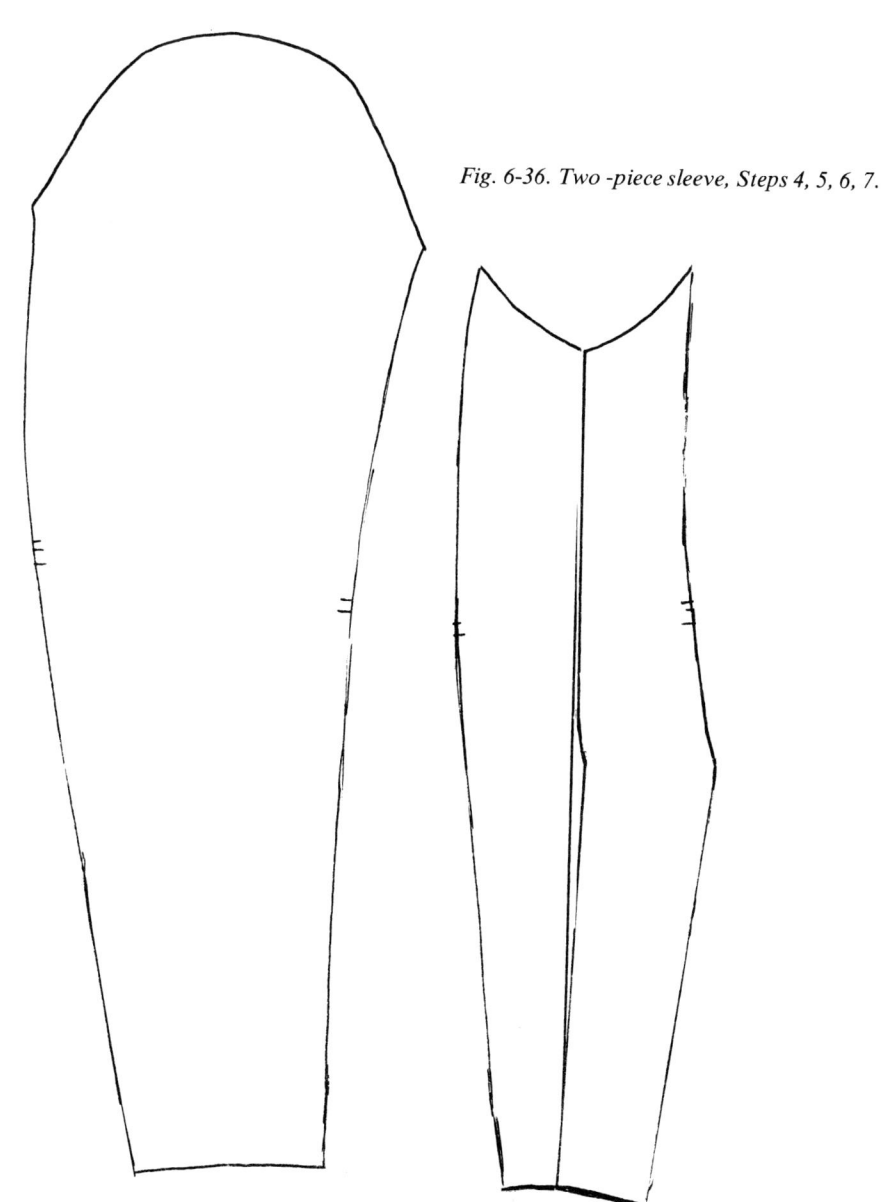

Fig. 6-36. Two-piece sleeve, Steps 4, 5, 6, 7.

Elizabethan Sleeve

The Elizabethan sleeve has no gathers but through a series of horizontal seams gradually becomes wider to the elbow and narrows down to the wrist. It was worn widely in the sixteenth century and is an attractive sleeve with design possibilities today (see Fig. 6-37).

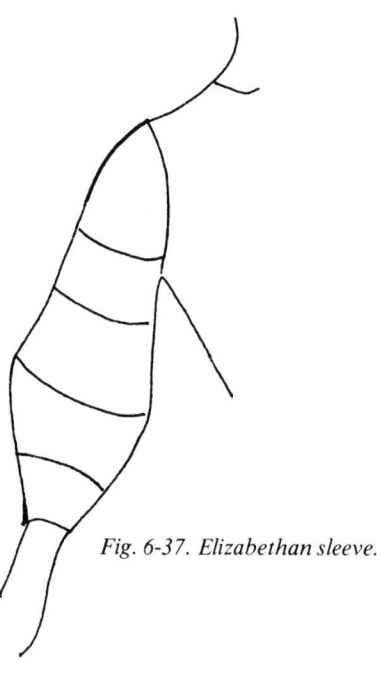

Fig. 6-37. Elizabethan sleeve.

STEP 1: Trace sloper (sleeve only).

STEP 2: Draw in new design lines; draw in horizontal lines first.

The sleeve is divided into five sections, labeled "a" through "e"; these sections are approximately equal in size.

Vertical lines (about four) cut the sleeve into approximately equal sections the other direction (see Fig. 6-38).

STEP 3: Cross-notch.

STEP 4: Cut on new design lines; add paper; start with section a.

Cut from lower edge to cap edge; do not cut through cap edge; spread lower edge, and add paper.

With section b, cut all the way through vertical lines; spread the top of this section to match the lower edge spreads on section a; spread the lower edge of section b wider that the top of section b.

Cut off section c, cut all the way through the vertical lines; spread the top of section c to equal the lower edge of section b; spread the lower edge of section c wider than the upper edge of this section.

Cut off section d; cut all the way through the vertical lines; spread the top of section d the same amount as the lower edge of section c; spread the lower edge of section d less than the upper edge of section d.

105 THE SLEEVE

Cut off section e; cut from upper edge of section e to wrist edge, not cutting through wrist edge.

Spread the top edge of section e to match the lower edge of section d (see Fig. 6-39).

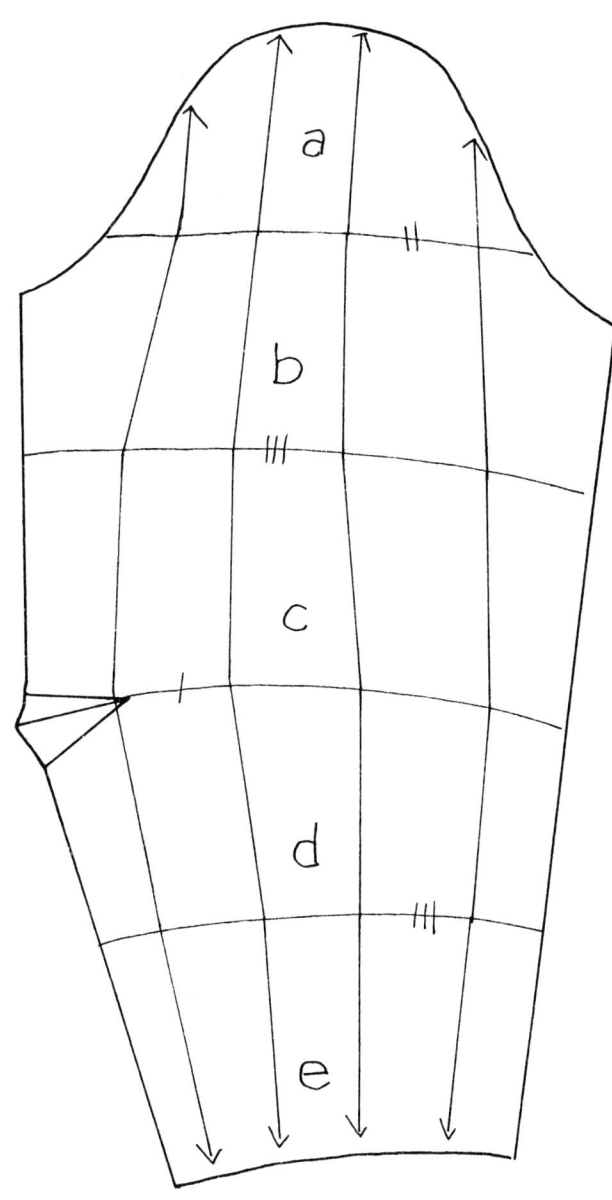

Fig. 6-38. Elizabethan sleeve, Steps 1, 2, 3.

THE COMPLETE GUIDE TO PATTERN-MAKING

STEP 5: Add fullness at elbow point.

Dart between section c and section d is cut away in the seam; a bulge is added here to emphasize the elbow, however; draw in this fullness bulge as shown.

The lower edge of section c and the upper edge of section d should exactly match when the drawing is completed (see Fig. 6-39).

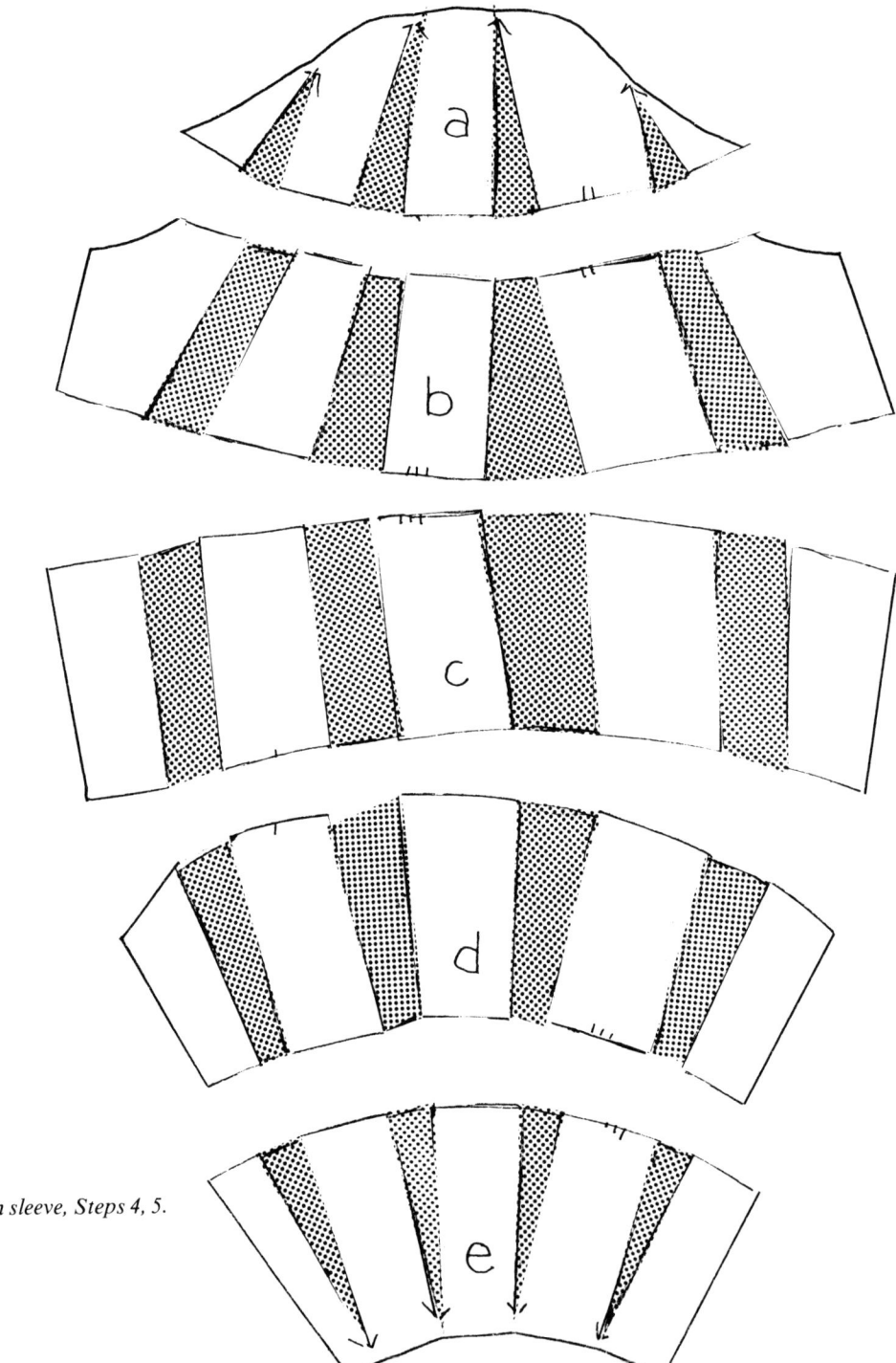

Fig. 6-39. Elizabethan sleeve, Steps 4, 5.

107 THE SLEEVE

Epaulet Sleeve

The epaulet sleeve has an extension over the shoulder which can give a very military look to a garment. It is most commonly combined with a bodice design that complements this look (see Fig. 6-40).

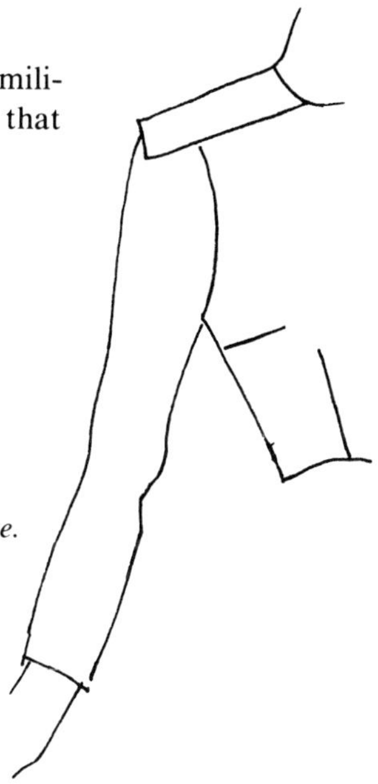

STEP 1: Trace sloper (bodice front, bodice back, sleeve).

STEP 2: Transfer back bodice shoulder dart to neck edge (see Fig. 6-41).

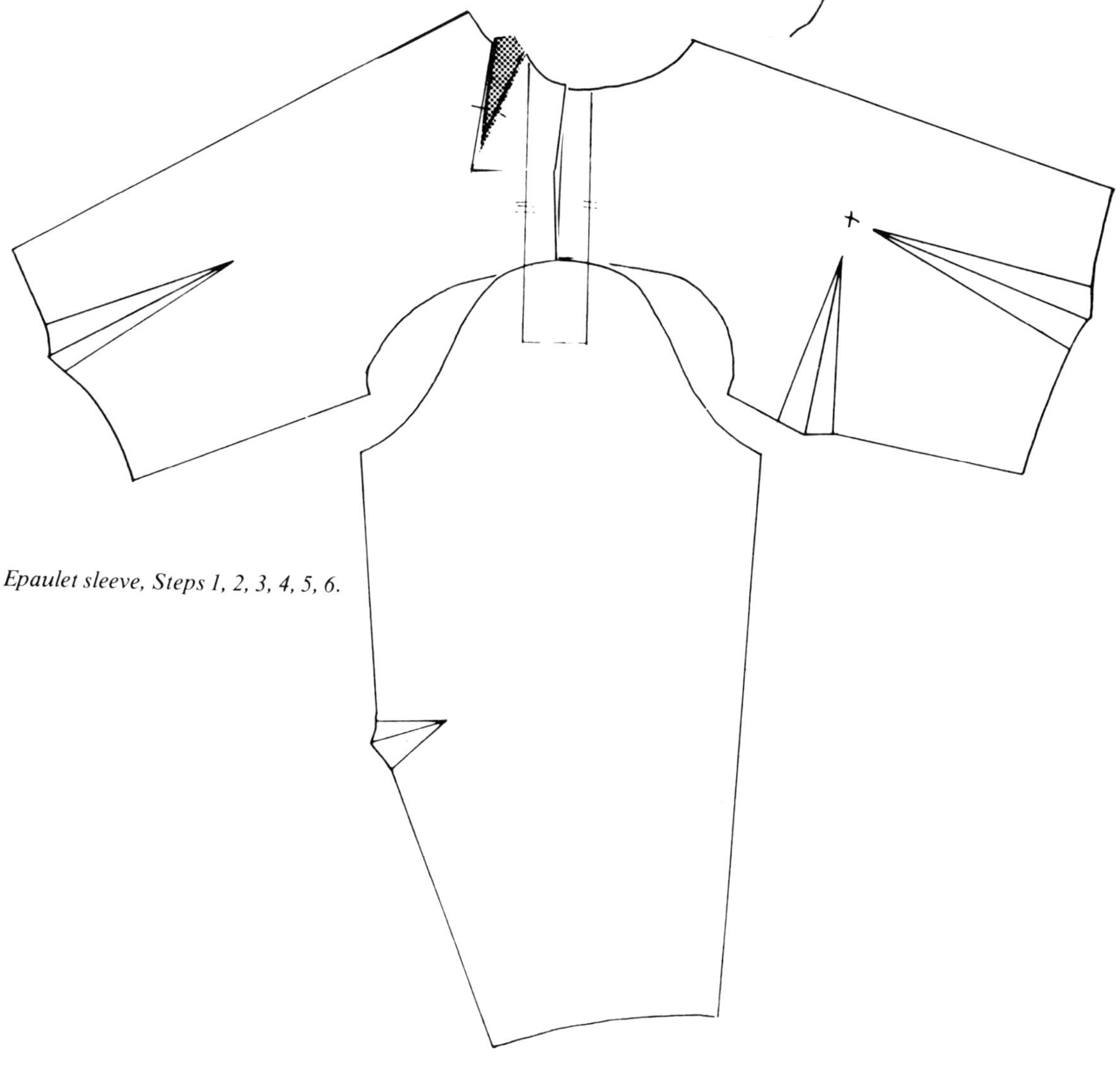

Fig. 6-40. Epaulet sleeve.

Fig. 6-41. Epaulet sleeve, Steps 1, 2, 3, 4, 5, 6.

THE COMPLETE GUIDE TO PATTERN-MAKING 108

STEP 3: Place bodice front and bodice back together at shoulder; tape or glue (see Fig. 6-41).

STEP 4: Place sleeve on bodice, making sure elbow dart is toward bodice back (see Fig. 6-41).

STEP 5: Draw in new design lines; draw epaulet lines from bodice neck over sleeve cap.

The epaulet is a rectangular piece and should extend approximately 1½" to 2" over sleeve cap (see Fig. 6-41).

STEP 6: Cross-notch.

STEP 7: Cut on new design lines (see Fig. 6-42).

STEP 8: Use original sleeve sloper. The epaulet extends freely over the shoulder (see Fig. 6-42).

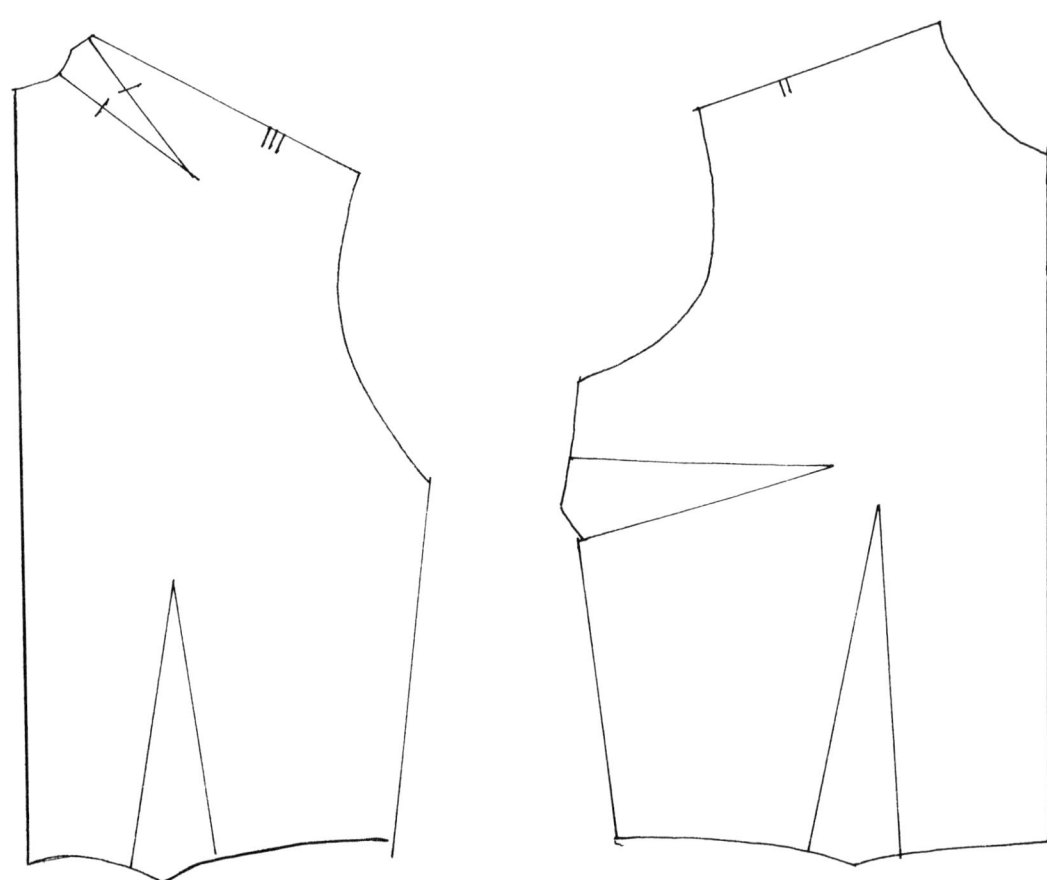

Sleeve with Short Top Puff

The short top puff has the fullness at the armhole edge and is smooth at the lower edge, fitting the arm (see Fig. 6-25).

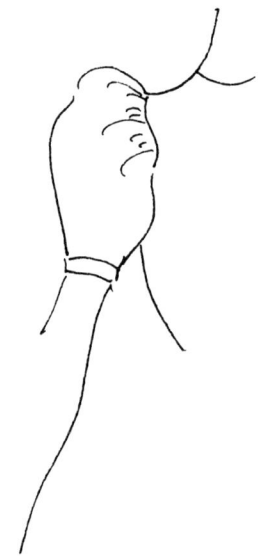

STEP 1: Trace sloper (sleeve only); shorten sloper.

STEP 2: Draw in new design lines; draw lines from cap edge to lower edge; space lines evenly across sleeve (see Fig. 6-26).

STEP 3: Cut on new design lines; cut from upper sleeve edge to lower edge, being careful not to cut through lower edge (see Fig. 6-33).

STEP 4: Spread, add paper. Any amount of spread is possible, but remember a soft fabric will take more fullness than a stiff one (see Fig. 6-27).

STEP 5: Smooth cap edge of sleeve with the help of the Dietzgen curve.

STEP 6: Write "gather" at cap edge of sleeve (see Fig. 6-27).

Fig. 6-25. Short top puffed sleeve.

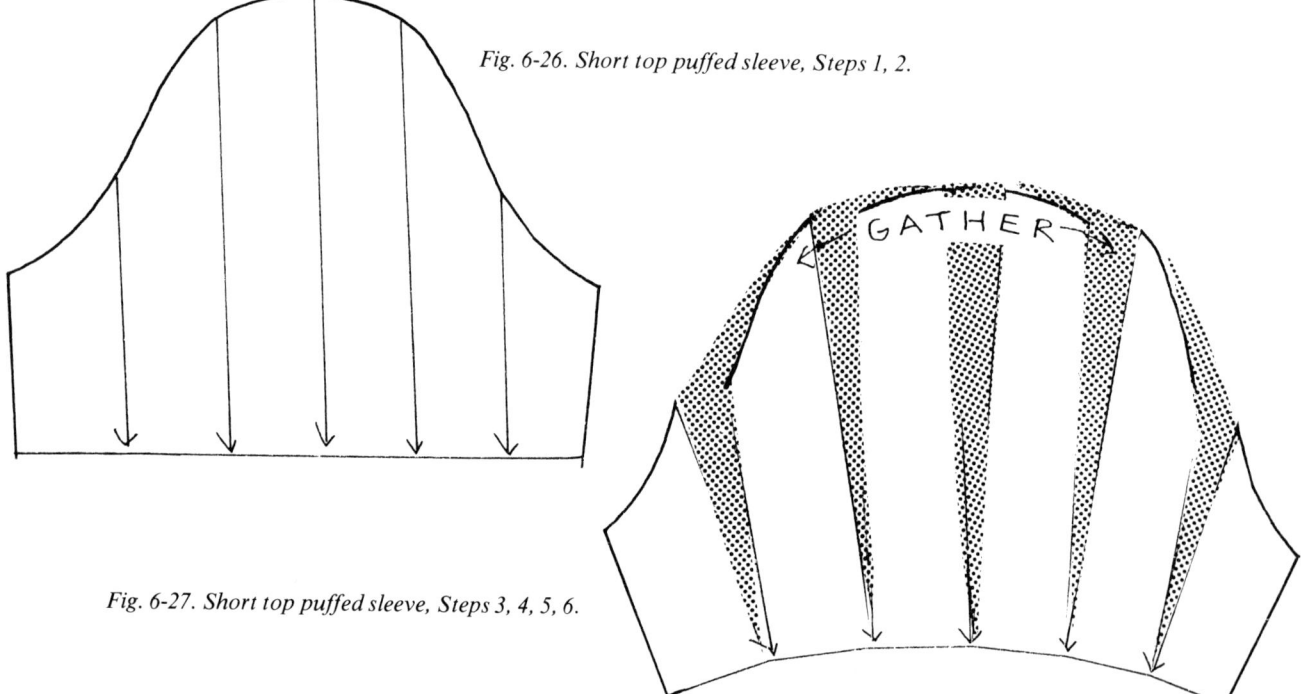

Fig. 6-26. Short top puffed sleeve, Steps 1, 2.

Fig. 6-27. Short top puffed sleeve, Steps 3, 4, 5, 6.

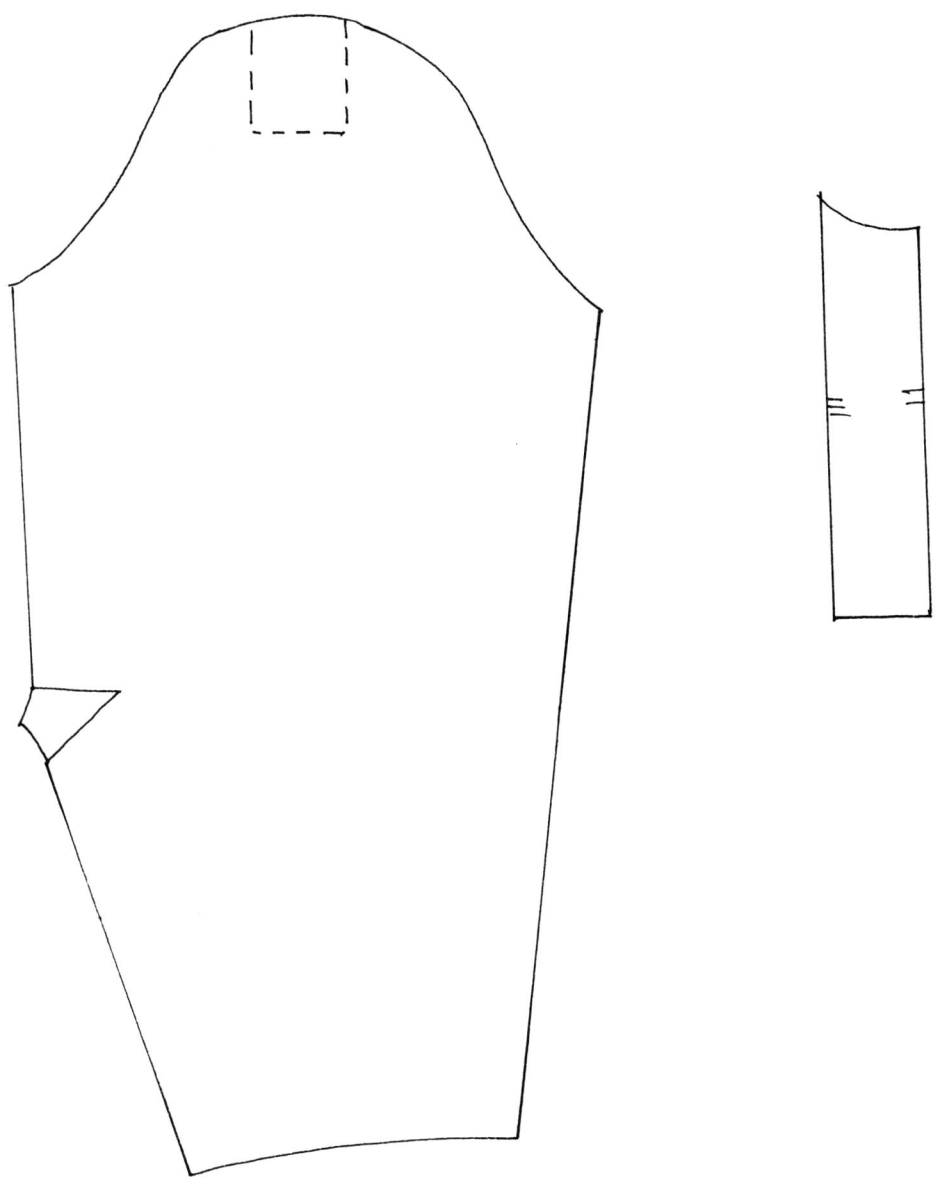

Fig. 6-42. Epaulet sleeve, Steps 7, 8.

Kimono Sleeve

The kimono sleeve is cut in one with the bodice. Fullness is added in the armhole area, which compensates for the sleeve cap lost when the sleeve is added to the bodice. The kimono sleeve derives its name from the Japanese kimono, a garment which has a sleeve cut with the bodice (see Fig. 6-43).

STEP 1: Trace sloper (bodice front, bodice back, sleeve).

STEP 2: Transfer back bodice shoulder dart to neck edge (see Fig. 6-44).

STEP 3: Place bodice front and bodice back together at shoulder edge, leaving a ½" gap at shoulder edge, matching exactly at neck edge; tape or glue (see Fig. 6-45).

STEP 4: Place sleeve on bodice armhole, making certain the elbow dart is towards the bodice back.

Place sleeve on bodice armhole so that the underarm points match; the sleeve cap will overlap the bodice; this ease will be lost. Additional ease is added from the middle of the armhole to the underarm; this will compensate for the cap ease that is lost (see Fig. 6-45).

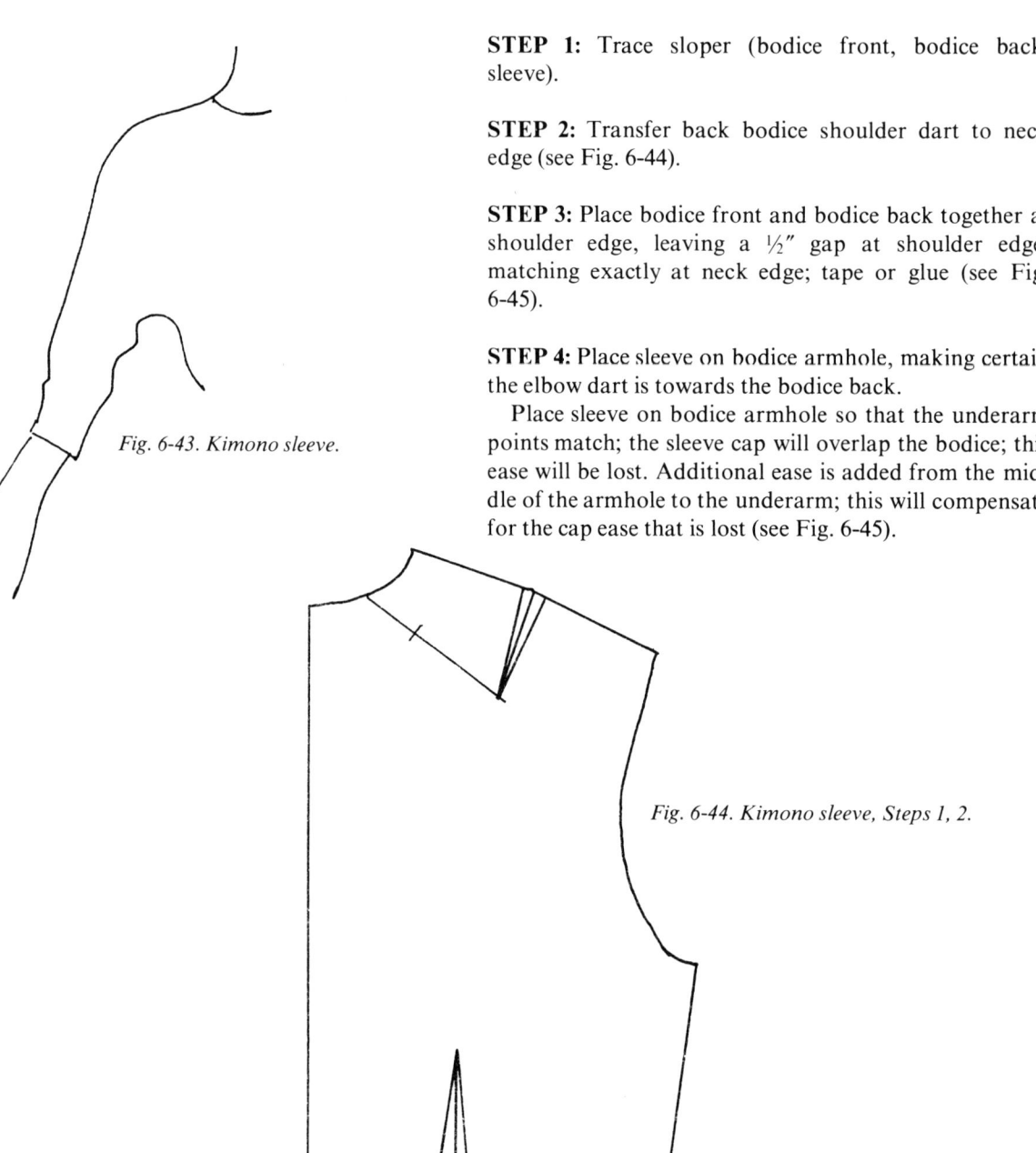

Fig. 6-43. Kimono sleeve.

Fig. 6-44. Kimono sleeve, Steps 1, 2.

111 THE SLEEVE

NOTE: If a seam is desired along the length of the sleeve, it can be drawn in at this point; the pattern then must be cross-notched and separated.

Fig. 6-45. Kimono sleeve, Steps 3, 4.

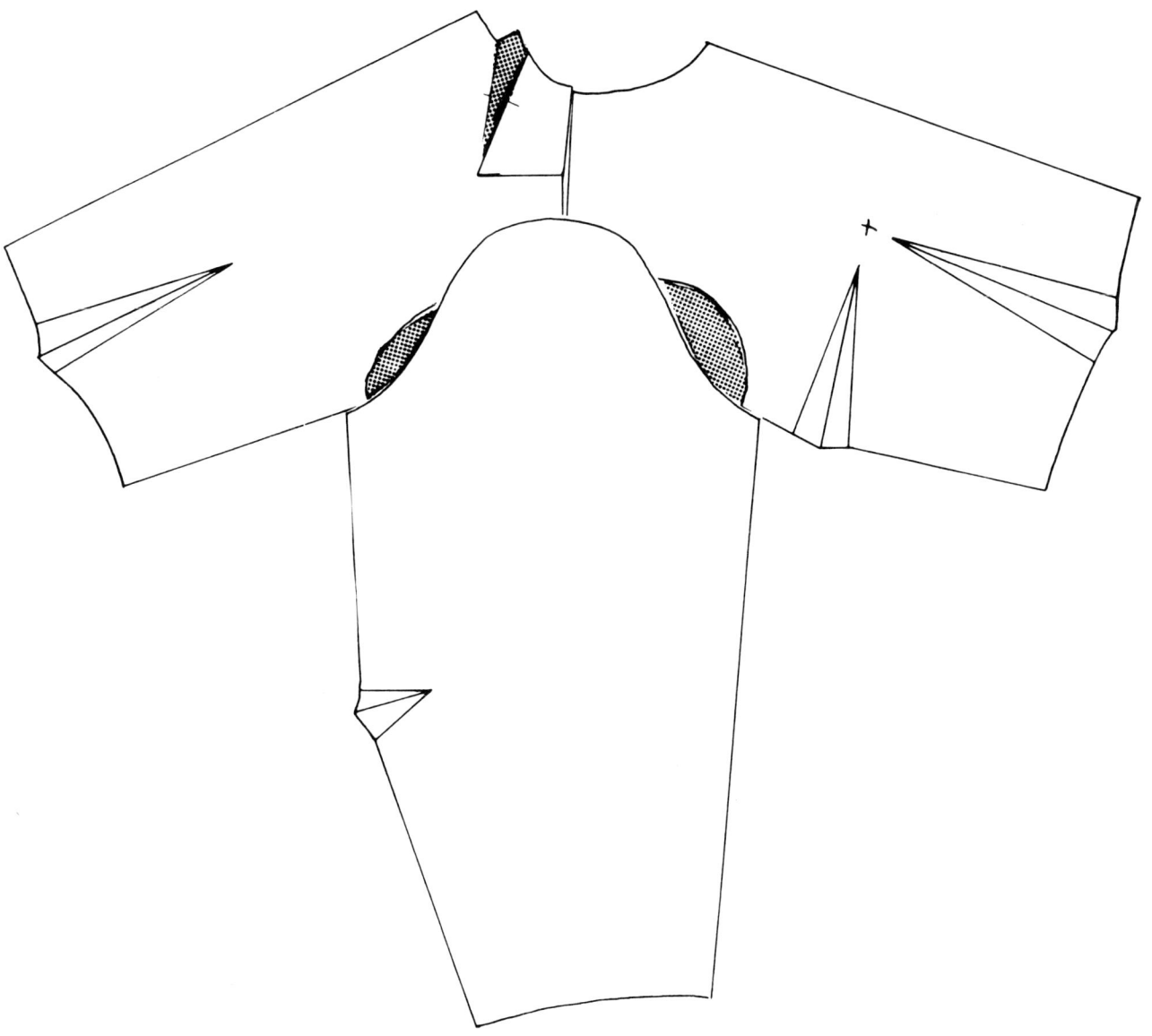

Dolman Sleeve

The Dolman sleeve is actually a variation of the kimono sleeve. To create interest in seams, the kimono sleeve as previously drawn is traced, and a sleeve seam is added in the manner shown here. The underarm may be dropped even lower if desired. This procedure is indicated by the dotted lines at the underarm seam (see Fig. 6-46).

STEP 1: Trace kimono sleeve sloper.

STEP 2: Draw in new design lines; draw a curved line from the center of the shoulder to above the bust point in front and above the back waist dart on bodice back; lower underarm seam if desired (see Fig. 6-47).

STEP 3: Cross-notch.

STEP 4: Cut on new design lines (see Fig. 6-47).

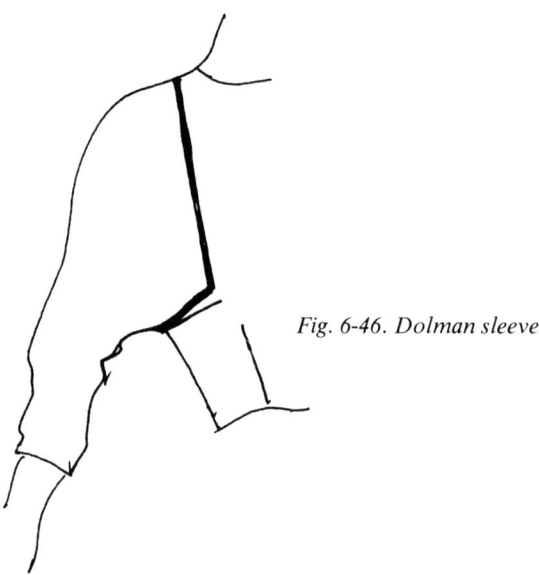

Fig. 6-46. Dolman sleeve.

113 THE SLEEVE

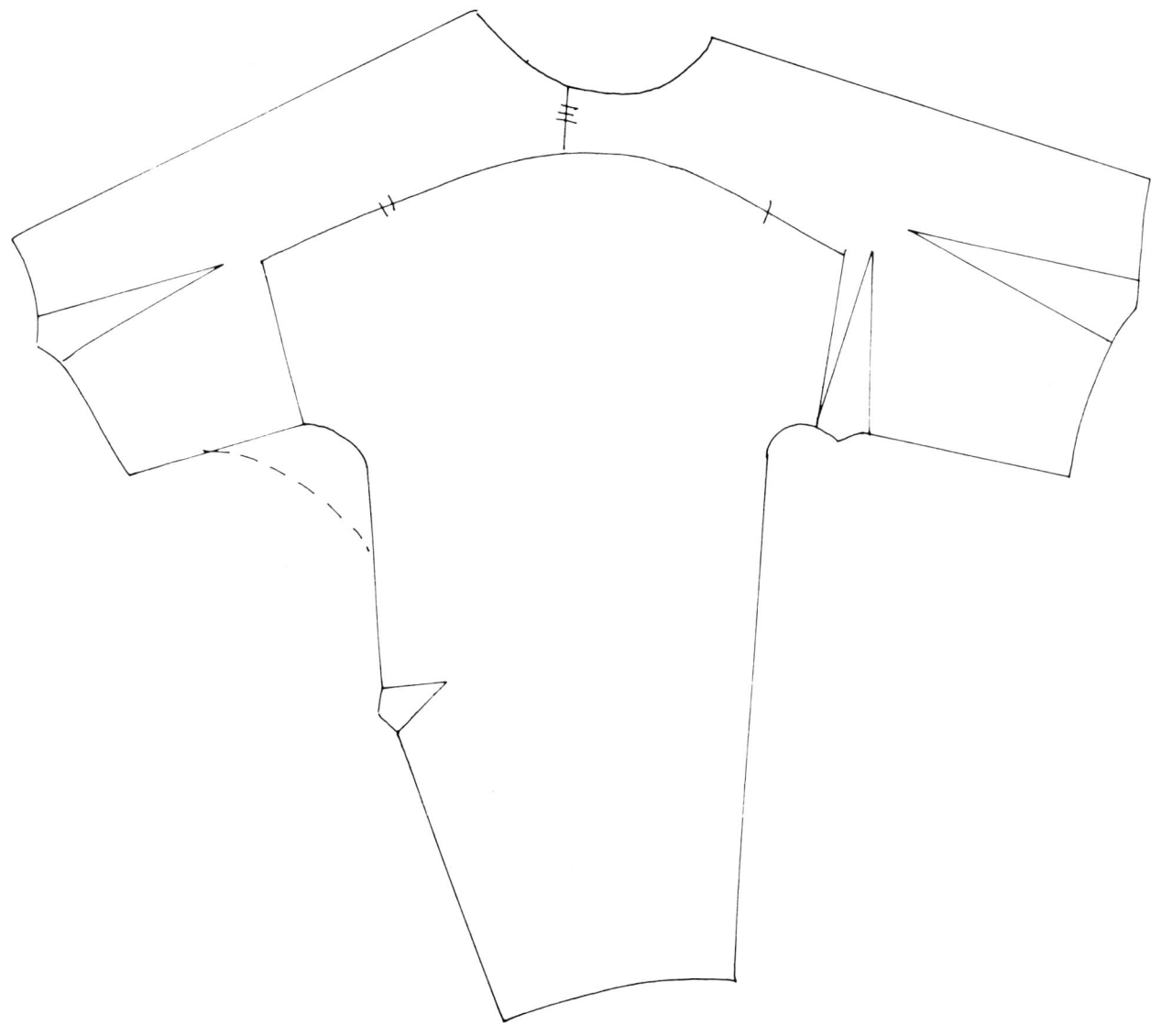

Fig. 6-47. Dolman sleeve, Steps 1, 2, 3, 4.

THE COMPLETE GUIDE TO PATTERN-MAKING

Kimono Sleeve with Gusset

The kimono sleeve can be uncomfortable to wear if its fits the body too tightly. If it is made with enough ease, there is sometimes an excessive amount of ease in the area right above the underarm. To avoid these problems, the kimono sleeve can be made with a gusset (see Fig. 6-48).

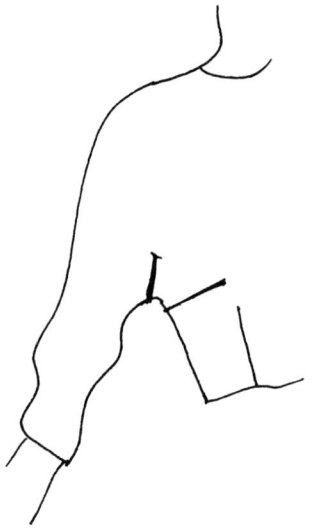

Fig. 6-48. Kimono sleeve with gusset.

STEP 1: Trace sloper (bodice front and back; sleeve).

STEP 2: Transfer back bodice shoulder dart to neck edge (see Fig. 6-49).

STEP 3: Fold sleeve in half; cross-notch, and cut apart (see Figure 6-49).

STEP 4: Place sleeve back on bodice back, overlapping at underarm so that triangular piece is overlapped, indicated by dotted lines in drawing (see Fig. 6-50).

STEP 5: Place sleeve front on bodice front, overlapping at underarm so that triangular piece is overlapped, indicated by dotted lines in drawing (see Fig. 6-51).

STEP 6: Tape or glue down. Some paper will be added at armhole on bodice front (see Figs. 6-50, 6-51).

STEP 7: Draw in gusset location, this is a line extending from underarm up 3" to 4" in full-size on front and back (see Figs. 6-50, 6-51).

STEP 8: Draw gusset; each side of gusset is 3" to 4" to equal the length of the gusset extension just drawn on pattern.

115 THE SLEEVE

A diamond-shaped piece should be drawn with a 70° to 80° angle at each side; the long side of the triangle will therefore measure about 4½" sides.

The gusset can be used in this manner with a seam at underarm, or it can be doubled and used without an underarm seam (see Fig. 6-52).

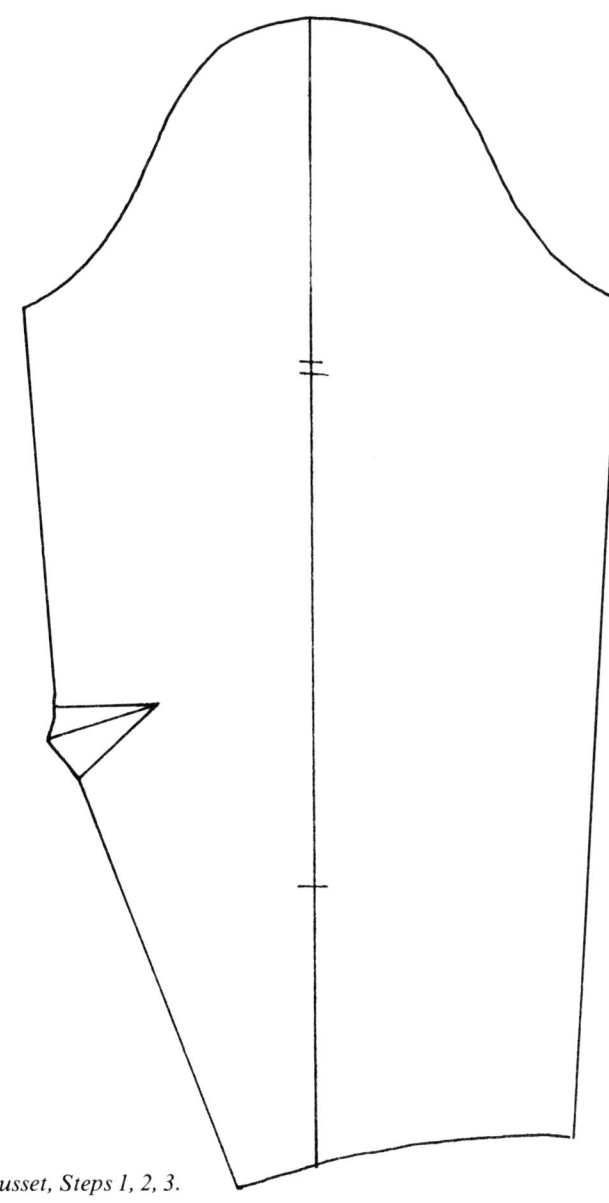

Fig. 6-49. Kimono sleeve with gusset, Steps 1, 2, 3.

THE COMPLETE GUIDE TO PATTERN-MAKING 116

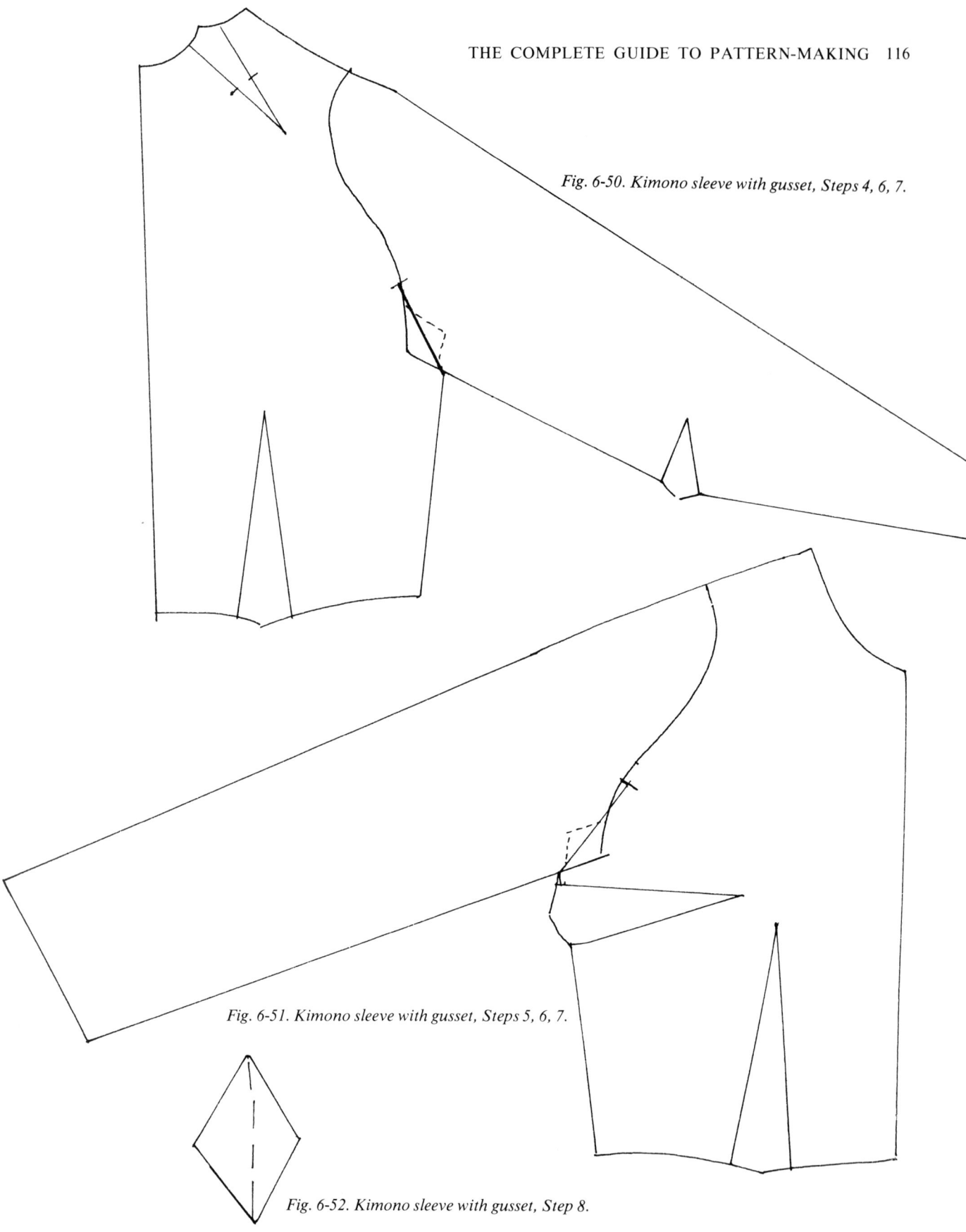

Fig. 6-50. Kimono sleeve with gusset, Steps 4, 6, 7.

Fig. 6-51. Kimono sleeve with gusset, Steps 5, 6, 7.

Fig. 6-52. Kimono sleeve with gusset, Step 8.

117 THE SLEEVE

Raglan Sleeve

The raglan sleeve is an adaptation of the kimono sleeve with gusset. Sleeve seams are drawn from the neck edge to underarm. When the underarm seam is drawn, it includes the curved pieces lost when the kimono with gusset was made and which were replaced by the gusset in that case. The raglan therefore needs no gusset and creates an interesting design line for the bodice (see Fig. 6-53).

STEP 1: Trace kimono sleeve with gusset pattern just completed; do not trace gusset pattern (see Figs. 6-54, 6-55).

STEP 2: Draw in new design lines; on bodice front, raglan sleeve extends from upper third of neck point in a slight curve toward the underarm; on bodice back, it extends from dart point in a slight curve toward the underarm.

Dart will be omitted as a seam (see Figs. 6-54, 6-55).

STEP 3: Cross-notch (see Figs. 6-54, 6-55).

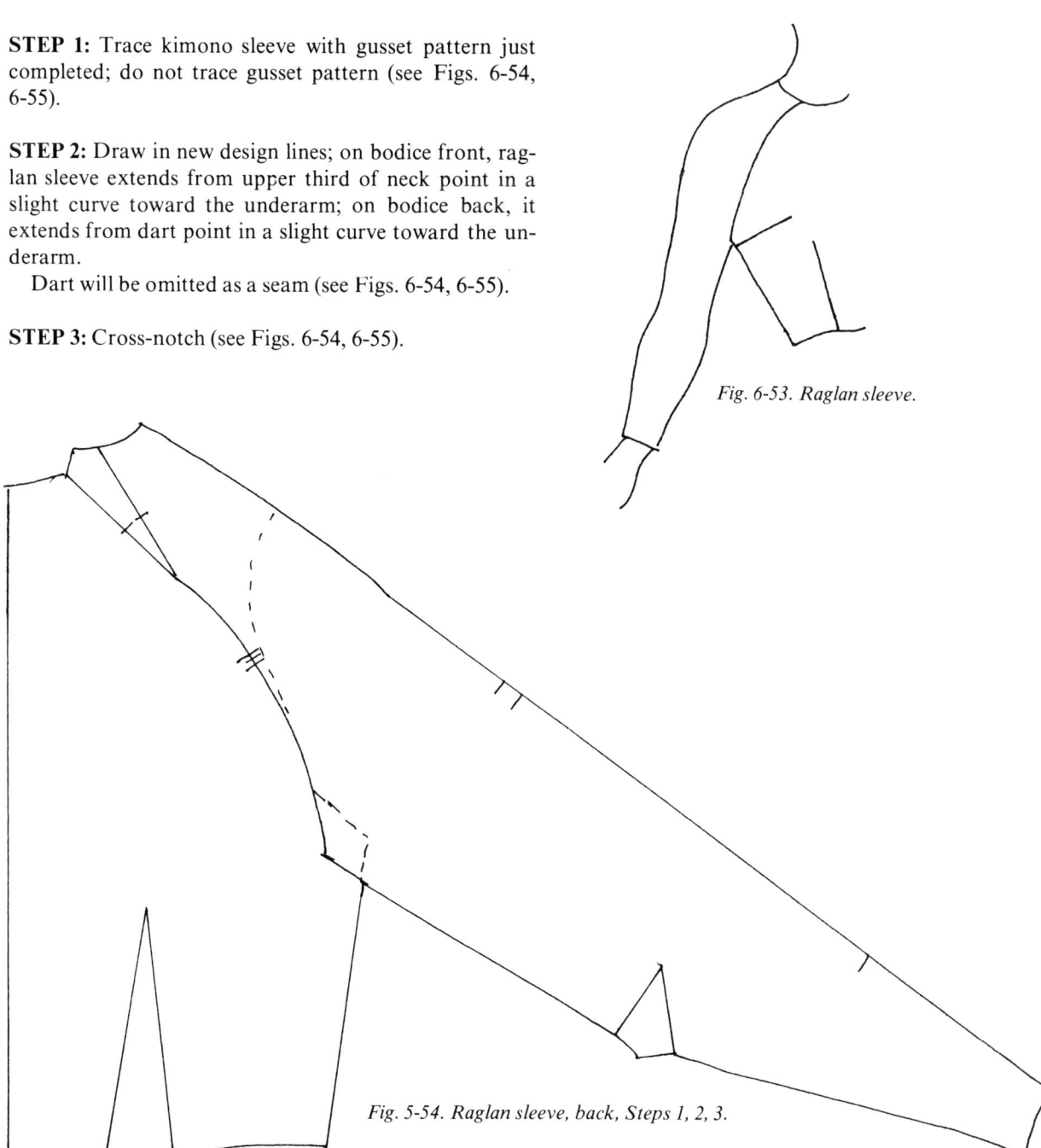

Fig. 6-53. Raglan sleeve.

Fig. 5-54. Raglan sleeve, back, Steps 1, 2, 3.

THE COMPLETE GUIDE TO PATTERN-MAKING 118

STEP 4: Trace; place tracing paper over drawing; bodice front is drawn along raglan sleeve line and includes upward curve of original bodice underarm.

Bodice front sleeve is drawn along raglan sleeve line and includes downward curve of original sleeve line.

Bodice back is drawn along edge of dart line over raglan curve and includes upward curve of original bodice back underarm.

Bodice back sleeve is drawn along upward edge of dart over raglan curve and includes downward curve of original sleeve underarm (see Figs. 6-56, 6-57).

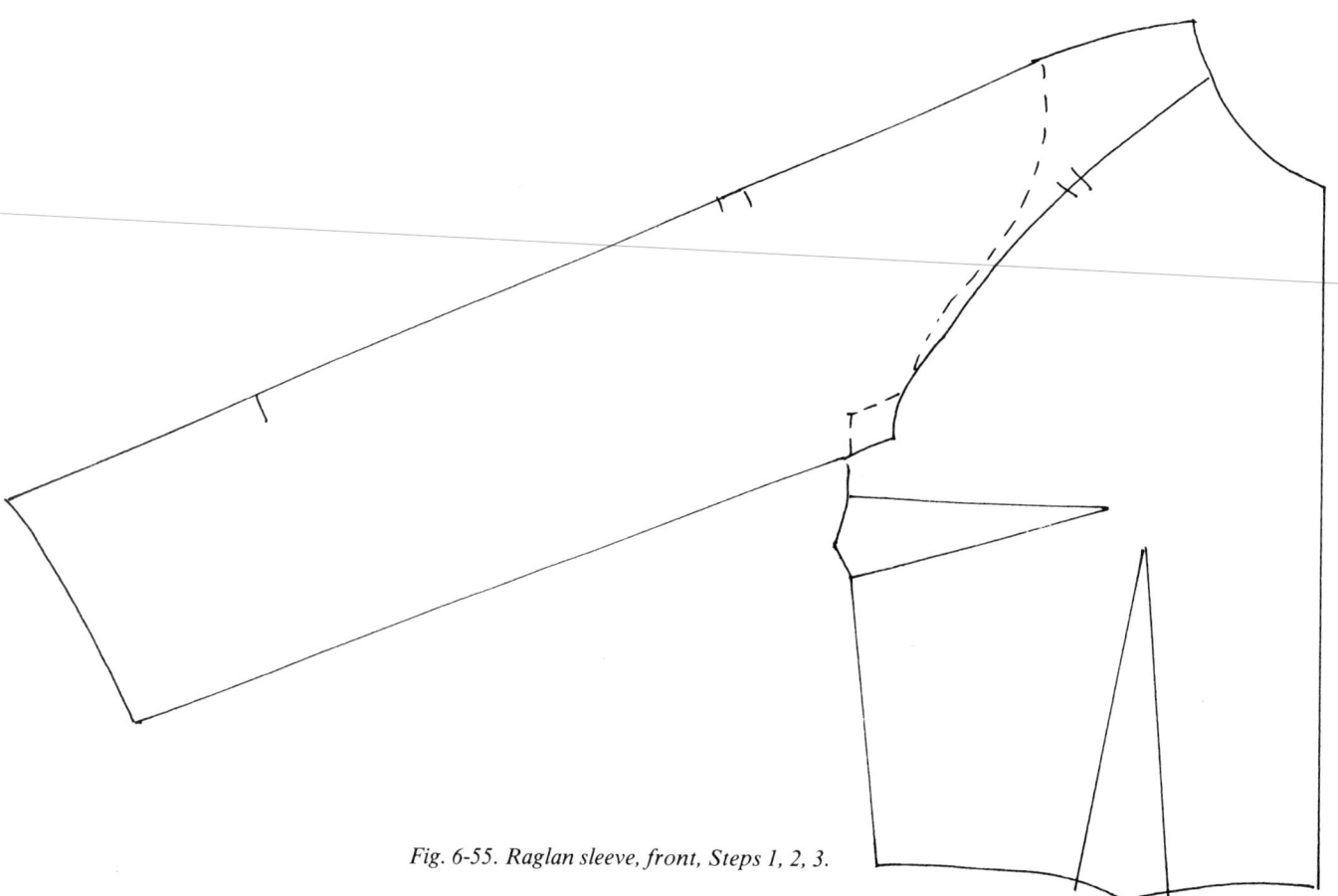

Fig. 6-55. Raglan sleeve, front, Steps 1, 2, 3.

Fig. 6-56. Raglan Sleeve, back, Step 4.

Fig. 6-57. Raglan sleeve, front, Step 4.

Cap Sleeve

The cap sleeve is not a true sleeve in that it is just an extension of the bodice. There is no sleeve seam and the sleeve sloper is not used to develop the pattern. It can be most comfortable to wear and is easy to construct (see Fig. 6-58).

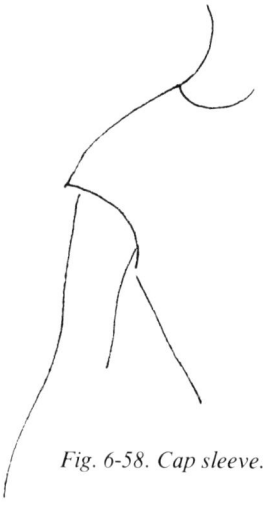

Fig. 6-58. Cap sleeve.

STEP 1: Trace sloper (bodice front, bodice back).

STEP 2: Transfer back shoulder dart to neck edge (see Fig. 6-5).

STEP 3: Place shoulder seams together, separating 1″ at armhole edge for ease (see Fig. 6-59).

STEP 4: Connect underarm side seams from point 1½″ down on underarm seam (see Fig. 6-59).

STEP 5: Draw line from neck shoulder point through center of added ease of shoulder seam to sleeve edge; then cross-notch (see Fig. 6-59).

STEP 6: Cut pattern apart (see Fig. 6-60).

STEP 7: Add 1½″ facing to lower sleeve edge (see Fig. 6-60).

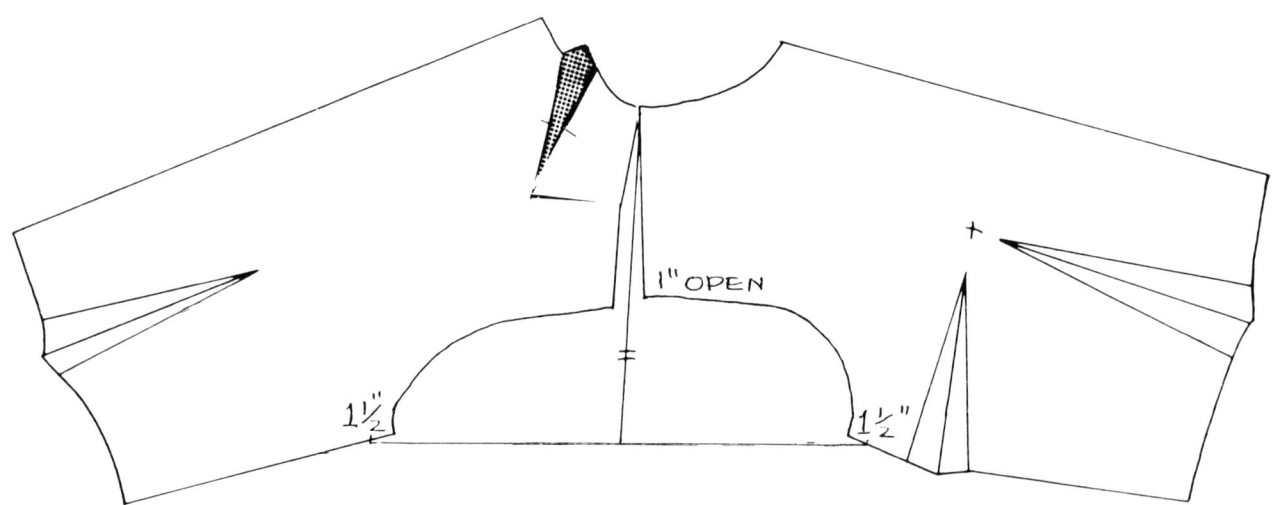

Fig. 6-59. Cap sleeve, Steps 1, 2, 3, 4, 5.

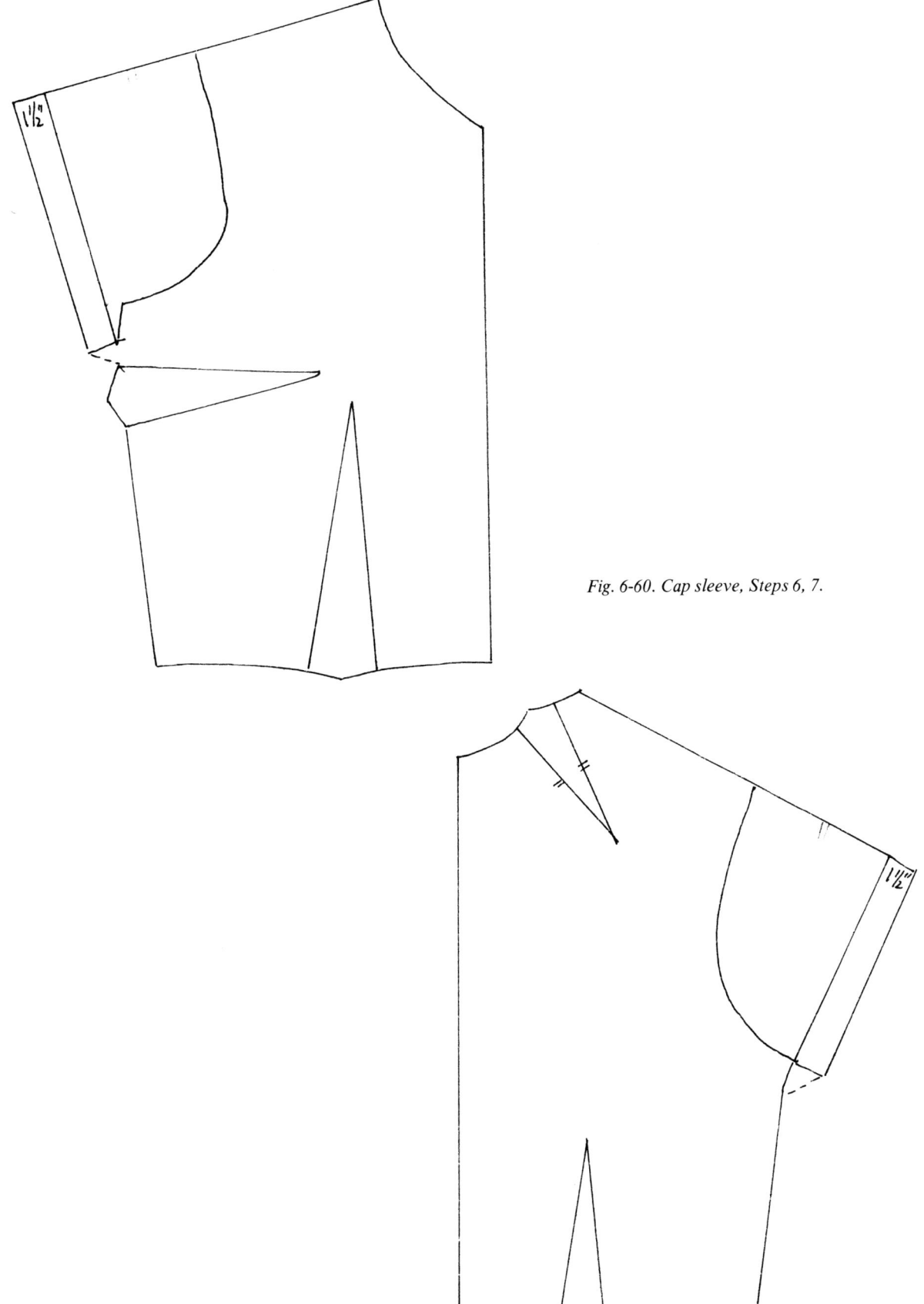

Fig. 6-60. Cap sleeve, Steps 6, 7.

CHAPTER **VII**

FACINGS AND BUTTON EXTENSIONS

Facings are produced by tracing over the pattern in the area where the facing is needed. The width of the facing varies, but generally speaking a neck and armhole facing should be 2″ to 2½″ wide and a front facing 3″ to 3½″ wide. Sleeve facings are often 1½″ wide.

Button extensions are drawn on the bodice or skirt and sleeve so that the front end of the button extends ⅛″ to ¼″ past the location where you want the button to stand when in hole. This allows room for the shank of the button. The width of the button extension is a design problem and depends somewhat on the size of the button, but ½″ to 1″ is common (see Fig. 7-1).

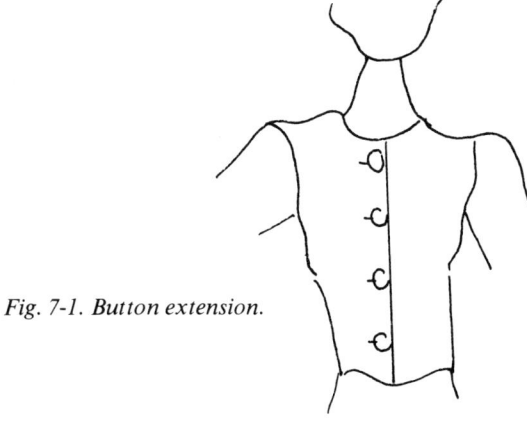

Fig. 7-1. Button extension.

Button Extension, Front Facing

STEP 1: Trace sloper (bodice front).

STEP 2: Add button extension; 1″ (full-size) added; buttons spaced evenly along edge.
Mark fold line (see Fig. 7-2).

STEP 3: Add facing.
Draw a line from shoulder edge to waistline, shown by dotted line (see Fig. 7-2).
Trace this area.

STEP 4: Add traced section to right edge of pattern (see Fig. 7-2).

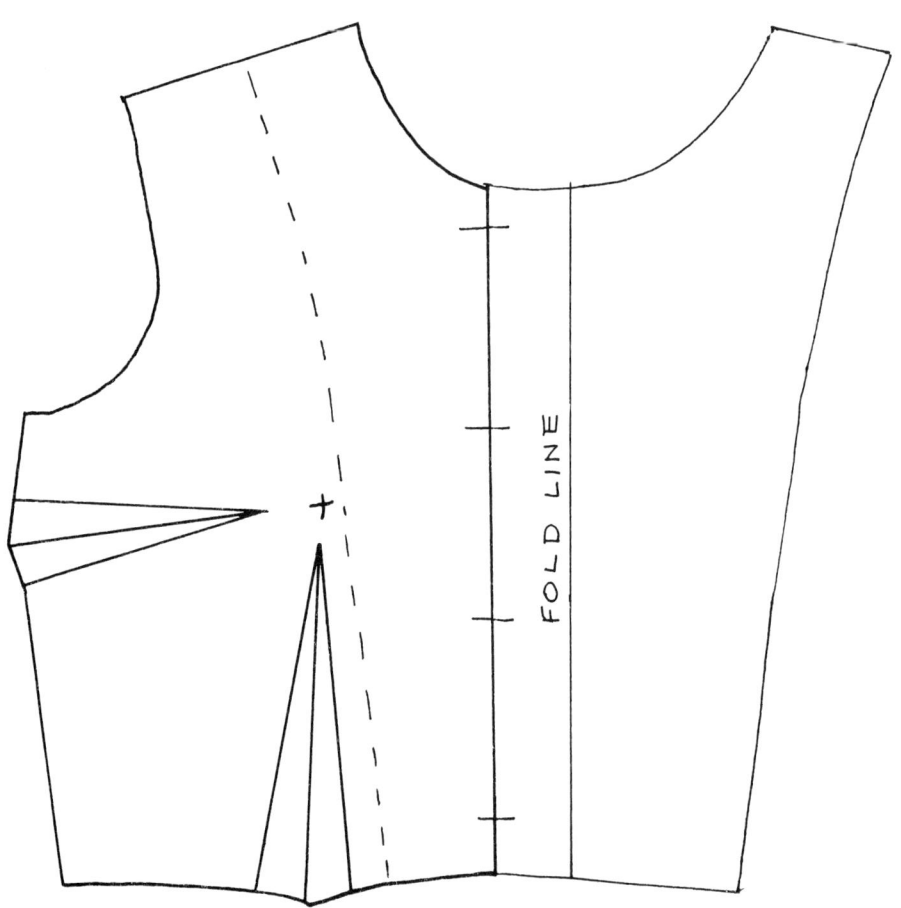

Fig. 7-2. Button extension, Steps 1, 2, 3, 4.

Neck and Armhole Facings for Bodice Front and Back

STEP 1: Trace sloper (bodice front, bodice back).

STEP 2: Draw in facings as shown; cross-notch; trace (See Figs. 7-3, 7-4).

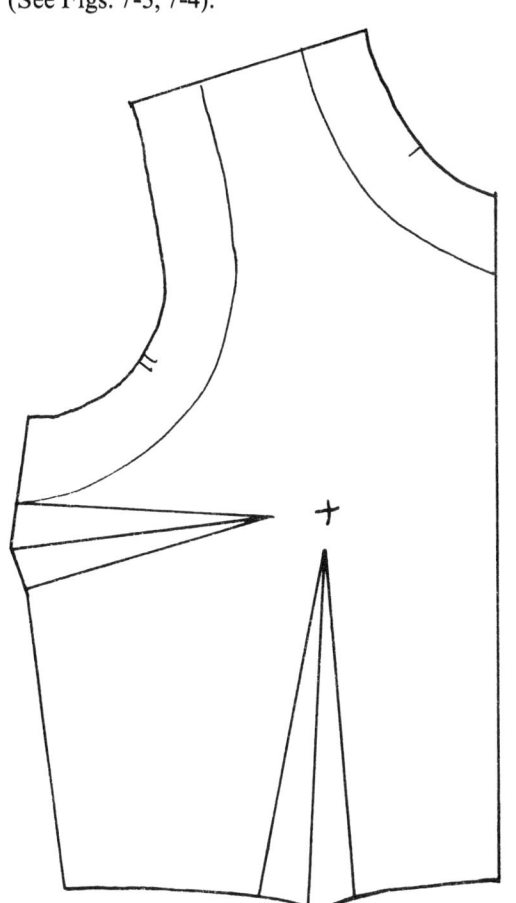

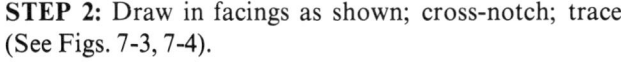

Fig. 7-3. Neck and armhole facings, bodice front, Steps 1, 2.

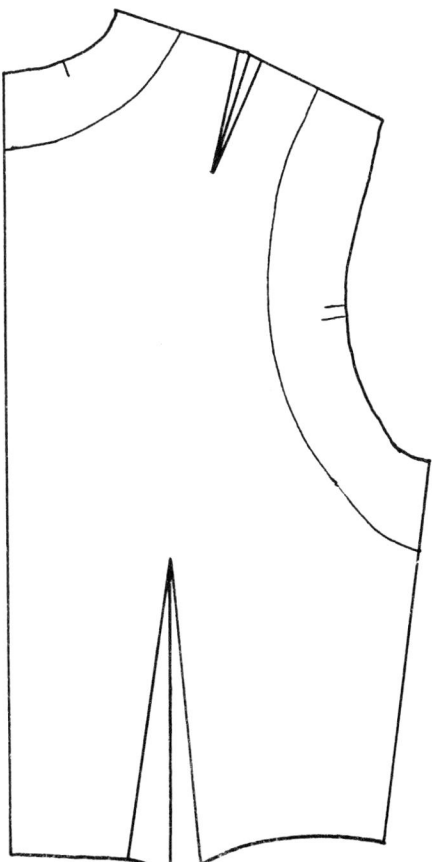

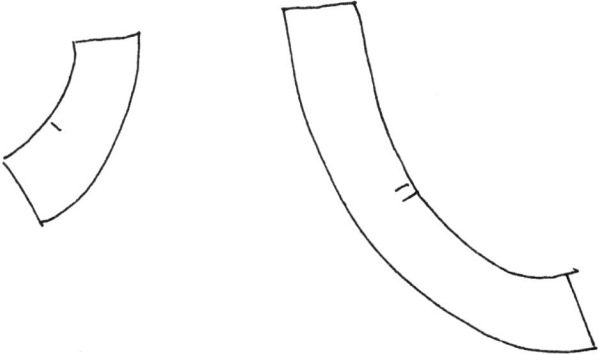

Fig. 7-4. Neck and armhole facings, bodice back, Steps 1,2.

THE COMPLETE GUIDE TO PATTERN-MAKING 126

Neck and Armhole Facings for Bodice Front and Back with Lowered Neckline

STEP 1: Trace sloper (bodice front, bodice back).

STEP 2: Lower neckline.

STEP 3: Draw in facings as shown; cross-notch; trace (see Figs. 7-5, 7-6).

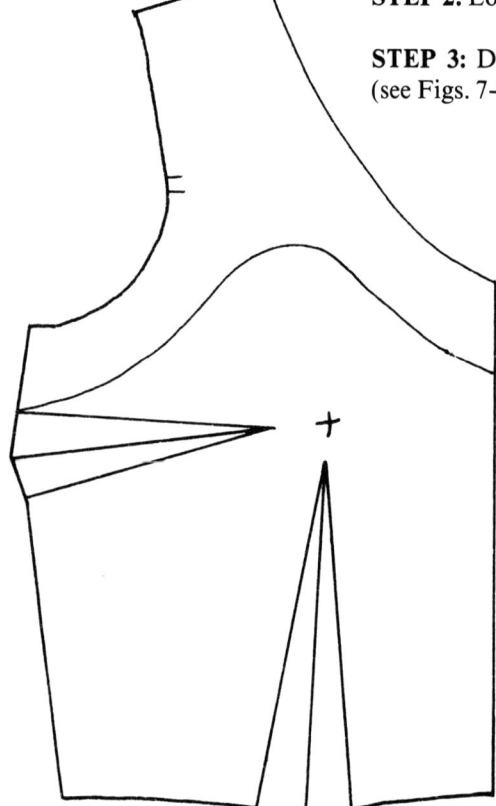

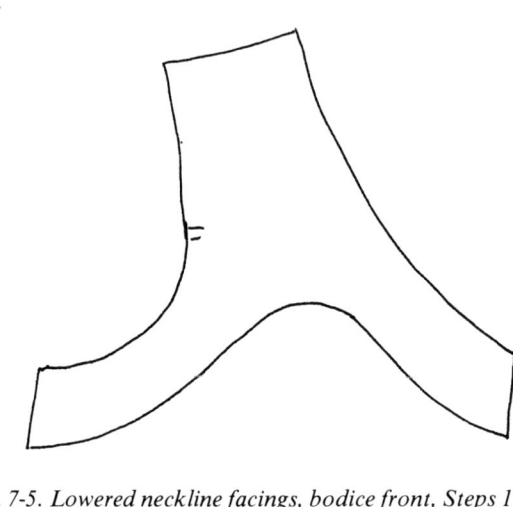

Fig. 7-5. Lowered neckline facings, bodice front, Steps 1, 2, 3.

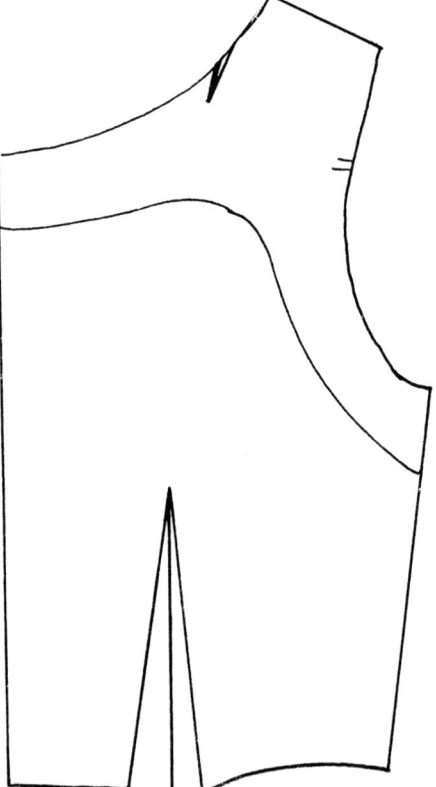

Fig. 7-6. Lowered neckline facings, bodice back, Steps 1, 2, 3.

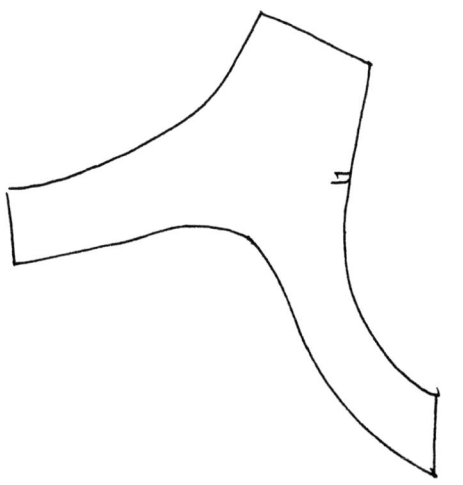

127 FACINGS AND BUTTON EXTENSIONS

Sleeve Facing

STEP 1: Trace sloper (sleeve only).

STEP 2: Draw in facing as shown; cross-notch; trace (see Fig. 7-7).

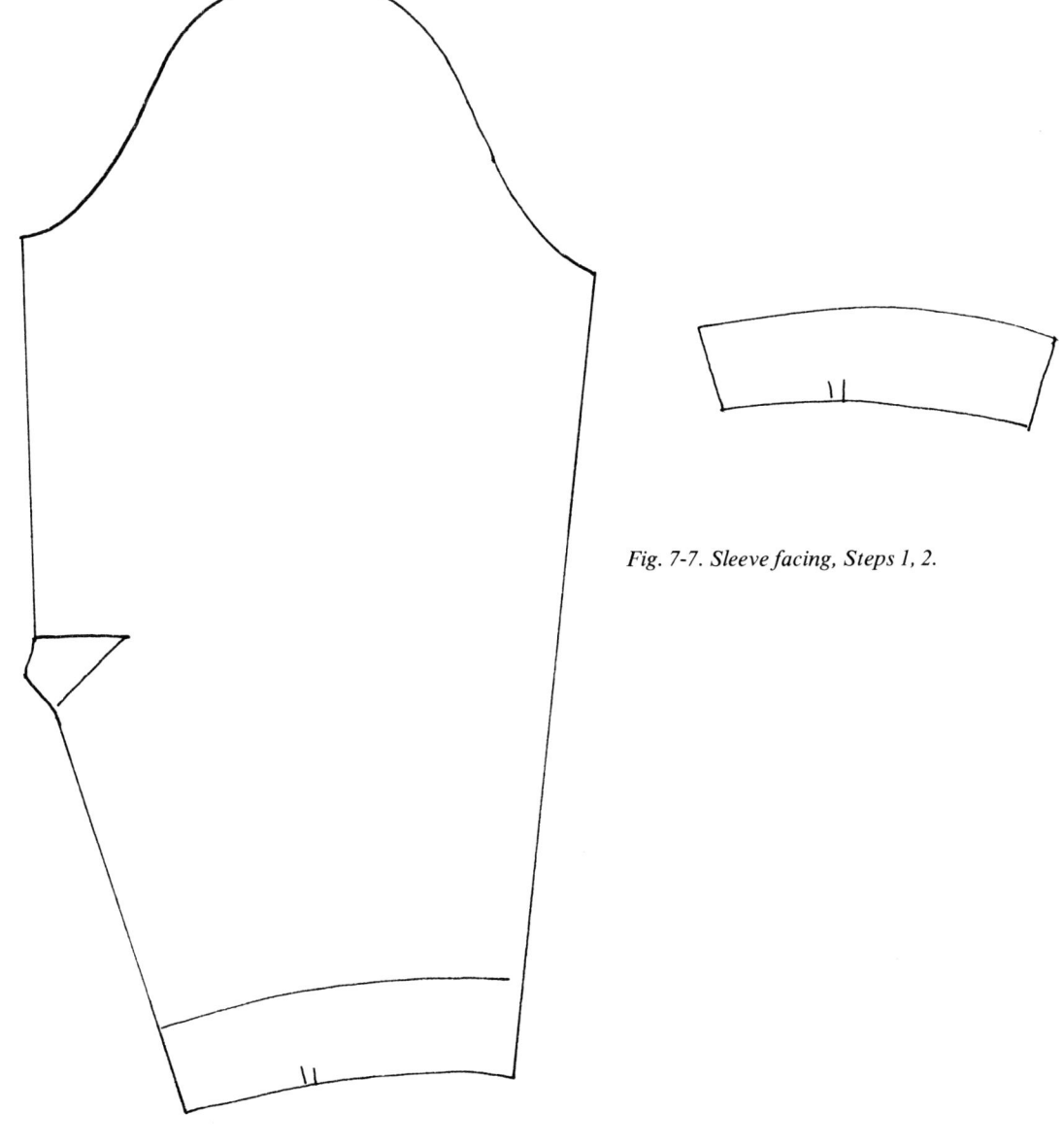

Fig. 7-7. Sleeve facing, Steps 1, 2.

CHAPTER VIII

SKIRTS

The basic skirt has one dart and a curved side seam. These create the third dimension. The curves involved are the waist and hips and sometimes stomach. If the waist is small in comparison with the hips, the dart will have to be larger to form a steeper curve, and the side seam will also often have to be more curved. If the derriere is large and the waist is small, the back dart will have to be large. If the hip bones are wide, but the derrière and stomach are flat, the pattern will have to have curved side seams but smaller darts (see Fig. 8-1).

The sloper for a person with a full derrière and a flat stomach will require a large dart in back and a curved side seam. The front will need a regular long dart and a side curve to match that in the back (see Fig. 8-2).

The sloper for a person with a full stomach and flat derrière will require a short dart in front and a curved side seam. The back should have a regular long dart and a curve at the side to match that in the front (see Fig. 8-3).

Large darts in front and back are required for a figure with a small waist and large hips. Side seams should have the normal curve (see Fig. 8-4).

An increased side curve will compensate for wide hip bones. Darts should be of normal width. This will give width at the side, but not at the front or back (see Fig. 8-5).

There are seven basic steps in making the skirt variations. The steps should be familiar to you by now, but do not omit any when working through the patterns. Pattern-making must be an exact and systematic process if a successful result is to be achieved.

THE COMPLETE GUIDE TO PATTERN-MAKING 130

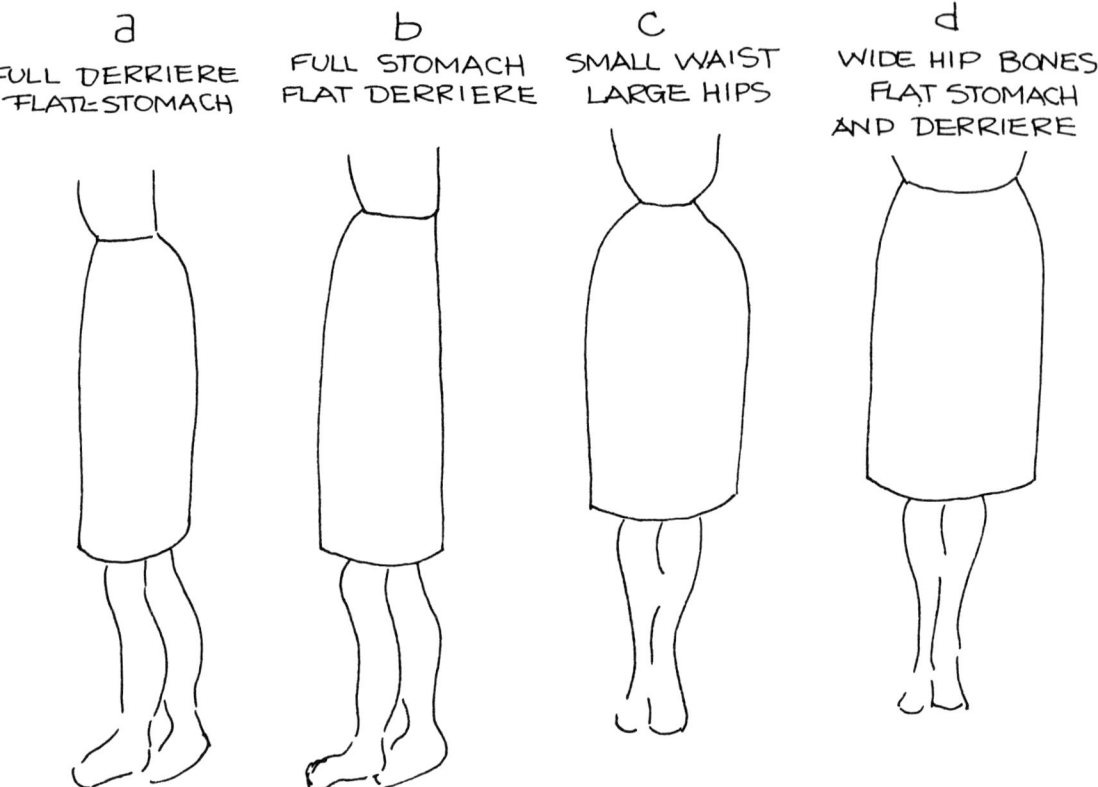

Fig. 8-1. Various ladies' skirt shapes.

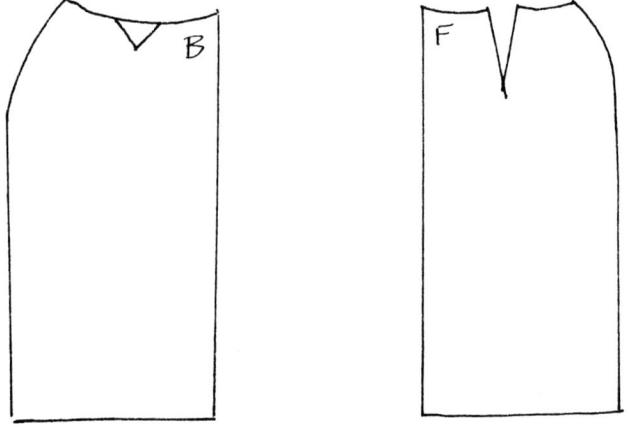

Fig. 8-2. Full derrière, flat stomach.

131 SKIRTS

 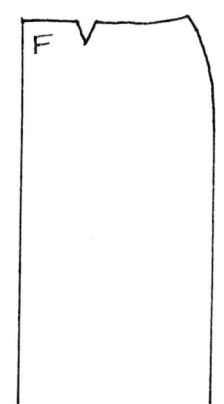

Fig. 8-3. Full stomach, flat derriere.

Fig. 8-4. Small waist, large hips.

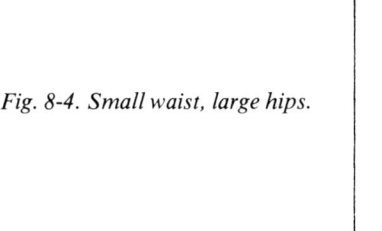 

Fig. 8-5. Wide hip bones.

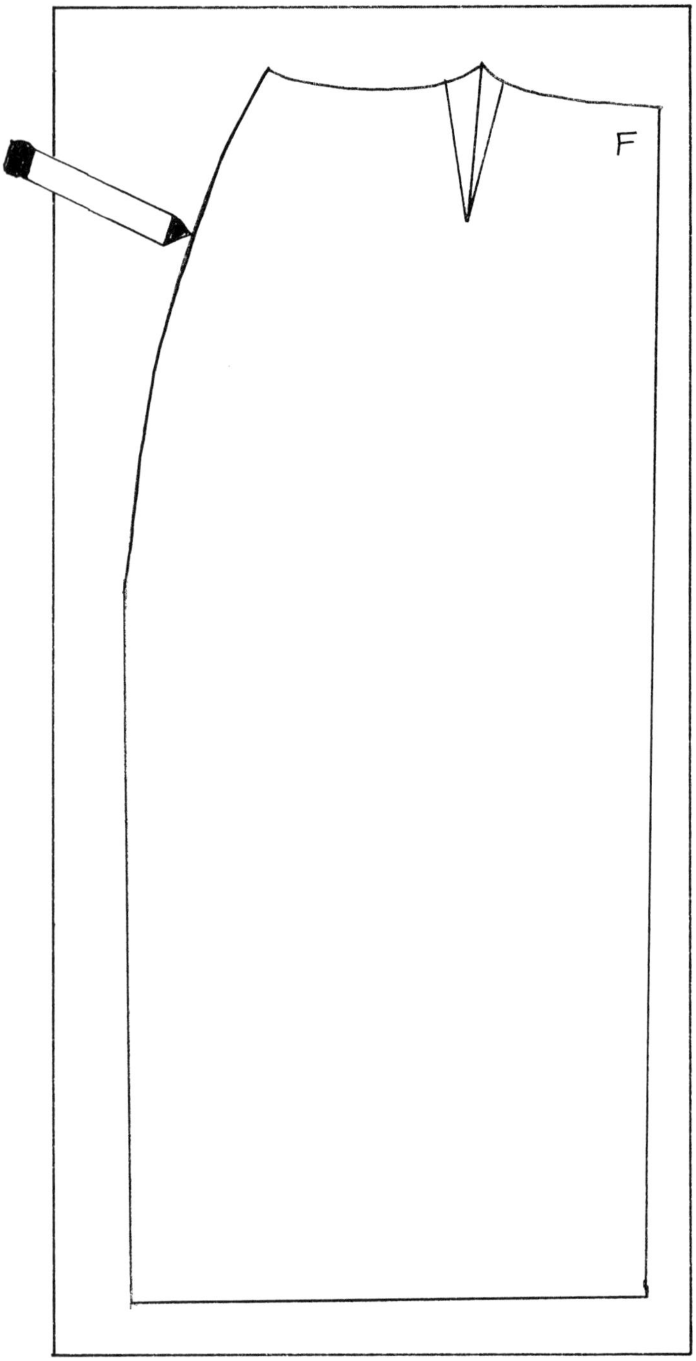

STEP 1: Trace sloper.

Use a medium-weight, good-quality paper to trace the sloper. Trace in the waist dart (see Fig. 8-6).

STEP 2: Draw in new design lines.

In the first example, the dart has been transferred to the center front location. For some designs you may add fullness, cut the skirt into gores, lengthen or shorten the skirt, or flare it. Draw in the design line location to the point of the original dart (see Fig. 8-7).

STEP 3: Cross-notch.

Cross-notch over the new design line(s) to aid in stitching the fabric together after the pattern is completed. In this example, the dart will require a cross-notch somewhere along its length (see Fig. 8-8).

Fig. 8-6. Step 1: Trace skirt sloper.

133   SKIRTS

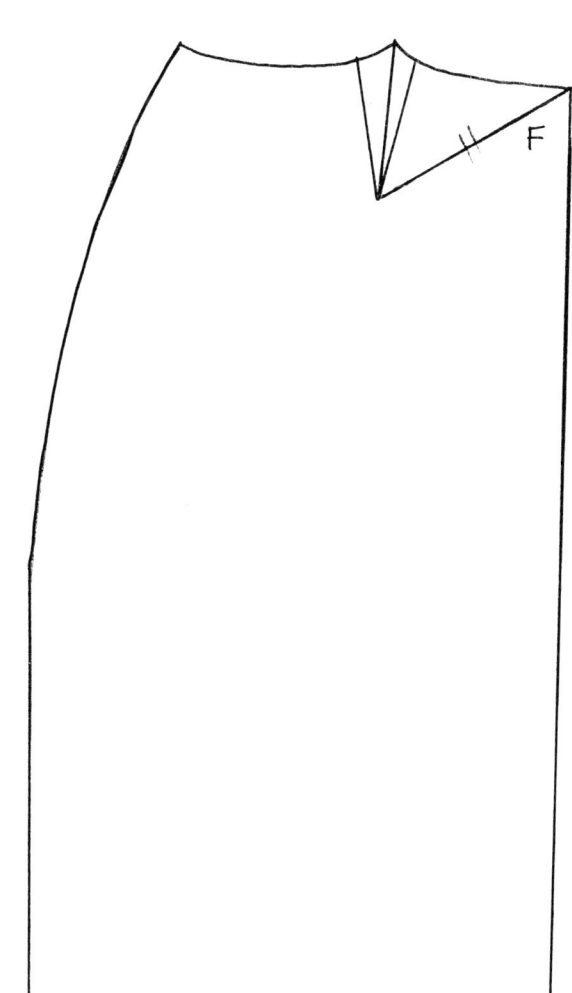

Fig. 8-7. Step 2: Draw in new design lines.

Fig. 8-8. Step 3: Cross-notch.

THE COMPLETE GUIDE TO PATTERN-MAKING 134

STEP 4: Fold out dart.

Cut on one side of the dart to the point. Lap one side of the dart over the other, and tape it down. The folded-out pattern will now be curved and will not lie flat on the working surface (see Fig. 8-9).

STEP 5: Cut on new design lines.

Cut on the new design lines. The pattern will open to lie flat and create the new dart (see Fig. 8-10). (In cases where you have a seam and no new dart, the pattern as it separates is the correct size.)

STEP 6: Add paper.

Add tissue paper to the open space created when you cut on the new design line. This step is omitted for gored skirts, as the darts become seams. Glue or tape the pattern to the tissue (see Fig. 8-11).

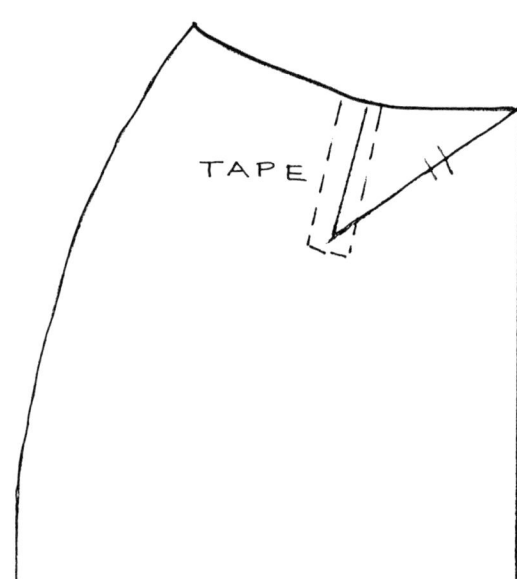

Fig. 8-9. Step 4: Fold out dart.

135 SKIRTS

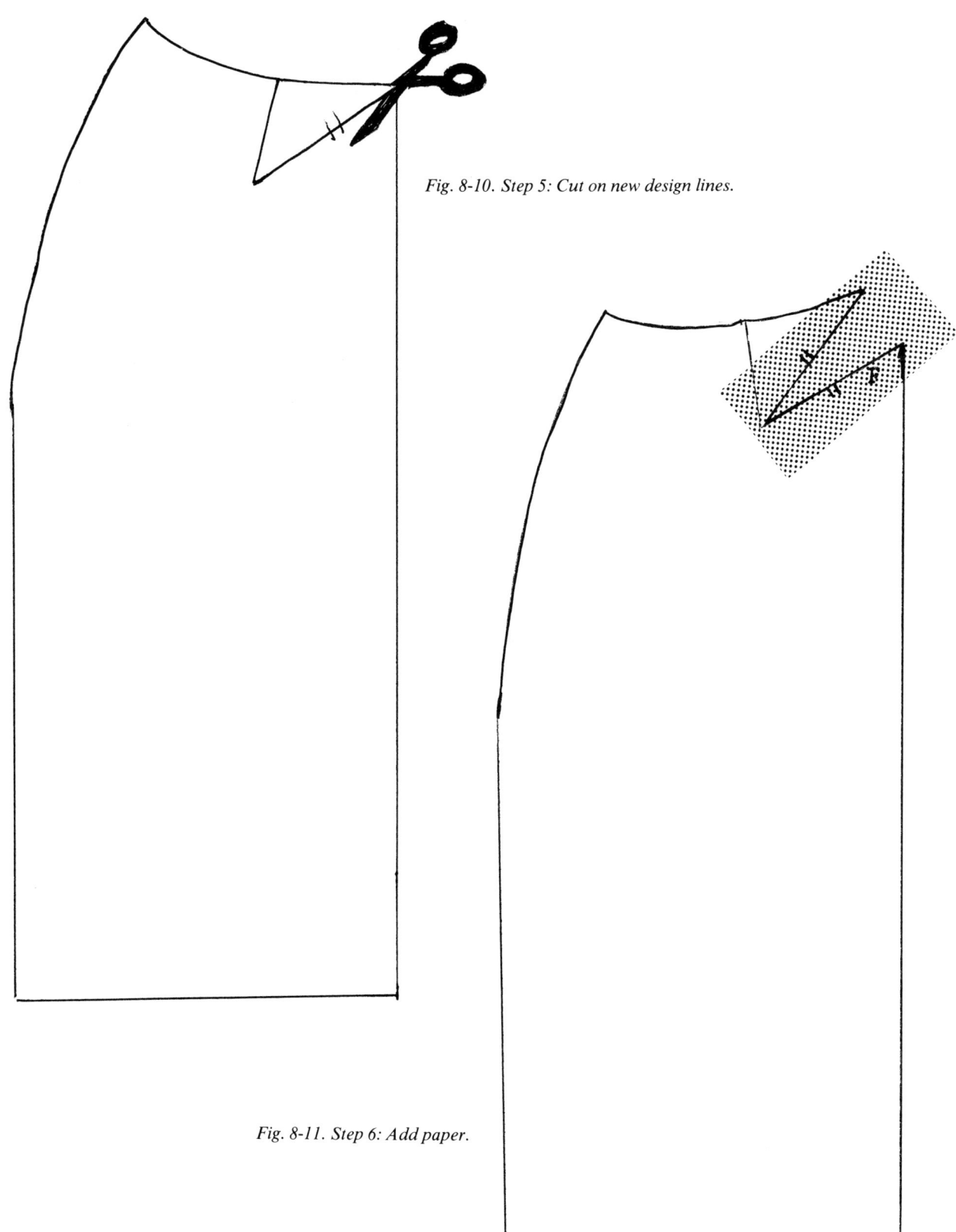

Fig. 8-10. Step 5: Cut on new design lines.

Fig. 8-11. Step 6: Add paper.

THE COMPLETE GUIDE TO PATTERN-MAKING 136

STEP 7: Fold out new dart(s), pleat(s), tuck(s), etc., to cut ends.

Draw in the center line for new darts, tucks, or pleats. Bring the cross-notches together, and fold out the dart on the new design lines. Fold the dart toward the side seam in this example. We then encounter the same problem we saw with the first example of the bodice front. If the dart is folded toward the center front for design purposes, it will create a flap that can only be secured if the skirt has a center front seam. By folding toward the side seam, you can stitch the dart end into the waistline seam.

After folding the new dart toward the side seam, cut the end as you did for darts on the bodice (see Fig. 8-12).

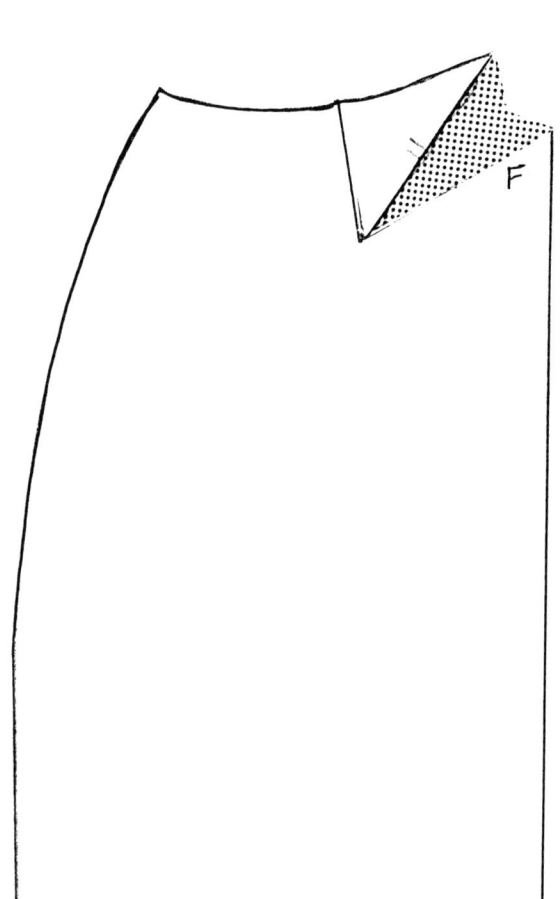

Fig. 8-12. Step 7: Fold out new dart to cut ends.

137 SKIRTS

Skirt with Three Darts

As with the bodice darts, the skirt darts can be divided into two or three darts for design variation. In this case three new darts are made from the original one dart (see Fig. 8-13).

STEP 1: Trace sloper (skirt front only).

STEP 2: Draw in new design lines; draw lines parallel to original dart and along original dart line (see Fig. 8-14).

STEP 3: Cross-notch (see Fig. 8-14).

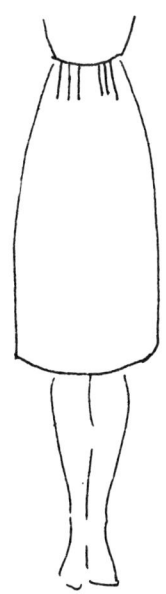

Fig. 8-13. Three darts.

Fig. 8-14. Three darts, Steps 1, 2, 3.

THE COMPLETE GUIDE TO PATTERN-MAKING 138

STEP 4: Fold out original dart.

STEP 5: Cut on new design lines; you must cut over to the point or tip of the original dart to release the fullness to the new darts (see Fig. 8-15).

STEP 6: Add paper.

STEP 7: Fold out new darts; cut ends (see Fig. 8-15).

Fig. 8-15. Three darts, Steps 4, 5, 6, 7.

Four-Gore or A-Line Skirt

To develop the four-gore or A-line pattern, the dart is transferred to the lower skirt edge. A four-gore skirt has a seam down the center front to create the four parts, or gores. The straight grain is parallel to the side seam. In the A-line, there is no seam down the center front, and the straight grain is parallel to the center front (see Fig. 8-16).

STEP 1: Trace sloper (skirt front only).

STEP 2: Draw in new design lines; draw line from tip to point of dart to lower edge of skirt. This line will be parallel to the center front line (see Fig. 8-17).

STEP 3: There is no need to cross-notch, because there will be no new dart or tuck to stitch in (see Fig. 8-17).

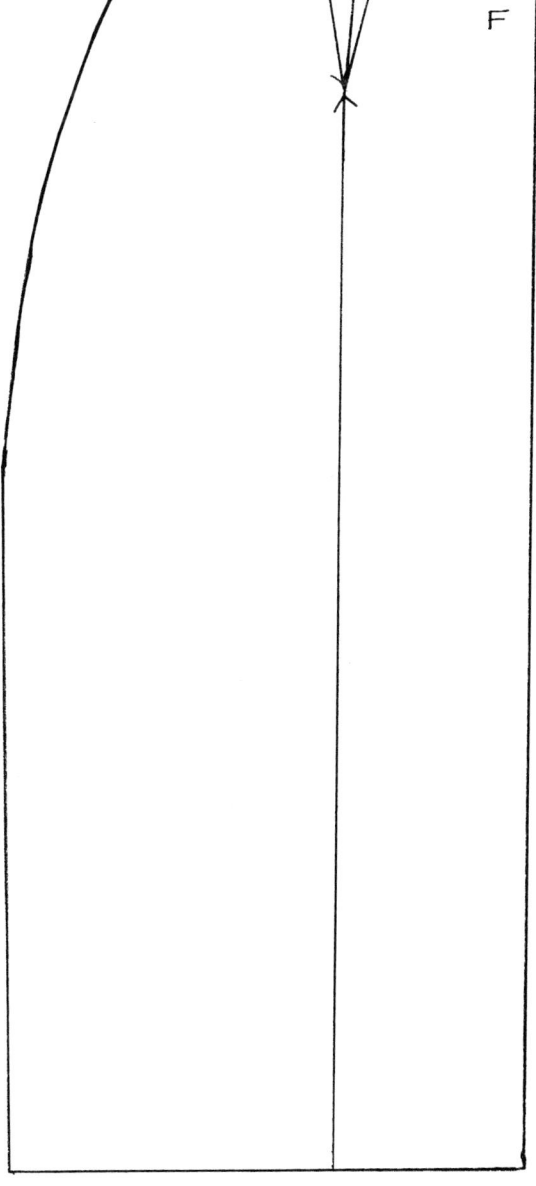

Fig. 8-16. Four-gore or A-line skirt.

Fig. 8-17. Four-gore or A-line skirt, Steps 1, 2, 3.

STEP 4: Fold out original dart.

STEP 5: Cut on new design lines (see Fig. 8-18).

STEP 6: Add paper.

STEP 7: Draw in a smooth curve on lower skirt edge with help of curve stick. Place grain marking for four-gore or A-line skirt (see Fig. 8-18).

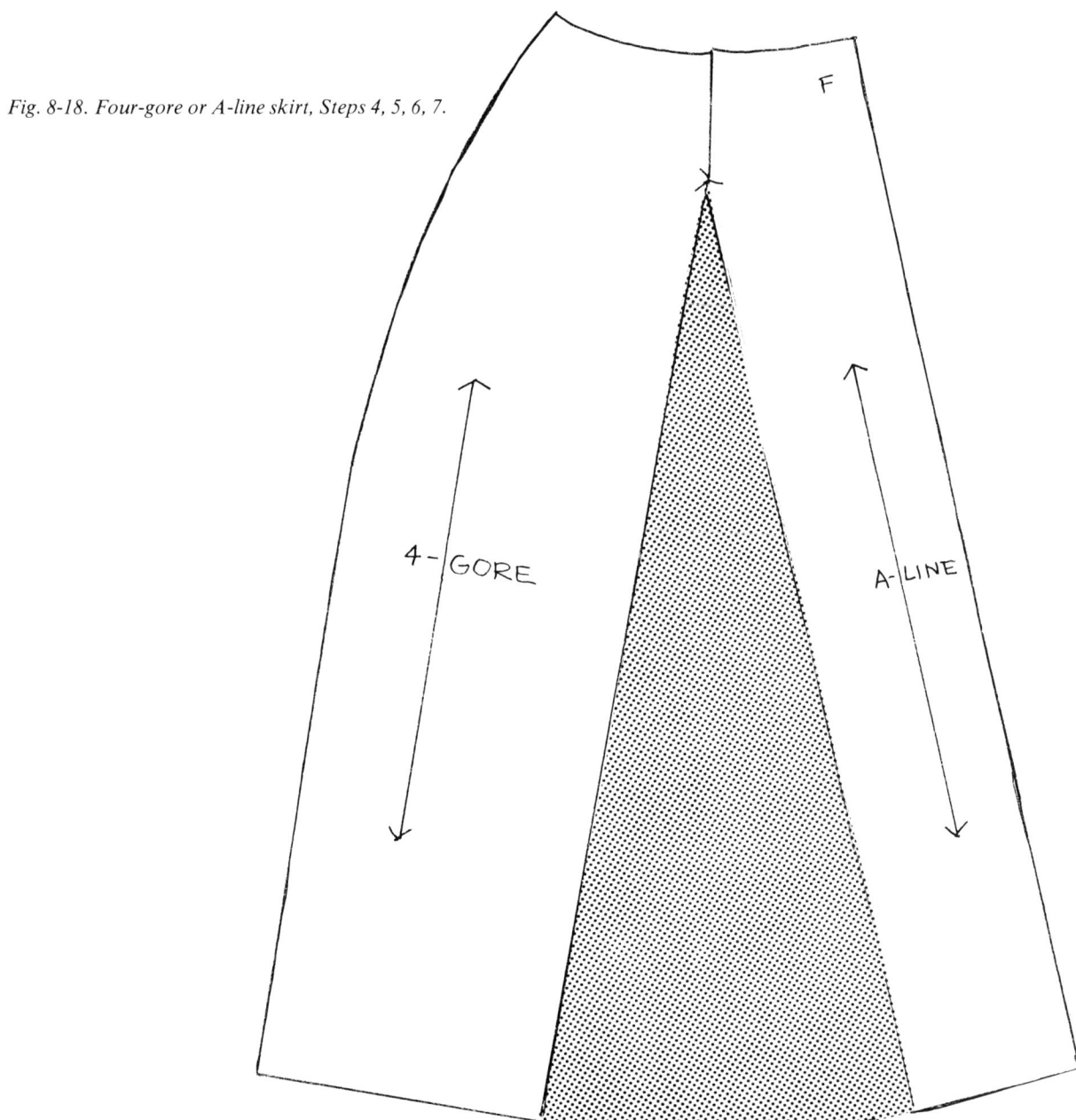

Fig. 8-18. Four-gore or A-line skirt, Steps 4, 5, 6, 7.

141 SKIRTS

Peg-Top Skirt

A peg-top, or "hobble," skirt has fullness added at the top and is tight at the lower edge. This skirt was fashionable during various periods in costume history and is used today in various ways for interest and variation (see Fig. 8-19).

STEP 1: Trace sloper (skirt front only).

STEP 2: Draw in new design lines; draw one line from tip of dart to lower edge; then draw three or four more lines from waist edge to lower edge (see Fig. 8-20).

STEP 3: Fold out original dart.

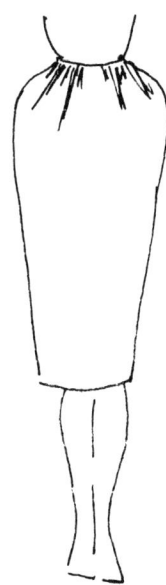

Fig. 8-19. Peg-top skirt.

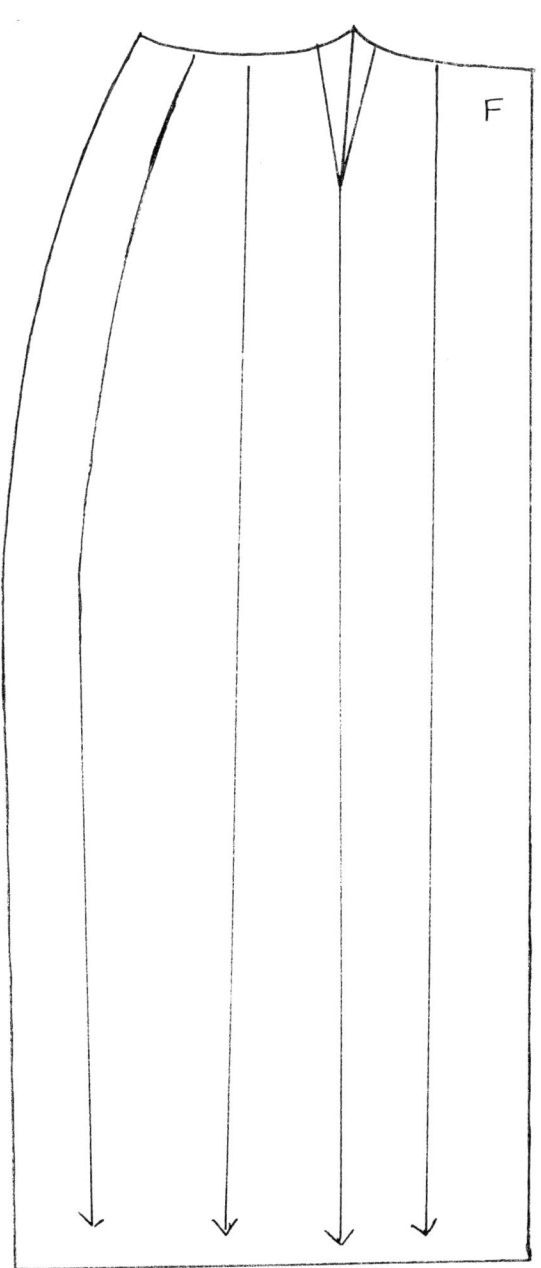

Fig. 8-20. Peg-top skirt, Steps 1, 2.

STEP 4: Cut on new design lines, and spread desired distance (see Fig. 8-21).

STEP 5: Add paper.

STEP 6: Draw in a smooth curve at waist edge. Write the word "gather" across waist edge (see Fig. 8-21).

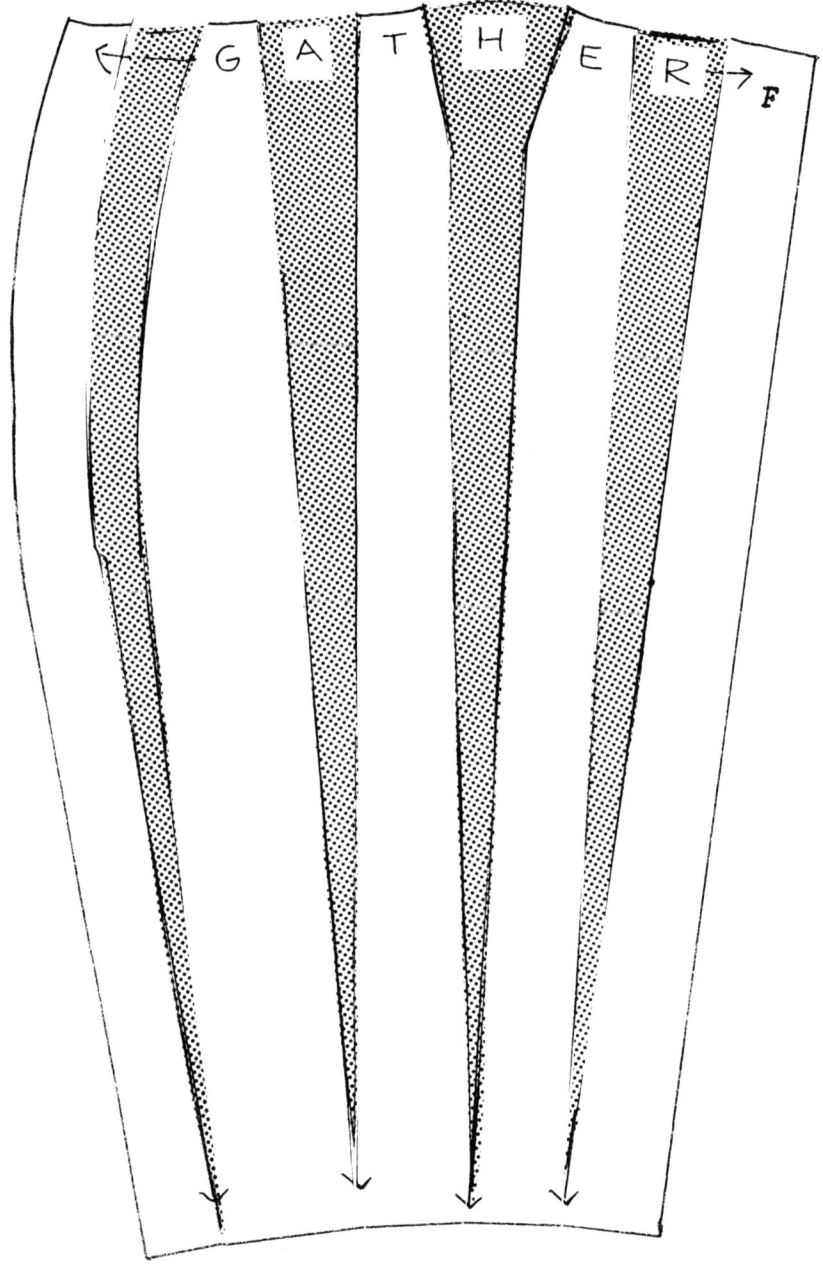

Fig. 8-21. Peg-top skirt, Steps 3, 4, 5, 6.

Peg-Top Skirt—Alternate Method

A second method of achieving fullness at the waist is shown in this example. The added fullness can be either gathered or tucked into the waistband or bodice waist. This method adds less fullness through the lower portion of the skirt and concentrates on the over-the-hip area (see Fig. 8-22).

STEP 1: Trace sloper (skirt front only).

STEP 2: Draw in new design lines; draw one line from tip of dart to lower edge of skirt; then draw three lines from waist to hip (see Fig. 8-23).

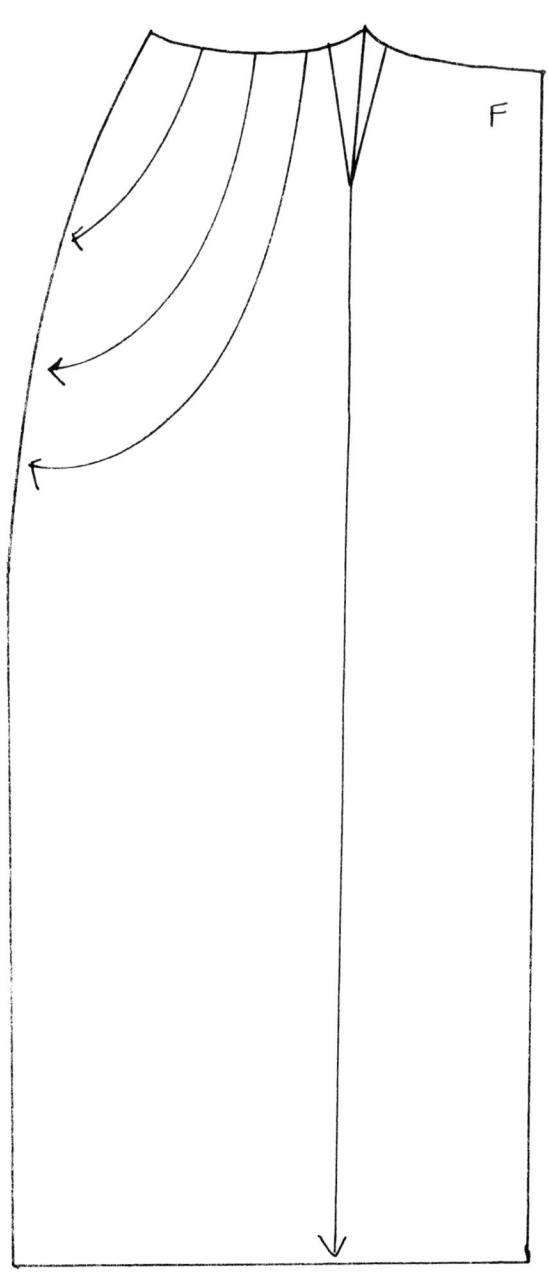

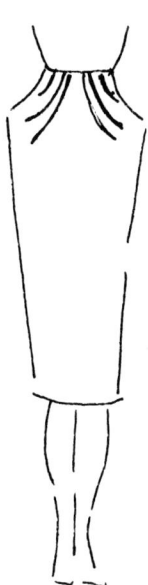

Fig. 8-22. Peg-top skirt, alternate method.

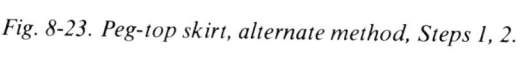

Fig. 8-23. Peg-top skirt, alternate method, Steps 1, 2.

STEP 3: Fold out original dart.

STEP 4: Cut on new design lines; do not cut through lower skirt edge or through the side seam. Spread the amount desired (see Fig. 8-24).

STEP 5: Add paper.

STEP 6: Draw in smooth line on upper skirt edge; write word "gather" along waist edge, or mark for tucks (see Fig. 8-24).

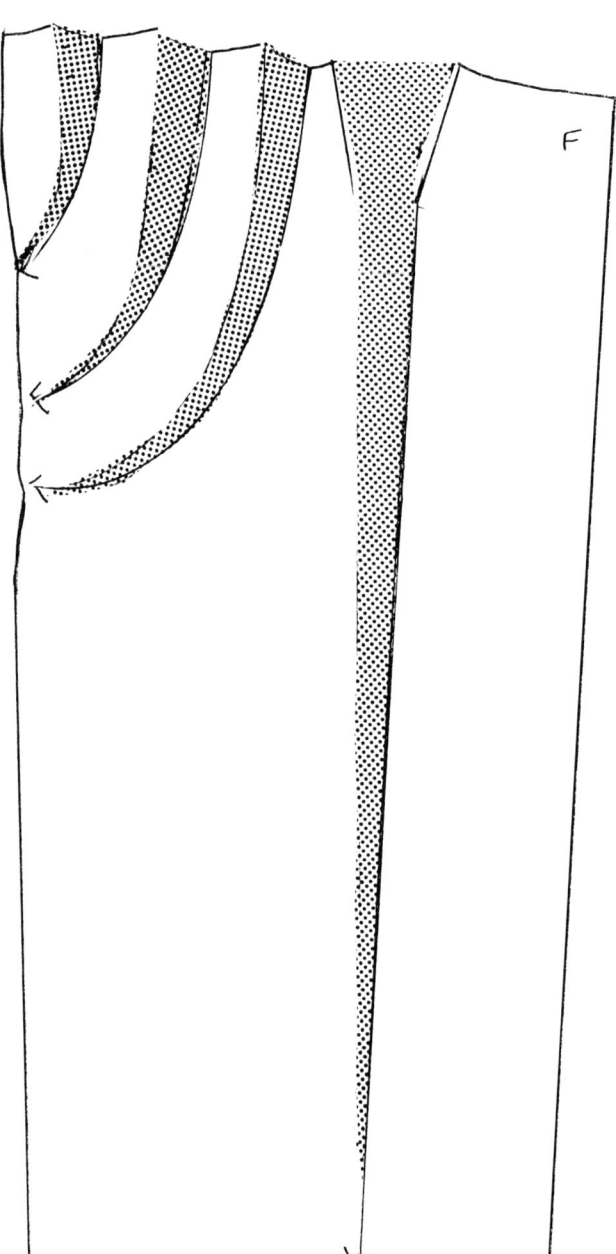

Fig. 8-24. Peg-top skirt, alternate method, Steps 3, 4, 5, 6.

145 SKIRTS

Six-Gore Skirt

The six-gore skirt has side seams and seams through the center of the front and back panels to make the six parts. The added vertical lines can help to create a slim illusion for the full figure (see Fig. 8-25).

STEP 1: Trace sloper (skirt front only).

STEP 2: Draw in new design lines; draw line from tip of dart to lower edge, parallel to center front (see Fig. 8-26).

STEP 3: Cross-notch.

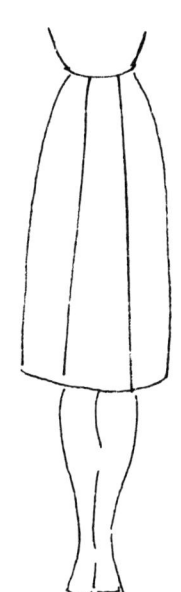

Fig. 8-25. Six-gore skirt.

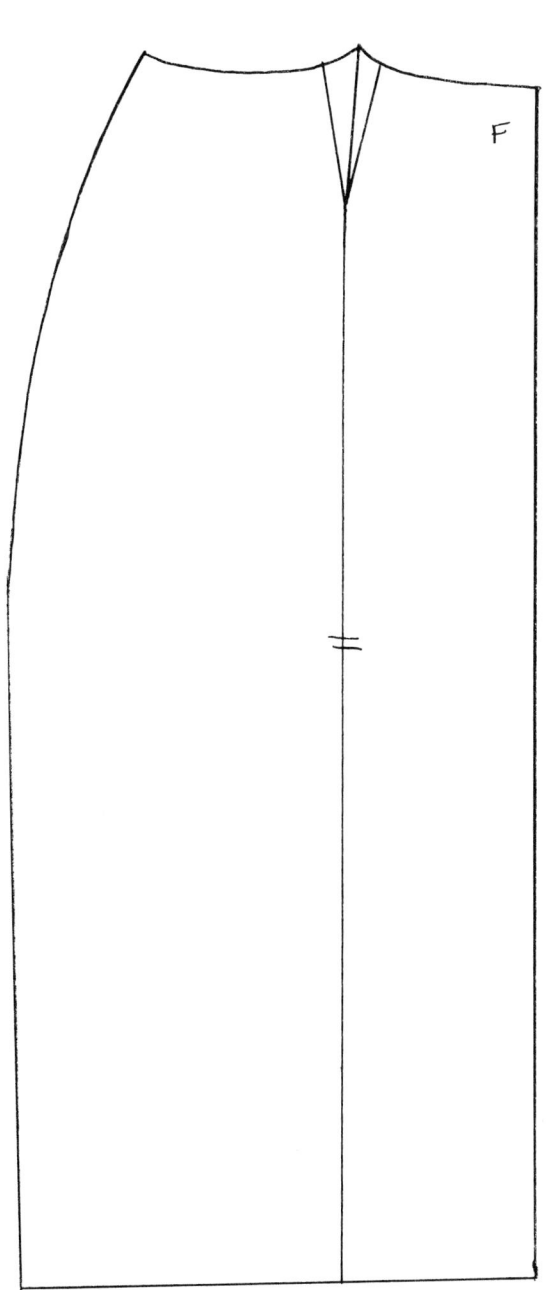

Fig. 8-26. Six-gore skirt, Steps 1, 2, 3.

STEP 4: Fold out original dart (see Fig. 8-27).

STEP 5: Cut on new design line (see Fig. 8-27).

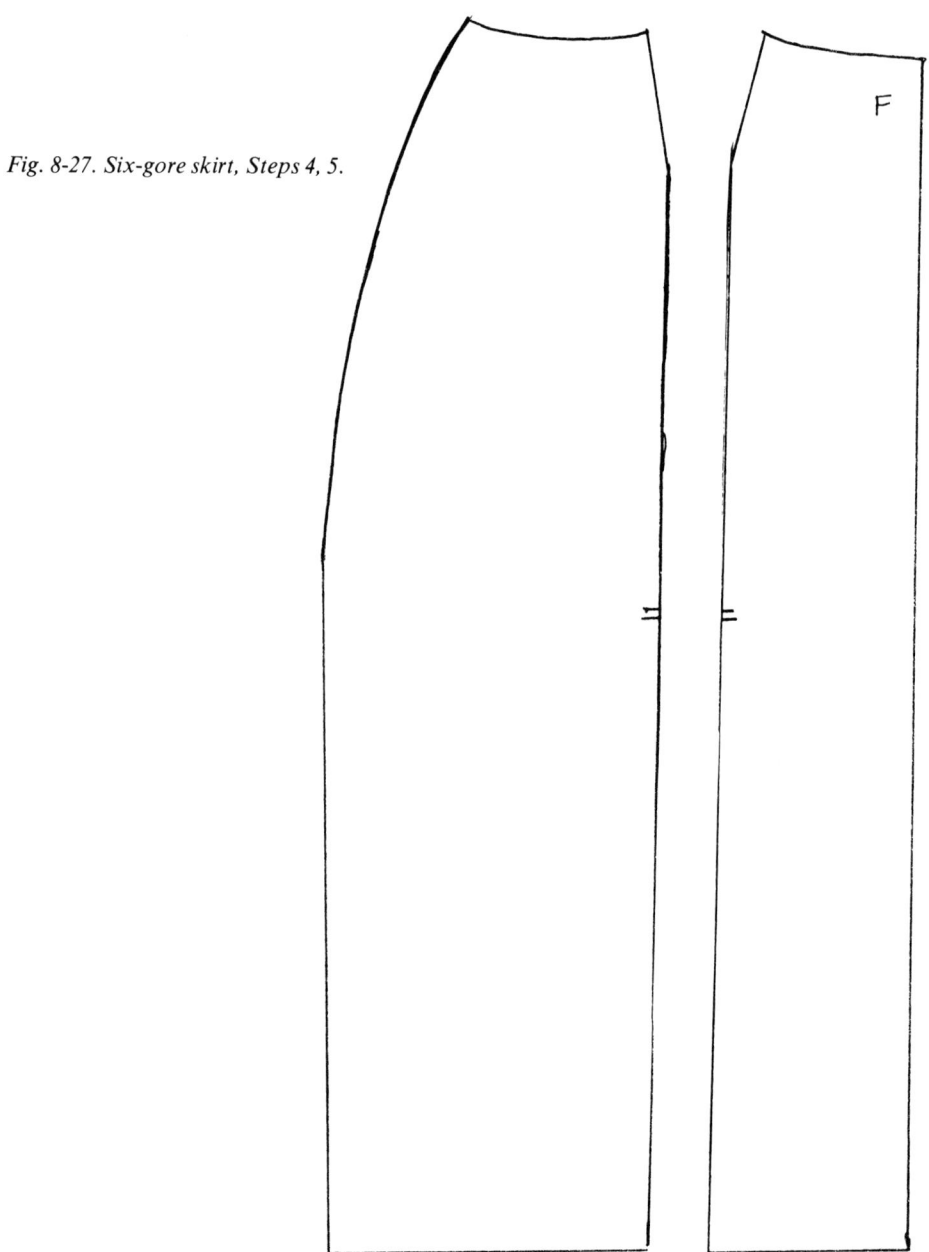

Fig. 8-27. Six-gore skirt, Steps 4, 5.

147 SKIRTS

Six-Gore Skirt with Flare

The six-gore skirt with flare can be attractive for the fuller figure and also is quite comfortable to wear. Be sure the same amount of flare is added to each panel. If differing amounts are added, the grain in the seam lines will be different, too, and this will produce construction problems (see Fig. 8-28).

STEP 1: Trace six-gore sloper just made (see Fig. 8-29).

Fig. 8-28. Six-gore skirt with flare.

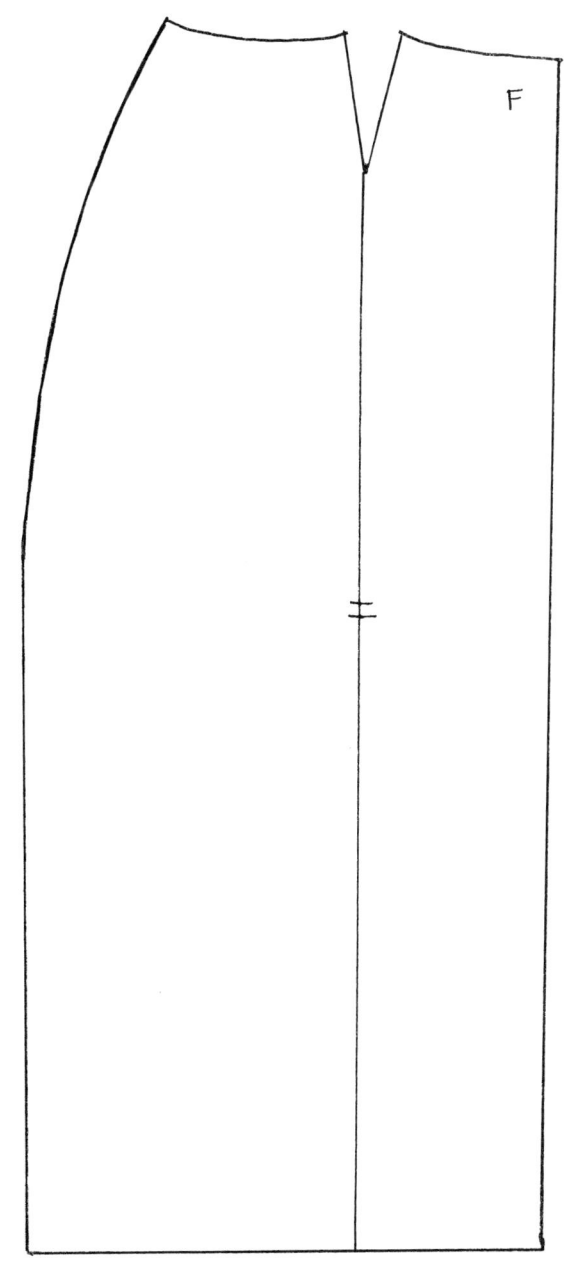

Fig. 8-29. Six-gore skirt with flare, Step 1.

THE COMPLETE GUIDE TO PATTERN-MAKING 148

STEP 2: Draw in new design lines; draw lines from lower skirt edge to point where you want flare to stop. In this example, lines are drawn to hip.

Angle line to seam edge (see Fig. 8-30).

STEP 3: Cut on new design lines; cut to edge but not through it (see Fig. 8-31).

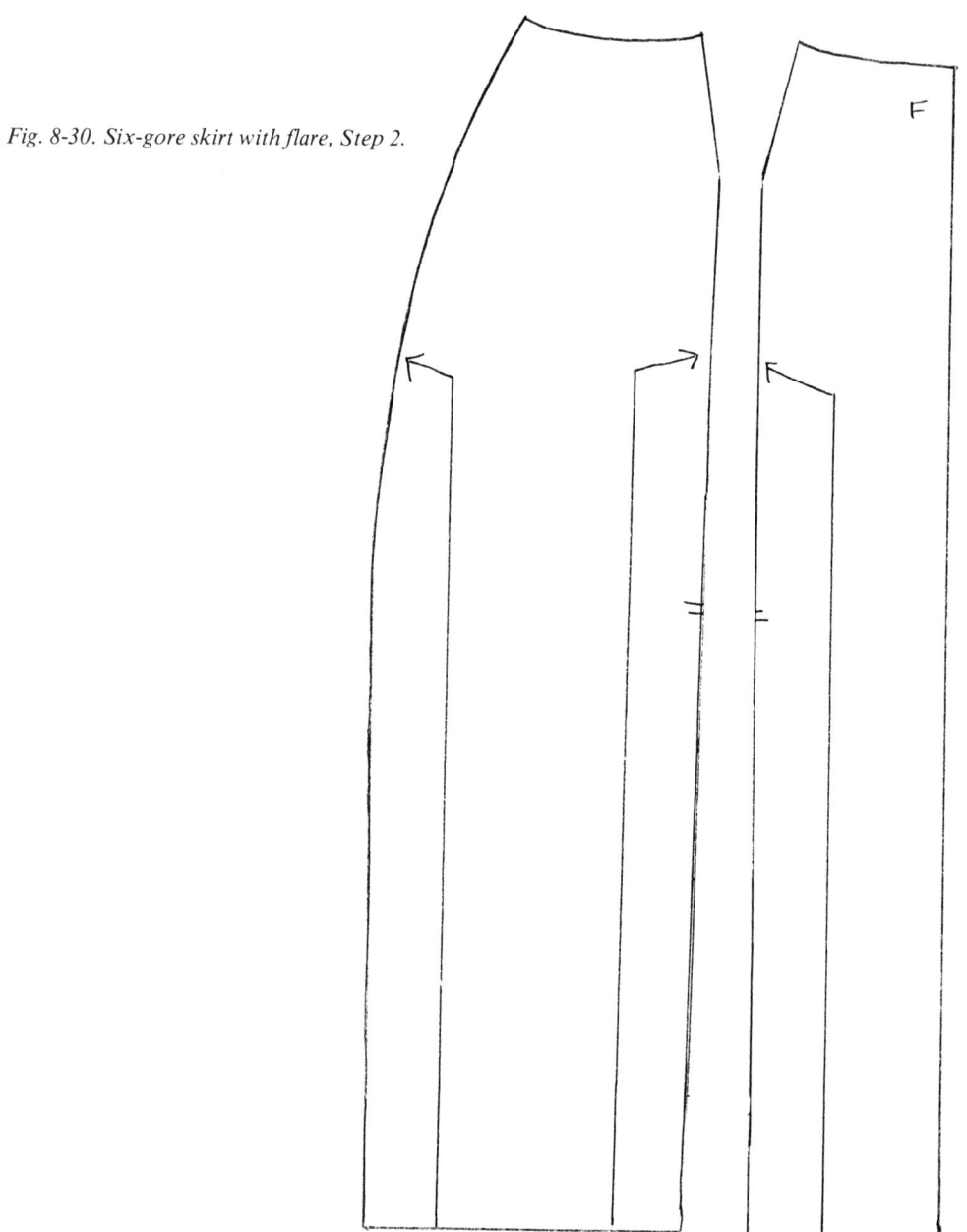

Fig. 8-30. Six-gore skirt with flare, Step 2.

STEP 4: Spread desired amount; be certain you spread each piece the same distance (see Fig. 8-31).

STEP 5: Add paper.

STEP 6: Smooth out lower edge with aid of curve stick (see Fig. 8-31).

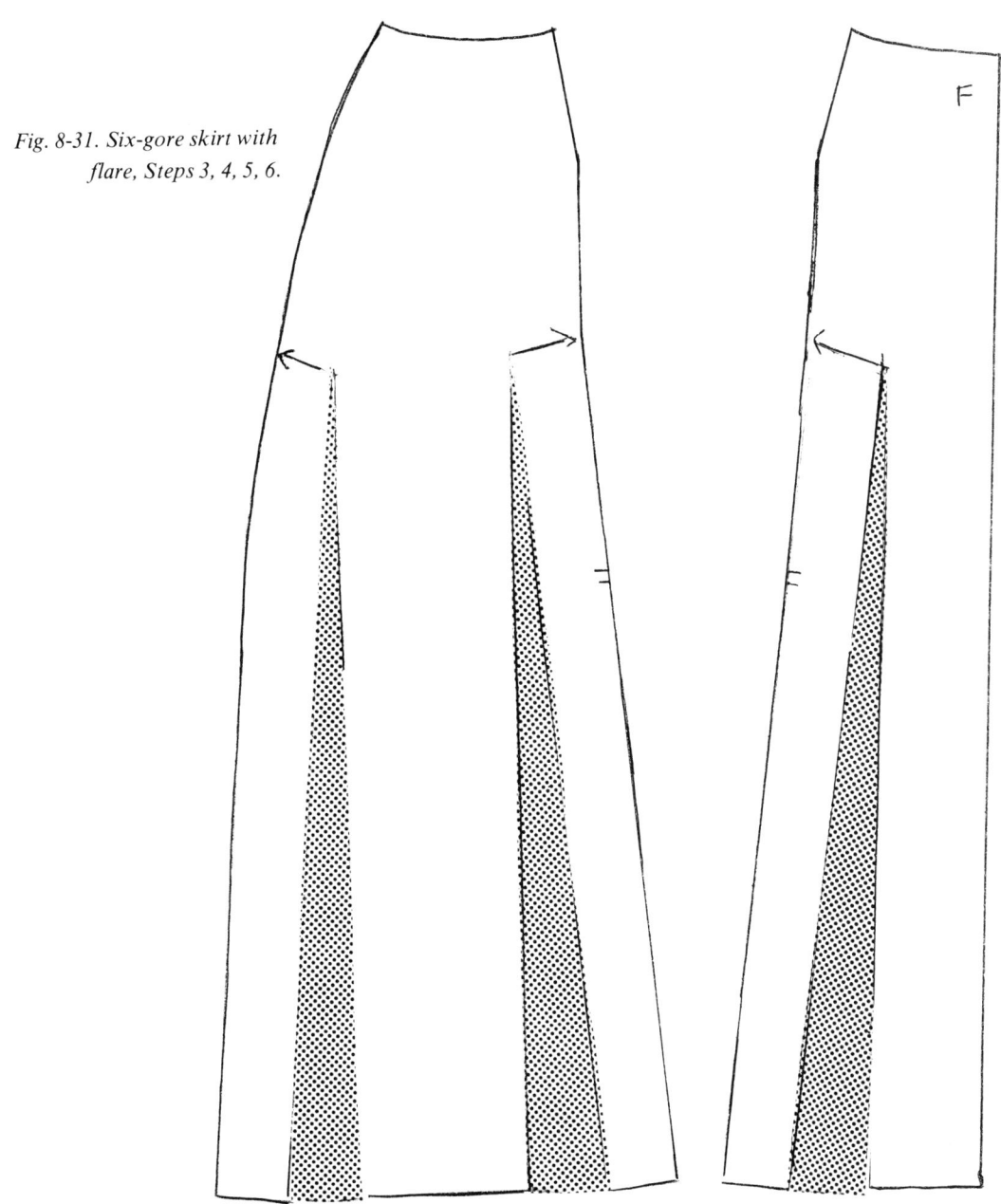

Fig. 8-31. Six-gore skirt with flare, Steps 3, 4, 5, 6.

THE COMPLETE GUIDE TO PATTERN-MAKING

Six-Gore Skirt with Flare and Gathers

The six-gore skirt with flare and gathers has more fullness at the lower edge than at the waist edge. This can be an advantage in reducing bulk at the waist edge when a full skirt is desired (see Fig. 8-32).

STEP 1: Trace six-gore skirt sloper with flare just completed.

STEP 2: Draw in new design lines; draw lines from waist edge to lower skirt edge; then draw one line through center of center front panel and two lines through side front panel (see Fig. 8-33).

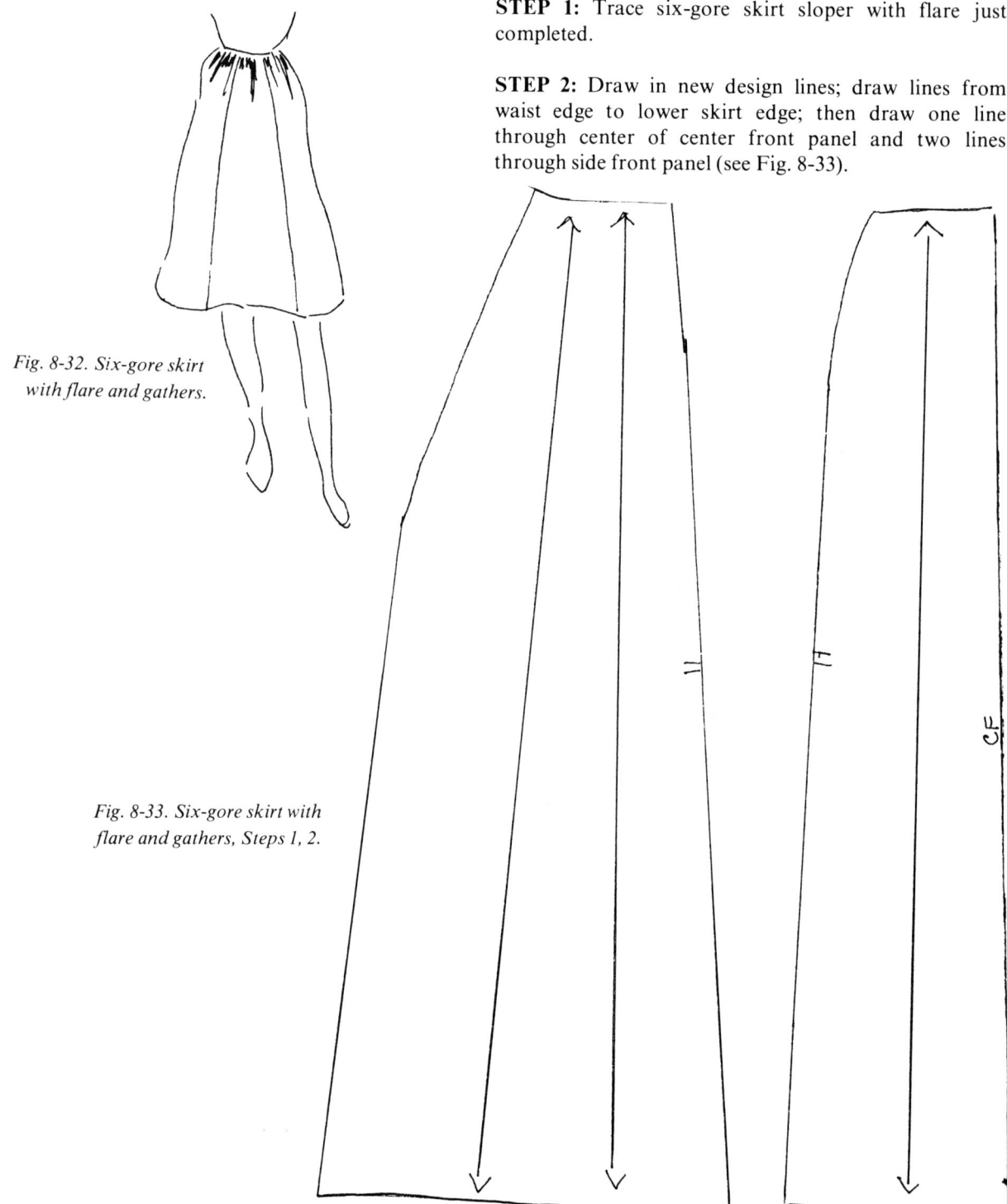

Fig. 8-32. Six-gore skirt with flare and gathers.

Fig. 8-33. Six-gore skirt with flare and gathers, Steps 1, 2.

STEP 3: Cut on new design lines; cut all the way through top and lower edges (see Fig. 8-34).

STEP 4: Spread and add paper; spread amount desired; twice the original measurement is a good guide (see Fig. 8-34).

STEP 5: Smooth waist and lower edge curves with aid of curve stick (see Fig. 8-34).

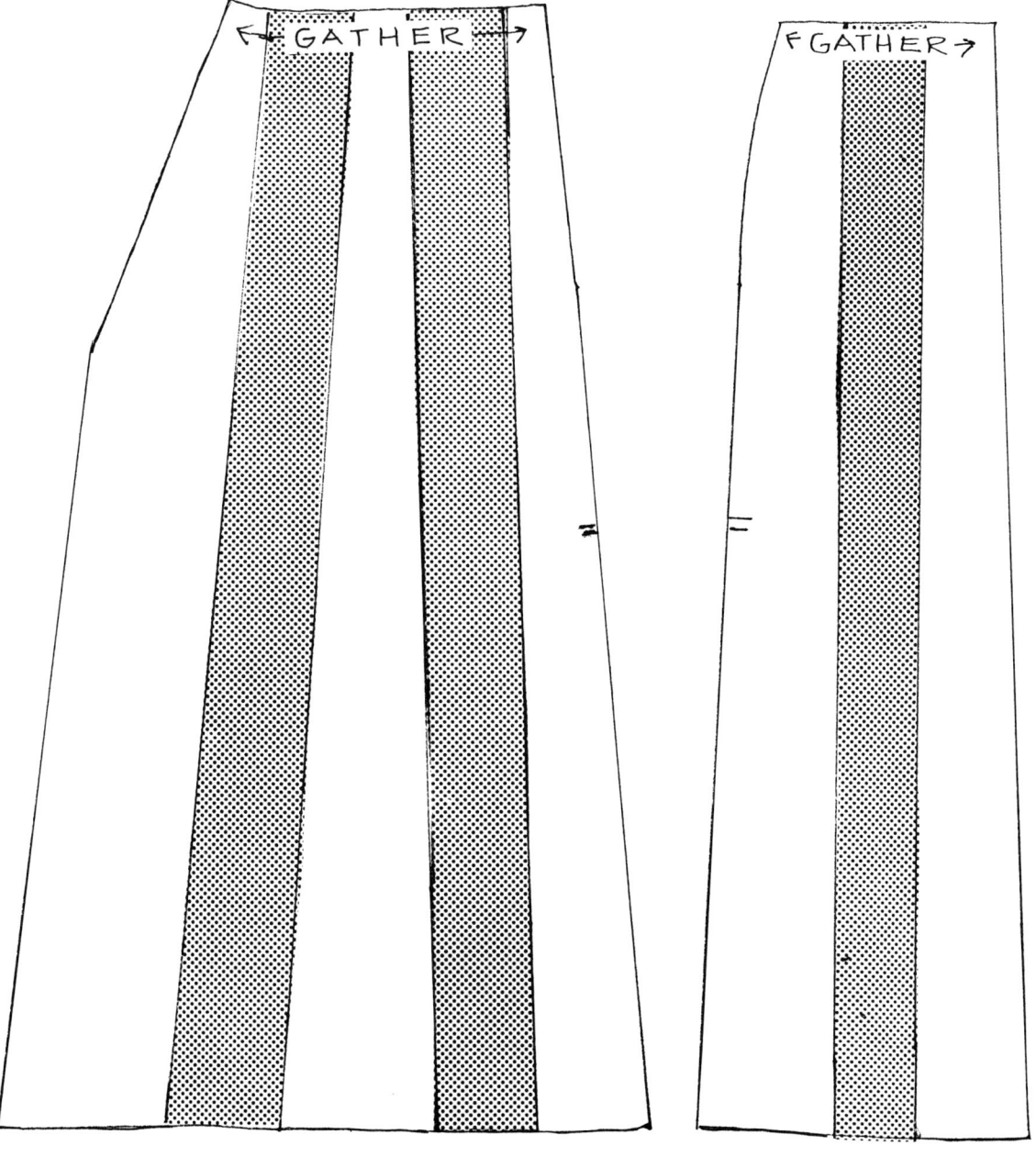

Fig. 8-34. Six-gore skirt with flare and gathers, Steps 3, 4, 5.

Twelve-Gore Trumpet Skirt

Any number of gores can be made in the skirt. (We once saw a skirt made of about forty men's ties; each gore was quite small, of course.) The twelve-gore trumpet skirt is flared at the lower edge and is named because of its resemblance to a trumpet (see Fig. 8-35).

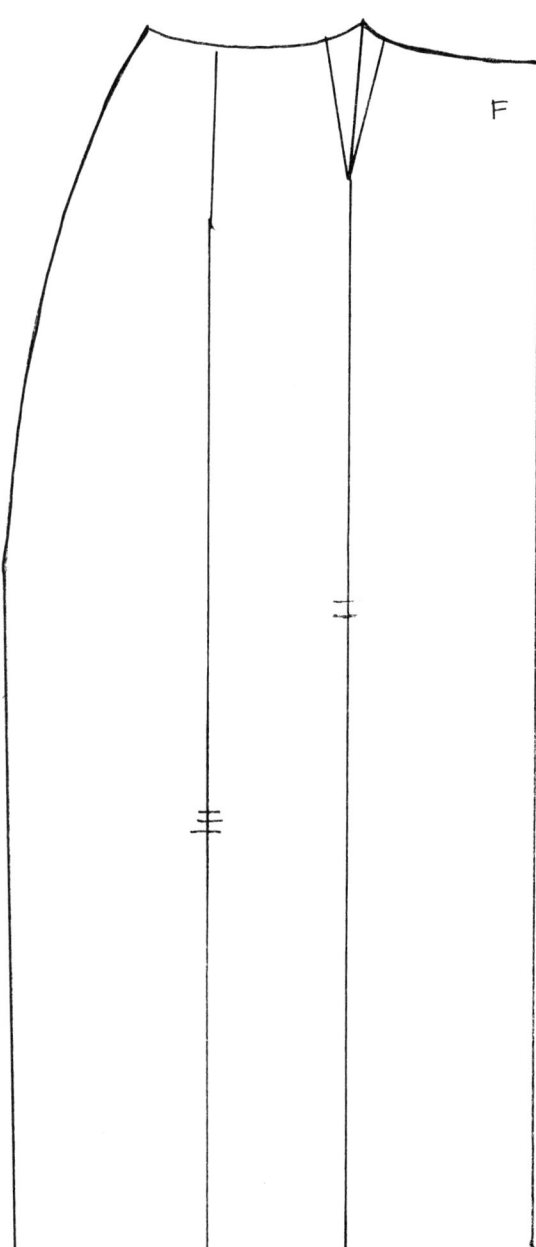

STEP 1: Trace sloper (skirt front only).

STEP 2: Draw in new design lines; draw one line from tip of dart to lower edge and parallel to center front; then draw another line parallel to the first and halfway between the first and the side seam (see Fig. 8-36).

STEP 3: Cross-notch (see Fig. 8-36).

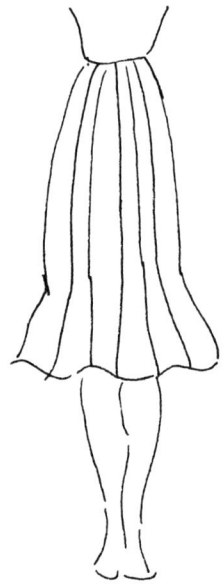

Fig. 8-35. Twelve-gore trumpet skirt.

Fig. 8-36. Twelve-gore trumpet skirt, Steps 1, 2, 3.

153 SKIRTS

STEP 4: Cut on new design lines (see Fig. 8-37).

STEP 5: Draw lines for flare from lower edge up 2″ to 4″ on full-size; draw lines at each edge; the center front is seamed (see Fig. 8-37).

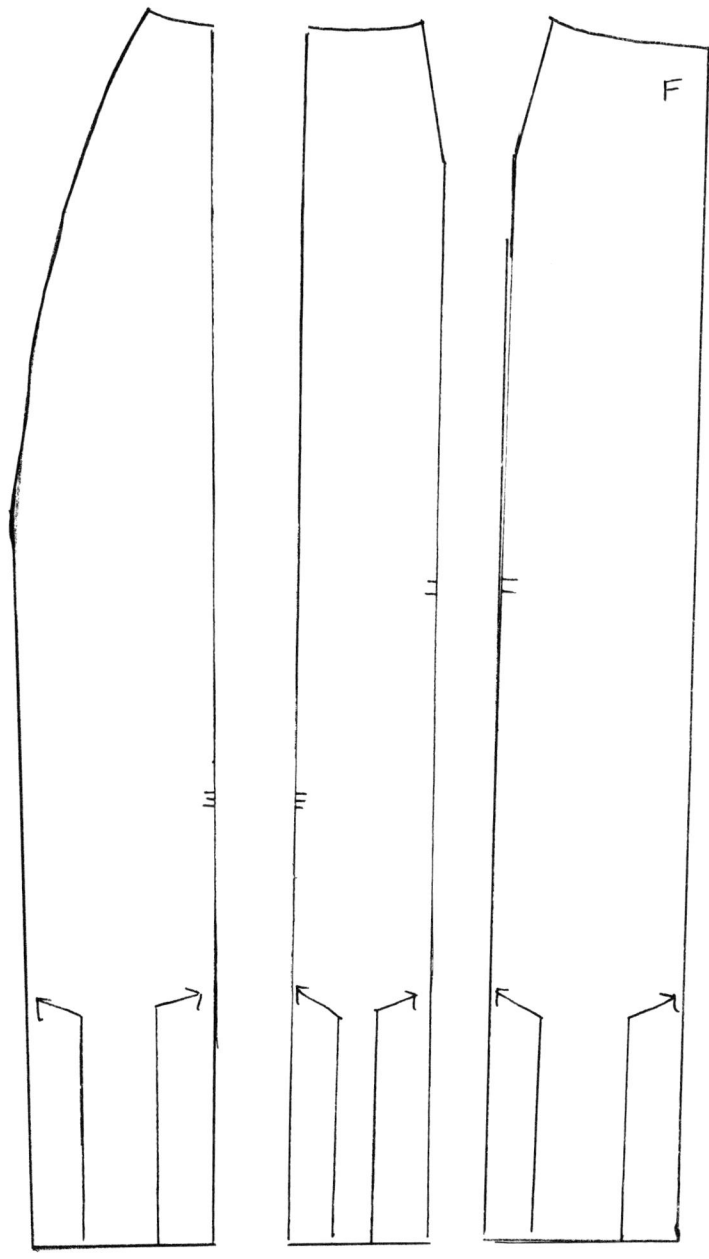

Fig. 8-37. Twelve-gore trumpet skirt, Steps 4, 5.

STEP 6: Cut on flare lines; cut to edge but not through it (see Fig. 8-38).

STEP 7: Spread and add paper; spread each section the same amount (see Fig. 8-41).

STEP 8: Smooth lower edge of skirt with the help of a curve stick (see Fig. 8-38).

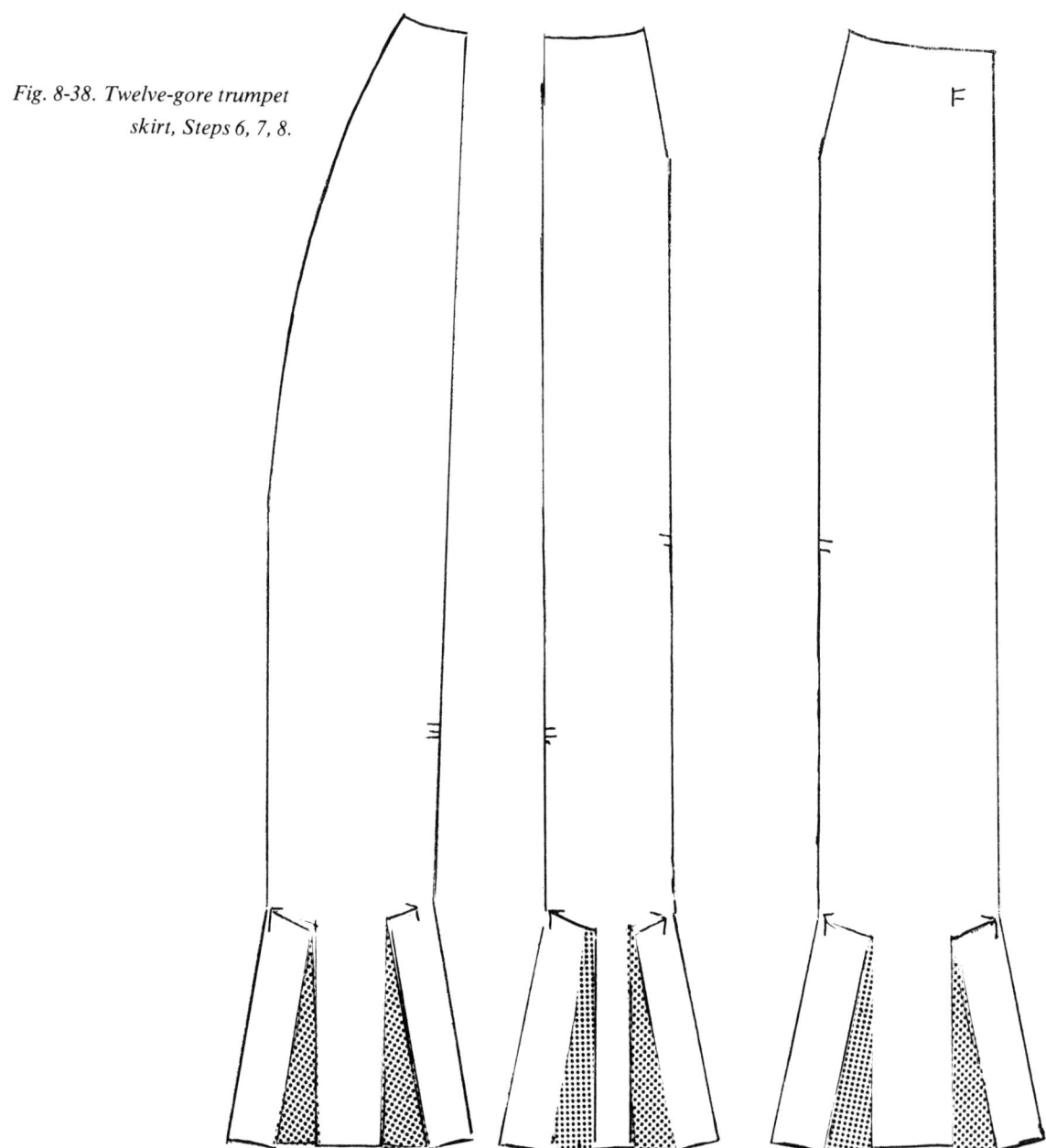

Fig. 8-38. Twelve-gore trumpet skirt, Steps 6, 7, 8.

155 SKIRTS

Full-Circle Skirt

The circular skirt is very full at the bottom but has no bulkiness at the waist. For this reason it can be a most attractive skirt when a very full lower edge is needed (see Fig. 8-39).

STEP 1: Trace sloper (skirt front only).

STEP 2: Remove side curve.

In order to make the circle skirt the sides of the pattern must be straight; the basic sloper has a side curve to allow for the hip curve. When the full circle skirt is completed there will be more than enough fullness to cover the hip curve, so it can be removed at this point to give a straight side seam.

Procedure shown with dotted line (see Fig. 8-40).

STEP 3: Draw in new design lines; draw lines from lower edge of skirt to waist; one line must meet tip of dart (see Fig. 8-4).

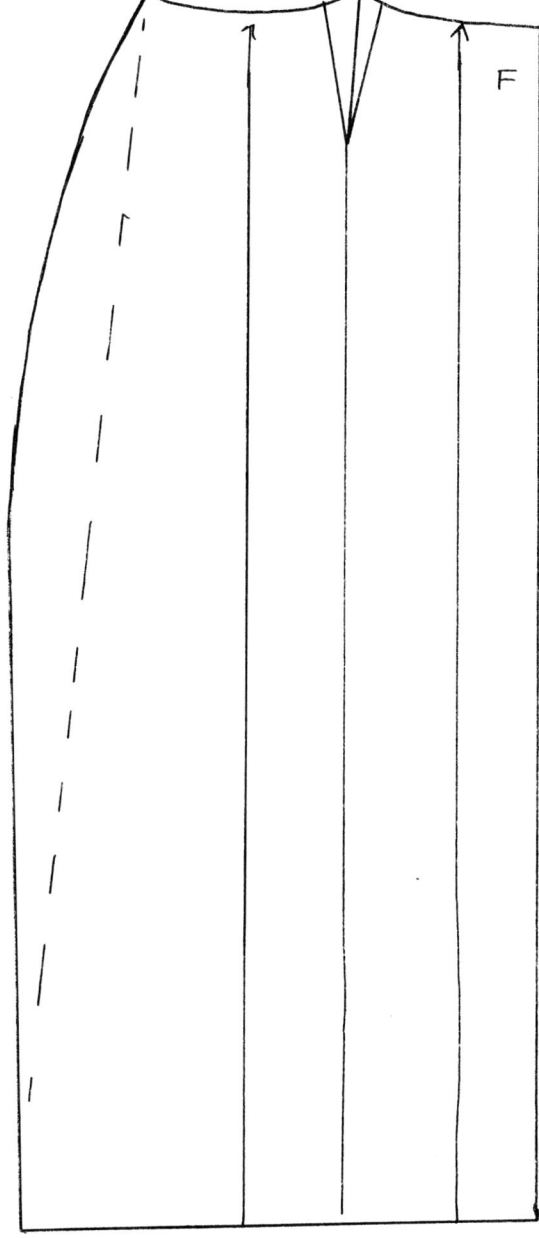

Fig. 8-39. Full circle skirt.

Fig. 8-40. Full circle skirt, Steps 1, 2, 3.

STEP 4: Fold out original dart (see Fig. 8-41).

STEP 5: Cut on new design lines; cut to but not through waist (see Fig. 8-41).

STEP 6: Spread so that sides of skirt form a 90° angle; this will give a full circle. If you should desire a double circle skirt, spread so that sides form a 180° angle (see Fig. 8-41).

STEP 7: Add paper.

STEP 8: Smooth lower edge of skirt with aid of curve stick (see Fig. 8-41).

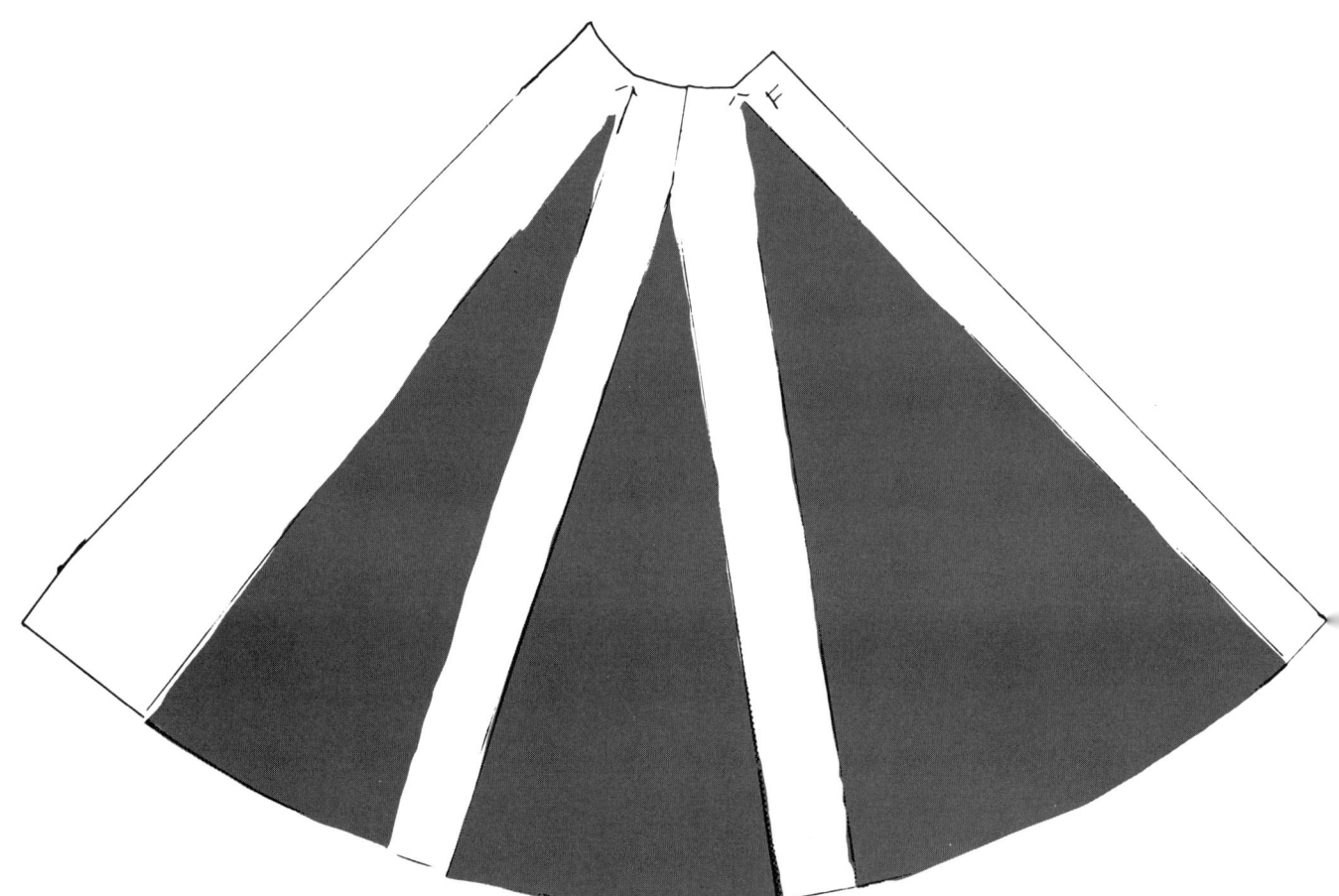

Fig. 8-41. Full circle skirt, Steps 4, 5, 6, 7, 8.

157 SKIRTS

Pleated Skirt

To be attractive a pleated skirt must hang smoothly from waist, over the stomach and hips to the hem. Pleating using only the waist measurement as a guide will never accomplish this end. The skirt as developed in the following illustration will make a pleated skirt that hangs perfectly, since it is developed from a sloper that hangs perfectly. It seems a bit complicated at first, but the result is well worth the time taken (see Fig. 8-42).

STEP 1: Trace sloper (skirt front and back).

STEP 2: The basic sloper usually has some flare from widest point of hip to hem; remove this if present by dropping a line from widest point of hip to hem, parallel to center front and center back (see Fig. 8-43).

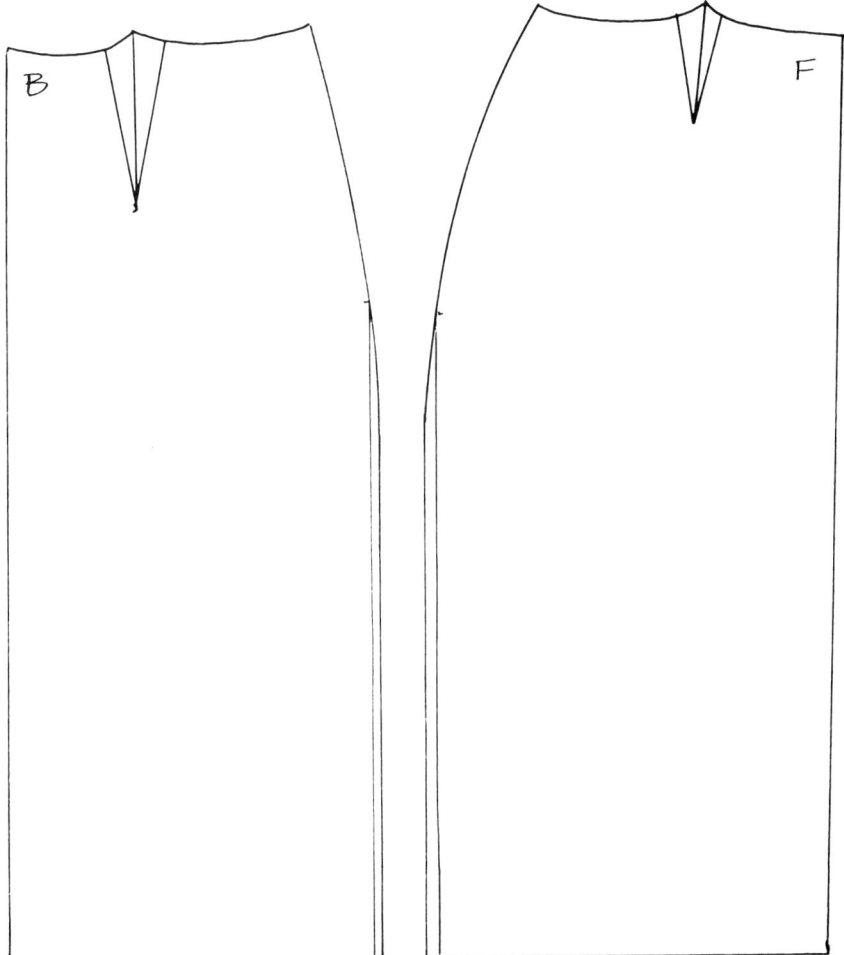

Fig. 8-42. Pleated skirt.

Fig. 8-43. Pleated skirt, Steps 1, 2.

STEP 3: Place side seams together; tape or glue in place (see Fig. 8-44).

STEP 4: Draw a horizontal line perpendicular to center front at widest point of hip; this will extend across back to center back line; then draw a second horizontal line at abdomen, halfway between hip line and waistline.

There are now three areas under consideration: hip, abdomen, and waist; each must be divided into equal sections, but the size of the sections will be different for each, because the waist is smaller than the abdomen, and the abdomen smaller than the hip.

The sections at the lower edge of skirt will equal the hip sections, since the pattern was made straight from hip to hem (see Fig. 8-44).

STEP 5: Decide on the number of pleats desired in the completed pattern; illustrated are six on one-half of the skirt or twelve on the completed skirt (see Fig. 8-44).

STEP 6: Divide the waist, abdomen, and hip into equal sections, omitting darts and side curve sections; in order to do this, it is sometimes helpful to cut a piece of paper the length of each of these lines and fold it into equal sections (see illustration 6); mark these six equal sections on the paper strip, and use this to mark off the six equal sections on each of the three lines, using the proper paper in turn (see Fig. 8-44).

Use the hip measurement to mark off six equal sections on lower edge of skirt (see Fig. 8-44).

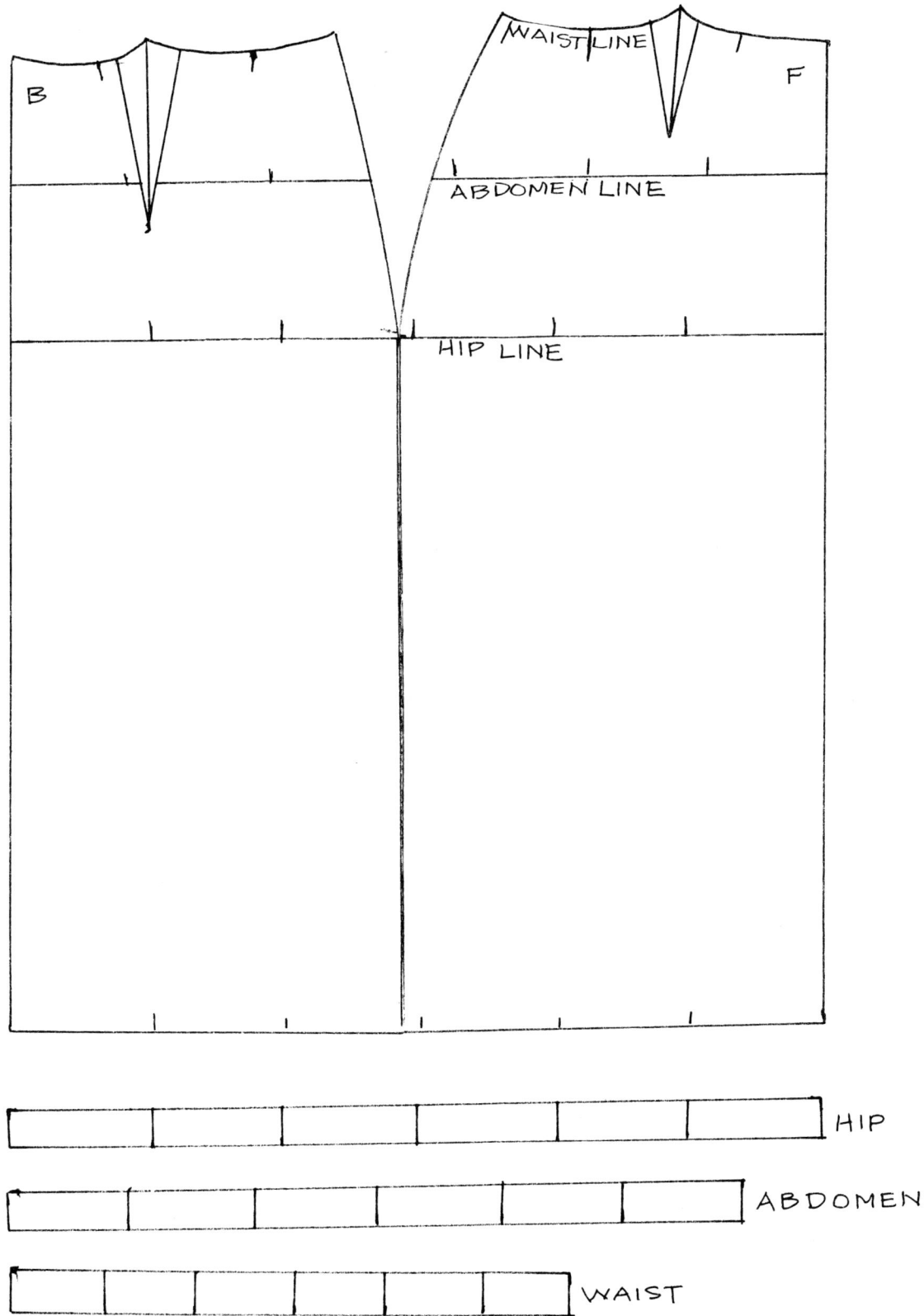

Fig. 8-44. Pleated skirt, Steps 3, 4, 5, 6.

THE COMPLETE GUIDE TO PATTERN-MAKING 160

STEP 7: Connect the sections with vertical lines as illustrated (see Fig. 8-45).

STEP 8: Cross-notch the vertical sections; number or letter each piece (see Fig. 8-45).

Fig. 8-45. Pleated skirt, Steps 7, 8.

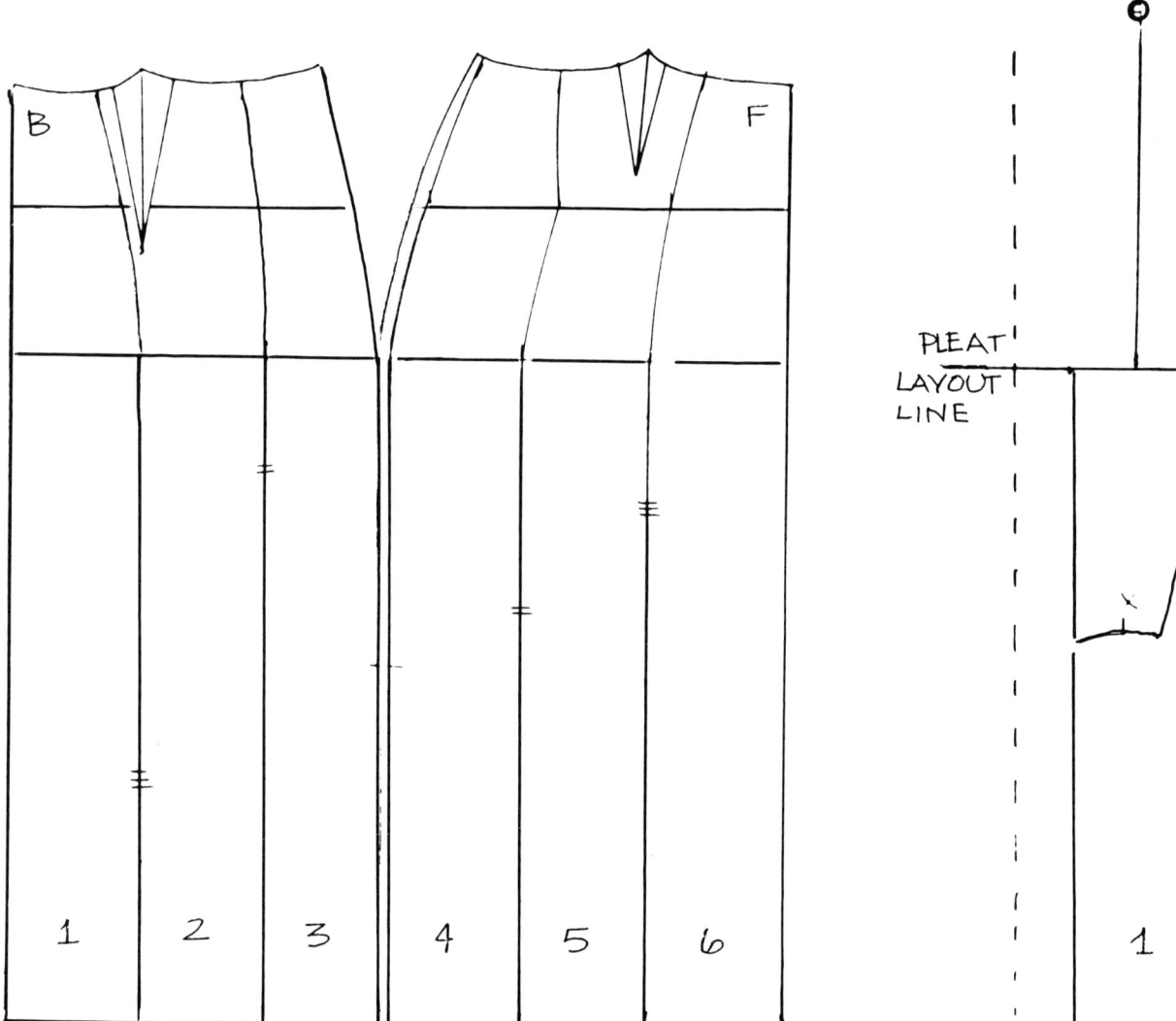

161 SKIRTS

STEP 9: Cut on vertical lines (see Fig. 8-46).

STEP 10: Lay out a piece of paper about 12″ x 18″ (for half-size pattern); on it draw a long horizontal line about 4″ from upper edge; label this "pleat layout line"; the hip line on the pattern will be matched to this line on the paper (see Fig. 8-46).

Fig. 8-46. Pleated skirt, Steps 9, 10, 11, 12, 13, 14, 15.

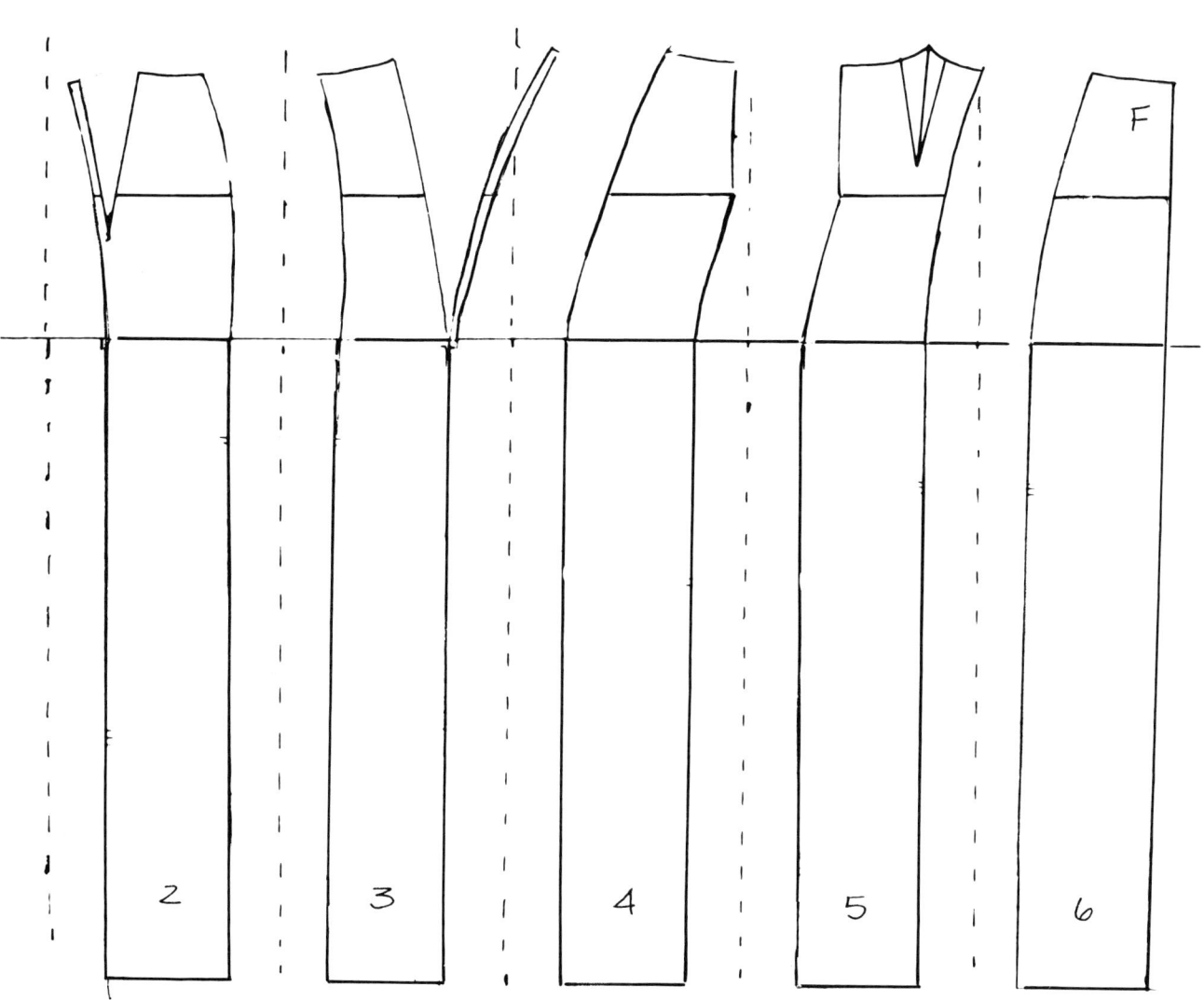

STEP 11: Place piece 1 on pleat layout line, matching hip line to pleat layout line. Glue or tape from hip to hem, leaving hip-to-waist area loose.

Decide type and width of pleat you desire; illustrated is a knife pleat ⅜″ wide; knife pleats require twice the finished width as they go in and back.

Box pleats require four times the finished pleat width as they go in and back on each side of the pleat (see Fig. 8-46).

STEP 12: Mark off pleat distance (⅜″), once on the left side (as this will be a fold line) and twice on the right side as this pleat will go in and out (knife pleat) (see Fig. 8-46).

STEP 13: Place piece 2 next to added portion, gluing down from hip to hem, leaving piece free from hip to waist (see Fig. 8-46).

STEP 14: Mark ⅜″ twice (or 6/8″) on right side of piece 2 (see Fig. 8-46).

STEP 15: Place piece 3 on right side of added portion, and continue on as for pieces 1 and 2 until you complete the six pleat sections (see Fig. 8-46).

STEP 16: Fold back pleat 1 at hip; draw a line perpendicular to pleat layout line in the center of the pleat (point "O").

Mark the center of the top of the pleat at waist with point "X"; repeat this process for each pleat (see Fig. 8-47).

STEP 17: Straighten each piece from hip to waist. First, fold out darts and join side seams with tape; when the pattern will not lie flat, clip from dart tip to side seam to release fullness; clip from side seam to hip curve of side seam.

Then bring points X and O into alignment on each pleat section; to do this you will have to clip from side to side, but not through both sides in order to make pattern line up. Some pleat sections require more clipping than others, and piece 2 is aligned without clips in this particular design (see Fig. 8-47).

Fig. 8-47. Pleated skirt, Steps 16, 17.

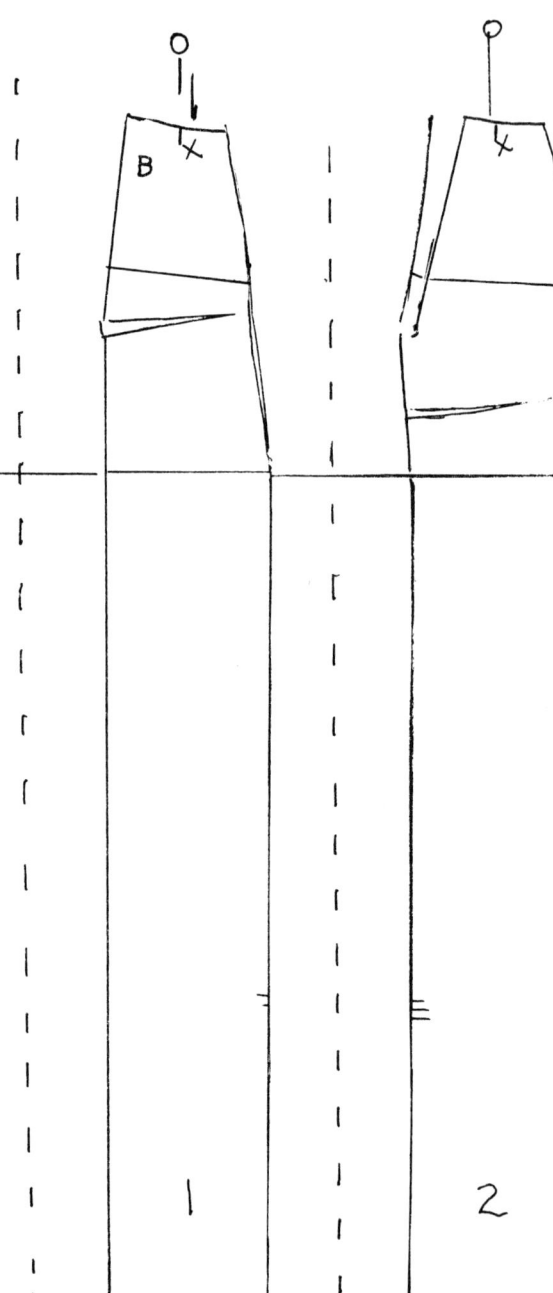

163 SKIRTS

THE COMPLETE GUIDE TO PATTERN-MAKING 164

STEP 18: Place a piece of tracing paper over pattern; trace completed pattern showing pleat edges and underlays; mark with arrows to indicate direction pleats are folded (see Fig. 8-48).

Fig. 8-48. Pleated skirt, Step 18.

165 SKIRTS

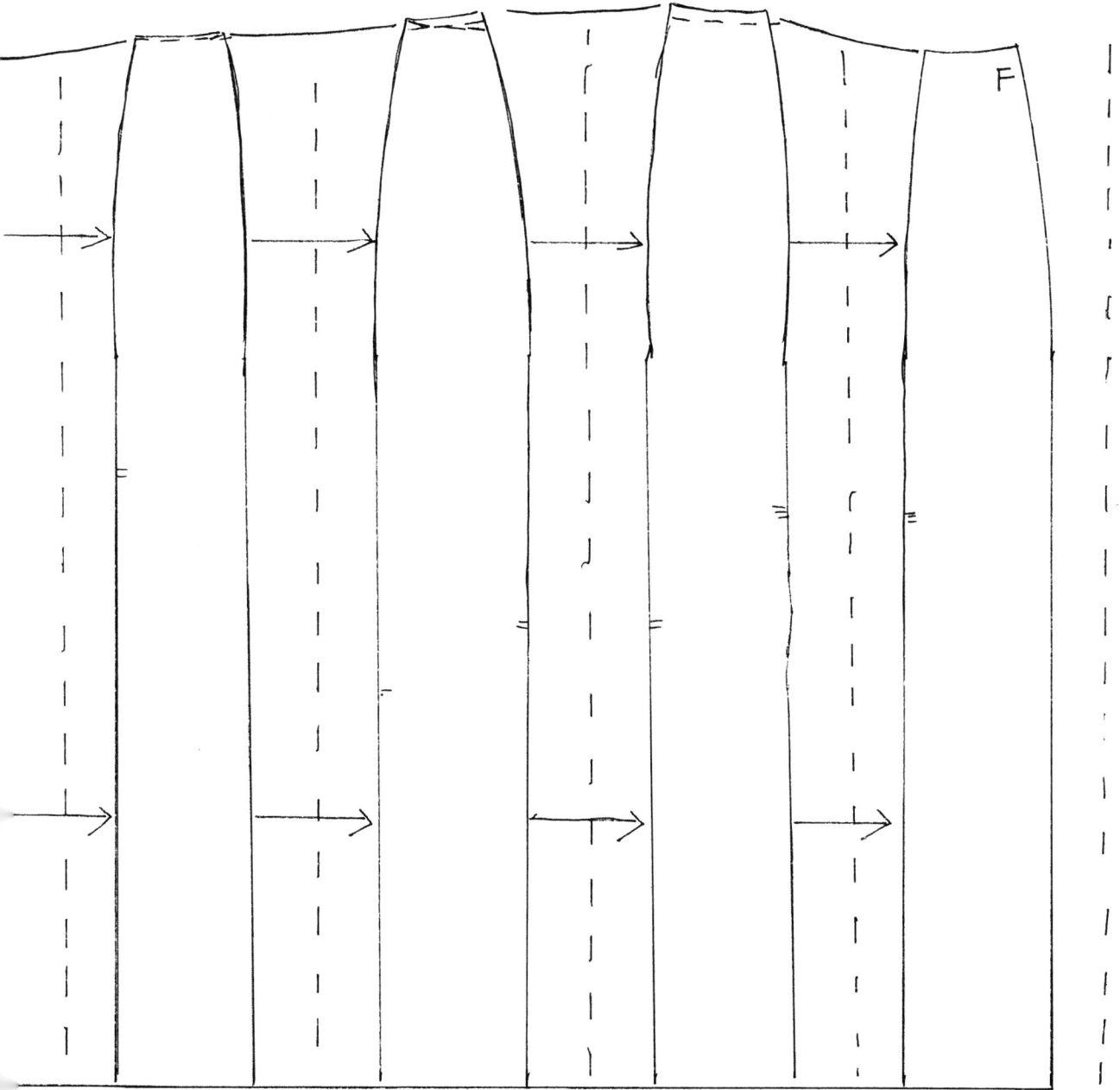

CHAPTER IX

ONE-PIECE GARMENTS

Sheath Dress

The sheath dress maintains the darts in bodice and skirt. When matching these, you may need to make some adjustments if the bodice darts are wider or narrower than the skirt darts. Remember that the side waist curve is also essentially a dart and therefore can be made to have more or less curve as necessary (see Fig. 9-1).

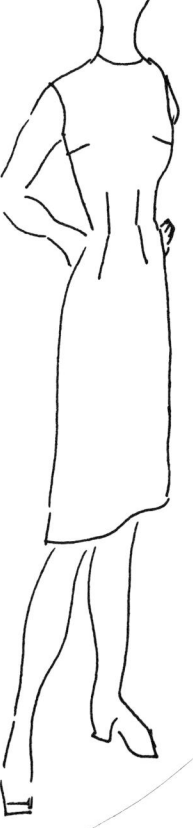

Fig. 9-1. Sheath dress.

STEP 1: Trace sloper (bodice front and back; skirt front and back).

STEP 2: Adjust bodice front to bodice skirt; in this case the bodice front waist dart is wider than the skirt front waist dart; to equalize them, cut from one edge of bodice front bust dart to bust point, and from one edge of bodice front waist dart to bust point; do not cut through bust point.

Adjust dart so that bodice front waist dart equals skirt front waist dart; this will increase the size of the bodice front bust dart (see Fig. 9-2).

STEP 3: Adjust bodice back to bodice skirt back; in this case the bodice back dart is too wide; to make it smaller, cut from the lower edge to the tip, then from the side seam to the tips; do not cut through the tip of the dart. Adjust the side curve so that the waist dart is made the same size at the waist dart of the skirt; there may be some overlapping at the waist (see Fig. 9-3).

STEP 4: Redraw darts; cut new ends at side seam of bust dart (see Figs. 9-2, 9-3).

STEP 5: If the side seams of the sheath dress front and back are not the same length because of overlapping at the waist, adjust them so that they will be equal. This may require lengthening one piece. It is because of these adjustments that sheath dresses often do not fit as well as the basic sloper from which they are made. The adjustments are minor, however, and will probably not be noticeable to the layman.

When a 'shift' dress is desired, simply omit stitching in the waistline darts; this will add the ease at the waist typical of the 'shift' style.

Fig. 9-2. Shealth dress, Steps 1, 2, 4. →

Fig. 9-3. Sheath dress, Steps 1, 3, 4. →

169 ONE-PIECE GARMENTS

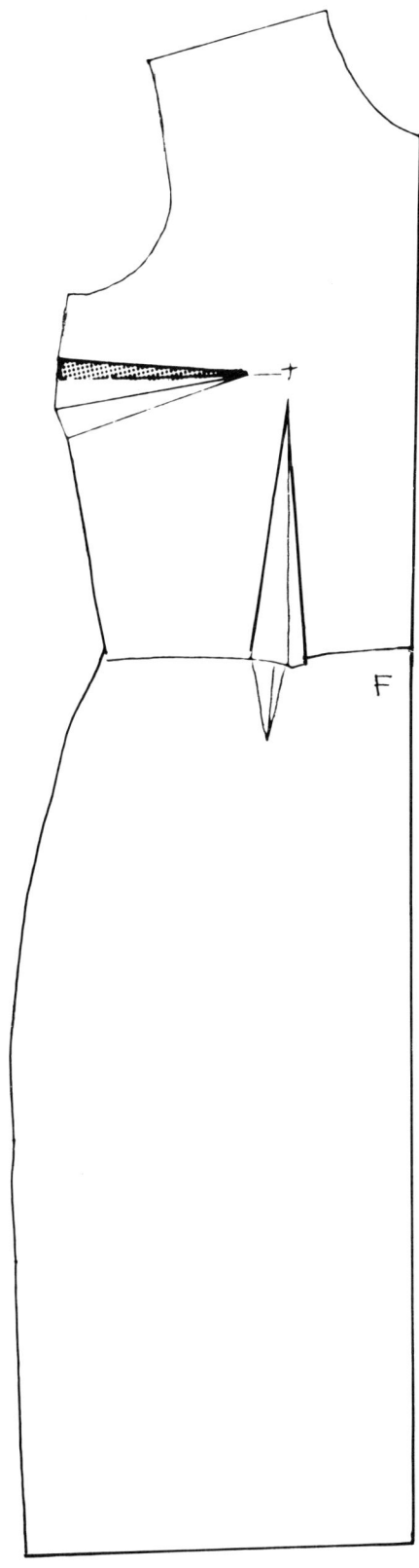
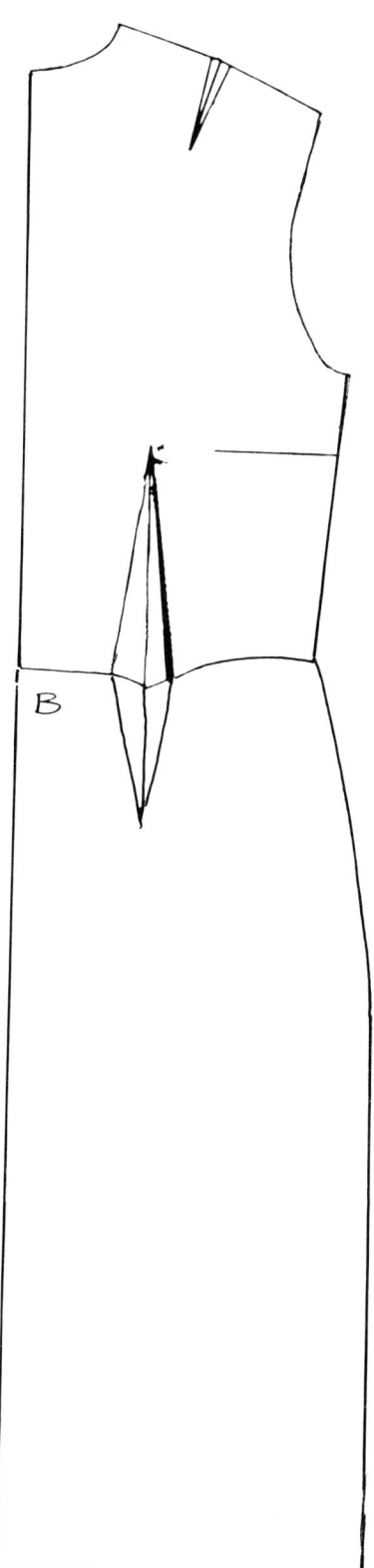

Princess-Line Back

The princess-line back will correspond to the front. The shoulder dart on the bodice back should line up with the mid-shoulder point on the front (see Fig. 9-4).

STEP 1: Trace sloper (bodice back, skirt back).

STEP 2: Draw in new design lines; draw princess lines, on bodice from tip of shoulder dart to tip of waist dart and to lower edge of waist dart, on skirt from tip of waist dart to hem (see Fig. 9-5).

STEP 3: Cross-notch.

STEP 4: Fold out original darts (see Fig. 9-6).

STEP 5: Cut on new design lines.

STEP 6: Place together at waist, making sure the center back is a straight line from neck to hem (see Fig. 9-6).

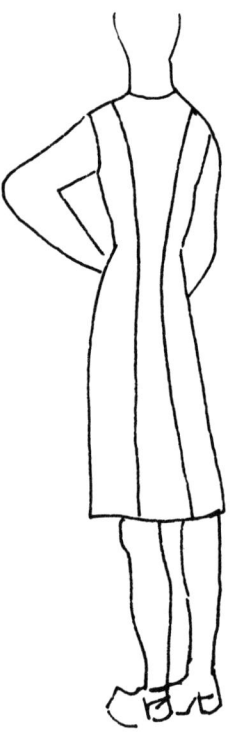

Fig. 9-4. Princess-line back.

Fig. 9-5. Princess-line back, Steps 1, 2, 3. ⟶

Fig. 9-6. Princess-line back, Steps 4, 5, 6. ⟶

171 ONE-PIECE GARMENTS

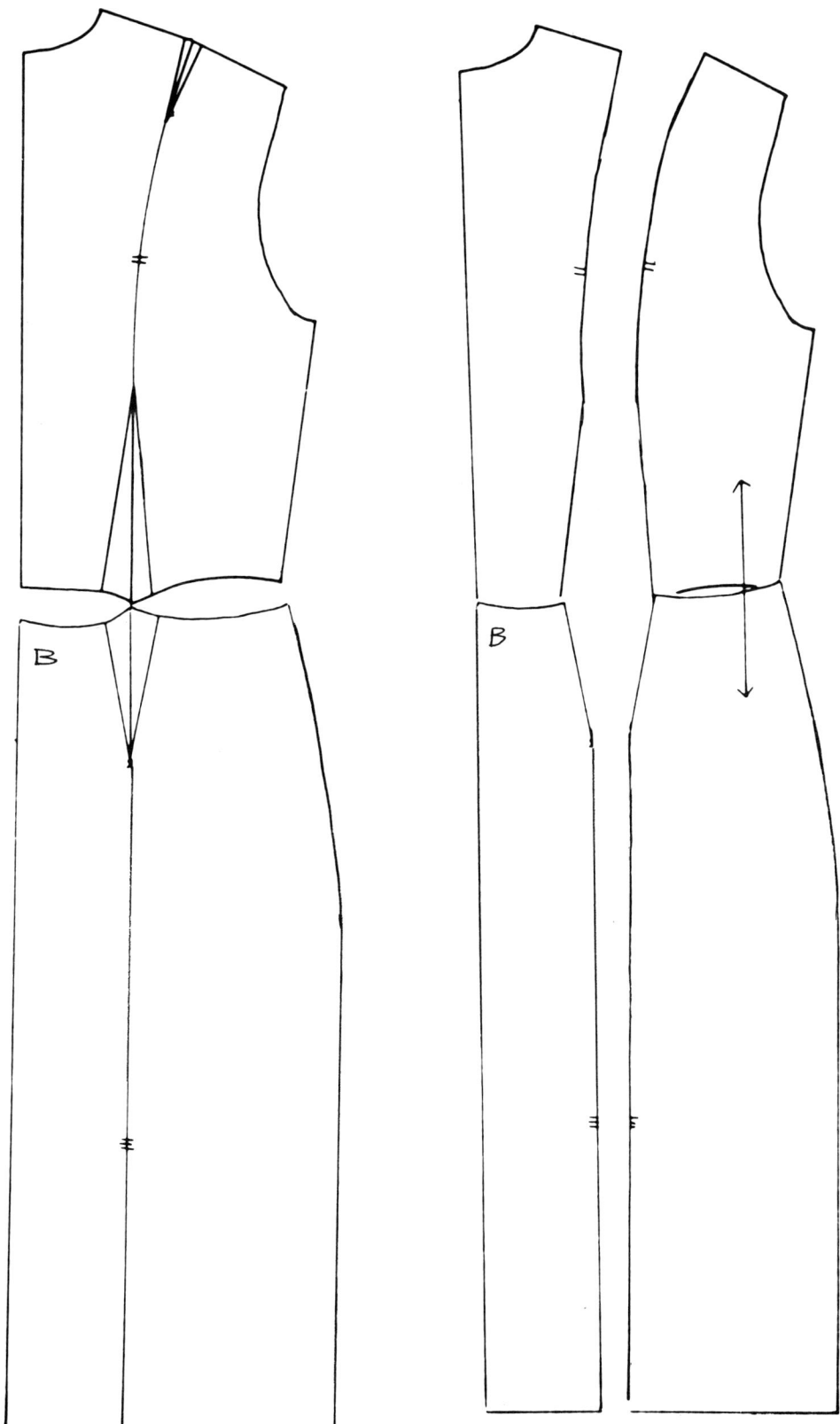

Princess-Line Front

The one-piece garment has no waistline seam. The basic sloper is put together at the waistline, and seams or darts are made to adjust the sloper to fit. If a person has a very curved waist, i.e., there is a very great difference between the waist and hip and especially if there is a large stomach or midriff section that has had ease allowed for in the sloper, the one-piece garment will not fit smoothly over these areas. This problem is often solved by making the one-piece garment fit with ease rather than snugly (see Fig. 9-7).

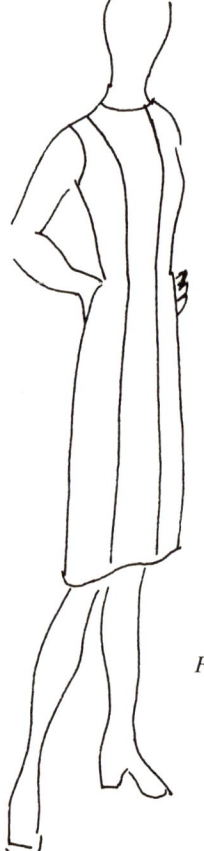

STEP 1: Trace sloper (bodice front, skirt front).

STEP 2: Draw in new design lines; draw in princess lines, on bodice from center of shoulder over point of bust to waist, on skirt from tip of dart to lower skirt edge (see Fig. 9-8).

STEP 3: Cross-notch.

STEP 4: Fold out original darts (see Fig. 9-9).

STEP 5: Cut on new design lines.

STEP 6: Bring bodice and skirt fronts together at waist; be certain center front is a straight line from neck to hem (see Fig. 9-9).

STEP 7: Add ease over bust (see Fig. 9-9).

Fig. 9-7. Princess-line front.

Fig. 9-8. Princess-line front, Steps 1, 2, 3. ⟶

Fig. 9-9. Princess-line front, Steps 4, 5, 6, 7. ⟶

173 ONE-PIECE GARMENTS

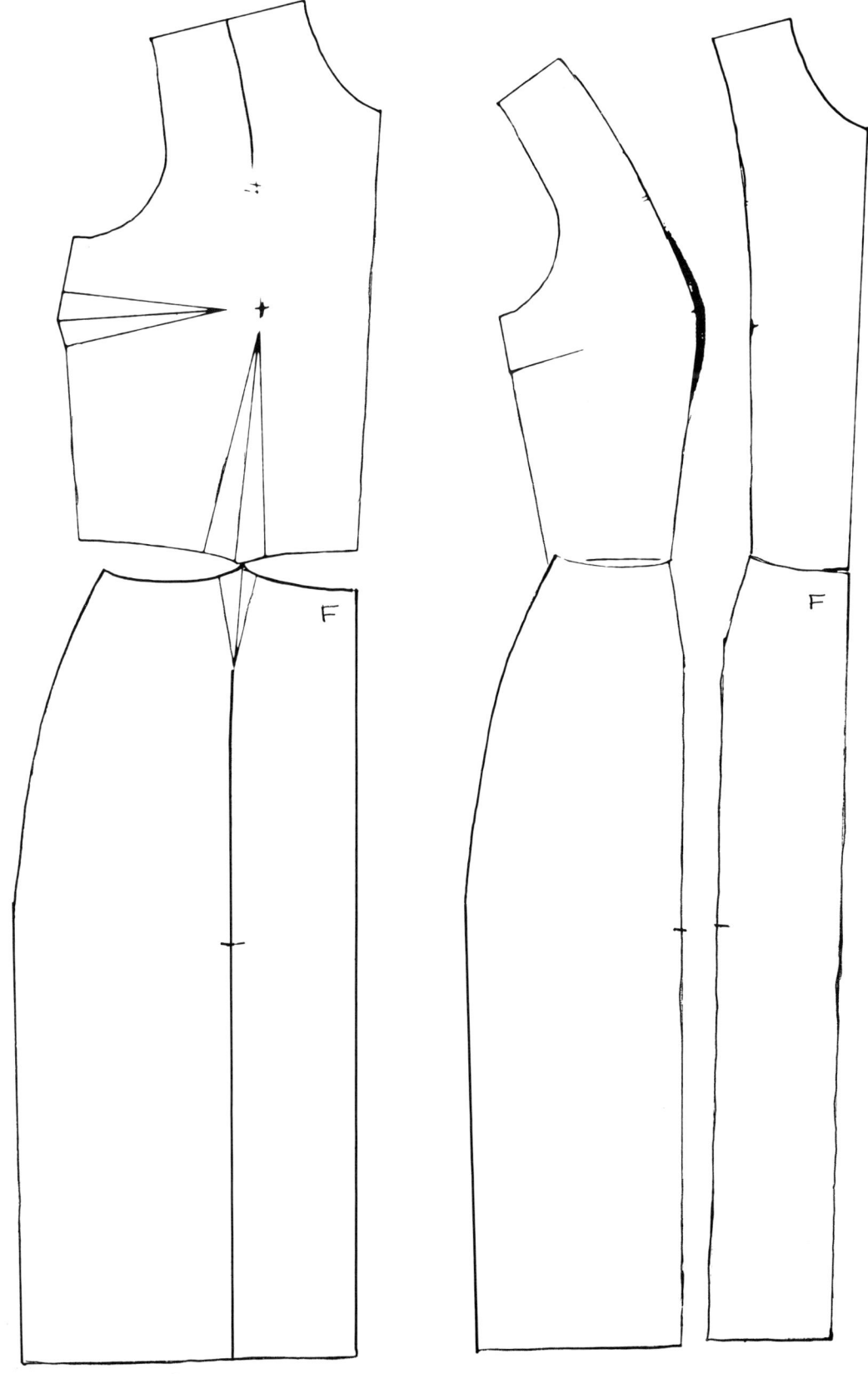

CHAPTER X

COLLARS

Full Roll and Peter Pan Collars

The designing of the collar first requires that the neck edge of the garment be planned. If you are to have a lowered neck edge, this change must be made before the collar is designed to fit it. A basic rule to remember about collars is that the neck edge of the collar and the neck edge of the garment must be the same length.

The collar has two parts, the *stand* and the *fall*. The stand is the part that stands up from the neck edge; the fall is the part that falls onto the garment from the crease of the stand. The shape and size difference of the outer edge will determine whether the collar will have any stand.

A collar that exactly reproduces the neck shape at both neck and outer edge will lie completely flat on the finished garment; that is, there will be no stand. A collar that fits the neck edge but is rectangular in shape will have the maximum amount of stand. In developing collars, the measurement for the neck edge remains stable. It is only the outer edge that can be changed to vary the amount of stand and fall on any given collar.

The collars illustrated in this first problem have two extremes of stand and fall. The rectangular collar will have a high stand. When it is stitched onto the neck edge, the outer edge will push up on the bodice until it reaches a point where it has the same measurement as the bodice. This is the neck edge, since it is the same size as the neck edge, and the bodice increases from the neck edge outward. It is for this reason that the collar will fold over at the back and create the stand and fall. Try it on a dress form, or cut and fold the paper pattern and tape the rectangular collar to it to see this process work.

The Peter Pan collar exactly reproduces the neck and outer edges of the garment and therefore it will have no stand. It will lie completely flat on the garment (see Fig. 10-1.

Most collars fall somewhere between these two extremes. Develop these two first, and then go on to the variations between.

STEP 1: Trace sloper (bodice front and back).

STEP 2: Put sloper together at shoulder, if you are going to change the neck shape, do it at this time (see Fig. 10-2).

STEP 3: Draw the Peter Pan collar. Measure the width desired and trace onto the bodice front and back as shown; then cut out or trace (see Fig. 10-2).

STEP 4: Draw the full roll (high-stand) collar; measure the neck edge; draw a line this length on the paper; develop a rectangle from this measurement, in the width desired (see Fig. 10-2).

Fig. 10-1. Peter Pan and full roll collars.

177 COLLARS

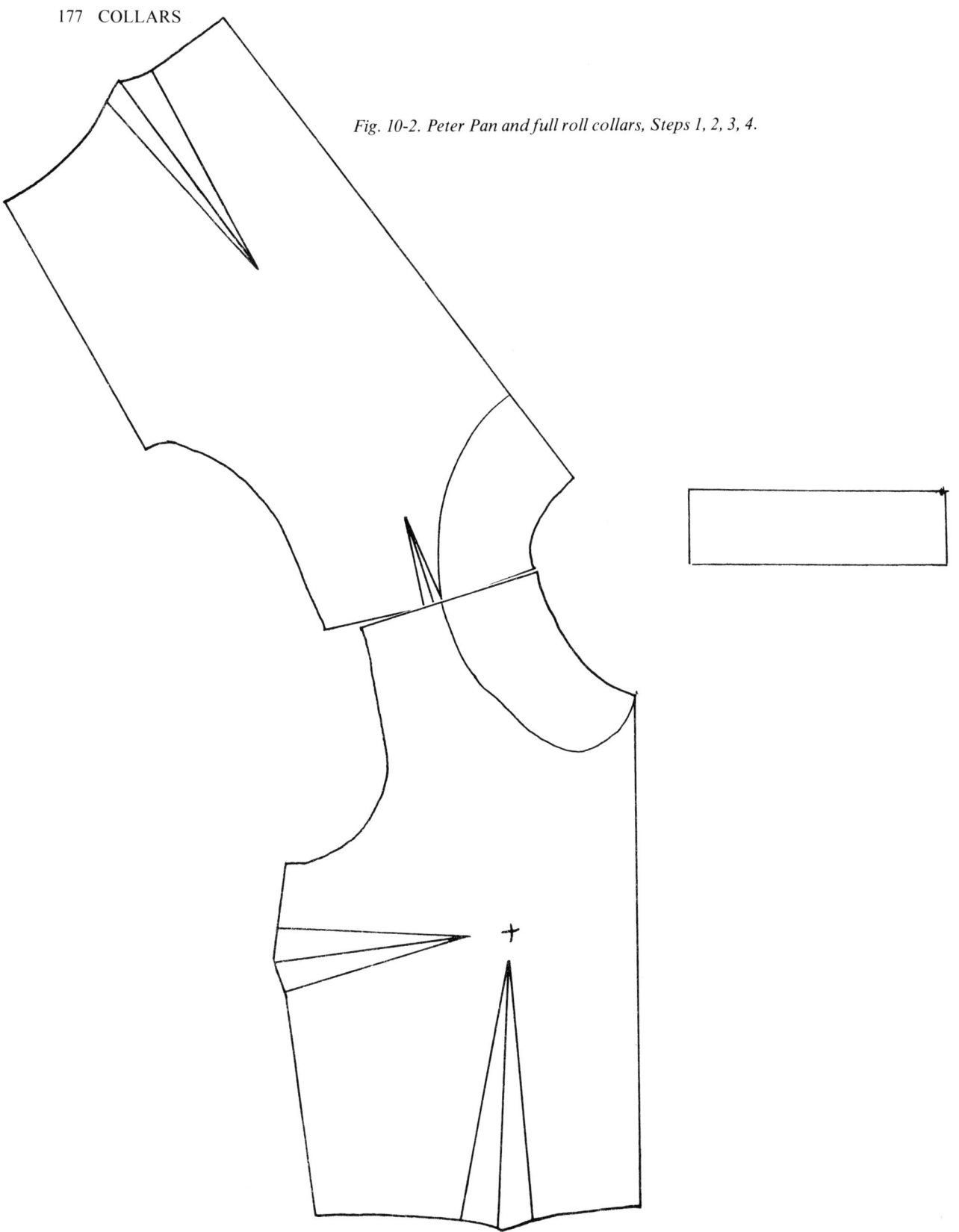

Fig. 10-2. Peter Pan and full roll collars, Steps 1, 2, 3, 4.

THE COMPLETE GUIDE TO PATTERN-MAKING 178

Five Variations on the Basic Collar

We have seen two extreme examples of collar stand in the previous example. Most collars have an amount of stand somewhere between these two extremes. A logical progression will include five variations from full roll (high-stand) to low-stand collar (see Fig. 10-3).

STEP 1: Trace sloper (bodice front and back).

STEP 2: Put slopers together at shoulder; change neckline at this point if desired (see Fig. 10-4).

STEP 3: Measure neck edge; draw a line this length on paper; develop a rectangle from this measurement; this is full roll collar (see Fig. 10-4).

STEP 4: Cut from outer edge to neck edge on collar just developed; do not cut through neck edge.

STEP 5: Spread; a progression of amounts of spread is shown.

As one spreads towards the full potential, one approaches duplicating the bodice design, as in the previous example of the Peter Pan collar (see Fig. 10-4).

STEP 6: Trace collars just developed (see Fig. 10-5).

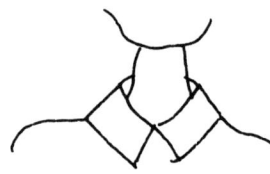

Fig. 10-3. Basic collars, five variations.

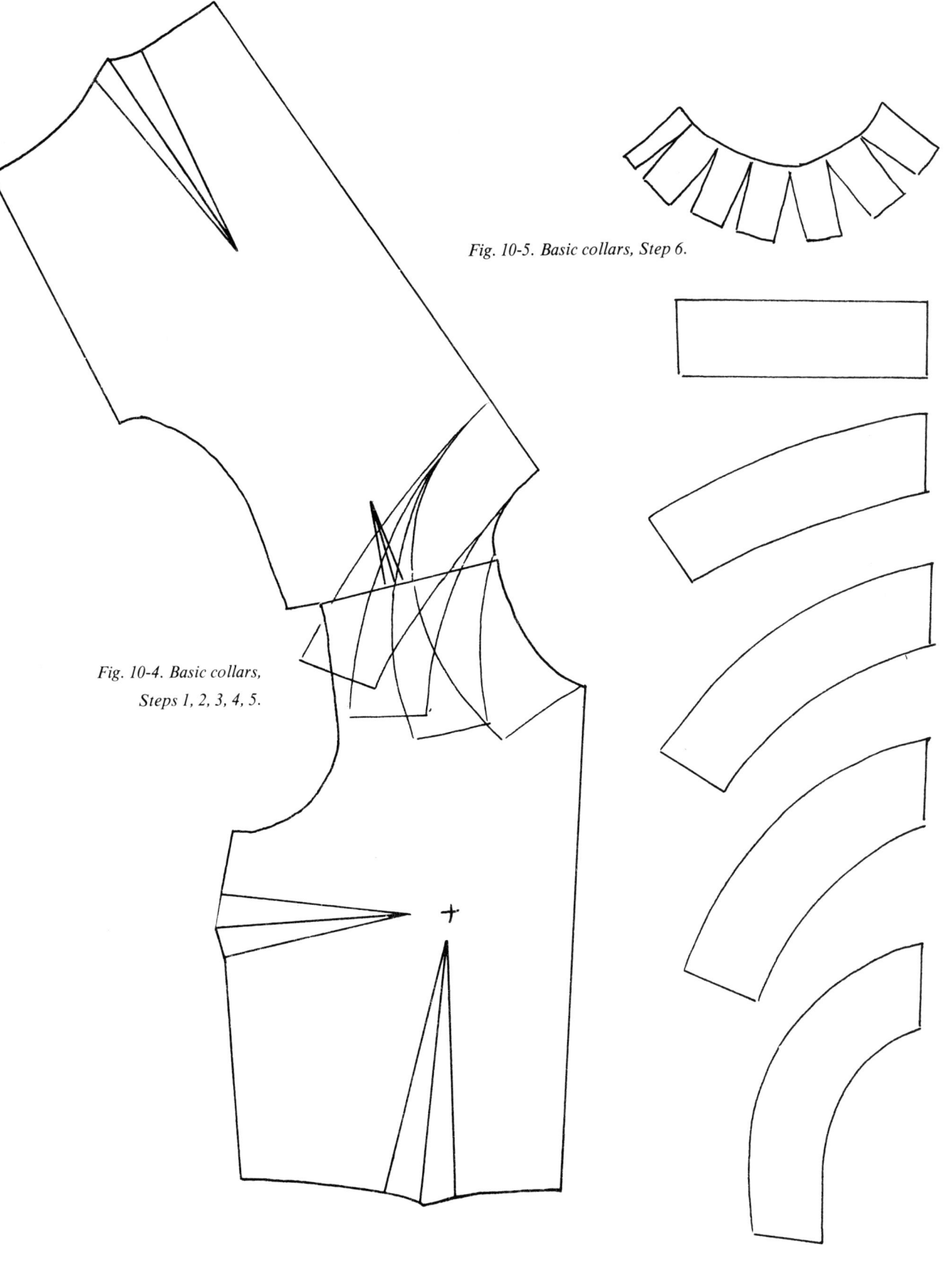

Fig. 10-5. Basic collars, Step 6.

Fig. 10-4. Basic collars, Steps 1, 2, 3, 4, 5.

Sailor Collar

The sailor collar derives its name from its use on sailor uniforms in the past and present times. A V-front bodice is used with a sailor collar. The depth of the fall on the bodice back can be easily changed by drawing it various widths (see Fig. 10-6).

STEP 1: Trace sloper (bodice front and back).

STEP 2: Put sloper together at shoulder (see Fig. 10-7).

STEP 3: Lower neckline (see Fig. 10-7).

STEP 4: Draw in sailor collar; on center back measure down depth desired; draw a perpendicular line to armhole from center back point; then connect shoulder with lowered bodice front neck; connect armhole point on bodice back with neck point at center front (see Fig. 10-7).

STEP 5: Trace collar (see Fig. 10-8).

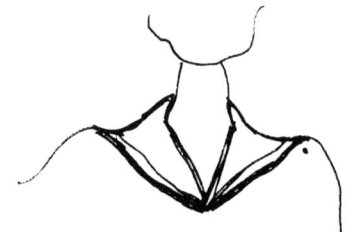

Fig. 10-6. Sailor collar.

To create a sailor collar with stand add the following step.

STEP 6: Cut from outer edge to neck edge, but not through neck edge; overlap outer edge a small amount to create a stand.

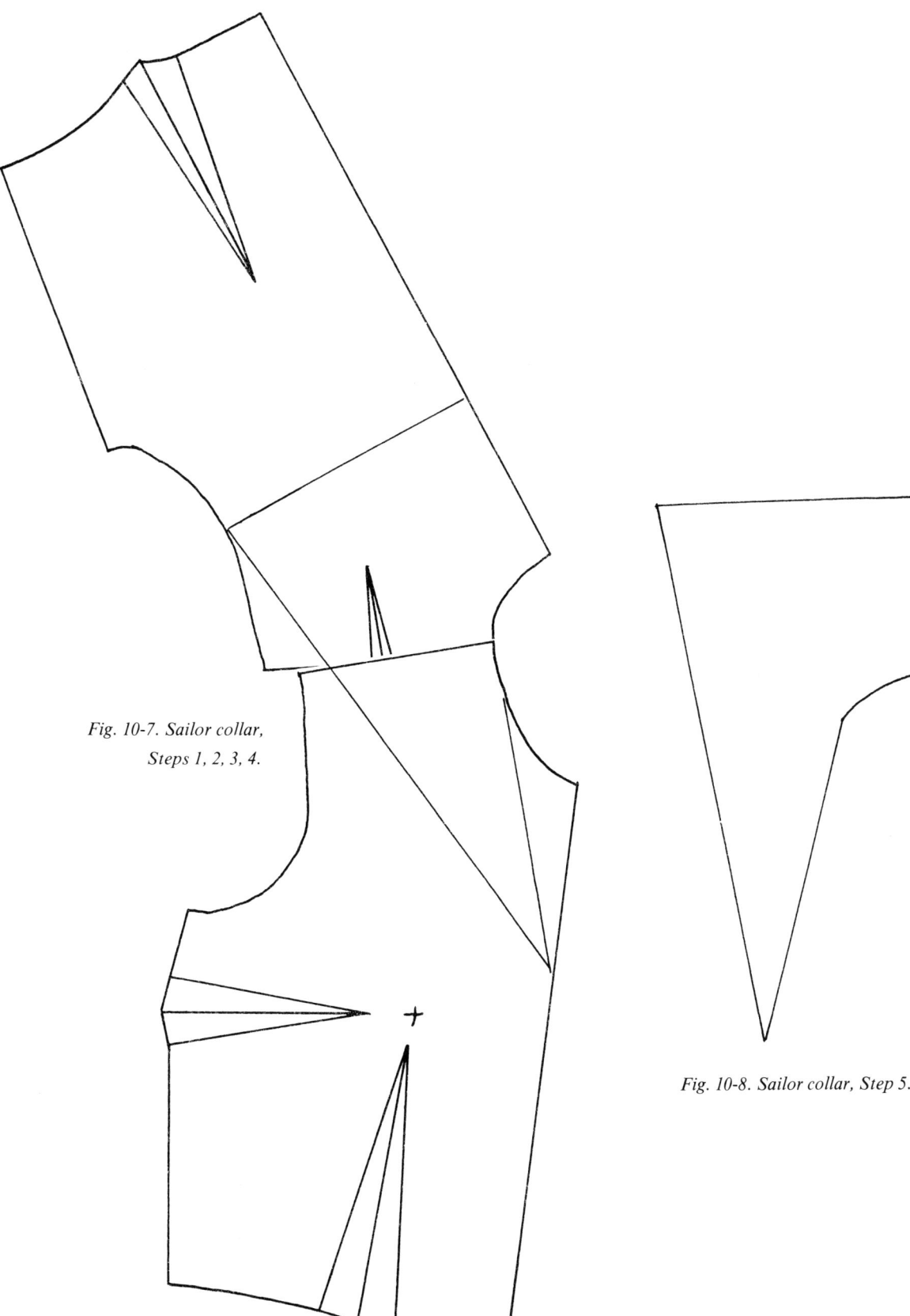

Fig. 10-7. Sailor collar, Steps 1, 2, 3, 4.

Fig. 10-8. Sailor collar, Step 5.

Turtle-Neck Collar

The turtle-neck collar stands up from the neck edge and hugs the neck because it is cut on the bias. The mardarin collar design (see p. 184) must be made smaller at the upper edge to accomplish this end (see Fig. 10-9).

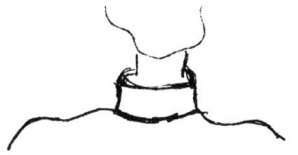

STEP 1: Draw a line the length of the neck edge.

STEP 2: Make a rectangle the width desired for the collar; double this to allow for a fold at the upper edge since a seam at the upper edge is undesirable (see Fig. 10-10).

STEP 3: Indicate the grain line to make the collar on the bias (see Fig. 10-10).

Fig. 10-9. Turtle-neck collar.

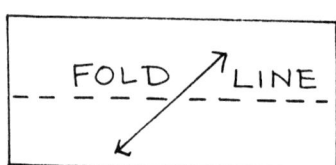

Fig. 10-10. Turtle-neck collar, Steps 1, 2, 3.

183 COLLARS

Ruffle Collar

The ruffle collar fits the neck edge but is full at the outer edge. This is an especially attractive collar when fullness is required, as it does not give bulk to the neck edge as a simple ruffle would (see Fig. 10-11).

STEP 1: Draw a line the length of the neck edge.

STEP 2: Make a rectangle the width desired for the collar (see Fig. 10-12).

STEP 3: Cut from outer edge to neck edge, but not through neck edge (see Fig. 10-13).

STEP 4: Spread the amount desired (see Fig. 10-13).

STEP 5: Trace collar (see Fig. 10-13).

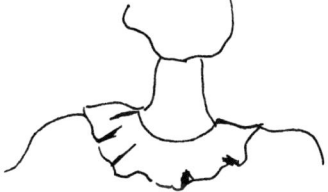

Fig. 10-11. Ruffle collar

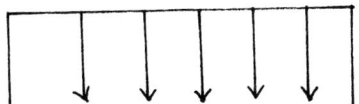

Fig. 10-12. Ruffle collar, Steps 1, 2.

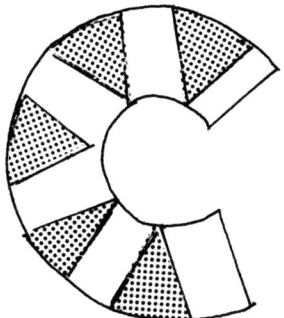

Fig. 10-13. Ruffle collar, Steps 3, 4, 5.

THE COMPLETE GUIDE TO PATTERN-MAKING

Mandarin Collar

The mandarin collar stands straight up from the neck edge. It is usually 1½" to 2" wide, and the center front edge is curved. In order to make the collar fit the neck snugly, the upper edge is cut and overlapped. This procedure gives a curve to the lower edge of the pattern (see Fig. 10-14).

STEP 1: Draw a line the length of the neck edge.

STEP 2: Make a rectangle the width desired (see Fig. 10-15).

STEP 3: Round off the front edge as shown (see Fig. 10-15).

STEP 4: Cut from upper edge to neck edge but not through neck edge (see Fig. 10-16).

STEP 5: Overlap to make upper edge shorter than neck edge (see Fig. 10-16).

STEP 6: Trace collar (see Fig. 10-16).

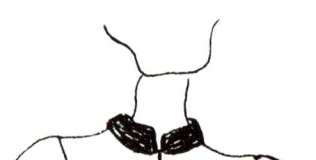

Fig. 10-14. Mandarin collar.

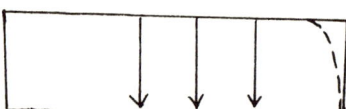

Fig. 10-15. Mandarin collar, Steps 1, 2, 3.

Fig. 10-16. Mandarin collar, Steps 4, 5, 6.

185 COLLARS

Shawl Collar

The shawl collar is a cut-on collar that rolls from the bodice front. The back portion of the collar is stitched to the back neck edge. Many sizes, shapes, and variations to the shawl collar are possible. The first example shows the basic steps for making a shawl collar (see Fig. 10-17).

STEP 1: Trace sloper (bodice front).

STEP 2: Draw in the break line on front sloper; the break line is the place where the collar will roll (see Fig. 10-18).

STEP 3: Measure the back neck edge; this length is represented by line A on diagram (see Fig. 10-18).

STEP 4: Draw the rectangle on the break line, making the collar the width desired; the lower edge may be squared or curved.

A notch may be added if such a design is desired (see Fig. 10-18).

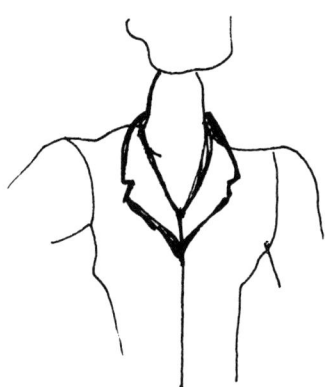

Fig. 10-17. Shawl collar.

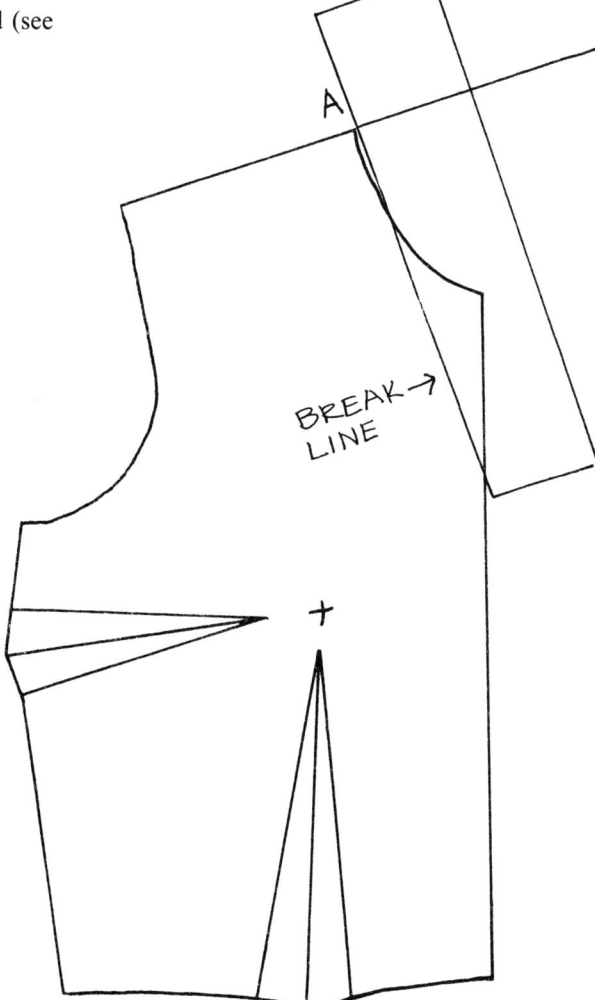

Fig. 10-18. Shawl collar, Steps 1, 2, 3, 4.

The collar as drawn has a high stand in back.
To create a shawl collar with less stand in back add the following steps:

STEP 5: Cut from outer edge to back neck edge but not through it (see Fig. 10-19).

STEP 6: Spread pattern, and add paper (see Fig. 10-20).

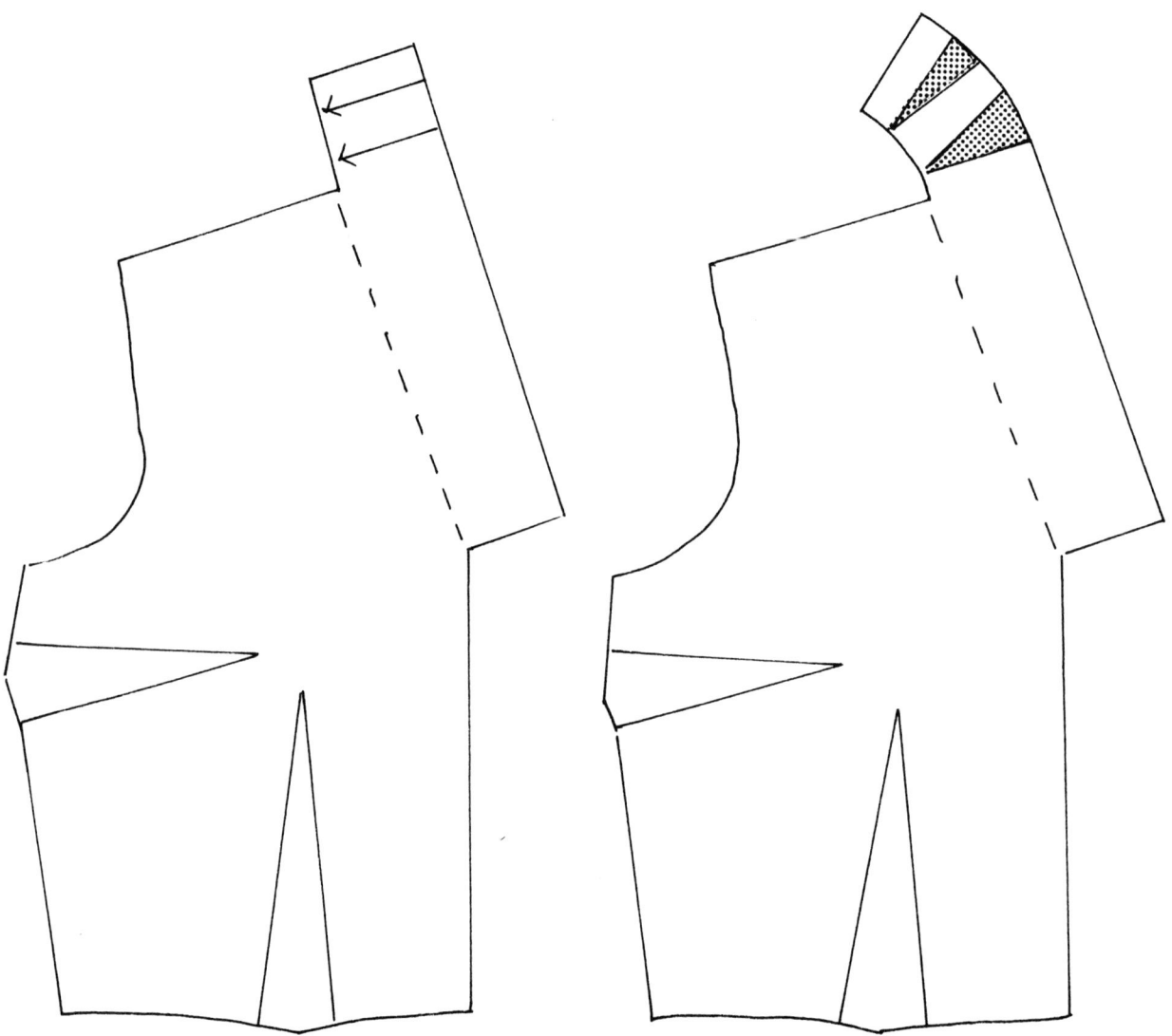

Fig. 10-19. Shawl collar, Step 5.

Fig. 10-20. Shawl collar, Step 6.

Shawl Collar with Center Front Closing

The shawl collar is more typically added to a garment with a center front closing. When this is the case, the center front extension must be added before the collar is drawn. The steps followed in the previous example are followed after the center front closing is added to the bodice front (see Fig. 10-21).

STEP 1: Trace sloper (bodice front).

STEP 2: Add center front closing, indicated on diagram as section A (see Fig. 10-22).

STEP 3: Draw in the break line.

STEP 4: Measure the back neck edge; add extension to break line to equal this length (see Fig. 10-22).

STEP 5: Draw on the collar; this collar has been given a notch and has been rounded at the lower edge.

STEP 6: A dart, labelled "c," can be stitched into the bodice front. It is often suggested that this procedure will make the shawl collar roll more effectively (see Fig. 10-22).

Fig. 10-21. Shawl collar with center front closing.

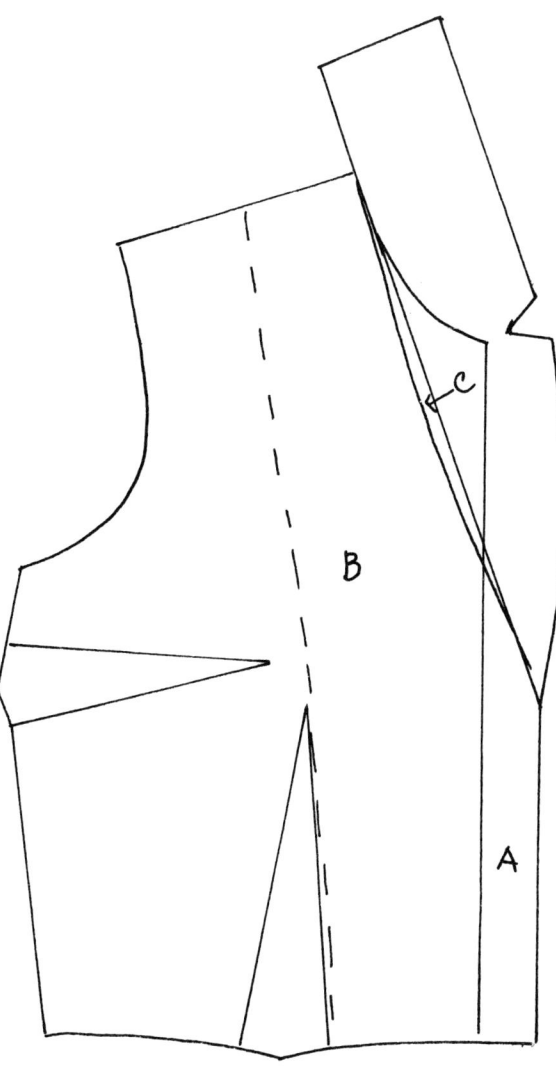

Fig. 10-22. Shawl collar with center front closing, Steps 1, 2, 3, 4, 5, 6.

THE COMPLETE GUIDE TO PATTERN-MAKING 188

STEP 7: Draw facing; the upper or outer collar on the shawl is included in one with the front facing.

Tracing over pattern just completed, add the facing indicated by dotted lines. This piece has been labelled "b" (see Fig. 10-23).

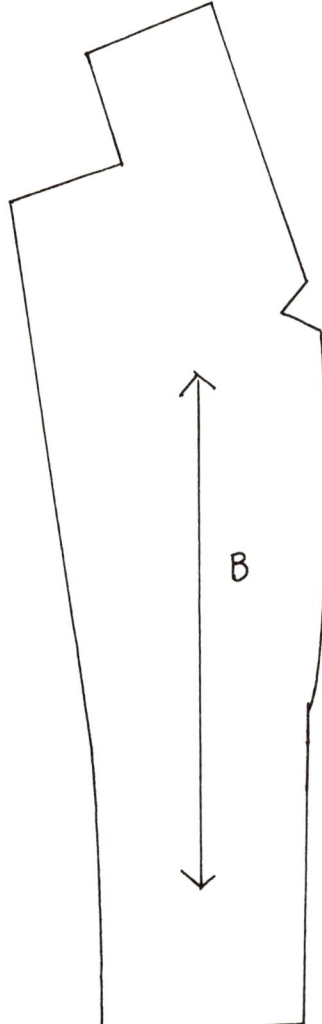

Fig. 10-23. Shawl collar with center front closing, Step 7.

Shawl Collar Variations

The actual sewing patterns for a shawl collar can be drawn in various ways. Pieces can be separated and stitched on to give seam lines in locations desired on the final design. The three examples shown here are all traced from the shawl collar with center front closing developed in the previous pattern (see Fig. 10-24).

Fig. 10-24 shows the collar as a separate piece. It would be stitched onto the bodice front, the dart being cut away in the seam.

Fig. 10-25 shows the collar cut on, with dart indicated by dotted lines.

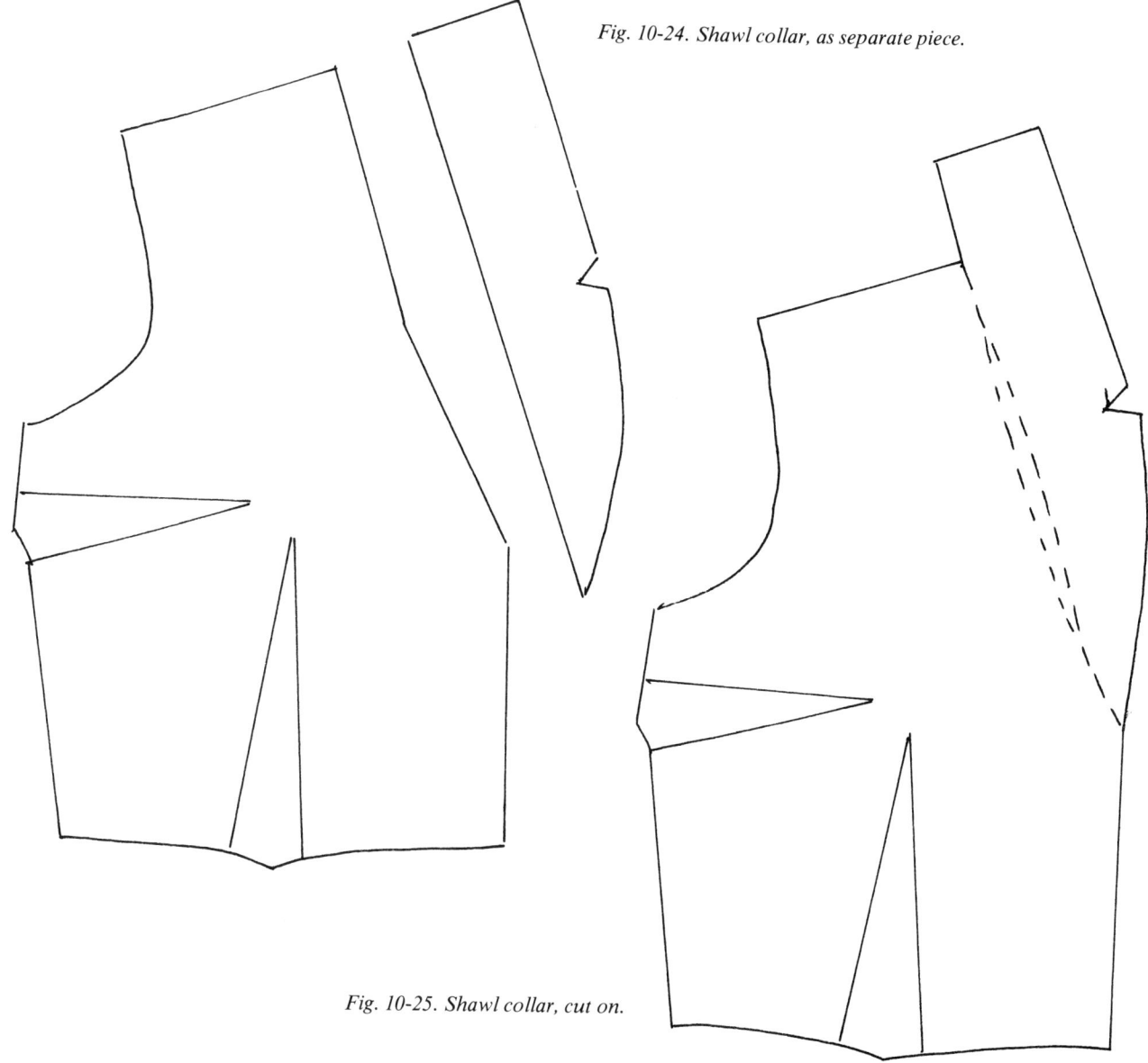

Fig. 10-24. Shawl collar, as separate piece.

Fig. 10-25. Shawl collar, cut on.

Fig. 10-26 shows the collar separated at the notch to create a seam in that place. The dart lines are indicated.

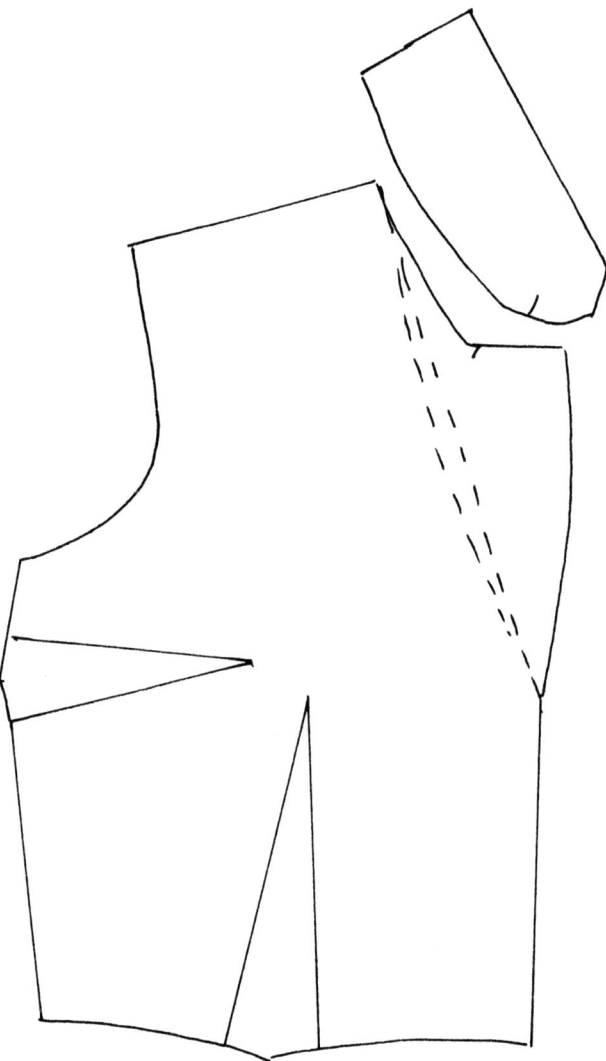

Fig. 10-26. Shawl collar, separated at notch.

CHAPTER **XI**

OUTER GARMENTS

Narrow Cape

The cape is an outer garment with rounded shoulders and no sleeves either cut in or set in. Use the bodice front and back slopers to develop the cape pattern (see Fig. 11-1).

Fig. 11-1. Narrow cape.

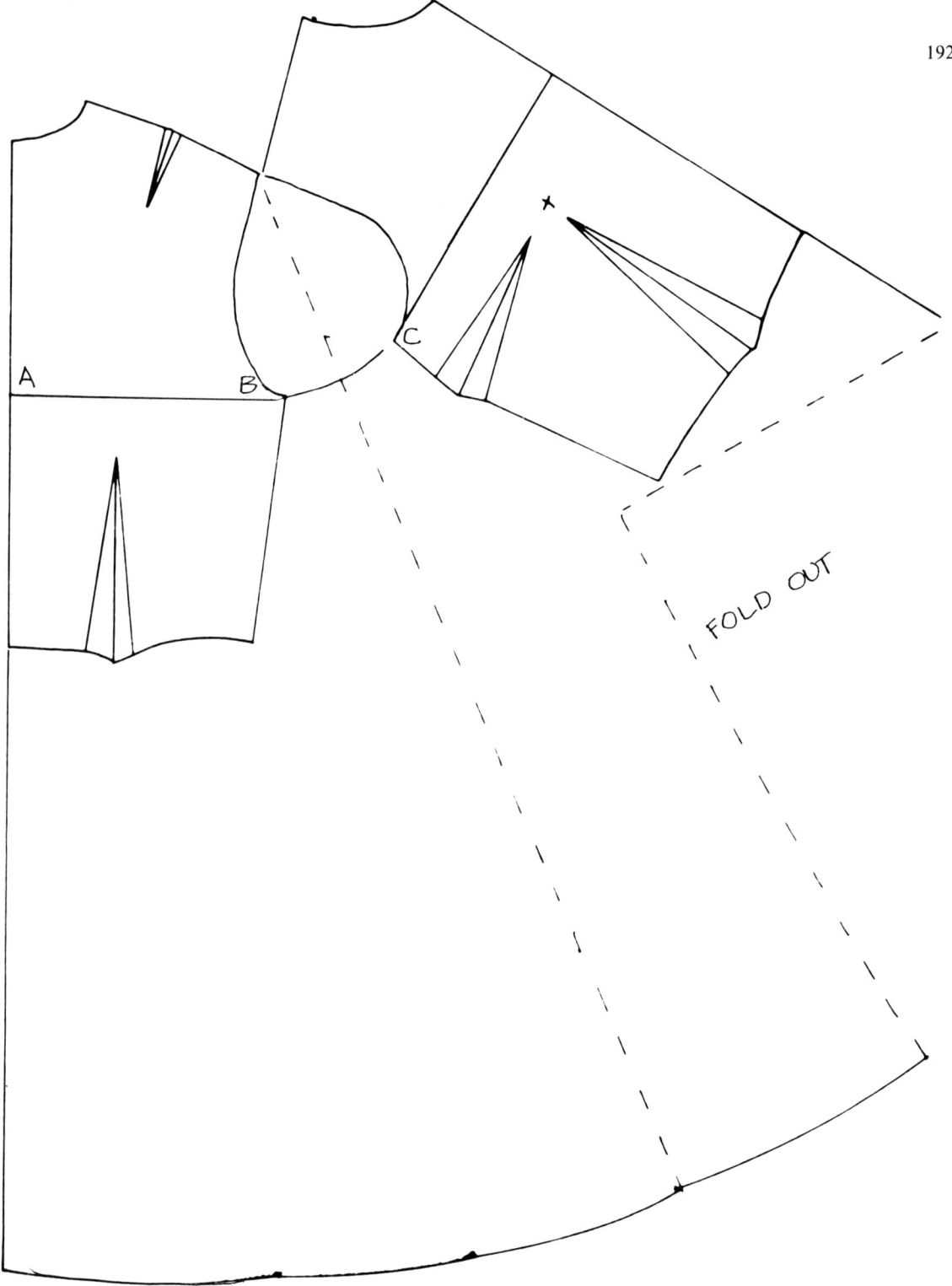

Fig. 11-2. Narrow cape, Steps 1, 2, 3, 4, 5.

193 OUTER GARMENTS

STEP 1: Trace sloper (bodice front and back).

STEP 2: Place together at shoulder edge as shown; B to C equals half the distance A to B (see Fig. 11-2).

STEP 3: Draw a line through the center of BC to shoulder and extend to length desired (see Fig. 11-2).

STEP 4: Lengthen center front and center back the amount desired; the amount added below the waistline should be equal on both front and back (see Fig. 11-2).

STEP 5: Connect center front and center back, crossing side extension line drawn in Step 3 (see Fig. 11-2).

STEP 6: Trace front and back separately, rounding shoulder seam slightly for better fit (see Fig. 11-3).

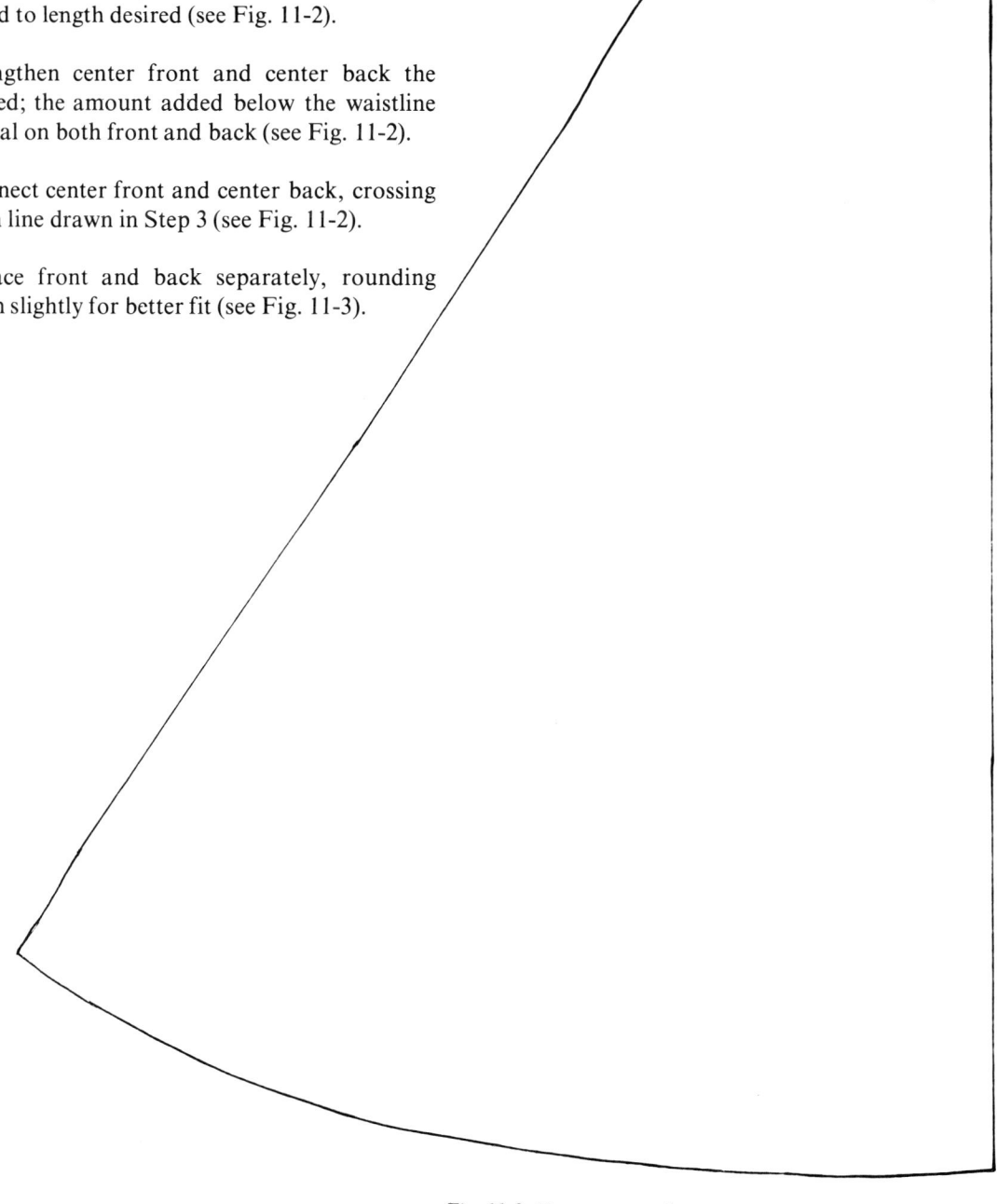

Fig. 11-3. Narrow cape, Step 6.

Jacket

The basic sloper can be used to develop a pattern for a jacket. The jacket usually goes over other clothing and therefore must have additional ease (see Fig. 11-4).

Fig. 11-4. Jacket.

STEP 1: Trace sloper (bodice front and back; skirt from and back).

STEP 2: Put bodice front and skirt front together as for sheath dress; put bodice back and skirt back together as for sheath dress.

Cut skirt off at length desired for jacket (see Fig. 11-5).

STEP 3: Make the following alterations for jacket design (see Fig. 11-5).

Add: ⅛" to side seams; ½" to shoulder width; ¾" to center front for single-breasted jacket or 3" to center front for double-breasted jacket.

Lower front neck ⅛" and armhole ½".

195 OUTER GARMENTS

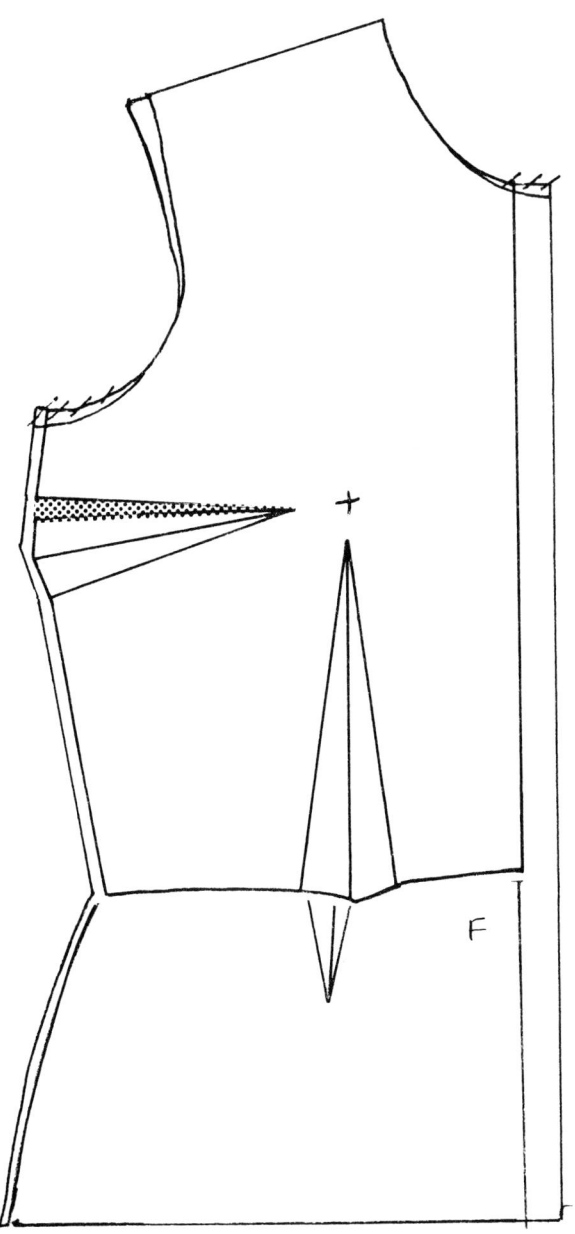
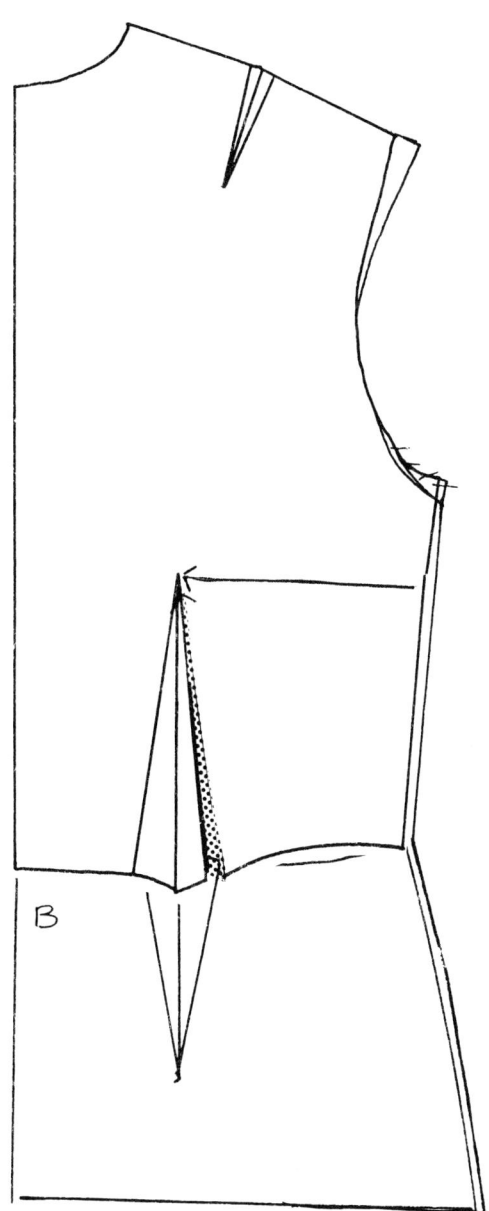

Fig. 11-5. Jacket, Steps 1, 2, 3.

Jacket Sleeve

STEP 1: Trace two-piece sleeve pattern (see Fig. 11-6).

STEP 2: Add ½" to cap (see Fig. 11-6).

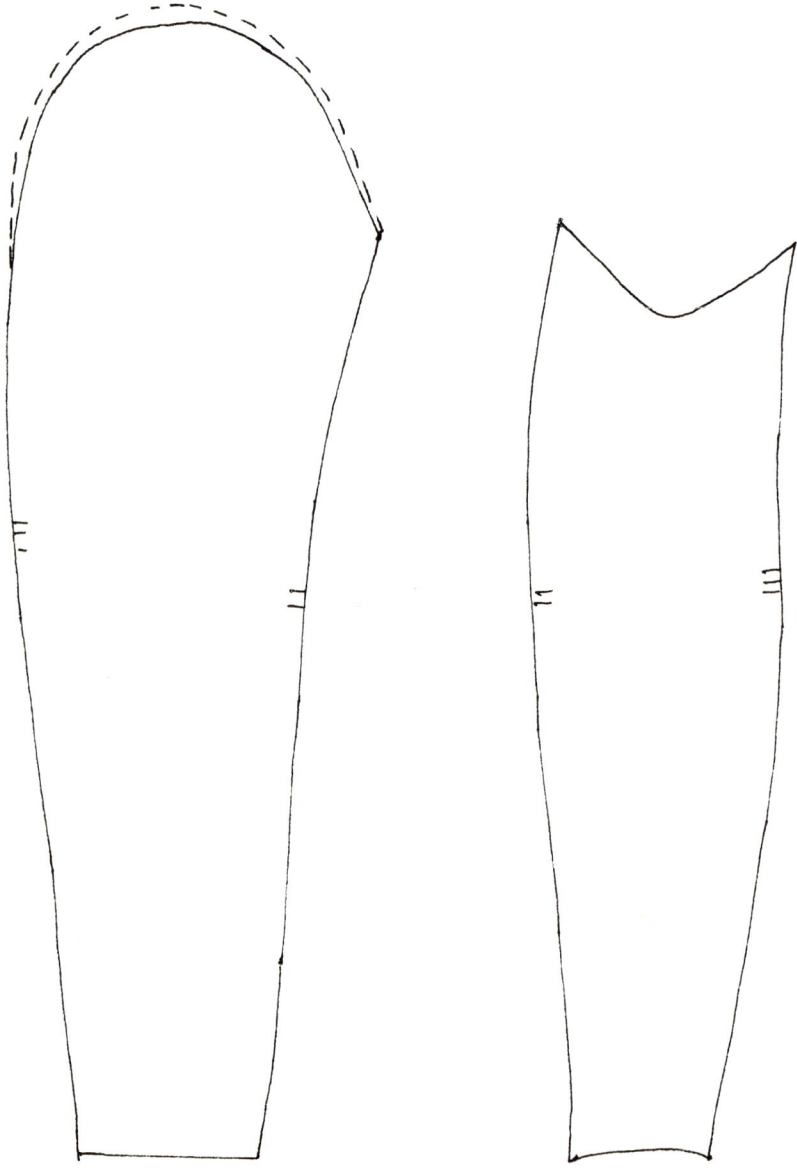

Fig. 11-6. Jacket sleeve, Steps 1, 2.

Coat

The basic sloper can likewise be used to develop a coat pattern. There must be additional ease in a coat since it will be worn on top of several layers of clothing (see Fig. 11-7).

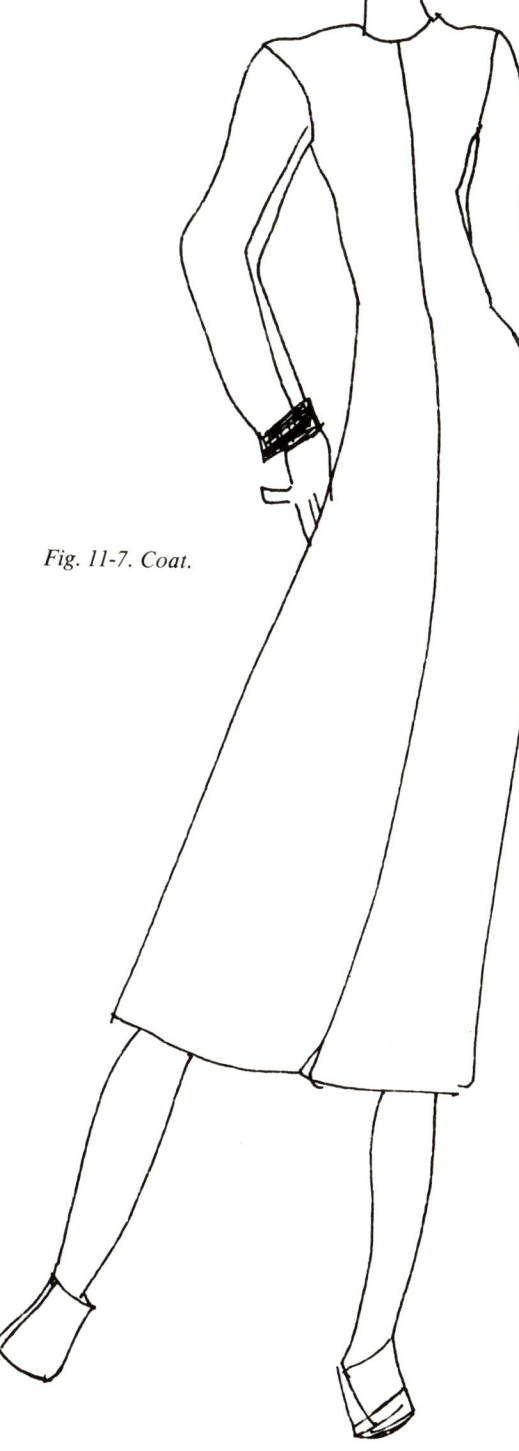

Fig. 11-7. Coat.

STEP 1: Trace sloper (bodice front and back; skirt front and back), or trace sheath dress pattern.

STEP 2: Put bodice front and skirt front together as for sheath dress; put bodice back and skirt back together as for sheath dress (see Fig. 11-8).

STEP 3: Make the following adjustments for coat design (see Fig. 11-8):

Add: ¼" to side seams; ½" to shoulder width; 1" to center front for single-breasted coat or 3½" to center front for double-breasted jacket.

Lower neckline ¼" and armhole 1".

Fig. 11-8. Coat, Steps 1, 2, 3.

199 OUTER GARMENTS

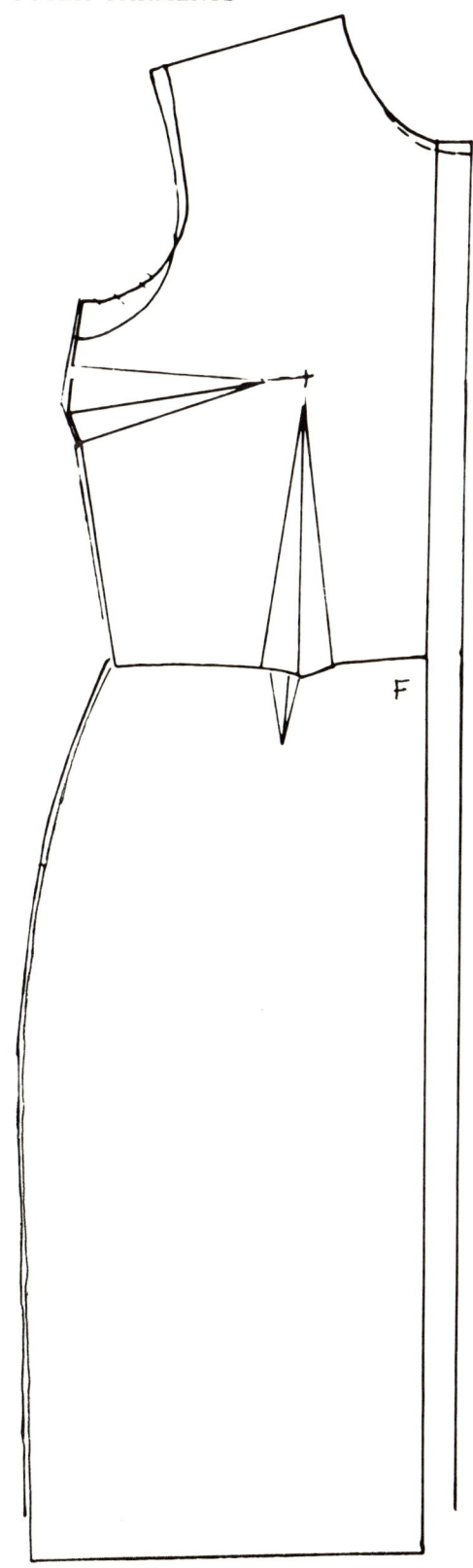
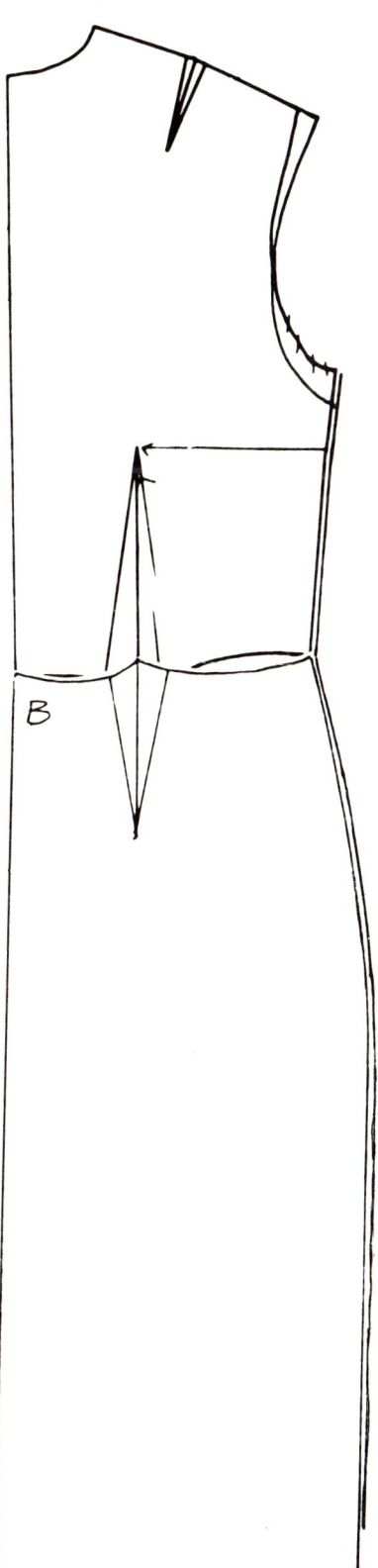

THE COMPLETE GUIDE TO PATTERN-MAKING

Coat Sleeve

STEP 1: Trace two-piece sleeve pattern (see Fig. 11-9).

STEP 2: Add 1″ to cap height (see Fig. 11-9).

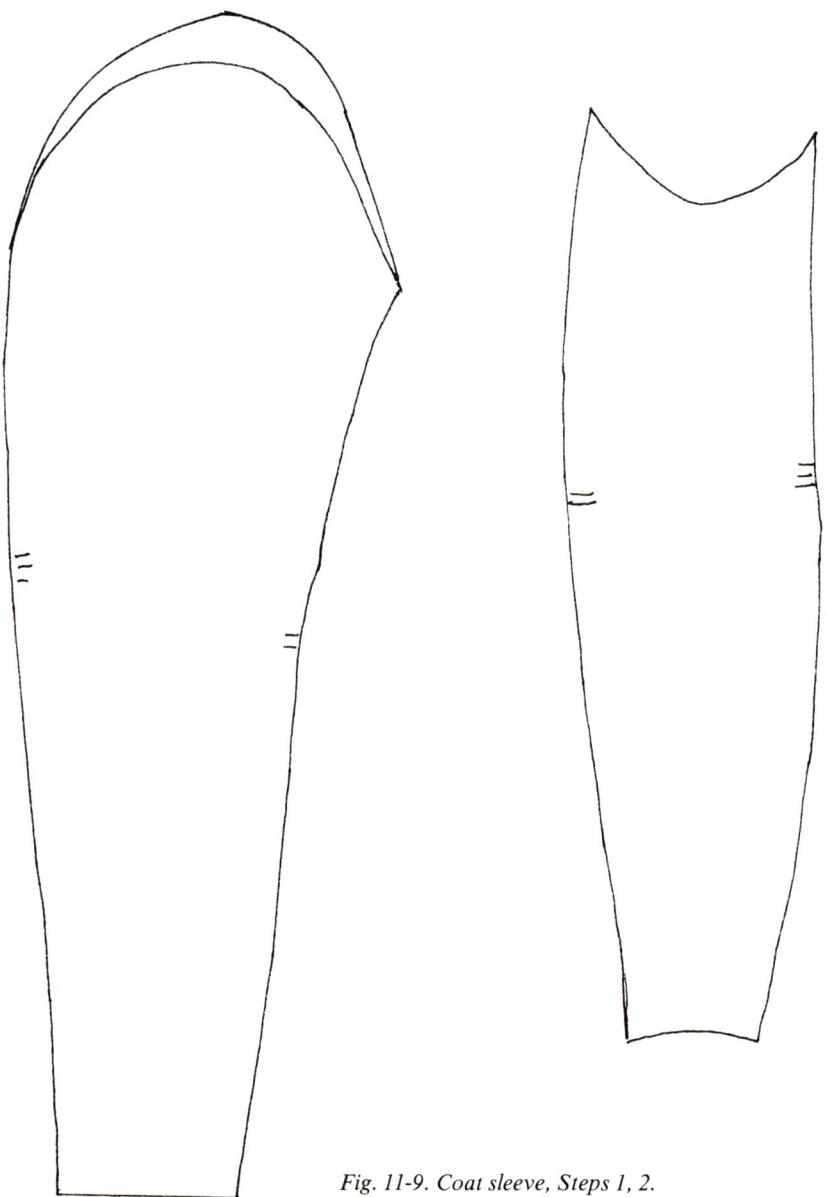

Fig. 11-9. Coat sleeve, Steps 1, 2.

CHAPTER XII

PANTS

The basic pants sloper has been developed with waist darts front and back. The basic sloper should fit the body smoothly, with ease enough to move comfortably.

From the basic pants sloper the designer can create any current or historical style. A common way to alter pants is to change their length. The diagram shows the relationship of lengths of some popular styles of the past or present (see Fig. 12-1).

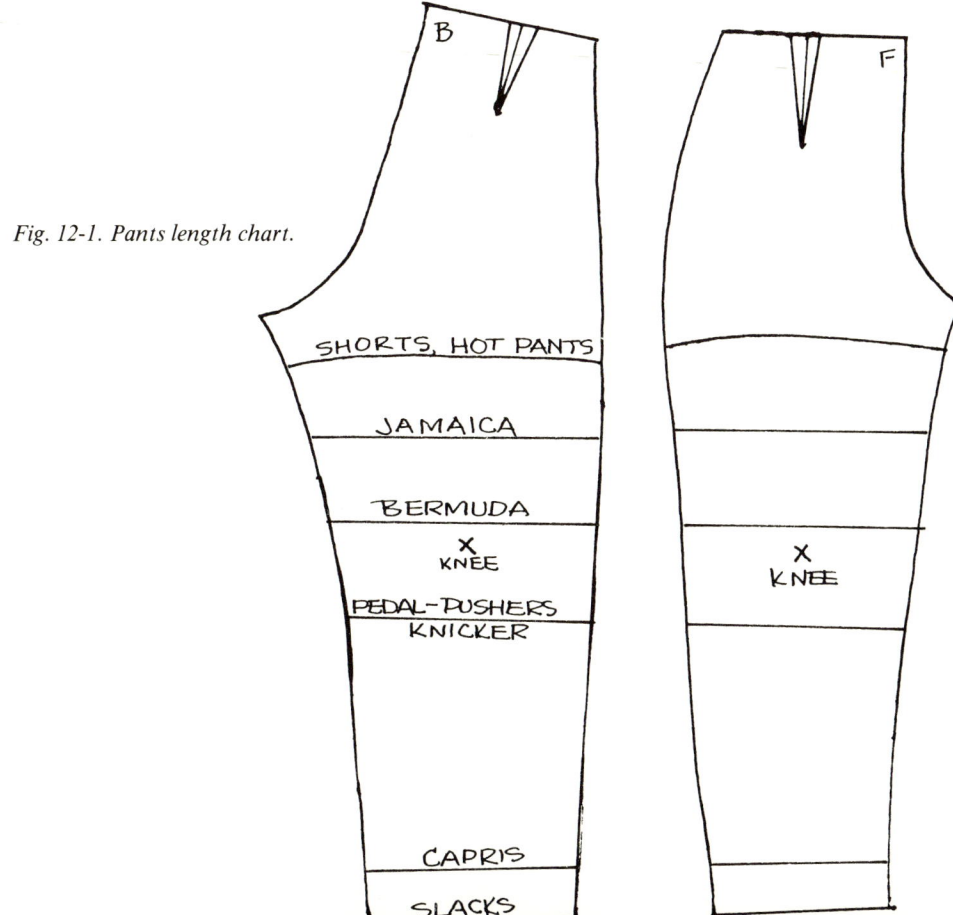

Fig. 12-1. Pants length chart.

Hip-Hugger Pants

As the name implies, the significant fact about hip huggers is that the upper edge begins at the hip rather than at the waist. Since there is often some ease in the hip area of the basic sloper, this must be removed in order to make the upper edge fit tightly (see Fig. 12-2).

STEP 1: Trace sloper (pants front and back).

STEP 2: Lower waistline 3″ to 4″. (This is not actually to the hip but is far enough to give the proper appearance.) (see Fig. 12-3).

STEP 3: Increase upper edges of dart to remove ease in this area and to make upper edge of pants hug the body (see Fig. 12-3).

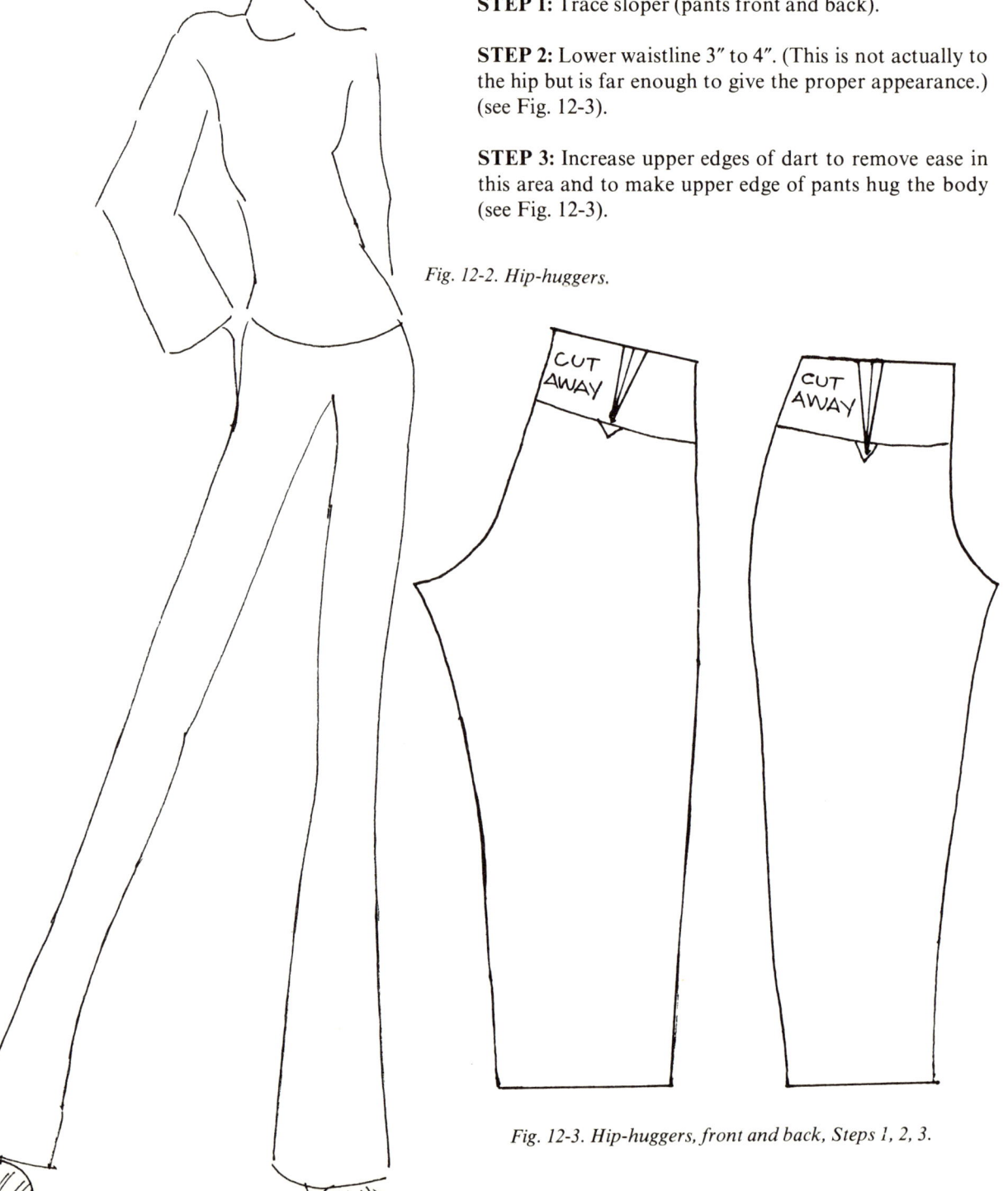

Fig. 12-2. Hip-huggers.

Fig. 12-3. Hip-huggers, front and back, Steps 1, 2, 3.

203 PANTS

Flared or Bell-Bottom Pants

The lower edge of pants may be flared any amount desired to create a new design. Bell-bottoms are flared from below the knee. They are an adaptation of the sailor uniform of historical note. The illustration shows the technique for flaring the bottom of trousers. The student should realize that this can be accomplished in a variety of places on the pants leg and with a variety of amounts of flare (see Fig. 12-4).

STEP 1: Trace sloper (pants front and back).

STEP 2: Draw in new design lines; draw a line up the center of the pants leg to the point from which you desire the flare to stem; in this example point X is placed at the knee.

Draw arrows to each side of pants leg from the center point X (see Fig. 12-5).

Fig. 12-4. Bell-bottom trousers.

Fig. 12-5. Bell-bottom trousers, Steps 1, 2.

THE COMPLETE GUIDE TO PATTERN-MAKING 204

STEP 3: Cut from lower edge to point X and over to each side seam; do not cut through the side and crotch seams (see Fig. 12-6).

STEP 4: Spread and add paper; spread each piece the same amount (see Fig. 12-6).

STEP 5: Smooth lower edge with help of a curve stick or Dietzgen curve (see Fig. 12-6).

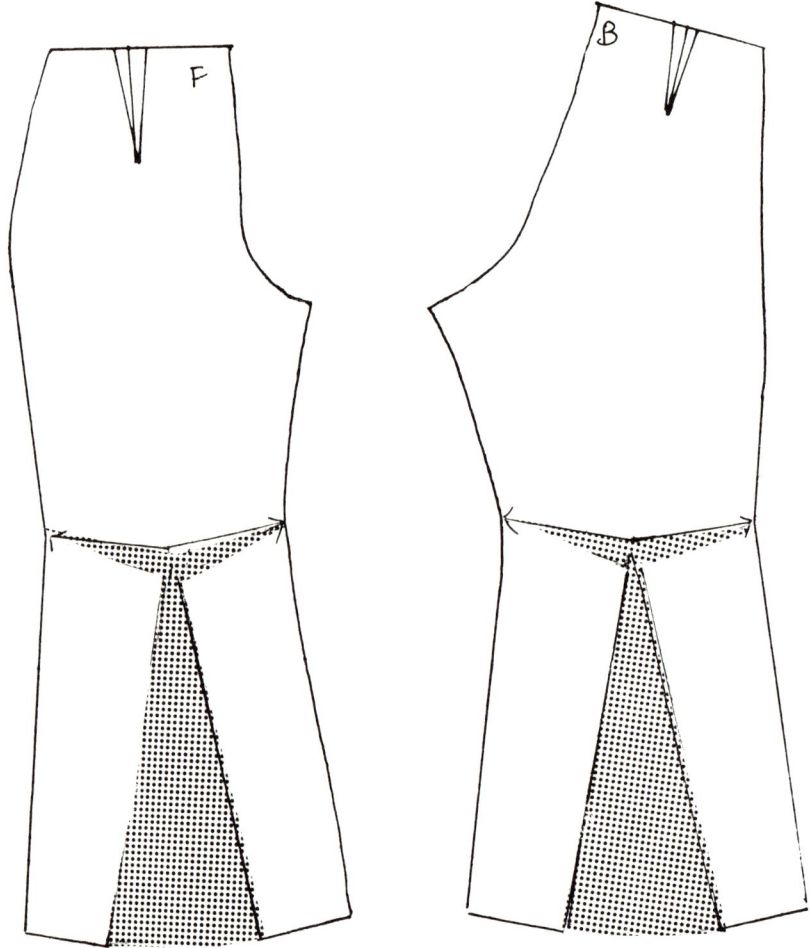

Fig. 12-6. Bell-bottom trousers, Steps 3, 4, 5.

Western-Style Slacks

Western-style slacks have a crotch reinforcement and hip pockets in the front. The crotch reinforcement serves to make the pants longer wearing when extensive horse-riding is done (see Fig. 12-7).

STEP 1: Trace sloper (pants front and back).

STEP 2: Draw in new design lines; draw in crotch reinforcement in pants front and back as shown.

Draw in pocket placement, outlining upper edge and with dotted lines showing pocket bag length (see Fig. 12-8).

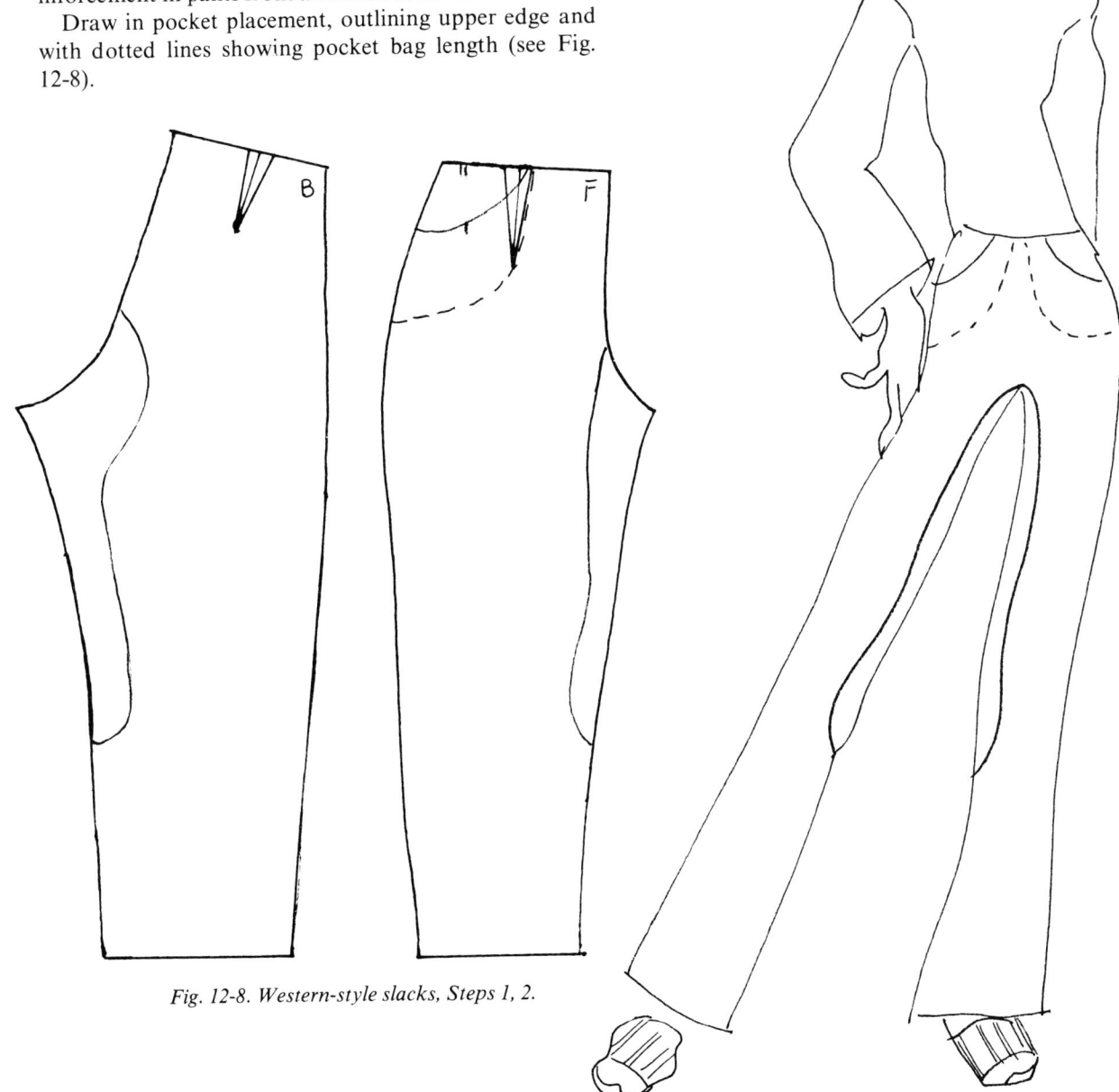

Fig. 12-7. Western-style slacks.

Fig. 12-8. Western-style slacks, Steps 1, 2.

STEP 3: Trace crotch reinforcement pieces for pants front and back; put them together on inseam; this will be sewn on as a patch without additional inseam (see Fig. 12-9).

STEP 4: Trace pocket pieces, facing, and pocket bag; a square patch pocket may be added to the pants back (see Fig. 12-10).

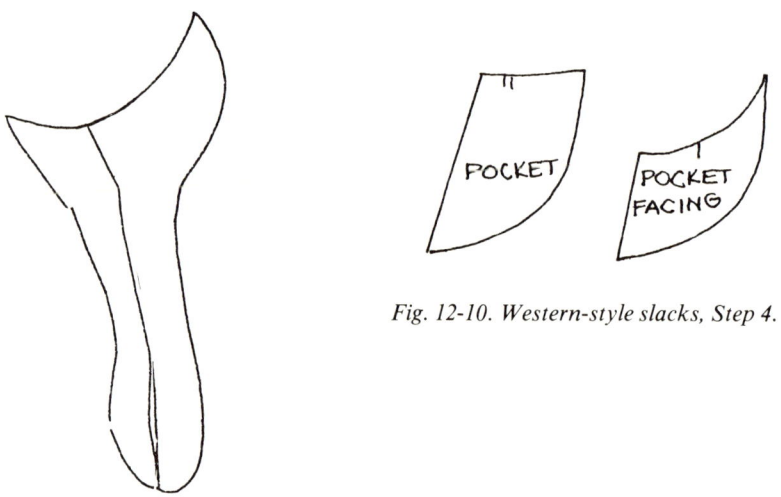

Fig. 12-10. Western-style slacks, Step 4.

Fig. 12-9. Western-style slacks, Step 3.

Pants with Yoke at Hip

Pants can have a yoke, the same as skirts and bodices. The most common yoke in pants is one passing below the lower edge of the darts, usually with curves or points at the center front and center back (see Fig. 12-11).

STEP 1: Trace sloper (pants front and back).

STEP 2: Draw in new design lines; draw yoke in pants front and back, making certain it is the same width on front and back at side seam (see Fig. 12-12).

STEP 3: Cross-notch.

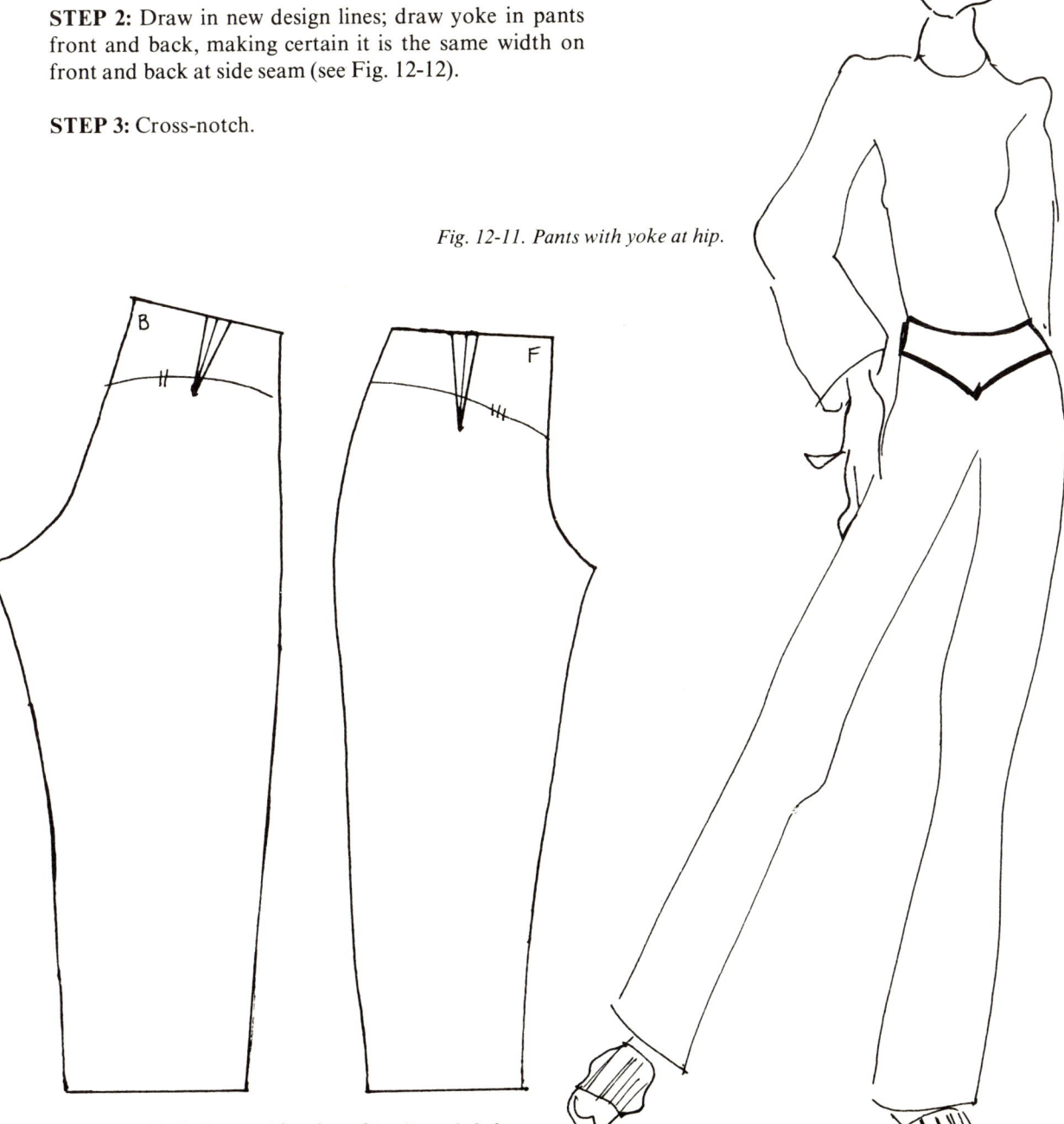

Fig. 12-11. Pants with yoke at hip.

Fig. 12-12. Pants with yoke at hip, Steps 1, 2, 3.

STEP 4: Fold out darts (see Fig. 12-13).

STEP 5: Cut off yoke (see Fig. 12-13).

STEP 6: If the yoke stops above the lower edge of dart, ease the remaining section of dart onto the yoke (see Fig. 12-13).

Fig. 12-13. Pants with yoke at hip, Steps 4, 5, 6.

Slacks with Front Pleats and Cuffs

Traditional trousers have added ease in the front, have straight legs, and are finished at the lower edge with a cuff (see Fig. 12-14).

STEP 1: Trace sloper (pants front and back).

STEP 2: Draw in new design lines; draw line through center of dart in front to lower edge of front (see Fig. 12-15).

STEP 3: Cross-notch.

Fig. 12-14. Slacks with front pleat and cuff.

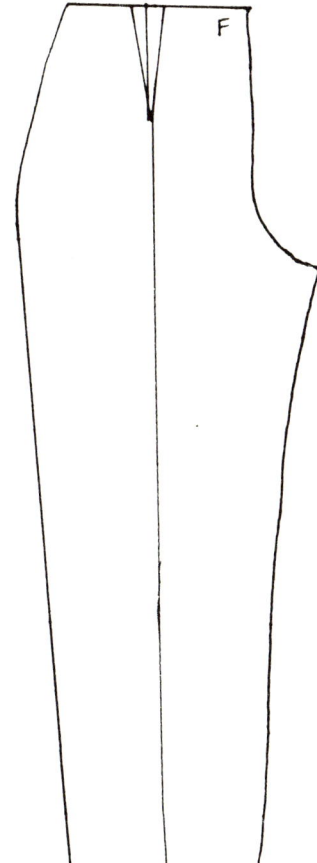

Fig. 12-15. Slacks with front pleat and cuff, Steps 1, 2, 3.

THE COMPLETE GUIDE TO PATTERN-MAKING 210

STEP 4: Cut on this line, and separate 1" or more depending upon amount of added ease desired (see Fig. 12-16).

STEP 5: Straighten leg panels; on side seams, add enough from hip to lower edge to allow pants leg to hang straight from hip to hem (see Fig. 12-16).

STEP 6: Add cuff; determine width of cuff desired; add twice this amount to lower edge of pants to allow for cuff and facing (see Fig. 12-16).

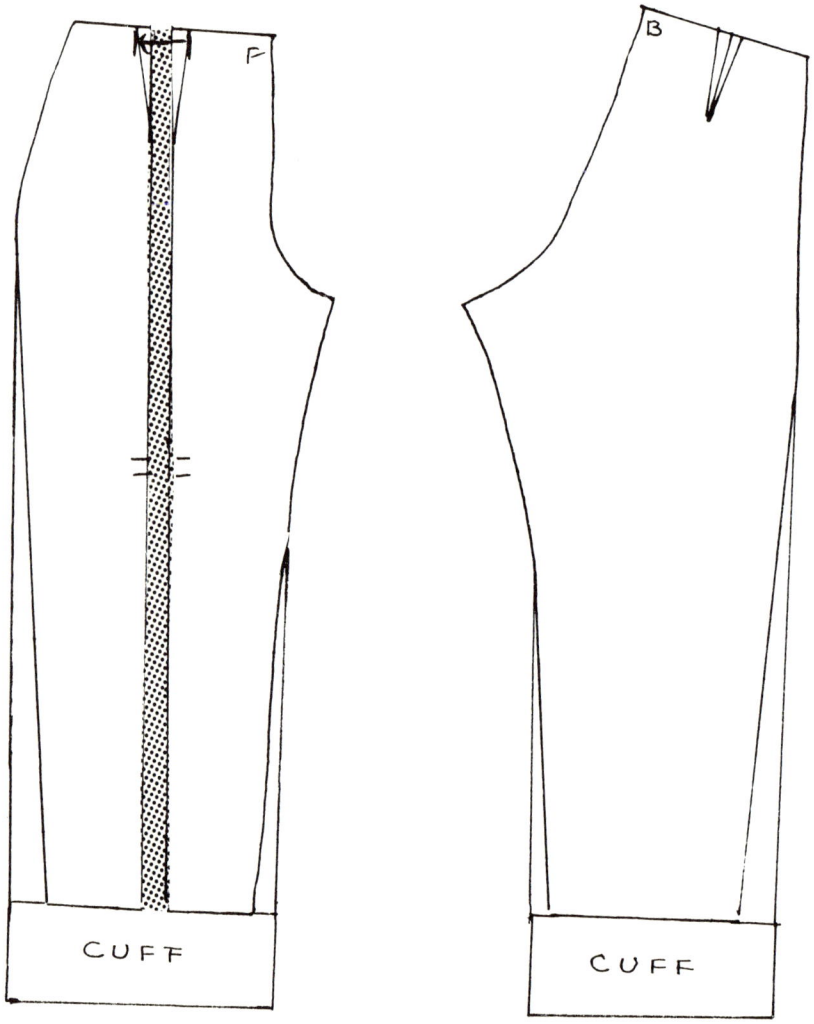

Fig. 12-16. Slacks with front pleat and cuff, Steps 4, 5, 6.

Pants with Leg Fullness

Pants with a fullness at the lower edge that stems from the waistline can be left to hang freely as in those termed hostess-style or palazzo pants, or they can be gathered to a band or elastic as in harem pants (see Fig. 12-17).

STEP 1: Trace sloper (pants front and back).

STEP 2: Draw in new design lines; draw lines from lower edge to waist, across width of pants leg; one line must go to lower edge of dart (see Fig. 12-18).

STEP 3: Fold out darts.

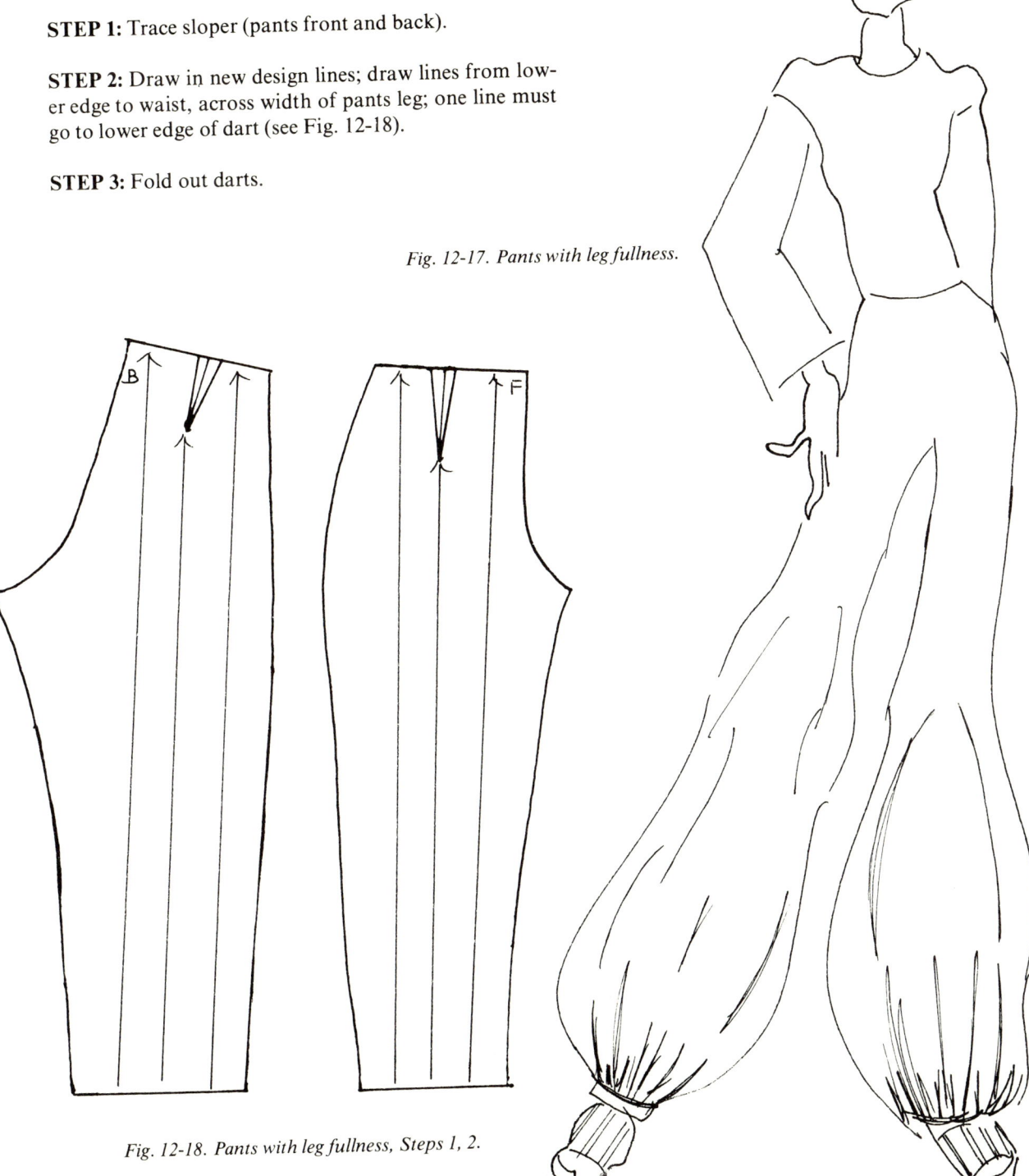

Fig. 12-17. Pants with leg fullness.

Fig. 12-18. Pants with leg fullness, Steps 1, 2.

THE COMPLETE GUIDE TO PATTERN-MAKING 212

STEP 4: Cut from lower edge to waist edge; do not cut through waist edge (see Fig. 12-19).

STEP 5: Spread amount desired; add paper.

STEP 6: Smooth lower edge with help of a curve stick or Dietzgen curve (see Fig. 12-19).

STEP 7: If pants legs are to be gathered onto a band, write word "gather" across lower pants leg.

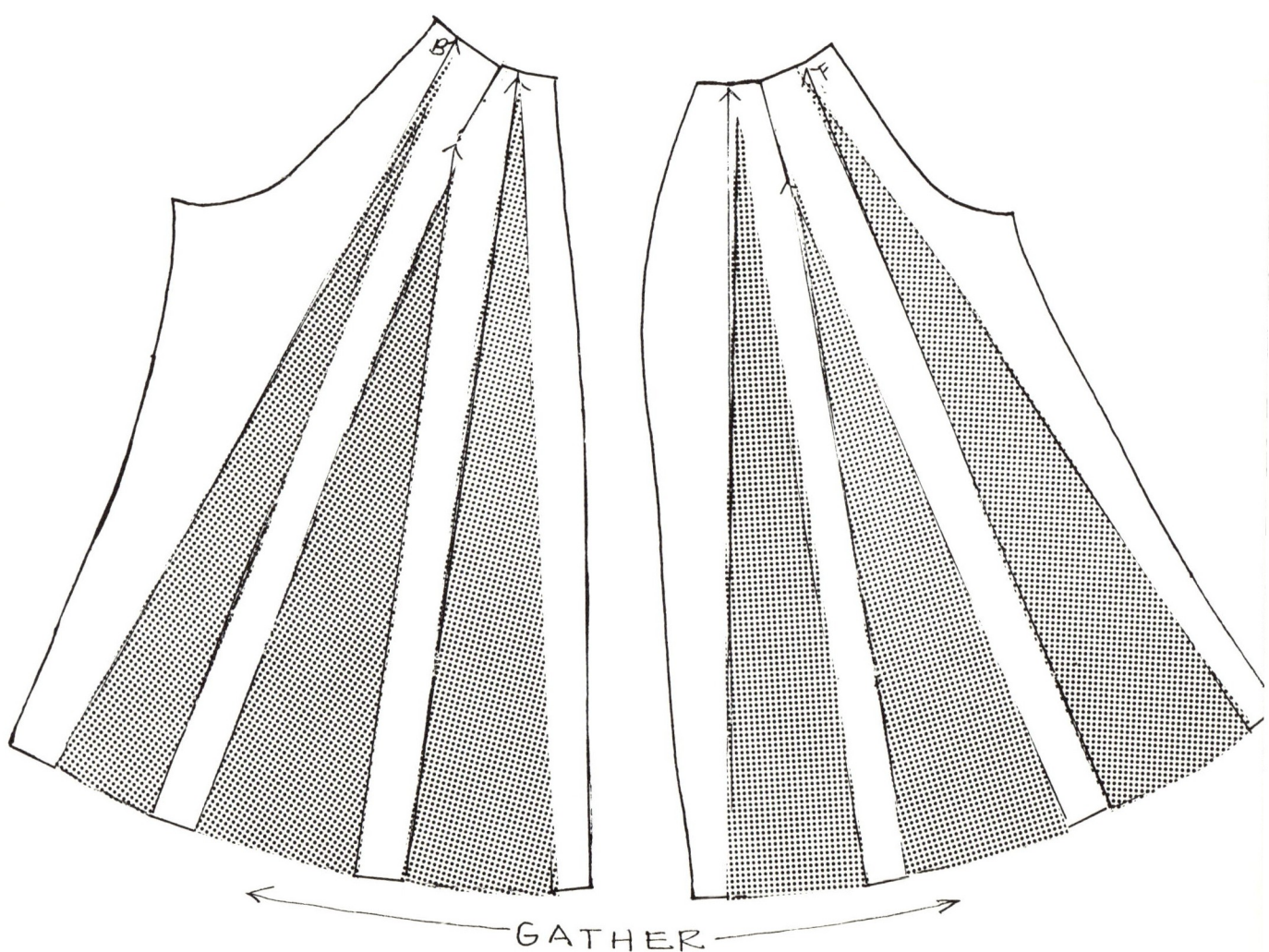

Fig. 12-19. Pants with leg fullness, Steps 3, 4, 5, 6, 7.

213 PANTS

Points of Leg Flare for Pants

This diagram shows the various points at which flare may begin on the pants leg. Pants so flared are given various names, such as elephant legs, trumpet, and so forth, according to fashion's dictates (see Fig. 12-20).

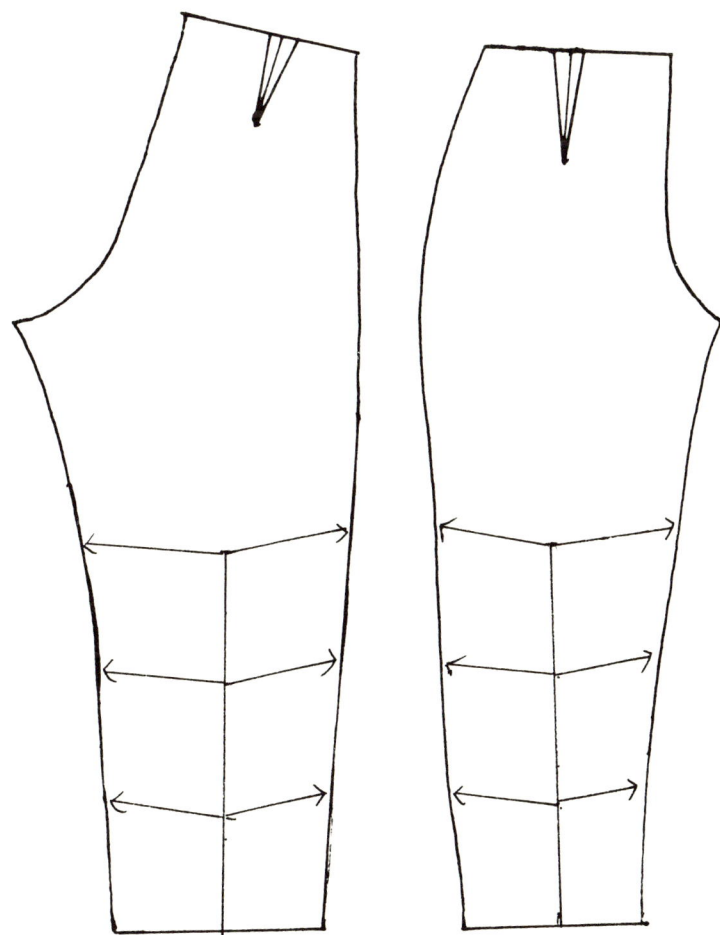

Fig. 12-20. Points of pants leg flare.

THE COMPLETE GUIDE TO PATTERN-MAKING 214

Jumpsuit Pants

The jumpsuit is a combination of pants and bodice. Jumpsuits can be designed in an infinite number of ways, but the principles will remain the same for any one. This example shows a jumpsuit with a lowered neckline, camisole-style top, and straight pants legs (see Fig. 12-21).

Fig. 12-21. Jumpsuit.

215 PANTS

STEP 1: Trace patterns (bodice front and back; pants front and back).

STEP 2: Put bodice front to pants front, adjusting darts as for sheath dress; put bodice back to pants back, adjusting darts as for sheath dress (see Fig. 12-22).

STEP 3: Draw in new design lines; lower neckline; square off armhole to make camisole-style top.

STEP 4: Cross-notch.

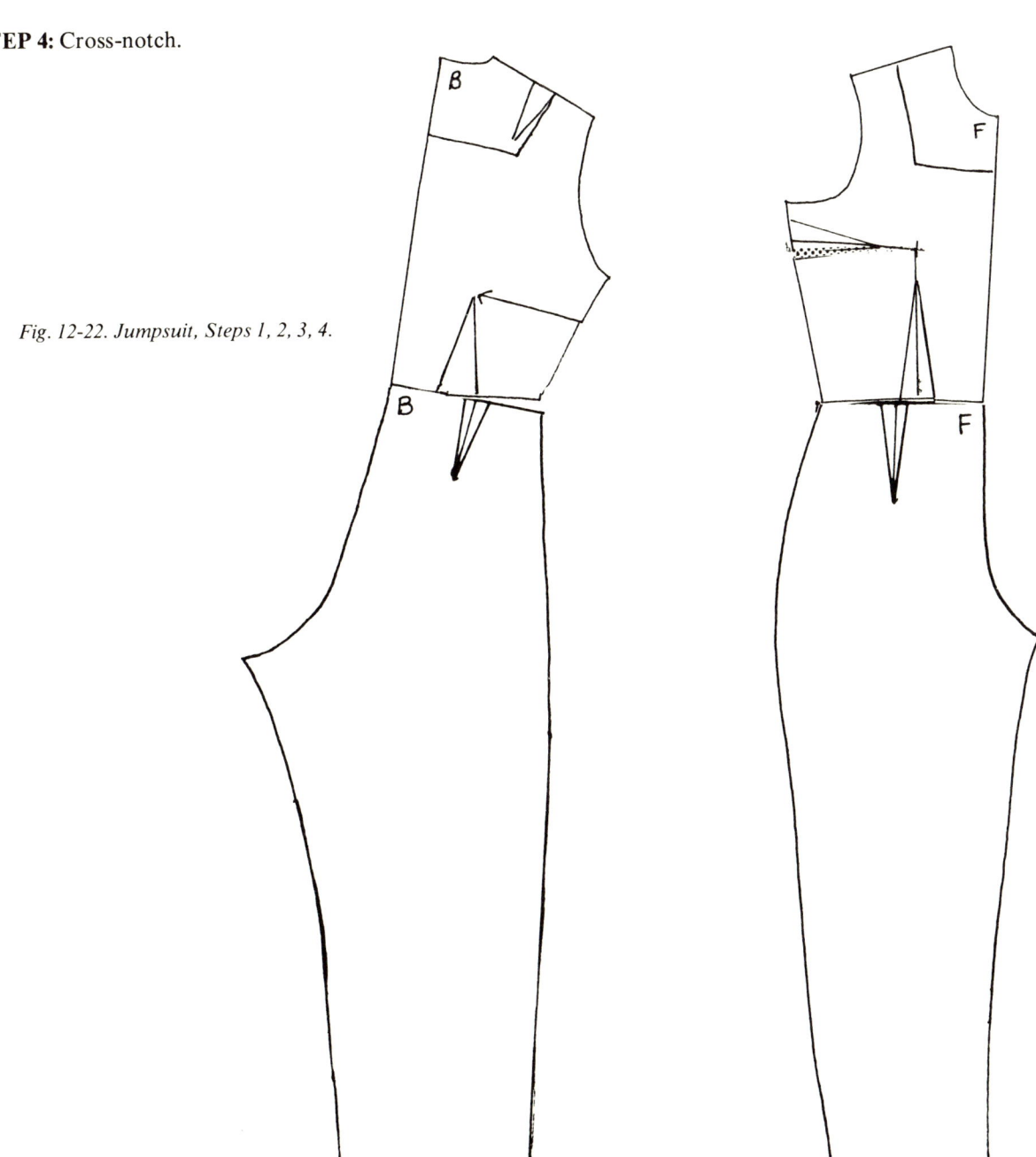

Fig. 12-22. Jumpsuit, Steps 1, 2, 3, 4.

THE COMPLETE GUIDE TO PATTERN-MAKING 216

STEP 5: Cut on new design lines (see Fig. 12-23).

STEP 6: Add paper for new darts; fold out new dart; cut points or ends (see Fig. 12-23).

Fig. 12-23. Jumpsuit, Steps 5, 6.

CHAPTER **XIII**

PUTTING IT ALL TOGETHER

You have now completed all the basic steps required in flat-pattern-making. It is now possible for you to see and make a complete garment. This may be a design you have created yourself or it may be a copy of a design from a magazine or clothing store.

Follow the basic steps required for each portion of the design. First, analyze what segments are included in the garment. Next, copy the sloper pieces required, and last, make the pattern according to the procedures you have learned.

For the example in this book, a historic garment has been chosen as the completed garment. This was done so that you would not react to the possibility of using this design for yourself, but would view it in purely objective terms. The dress is one shown in *Le Moniteur de la Mode* in 1892.

The dress has a yoke in the bodice which crosses the bust line. A modified sheath completes the lower portion of the garment, the left side having a button placket opening covering the dart. Leg o'mutton sleeves and a high turtle-neck collar complete the style (see Fig. 13-1). (The lace fichu at the neck would not require a pattern.)

Fig. 13-1. 1892 Ladies' dress. After Le Moniteur de la mode.

THE COMPLETE GUIDE TO PATTERN-MAKING 218

STEP 1: Trace sloper (bodice front and back; skirt front and back; sleeve required) (see Figs. 13-2, 13-3).

STEP 2: Draw in yoke in bodice front and back; cross-notch yoke (see Figs. 13-2, 13-3).

STEP 3: Fold out bust dart in bodice front; cut on new design lines (see Fig. 13-4).

STEP 4: Match lower portion of bodice front with skirt front; cut on waist dart line, and fold out so that waist dart of bodice matches waist dart of skirt (see Fig. 13-4).

STEP 5: Match bodice back and skirt back (see Figs. 13-4, 13-5).

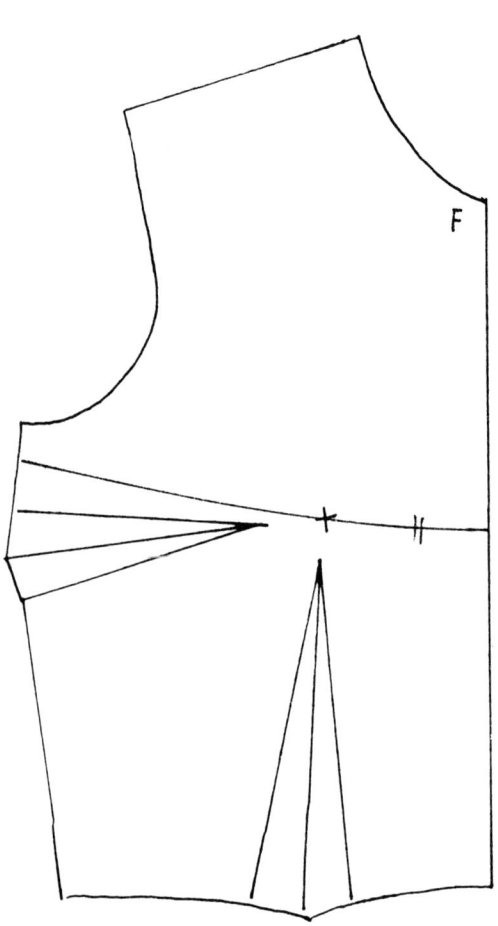

Fig. 13-2. 1892 Ladies' dress, Steps 1, 2.

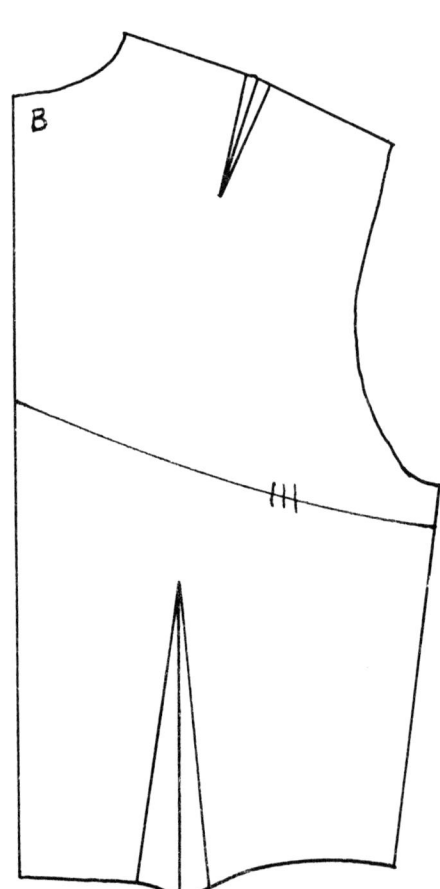

Fig. 13-3. 1892 Ladies' dress, Steps 1, 2.

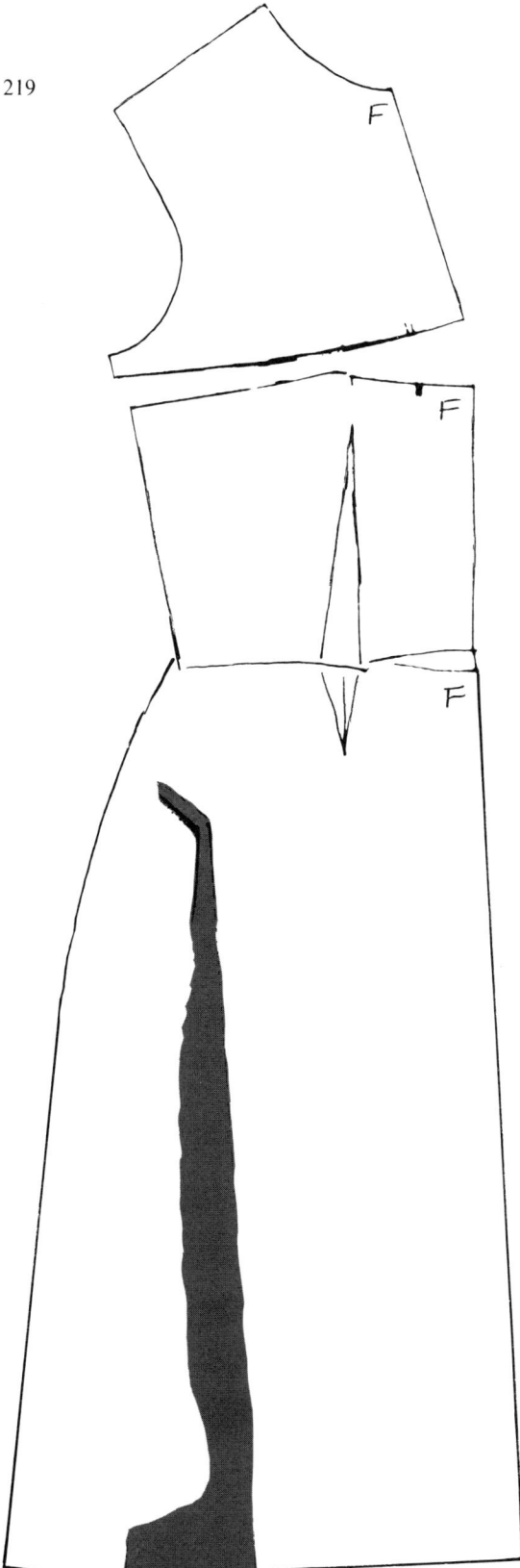

Fig. 13-4. 1892 Ladies' dress, Steps 3, 4, 5.

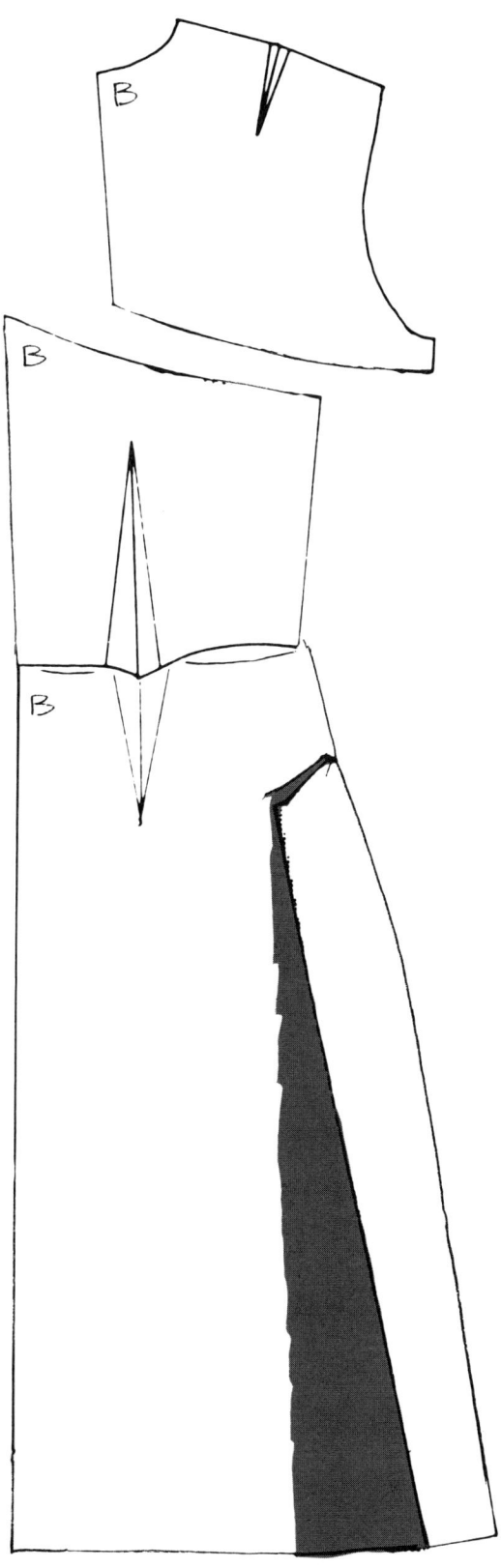

Fig. 13-5. 1892 Ladies' dress, Step 5.

THE COMPLETE GUIDE TO PATTERN-MAKING 220

STEP 6: Draw line for skirt flare on skirt front and back; cut and spread desired amount (see Figs. 13-6, 13-7).

STEP 7: Develop leg o'mutton sleeve by drawing in new design lines across sleeve cap; cut on new design lines, and spread (see Figs. 13-8, 13-9).

STEP 8: Develop collar by measuring neck edge and making rectangular piece desired width; the grain will be on the bias for this collar (see Fig. 13-10).

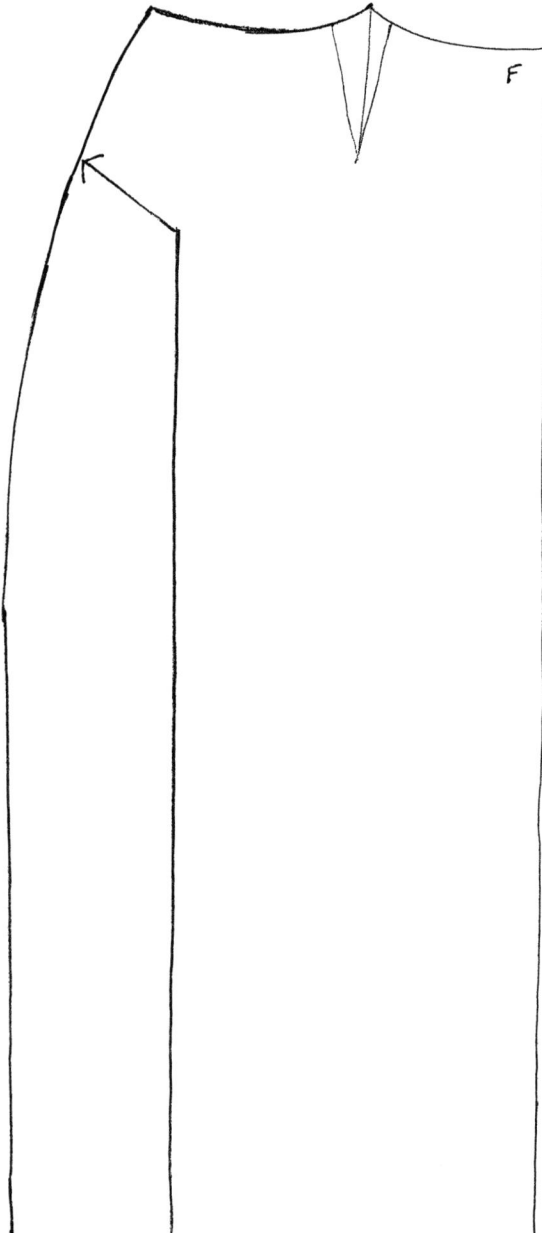

Fig. 13-6. 1892 Ladies' dress, Step 6.

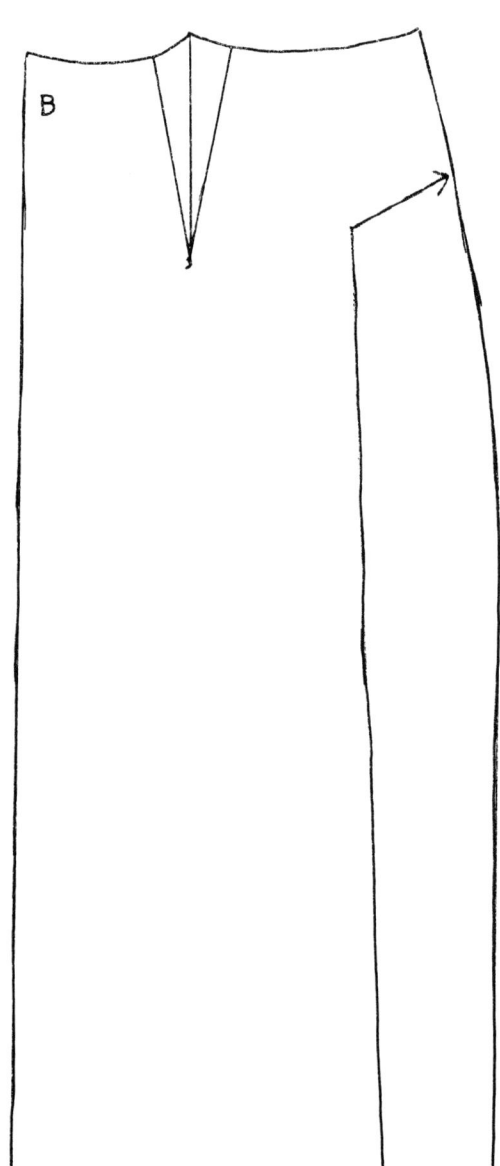

Fig. 13-7. 1892 Ladies' dress, Step 6.

221 PUTTING IT ALL TOGETHER

STEP 9: Draw dress button tab the desired width, and indicate on dress front the location for stitching tab onto garment.

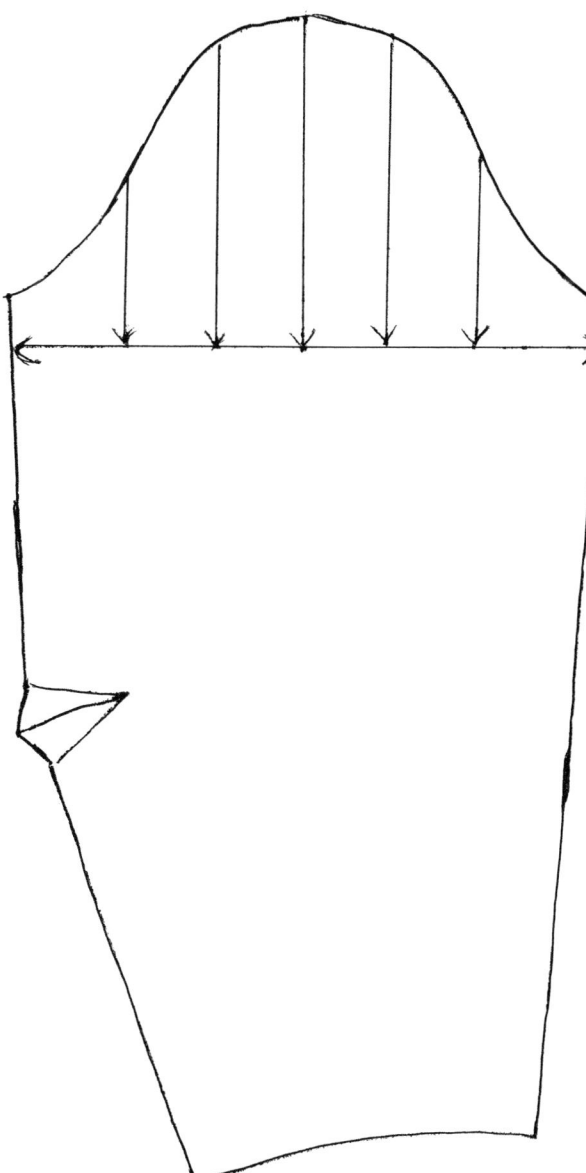

Fig. 13-8. 1892 Ladies' dress, Step 7

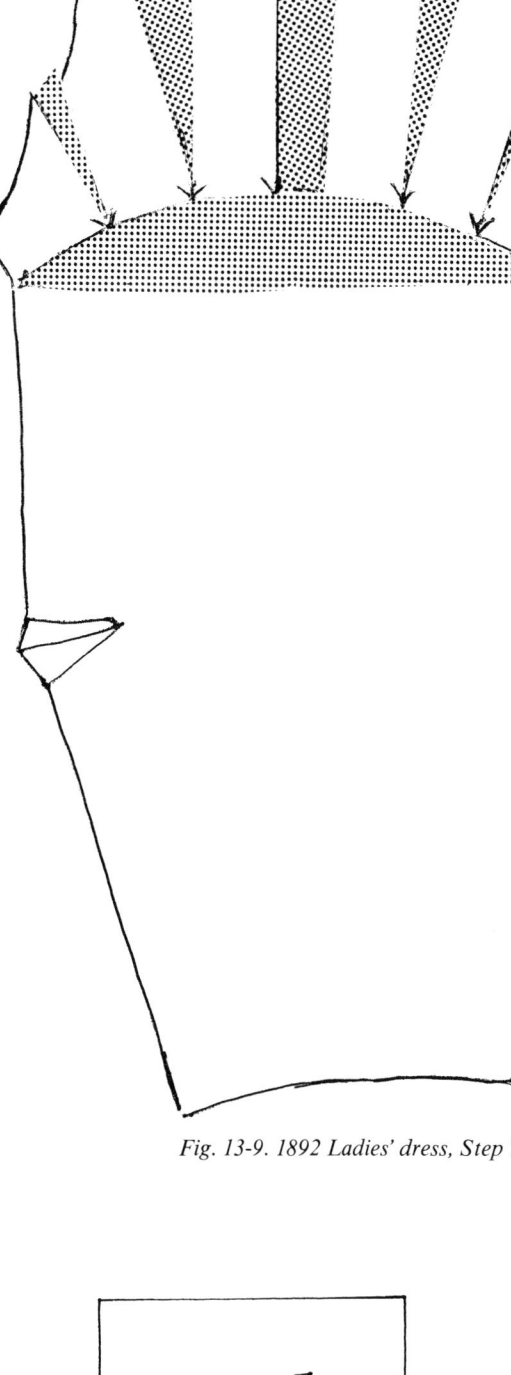

Fig. 13-9. 1892 Ladies' dress, Step 7.

Fig. 13-10. 1892 Ladies' dress, Step 8.

CHAPTER **XIV**

MAKING A PERSONALIZED SLOPER

Until now, we have been working with half-scale or quarter-scale slopers. After working through all the patterns given in the text you should now be able to make nearly any design you see or imagine. You are ready to develop a sloper to fit your own figure or that of another person whom you wish to fit.

It is easiest to begin with a commercial basic pattern. The various pattern companies all make what they call "Basic Patterns." Select the pattern that most closely resembles the half-scale or quarter-scale slopers you have been using, *i.e.,* waist and bust dart in bodice front, waist and shoulder dart in bodice back, one (or two) waist darts in straight skirt front, and (or two) waist darts in straight skirt back, one (or three) elbow darts in fitted full-length sleeve.

Cut the pattern you have chosen from a good-quality muslin, leaving 1" to 1½" seams. Do not mark darts or seams.

Beginning with the bodice front, draw in the grain lines with a pencil. If you sharpen a medium lead pencil and place it in the groove between two warp yarns, pulling down the cloth, you can draw a straight line without using a ruler. This is a more accurate way to determine the straight grain than with a ruler as the warp yarns are the straight grain (see section on grain, p. 15). Put straight lengthwise grain markings down the center front and midriff. Put crosswise grain markings across the shoulder and midriff (see Fig. 14-1).

Working with another person, and clothed in your slip and other undergarments (or a bodyshirt), stand quietly while your partner pins the muslin bodice front to you.

Pin the muslin at the shoulder, making certain the center front straight grain falls in a plumb line to the floor. Adjust the shoulder crosswise grain with an additional pin at the slip top if necessary.

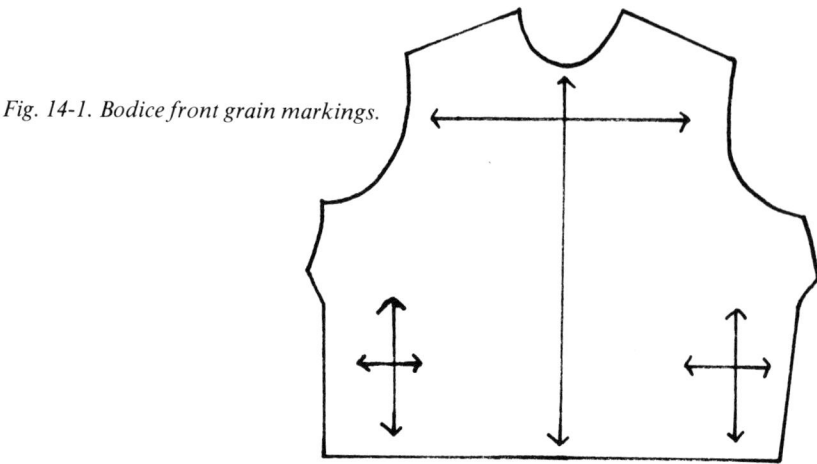

Fig. 14-1. Bodice front grain markings.

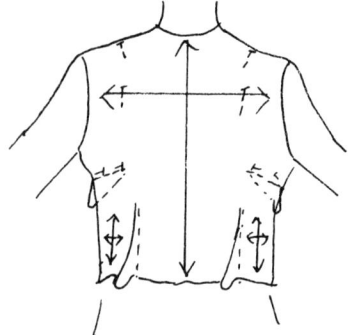

Fig. 14-2. Bodice front control darts.

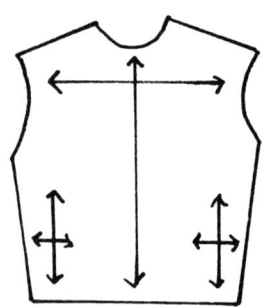

Fig. 14-3. Bodice back grain markings.

Adjust the midriff grain so that the lengthwise grain falls in a plumb line to the floor and crosswise grain is parallel to the floor. There will automatically now be two areas of excess fabric. These become the two basic darts. It is with these darts that you change the two-dimensional fabric to fit the three-dimensional figure.

Pin in these control darts, pinning to within ½" to 1" of the bust point (see Fig. 14-2).

On the bodice back mark the straight grain down the center back and in the midriff sections. Mark the crosswise grain over the shoulder and in the midriff region (see Fig. 14-3).

Pin the center back seam together. Place the muslin on the individual, pinning at the shoulder, and being certain the center back straight grain falls in a plumb line to the floor. Adjust the shoulder grain so that it falls parallel to the floor. You will now have excess fabric at the shoulder. This is for the shoulder curve and becomes the shoulder dart. Pin out this excess (see Fig. 14-4).

Adjust the midriff grain so that the lengthwise grain falls in a plumb line to the floor, and the crosswise grain is parallel to the floor. You will now have excess fabric at the waist, caused by the curve of the waist. Pin out the excess as the waist control dart.

NOTE: It will be a temptation to join this waist dart and the shoulder dart as you find you can get excess all the way up the back. Do not do this. Stop the waist dart below the shoulder blades. You need this extra bit of fullness in the back shoulder area because the arms move forward most often and cause a strain on the back of the garment. This is more of a problem when a sleeve is set in, but it even causes problems in a sleeveless dress when the dart extends too far up the back.

After completing this step, you will be able to see why the two back darts can never be combined in pattern design. In the bodice back you are dealing with two separate curves—the shoulder and the waist. In the bodice front you were dealing with one main curve—the bust—and therefore the bust darts were able to be combined.

Pin the side and shoulder seams. The shoulder seam should fall just behind the back of the ear. The side seams should be directly under the arm (see Fig. 14-5).

Remove the bodice by unpinning the center back seam, and sew up the darts and seams. Try on the bodice to be sure you have an accurate fit. If the bodice does not fit at this point, adjust until you get a fit that pleases you.

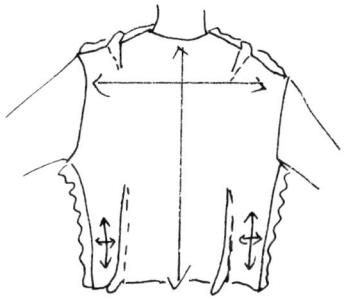

Fig. 14-4. Bodice back control darts.   *Fig. 14-5. Pin side and shoulder seams.*

Fit the skirt front next. Draw in lengthwise grain at the center front and in the side section. Draw in crosswise grain at the hip and in the side section (see Fig. 14-6).

Pin the skirt at the waist, adjusting the center front so that the lengthwise grain falls in a plumb line to the floor, and the crosswise grain at hip is parallel to the floor.

Adjust the grain lines at the side; the lengthwise grain should hang perpendicular to the floor and the crosswise grain parallel to the floor.

You will now have excess fabric between the side adjustment and the center front. This becomes the waist control dart. Fold out this dart, being sure to stop when over the stomach region. Again, it is a temptation to continue the dart on down so that you begin to curve the skirt inward under the stomach. This would result in an unattractive end-product, as you want the skirt to hang over the stomach to the floor (see Fig. 14-7).

Fit the skirt back next. Draw in the lengthwise grain at the center back and in the side section of the back. Draw in crosswise grain at the hip and in the side section (see Fig. 14-8).

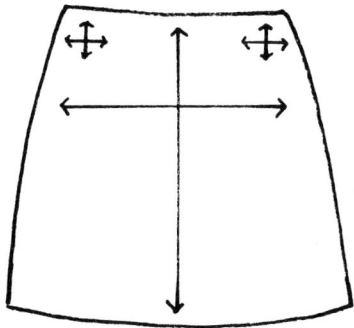 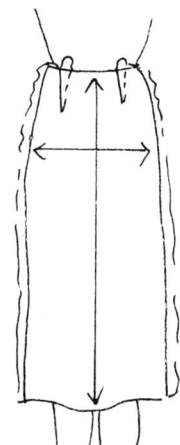 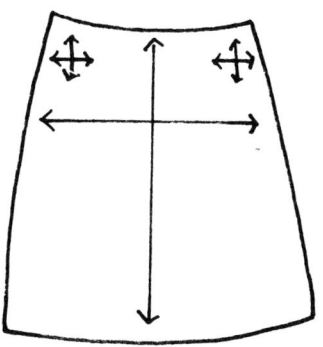

Fig. 14-6. Skirt front grain markings.   *Fig. 14-8. Skirt back grain markings.*

Fig. 14-7. Skirt front control markings.

THE COMPLETE GUIDE TO PATTERN-MAKING 226

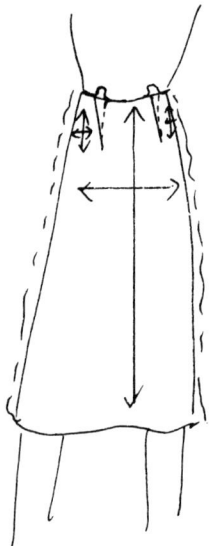

Fig. 14-9. Skirt back control dart.

Pin the skirt at waist, adjusting the center back so that the lengthwise grain falls in a plumb line to the floor, and the crosswise grain at hip is parallel to the floor.

Adjust the side grain lines so that the lengthwise grain is perpendicular to the floor, and the crosswise grain is parallel to the floor.

Again, you will have excess fabric at the waist between the side section and the center back. This becomes the back waist control dart. Stop this dart above the widest portion of the hip (see Fig. 14-9).

Pin the side seams of the skirt. You will notice that above the hip to the waist the seam will be curved. This is in lieu of another control dart and takes care of the waist curve in the hip area. The skirt should hang straight down from the widest point of the hip. Do not curve it in under the hip as this will give an exaggerated curve to the hip. Be certain the skirt side seam matches the location of the bodice side seams. Waist darts should match the waist darts of the bodice as well (see Fig. 14-10).

Remove the skirt, and sew up the darts and side seams. Try on the skirt, and be sure it fits correctly.

To secure the waist marking, place a string or other sturdy yarn around your waist when you have the bodice and skirt on. Adjust the string so that it is comfortable. Mark with a pencil both the bodice and skirt waist (see Fig. 14-11).

Remove the muslin, and sew the waist seams. Try on the garment and be sure it fits correctly.

Begin the sleeve next. Mark the lengthwise grain from the center of the sleeve cap. The grain will go straight to the elbow; at this point the sleeve will curve forward, and the grain line will seem to fall to the back. This occurs because we do not hold our arms stiffly at the side. If you let your arm hang loosely at your side, you will see that from the elbow your arm hangs forward and not straight down to the side. The pattern will therefore have straight grain to the elbow. Below that point it will hang in a plumb line to the floor, but not down the center of the sleeve pattern. The crosswise grain should be marked in the upper cap region (see Fig. 14-12).

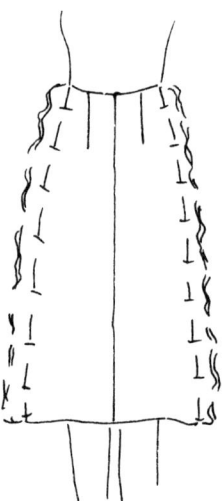

Fig. 14-10. Pin side seams.

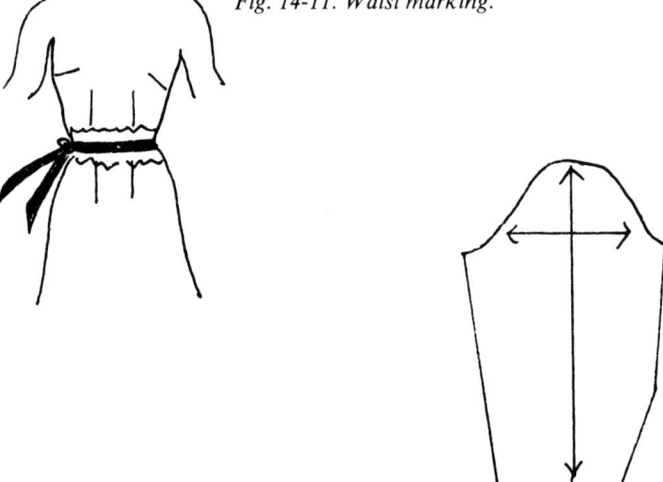

Fig. 14-11. Waist marking.

Fig. 14-12. Sleeve grain markings.

227 MAKING A PERSONALIZED SLOPER

Put an ease thread in the cap of the sleeve, and sew the underarm seam to the elbow. Pull up the ease thread and pin the sleeve on the bodice, matching the center top mark with the shoulder seam. Adjust the crosswise grain so it hangs parallel to the floor. Ease in the fullness and pin. Pin the underarm of the sleeve to the underarm of the bodice. Bend the elbow, and mark the position for the elbow dart.

Remove the bodice and stitch in the sleeve at the armhole. Stitch in the dart and remainder of the underarm seam.

Replace the bodice and mark the sleeve length. (Normally, a full-length sleeve ends just at the wrist.)

Replace the garment, and pin it up the center back. Mark the neck, the bust area, the shoulder straps (if the person usually wears a bra and slip), the top of the bra and slip (this will be helpful when designing low-cut dresses to avoid the need for special bras and other undergarments), and the skirt length. When you mark the skirt length, you may wish to make your sloper in a 'normal' or 'average', length. So many lengths are used today that one length on the sloper will not suffice so indicate on the lower edge of the sloper how much to add for a maxi, midi, below the knee, mini, micro-mini, and so forth (see Fig. 14-13).

Fig. 14-13. Bodice markings.

You are now ready to transfer your muslin to the posterboard. Buy a medium-weight posterboard, one that is not too difficult to cut and yet is sturdy enough to withstand continued use.

Separate the parts of the sloper, cutting on the seams. Remember, a sloper does not have seams and so these are cut off when you make your own sloper. Take the stitching out of the darts, and mark the seam lines with a pencil. Cut the bodice apart at the center front. Cut the skirt apart at the center front. Use one sleeve, one bodice back, one skirt back. Unless you are quite asymmetrical on the right and left sides, use only half of your garment. Only rarely is someone so differently shaped on the two sides that she needs to have a separate sloper for the right and left sides.

Press the muslin lightly, taking care not to stretch the pieces.

Begin with the bodice front. Place it on the posterboard with the center front on the cut edge. Pin it in place, again being careful not to stretch the pieces. Adjust the crosswise grain markings so that they form a right angle to the lengthwise grain markings. An L-square is quite helpful in this case. Pin lightly on the edges (see Fig. 14-1).

Trace around the edges with a pencil. Mark the darts and the bust point with pins, or put carbon paper under the muslin and use a tracing wheel to mark them. Remove the muslin and straighten the lines you have just drawn on the cardboard with a ruler, Dietzgen curve, and curve stick if necessary.

The bodice back is placed on the posterboard so that the center back is on a cut edge. Again, adjust the crosswise grain so that it is perpendicular to the lengthwise grain. Pin around the edges. Trace. Mark the darts, notches, and so forth (see Fig. 14-15).

Next transfer the skirt front and back to the posterboard. Place the pieces on the posterboard with the center front and the center back on the cut edges. Adjust the crosswise grain at the hip and side sections. Pin around edges. Trace, and mark the darts (see Fig. 14-16).

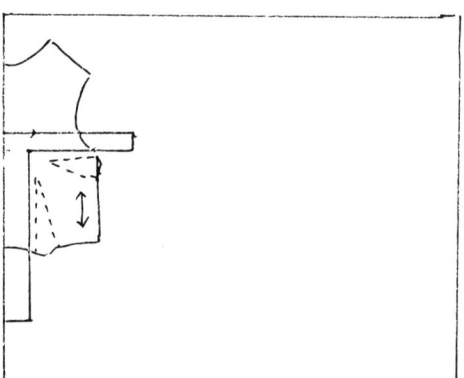

Fig. 14-14. Bodice front on posterboard.

Fig. 14-15. Bodice back on posterboard.

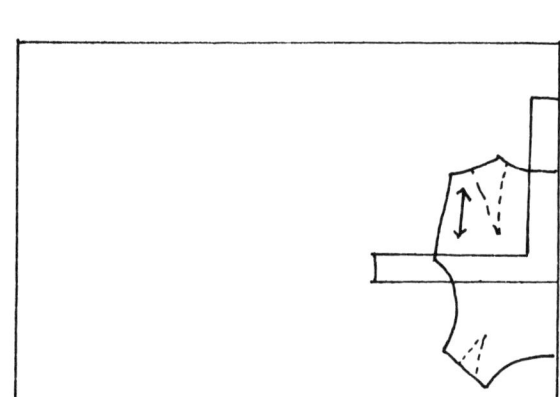

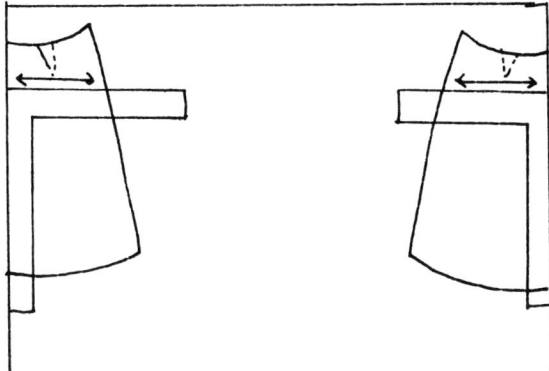

Fig. 14-16. Skirt front and back on posterboard.

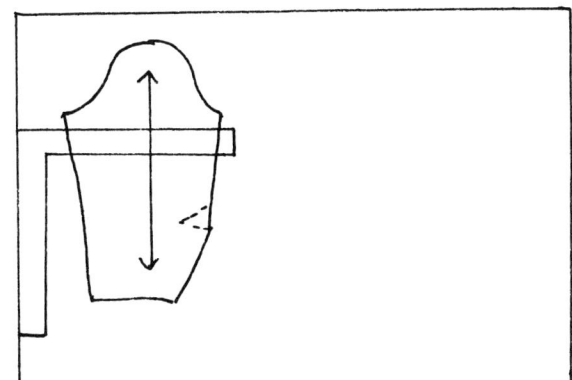

Fig. 14-17. Sleeve on posterboard.

Put the sleeve on the posterboard and adjust the lengthwise grain so that it is parallel to a cut edge. Be certain the crosswise grain is perpendicular to the lengthwise grain. Pin, trace around the edges, mark the notches, and the dart (see Fig. 14-17).

Cut out the posterboard roughly. Measure the side seams to be certain that they match front and back. Be sure the waist seams match. Check the underarm seam to see that it is the proper length. Cut out, and cut in notches.

You are now ready to begin making patterns for yourself. Anything you have done in half-scale you can do in full-scale. From the patterns you have done in half-scale, you have learned the basic principles necessary to make nearly any design you should desire. You have made this information your own and will not even need to refer to the text at this point. If you forget a point or two, it is available for your consultation.

Buy a big roll of shelf paper and begin!

CHAPTER **XV**

VARIOUS LADIES' SHAPES

The sloper that has been used in the text has darts and side curves which represent those needed for a woman with a so-called average shape. Upon the completion of your personalized sloper you may have found that your pattern pieces do not exactly resemble those used in the text. This is of course because women are not all average, and the darts and side curves must adjust to whatever shape one has.

Some common alternatives to the average ladies' shape are presented in this section. Refer to Chapter VII for alternate skirt shapes (see Fig. 15-1).

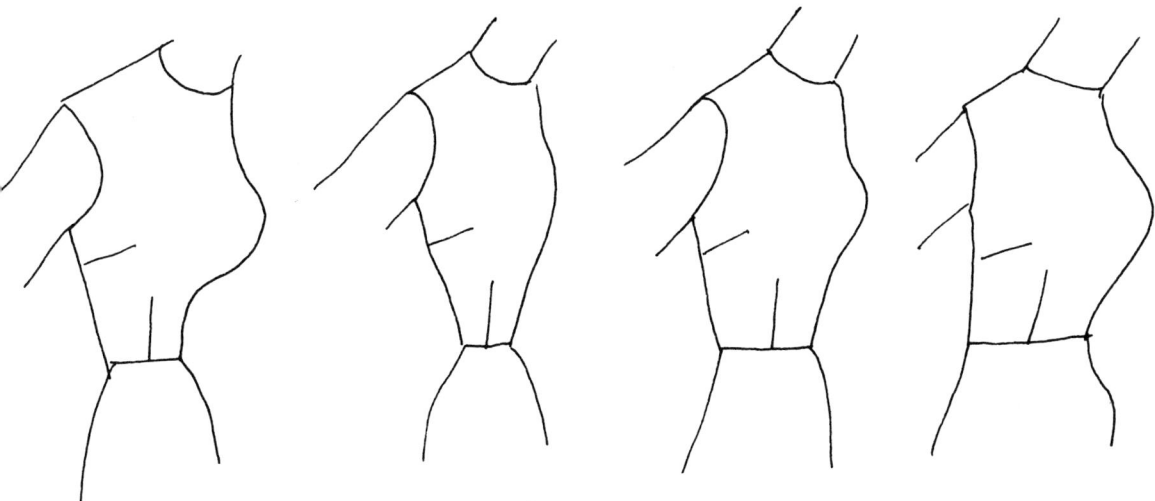

Fig. 15-1. Various Ladies' Shapes: (left to right) large bust, small waist; small bust, small waist; normal, or average; large bust, large waist.

For a large bust and a small waist, the curves are very great and therefore the darts must be large. There is more area to cover, because of the large bust, and so the area denoted by the dots must be larger. The fabric must be curved in more because of the small waist, and the ends of the darts become broadly spaced to compensate (see Fig. 15-2).

For a small bust and a small waist, very little curve is needed. The third dimension is small, and the size of the darts is therefore small. The bust area, denoted by dotted lines, is correspondingly small. The pattern is as broad at the shoulder as the first one, but the shape below the armhole is quite different (see Fig. 15-3).

For the so-called normal figure, the pattern appears with a curve between the previous two. Normal, or average, sizes are determined by the National Bureau of Standards by measuring a large number of people. A mean proportion is then determined. Pattern companies and clothing manufacturers usually use these measurements to develop their slopers (see Fig. 15-4).

The person with a large bust and large waist needs a large dart to secure extra fabric for covering the bust. However, the side section will come straight down to

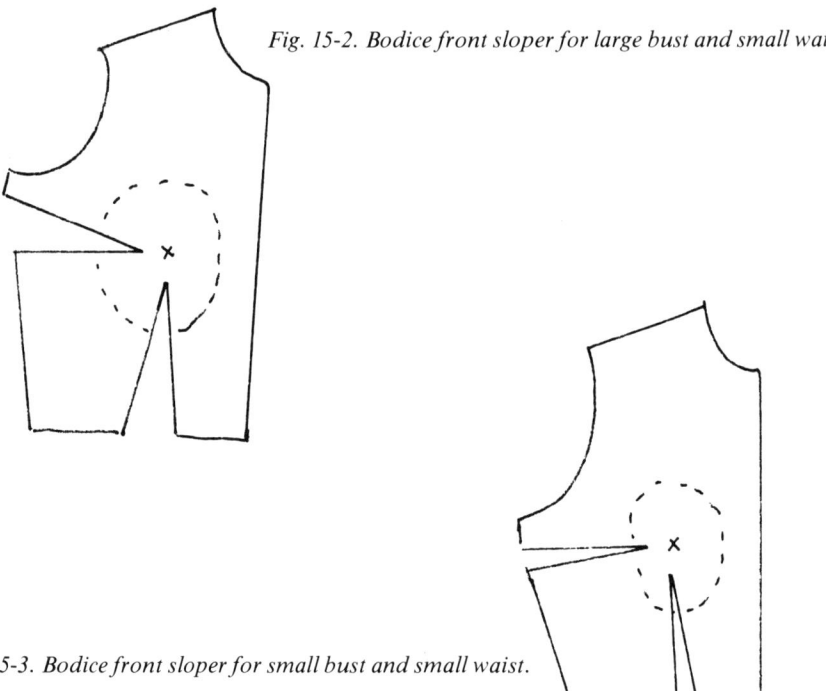

Fig. 15-2. Bodice front sloper for large bust and small waist.

Fig. 15-3. Bodice front sloper for small bust and small waist.

give extra fabric at the waist edge. The bust area denoted by the dotted circle is as large as for the first illustration (see Fig. 15-5).

The illustrations in the text use the normal, or average, dart combination. When the patterns are done in full-size to fit a specific person, the processes will be the same. The only varying factor will be the size and shape of the darts.

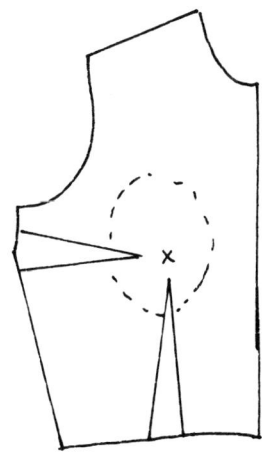

Fig. 15-4. Bodice front for normal figure.

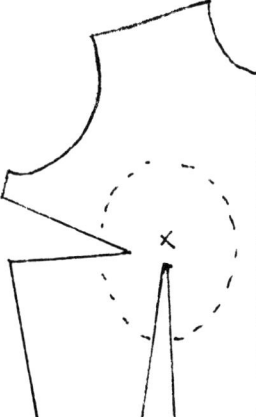

Fig. 15-5. Bodice front for large bust and large waist.

CHAPTER **XVI**

PERSONALIZED SLOPER FOR SLACKS

Select a basic slacks pattern, preferably one that fits your figure and hangs with straight legs (not tapered or flared).

Cut the pants out of a good-quality muslin, leaving at least 2" extra on all edges for fitting. Do not mark the darts or the seams.

Beginning with the pants front, draw in the grain lines with a pencil, carefully following the grain of the fabric. Do this on the right side of the fabric. Work with the right side out throughout. Put the straight lengthwise grain markings down the center and at the side of the pieces. Put the crosswise grain markings at the hip line (see Fig. 16-1).

Match the back and front crotch seams, and sew the inner leg seam, or inseam.

You now have only the waist and side seams to adjust to your figure, which includes front and back darts.

Working with another person, stand comfortably while the slacks are fit to you.

Begin the fitting by pinning the center front and the center back waist to your undergarments. (A bodyshirt or leotard makes an excellent undergarment to wear while you are being fitted.) Adjust the length of the crotch so it is comfortable. You have cut at least 2" extra at the waist and therefore you should have plenty of fabric with which to work. After pinning at your waist, sit down in the pants to be sure you have left enough room for movement (see Fig. 16-2).

Next, pin at the hip line, adjusting the crosswise grain so that it is parallel to the floor. Again, sit down and bend over to be certain you have left enough ease (see Fig. 16-3).

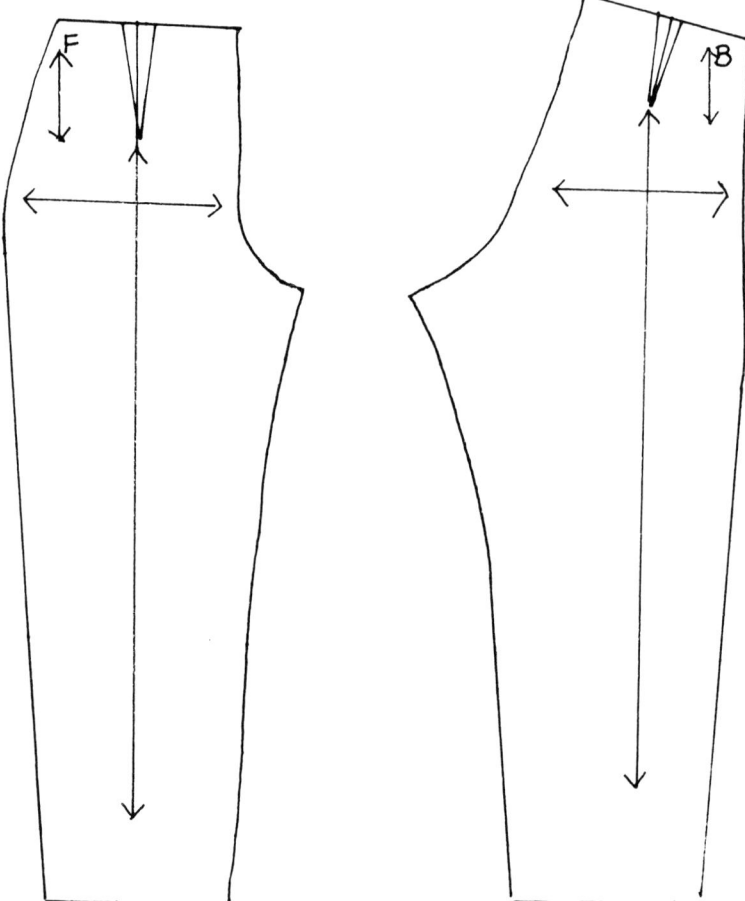

Fig. 16-1. Slacks grain markings.

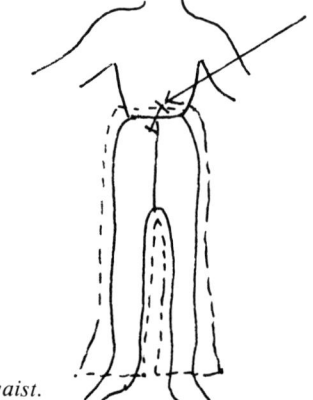

Fig. 16-2. Pin slacks at waist.

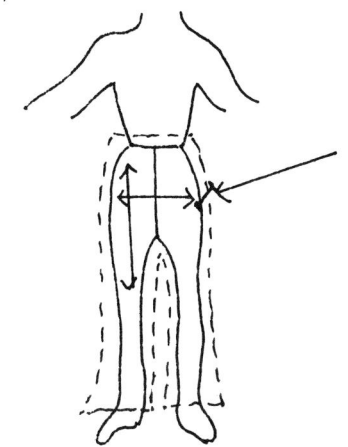

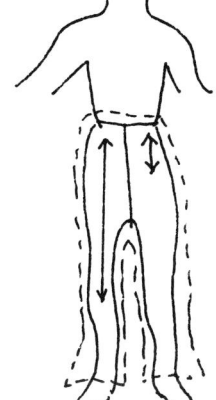

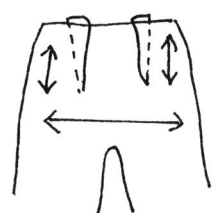

Fig. 16-4. Pin in front and back waist darts.

Fig. 16-3. Pin slacks at hip line.

Fig. 16-5. Put cord around waist.

Adjust the lengthwise grain so that it is perpendicular to the floor, and put in another pin at the waist. Adjust the lengthwise grain at your sides. The excess fabric is now pinned as a dart in both your front and back. The dart in the slacks back will be longer than in its front. The amount of difference will depend upon the curve of the derrière (see Fig. 16-4).

From the hip line, pin the slacks legs straight. (Flared and tapered variations can be worked from the basic sloper.)

Put a rope or a cord around your waist, and mark the waist location (see Fig. 16-5).

Mark the darts and side seams with a pencil or pen. Now take off the slacks. Stitch up the darts and the side seams, leaving an opening at the left side of 7″ to 9 ″.

Put the slacks back on with the seams and darts exposed. Sit, bend over, and move about in them. Check the grain lines. Make adjustments as necessary.

Mark the hems and knee locations. Take off the slacks again. Cut them apart, and remove the seam allowances, as you did previously for the basic dress.

Lightly press the slacks front and back. Be careful not to stretch the muslin.

Place the slacks thus prepared on a posterboard. Adjust the crosswise and lengthwise grain with an L-shape, T-square, or yardstick. Pin the edges lightly. Trace around the slacks. Mark the darts and the grain lines. Cut out the slacks front and back including notches, if desired (see Fig. 16-6).

This sloper method will work equally well for woven or knitted fabrics. Knits can be fit more tightly, so you may find that you can take up a ⅛" on each seam when you sew the pants together in a knit. Stretch fabrics likewise can be fitted more tightly. Take up a ⅛" on each seam when you sew the pants together.

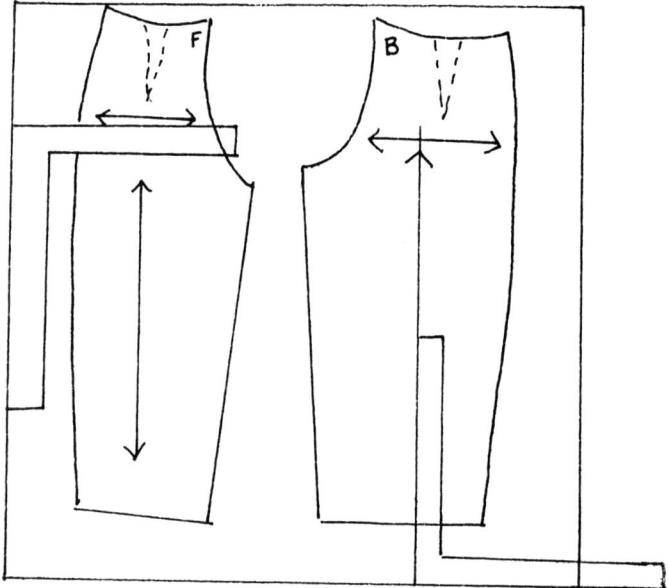

Fig. 16-6. Slacks front ane back on posterboard.

CHAPTER XVII

CHILDREN'S GARMENTS

Since the time when Western clothing was specifically designed with the child in mind, which was probably in the middle eighteenth century, children's fashion has undergone various changes in style and function. Prior to the eighteenth century, wealthy children were usually dressed as small adults. Marie Antionette is thought to be the first wealthy woman to take into account her child's activities and feelings in dressing him. She apparently allowed her child to wear trousers and a jacket for play. It took time and effort from that time until now to develop sensible and practical clothing for children.

We profess today to be interested in the individual and to provide for him in the best way possible at every stage to meet his specific needs. For children, to whom clothing is very important, this means comfortable, correctly fitting, desirable, and acceptable garments. For adults this means easy-to-care-for, attractive, appropriate clothes.

It is highly desirable, of course, that these two sets of objectives coincide. They can if some effort is made.

The children's clothing designer needs to be aware of the research in the field of clothing sociology. He needs to be aware that research shows that infants and toddlers do not like restrictive clothes. He needs to be aware of the fact that most children at around age two are undergoing toilet training. At this time it is most important that the child be able to get his clothes out of the way and get himself onto the toilet with a minimum amount of trouble and fuss. In walking through the toddlers' section of children's stores one finds the most respected children's clothing designers turning out one-piece outfits for little boys and girls which button at the shoulder. What could be more impractical for a child at this important stage of his development?

When the child is a preschooler (2-6) he has a growing interest in his clothes. At this time clothes are a means to elicit favorable attention, a means to imaginative role playing, and a means to secure peer approval.

For example, recent research studies have shown that children one, two, and even three years old enjoy small decorative details on their garments which they can see and feel. Placing a little embroidered flower or similar object on a pocket or far enough down on a shirt or bodice front for the child to see will give the child great pleasure. Decorative details placed in locations where the child can neither see nor feel them may give the viewer pleasure, but probably not the child.

At the preschool age, the child is also learning to dress himself and should be encouraged to do this by providing clothes that are easy for him to get on and off.

The child's clothing designer is encouraged to read the results of research in *Clothing: A Study in Human Behavior* by Mary Shaw Ryan (Holt, Rinehart and Winston, 1966).

The garments presented in this section reflect some traditional children's styles for the child from ages 1 to 6. Slopers for bodices, sleeves, and slacks are included.

The chart of children's garment lengths is helpful in designing for children. Refer to this when developing styles.

CHILDREN'S GARMENT LENGTHS

Garment, where measured	Size (number)					
	2	3	4	5	6	6X
Coat, at center back	17½	19	20½	22	23½	25
Dress, at center back	17	18½	20	21½	23	24½
Bottom of dress falls above knee (approx.)	2	2	2	2½	2½	2½
Skirt, at center back	10	11	12	13	14	15
Distance garment extends above waist height	1¾	1	¾	½	½	½
Bottom of skirt falls, above knee (approx.)	2½	2	2	2	2	2
Slacks, out seam, including waistband	20	21½	23½	25½	27½	29
Distance garment extends above waist height	1¾	1	¾	½	½	½
Bottom of slacks, clearance above soles of feet	1	1	1	1	1	1

Length in inches

For children's garments, use the full-size (1-6) slopers on pp. 274-279. Illustrations in this chapter are quarter-scale.

The shirts, coat, and pants can be used for either girls or boys.

To develop slopers for older children purchase a commercial basic pattern in the correct size and fit a muslin as described for women, pp. 223-230.

Child's Dress with Smocking

This traditional girl's dress has a yoke in front and back, smocking in front and back, short puffed sleeves, a Peter Pan collar, and a button band down the center front (see Fig. 17-1).

STEP 1: Trace sloper (bodice front and back; sleeve).

STEP 2: Draw line across bodice front and bodice back for yoke; cross-notch; cut apart (see Fig. 17-2).

STEP 3: Draw lines through width of lower front and back; cut through; add paper to three times original width (see Fig. 17-2).

Fig. 17-1. Child's dress with smocking.

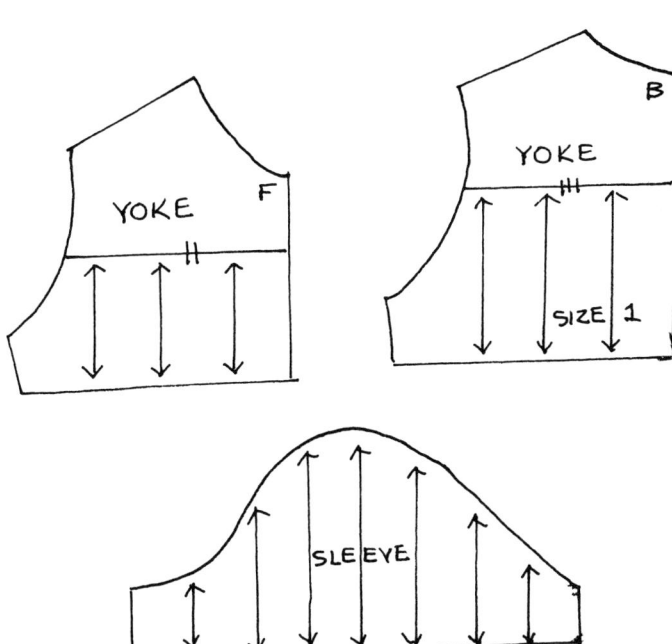

Fig. 17-2. Child's dress with smocking, Steps 1, 2, 3.

THE COMPLETE GUIDE TO PATTERN-MAKING 242

STEP 4: Lengthen sides to full skirt length (see Fig. 17-3).

STEP 5: Develop full puffed sleeve (see Fig. 17-4).

STEP 6: Develop Peter Pan collar (see Fig. 17-5).

STEP 7: Cut button extension off dress and yoke fronts; double width of extension for fold at outer edge (see Fig. 17-6).

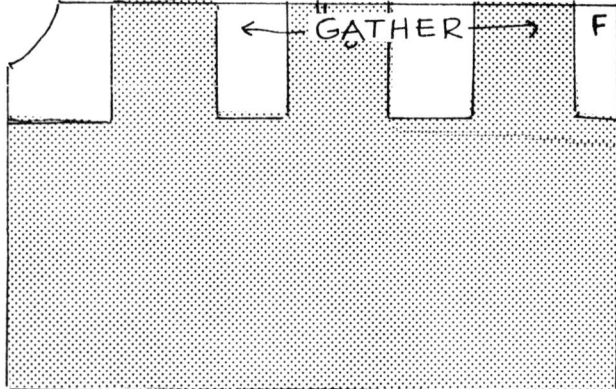

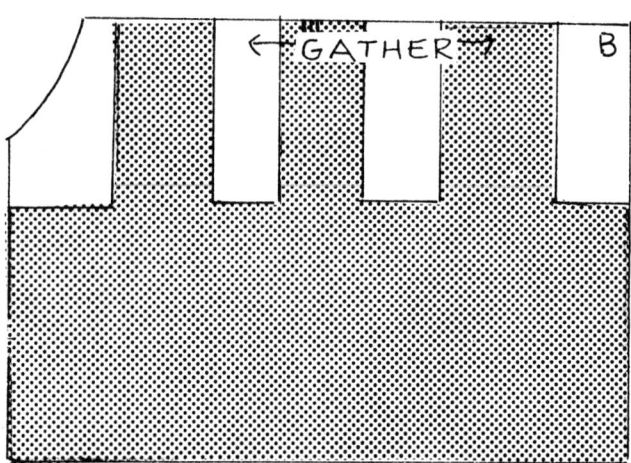

Fig. 17-3. Child's dress with smocking, Step 4.

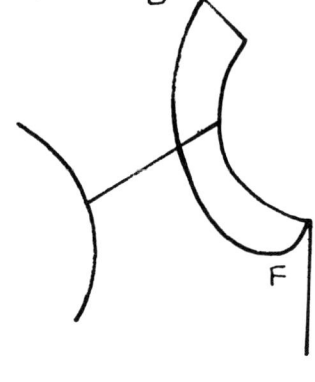

Fig. 17-5. Child's dress with smocking, Step 6.

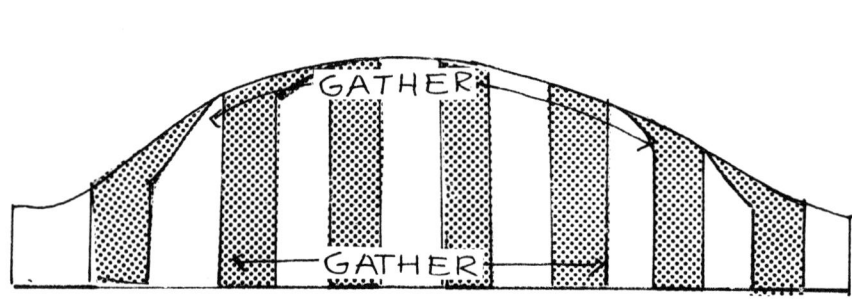

Fig. 17-4. Child's dress with smocking, step 5.

Fig. 17-6. Child's dress with smocking, Step 7.

Child's Pinafore with Front and Back Yokes

The pinafore is a very comfortable style for the young child. It allows freedom of movement since it hangs from the shoulder. The butterfly sleeve is comfortable to wear and adds a unique feature to the garment (see Fig. 17-7).

STEP 1: Trace slopers (bodice front and back).

STEP 2: Draw in new design lines; draw yoke location on bodice front and back; the yoke is usually narrower on the bodice back than in the bodice front (see Fig. 17-8).

STEP 3: Cross-notch; cut yoke away (see Fig. 17-8).

Fig. 17-7. Child's pinafore with front and back yoke.

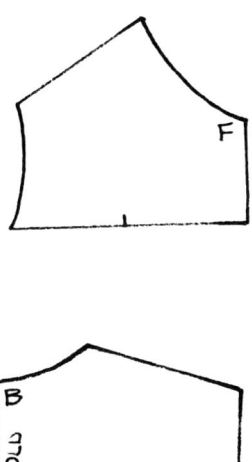

Fig. 17-8. Pinafore, Steps 1, 2, 3.

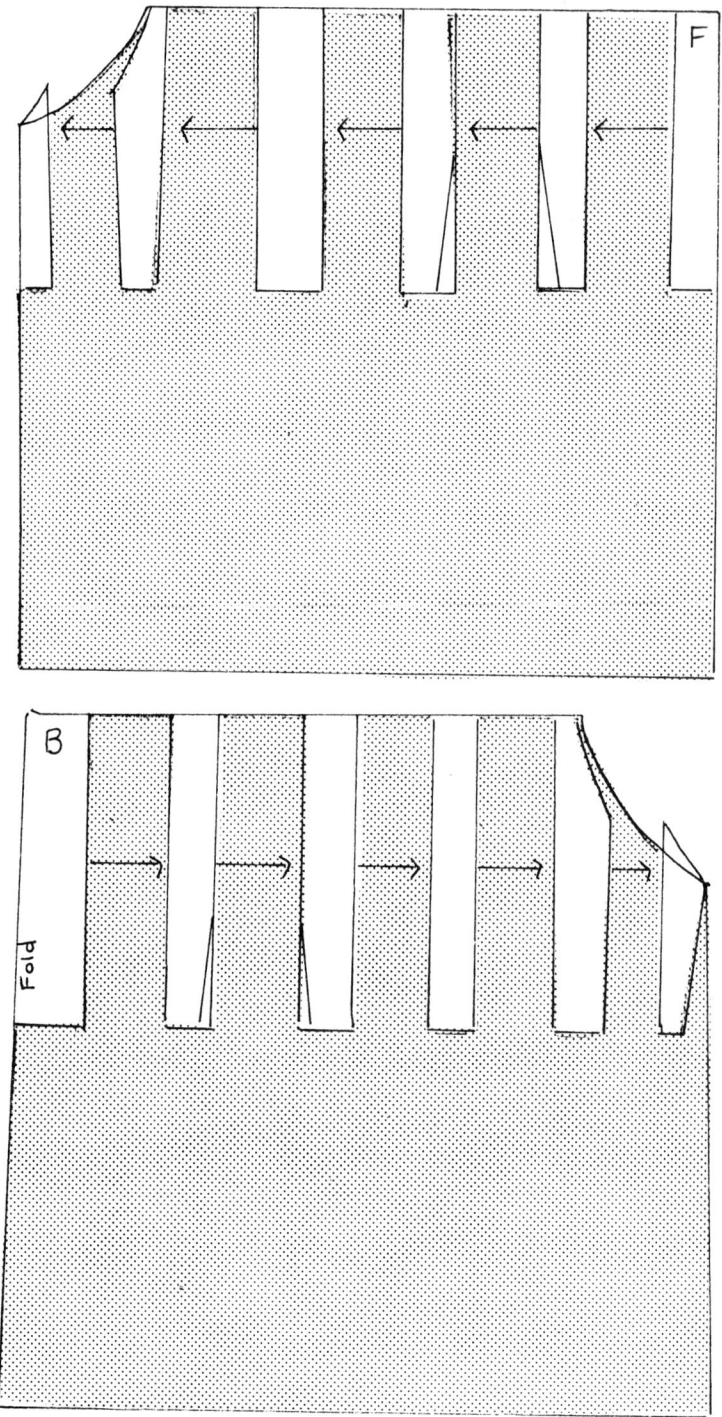

Fig. 17-9. Pinafore, Step 4.

245 CHILDREN'S GARMENTS

STEP 4: For skirt, measure lower edge of yoke on bodice front; mark twice to three times this distance on paper; draw lines through remaining section of bodice front from lower to upper edge. Cut through sections, and spread distance measured on paper; then straighten armhole.

Length of skirt is length of bodice plus skirt length taken from chart; square off a rectangle as shown.

Repeat process for back (see Fig. 17-9).

STEP 5: For front band, draw line length of front skirt section and front yoke section width desired (approximately 1½"); cross-notch; cut away. Double this piece to make the front band (see Fig. 17-10).

STEP 6: For butterfly sleeve, measure total armhole, front and back; double or triple this length; mark on paper with straight line; square a line on top and bottom, 3" wide; at center point of line draw a perpendicular line 5" wide; connect these lines to make pattern as shown.

The center line will be the fold line, and the two raw edges will be sewn into the armhole after being gathered or pleated (see Fig. 17-11).

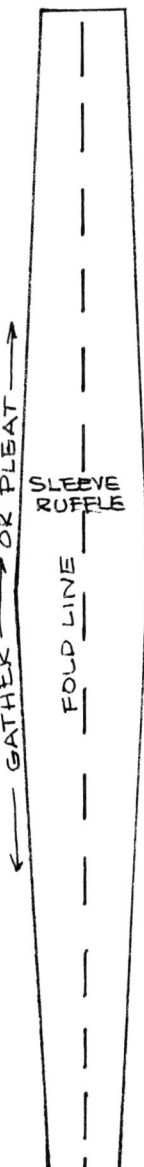

Fig. 17-11. Pinafore, Step 6.

Fig. 17-10. Pinafore, Step 5.

Child's Dress with Puffed Sleeve and Gathered Skirt

The illustration shows a traditional child's garment with Peter Pan collar, gathered skirt, and full puffed sleeve. The fullness in the skirt can vary according to the designer's wish. Two to three times the waist measurement is usually suitable. In very sheer or soft fabrics up to four times the waist measurement can be used, but it is not necessary for an attractive finished product.

The sleeve fullness is usually twice the original ungathered measurement. The sleeve can be any of the three puff styles—full puff, top puff, or bottom puff.

The embroidery shown in the illustration is at the waistline. This is a good location for both the child and the viewer. A tuck near the lower edge of the skirt can be both a growth feature and an attractive design detail (see Fig. 17-12).

STEP 1: Trace sloper (bodice front and back, sleeve).

STEP 2: For bodice, put shoulder seams together, trace collar following principles learned in section on collars (see Fig. 17-13).

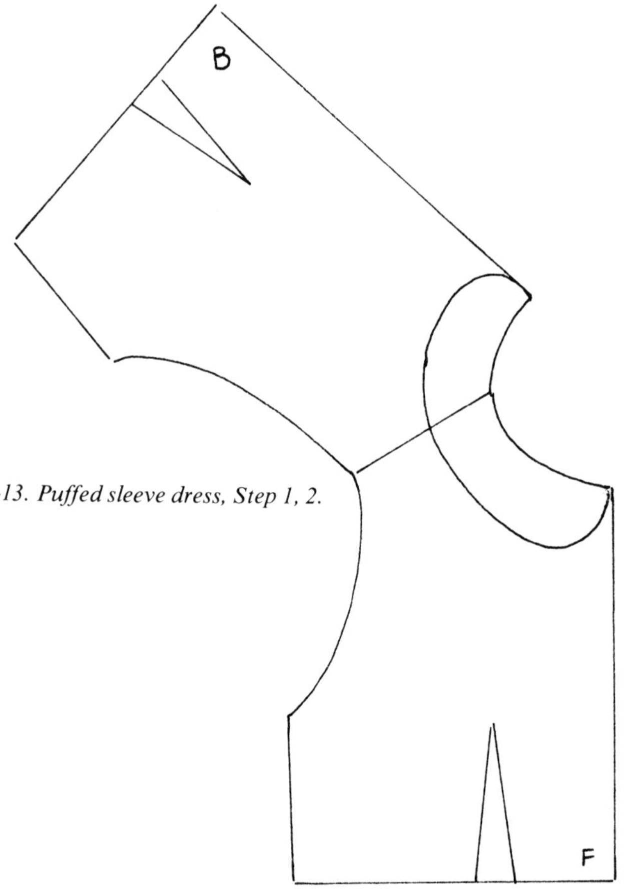

Fig. 17-13. Puffed sleeve dress, Step 1, 2.

Fig. 17-12. Child's dress with puffed sleeve and gathered skirt.

247 CHILDREN'S GARMENTS

STEP 3: For sleeve, draw lines from upper to lower edge across sleeve width; cut through; spread and add paper (see Fig. 17-14).

STEP 4: For skirt, from chart select proper length for child's skirt; add hem; measure waist seam of sloper; multiply by 2, 3, or 4, depending upon fullness desired; trace rectangle using length and width measurements just determined (see Fig. 17-15).

STEP 5: As drawn, dress will zip up center back.

If button closure is desired, draw button closure following principles learned in section on closures.

Fig. 17-14. Puffed sleeve dress, Step 3.

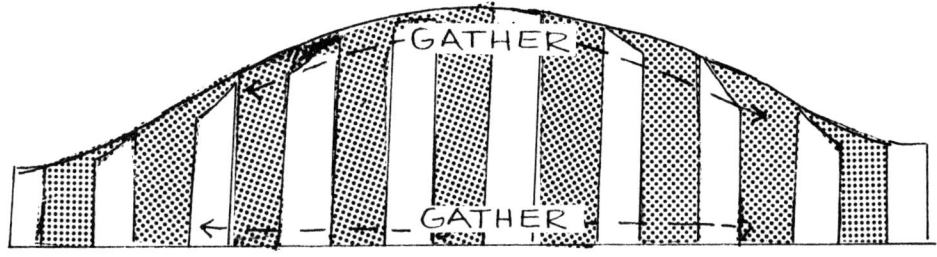

Fig. 17-15. Puffed sleeve dress, Step 4.

THE COMPLETE GUIDE TO PATTERN-MAKING 248

Child's Shirt or Blouse Without Shoulder Seams

This shirt or blouse without shoulder seams is a very comfortable style for the small child. It allows the child to put the garment on easily over the head and is nonrestrictive during active play (see Fig. 17-16).

STEP 1: Trace sloper (bodice front and back; sleeve).

STEP 2: Put sloper together at shoulder seam (see Fig. 17-17).

STEP 3: Draw in new design lines; measure half the distance of the armhole from the back shoulder then to the back side seam.

Repeat procedure on front armhole; then connect these two points with a circle that touches the neck edge at the shoulder (see Fig. 17-17).

Fig. 17-16. Skirt or blouse without shoulder seam.

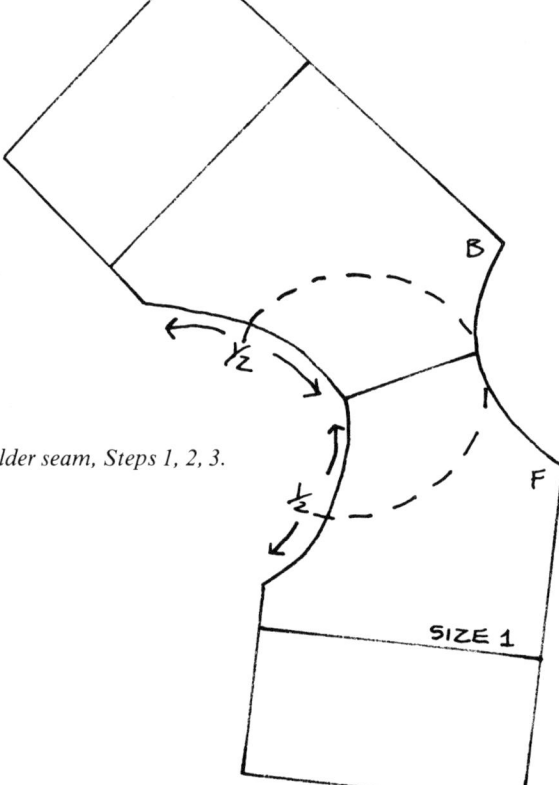

Fig. 17-17. Shirt or blouse without shoulder seam, Steps 1, 2, 3.

STEP 4: Trace front and back, adding circular area and omitting the shoulder seam as shown (see Fig. 17-18).

STEP 5: For sleeve, lower cap by ¼" (see Fig. 17-19).

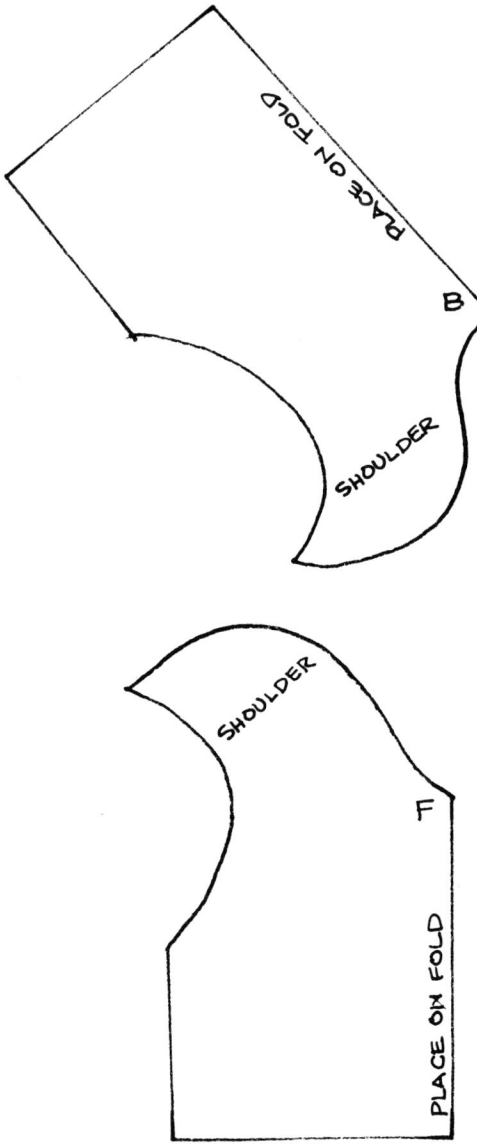

Fig. 17-18. Shirt or blouse without shoulder seam, Step 4.

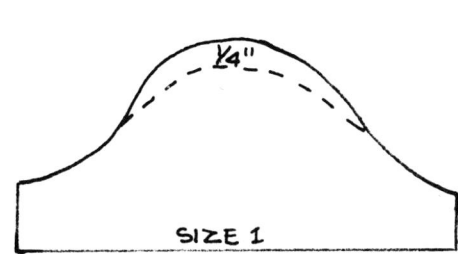

Fig. 17-19. Shirt or blouse without shoulder seam, Step 5.

THE COMPLETE GUIDE TO PATTERN-MAKING 250

Child's Trapeze Dress

This trapeze, or tent, dress flares out from the shoulder, which makes it comfortable for the young, active child. The neck has been lowered so that the completed design will need no closures. With a raised neck line, a zipper can be put in the center back (see fig. 17-20).

STEP 1: Trace sloper (bodice front and back).

STEP 2: Lower neckline on bodice front and back (see Fig. 17-21).

STEP 3: Draw lines from lower edge to neck and armhole edge as illustrated; be sure one line passes through the center of the waistline darts (see Fig. 17-21).

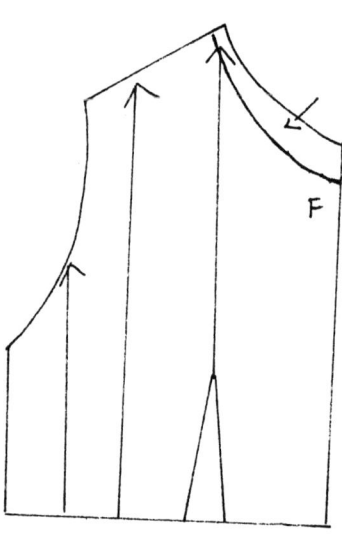
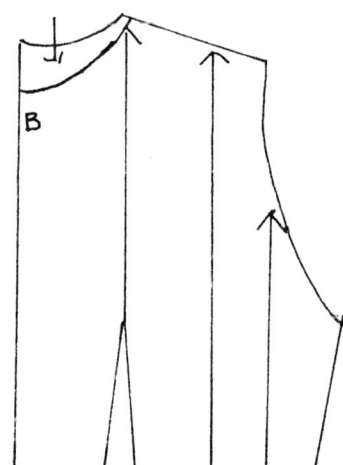

Fig. 17-21. Child's trapeze dress, Steps 1, 2, 3.

Fig. 17-20. Child's trapeze dress.

251 CHILDREN'S GARMENTS

STEP 4: Cut from lower edge to upper edge, do not cut through upper edges of pattern (see Fig. 17-22).

STEP 5: Spead and add paper to amount of flare desired; flare the front and back the same amount so that the grain of the side seam is the same on both pieces (see Fig. 17-22).

STEP 6: Smooth lower edge with the aid of a curve stick (see Fig. 17-22).

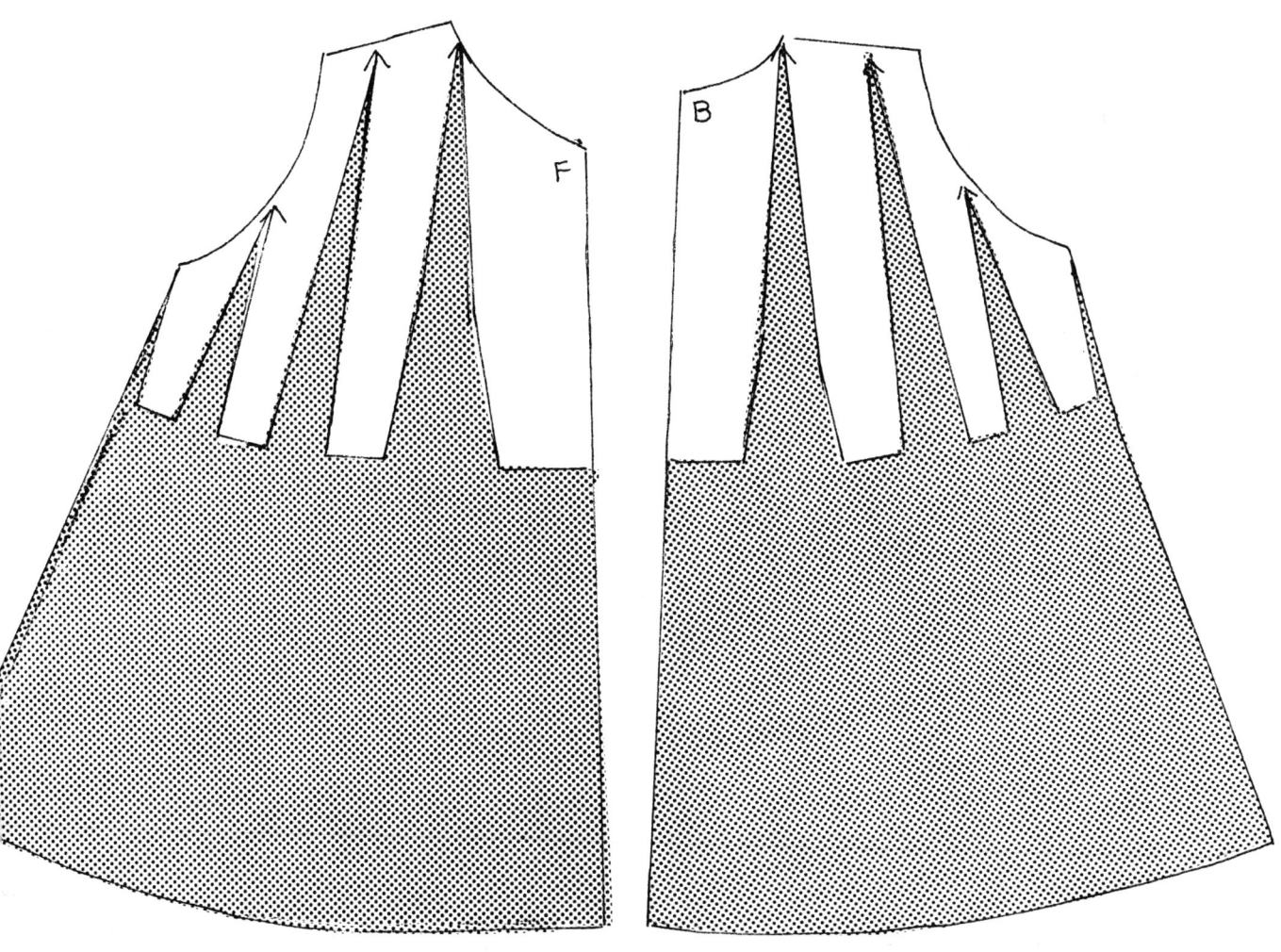

Fig. 17-22. Child's trapeze dress, Steps 4, 5, 6.

Child's Traditional Shirt

This is a traditional shirt, suitable for boys or as a girl's tailored cowgirl shirt (see Fig. 17-23).

Fig. 17-23. Child's traditional shirt.

STEP 1: Trace sloper (bodice front and back) (see Figs. 17-24, 17-25).

STEP 2: Draw in new design lines; for bodice back, cut yoke across bodice back, cross-notch, and separate.

Draw line from lower edge of bodice back to upper edge, to make tuck; separate and add paper.

Straighten side seam and lengthen so that shirt will extend to hip area; square across to center back (see Fig. 18-25).

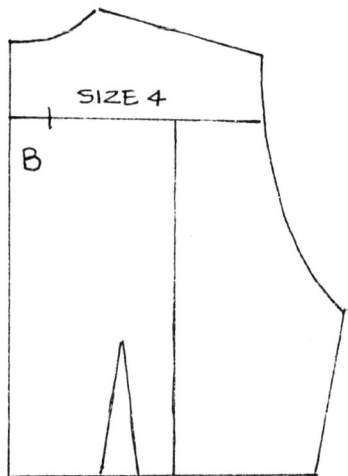

Fig. 17-24. Child's traditional shirt, front, Step 1.

STEP 3: Draw in new design lines; for bodice front, square down sides and lengthen bodice front the same amount as bodice back.

Add button extension (see Fig. 17-26).

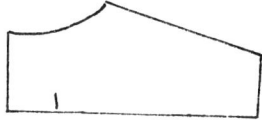

Fig. 17-25. Child's traditional shirt, back, Steps 1, 2.

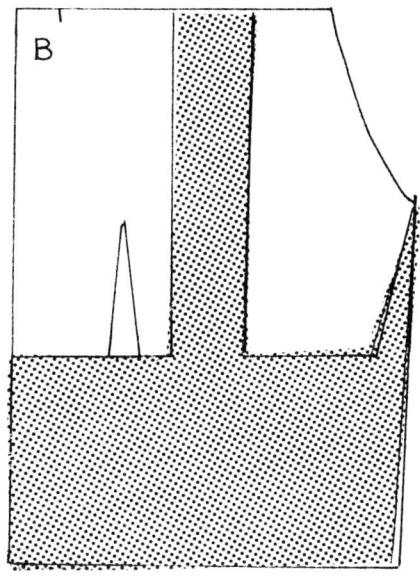

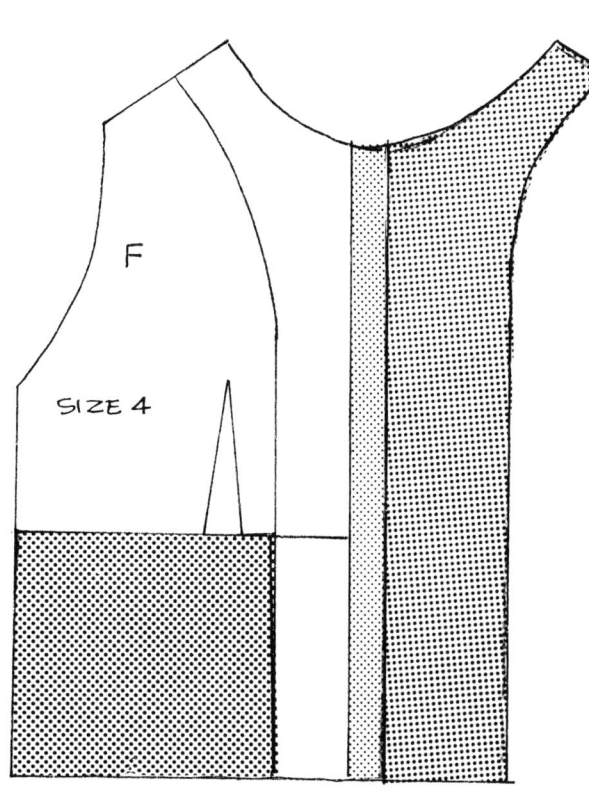

Fig. 17-26 Child's traditional shirt, front, Step 3.

THE COMPLETE GUIDE TO PATTERN-MAKING 254

Develop front facing following porcedures used on women's garments. (see Fig. 17-27).

STEP 4: Make collar with high stand or intermediate amount of stand, following procedures learned in section on collars (see Fig. 17-28).

STEP 5: Lengthen sleeve to give short sleeve with cuff. A long sleeve can also be used for the shirt (see Fig. 17-29).

STEP 6: Draw pocket for bodice front (see Fig. 17-30).

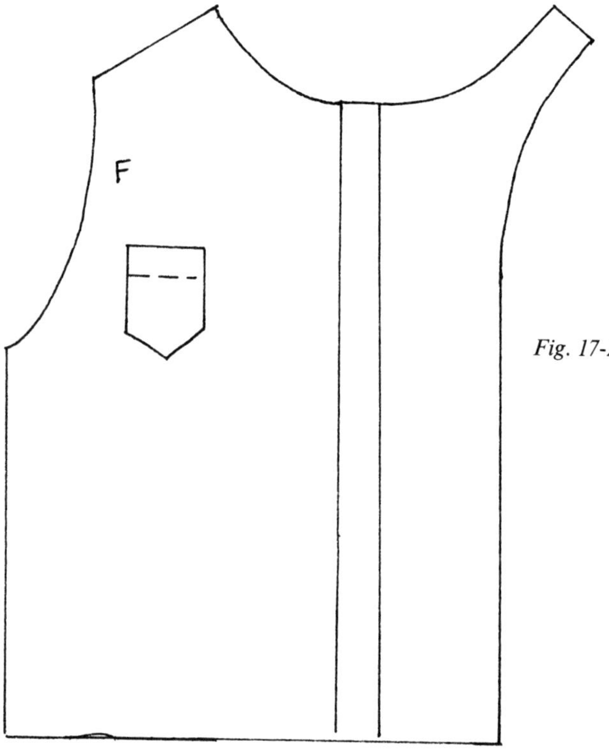

Fig. 17-27. Child's traditional shirt, front completed, Step 3.

Fig. 17-28. Child's traditional shirt, Step 4.

Fig. 17-29. Child's traditional shirt, Step 5.

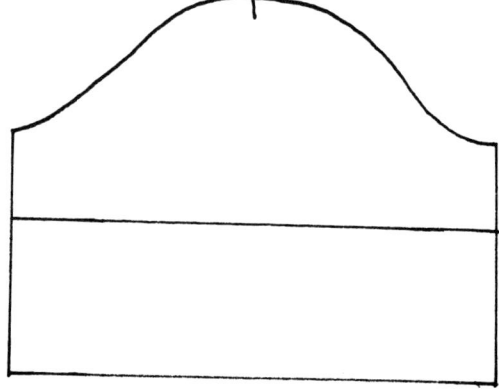

Fig. 17-30. Child's traditional shirt, Step 6.

255 CHILDREN'S GARMENTS

Child's Apron with Flare from Shoulder

This apron cover-up is a most practical garment for the young child, especially when made from either a disposable paper material or from a soft oilcloth or vinyl (see Fig. 17-31).

Fig. 17-31. Child's apron with flare from shoulder.

STEP 1: Trace sloper (bodice front and back).

STEP 2: Put shoulder seams together (see Fig. 17-32).

STEP 3: Lower neckline (see Fig. 17-32).

STEP 4: Flare sides by cutting from lower edge to side seam; flare front and back the same amount (see Fig. 17-32).

STEP 5: Add length appropriate to size; measurements can be taken from chart at beginning of section (see Fig. 17-32).

STEP 6: Connect the armhole halfway from the shoulder on both front and back as shown by straight line; cut out remaining half of armhole as shown by dotted lines to allow for ease. (The apron will go over another garment and thus the extra ease is desirable.)

STEP 7: Trace the pocket on front; as shown by dotted line (see Figs. 17-32, 17-33).

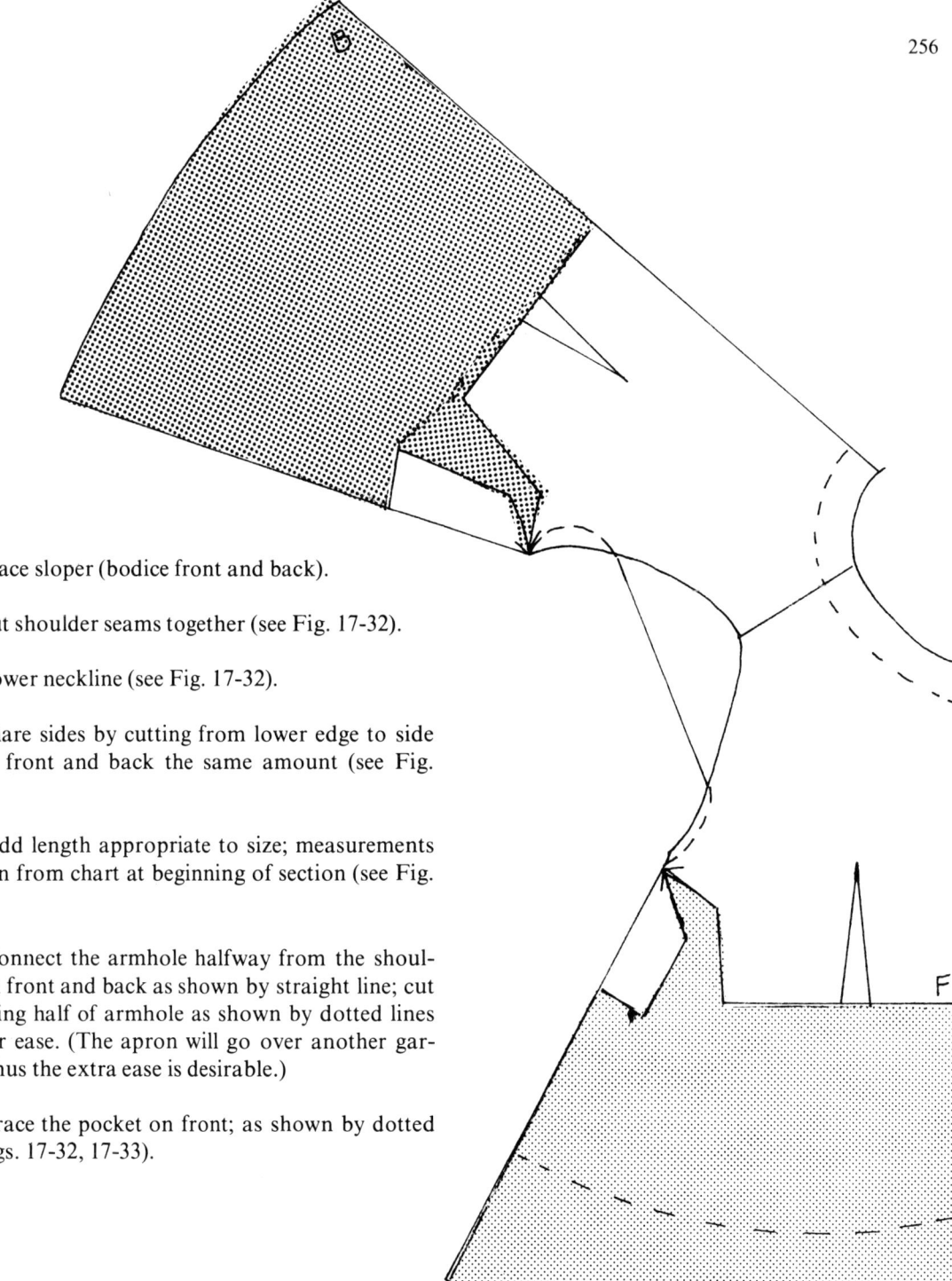

Fig. 17-32. Child's apron, Steps 1, 2, 3, 4, 5, 6, 7.

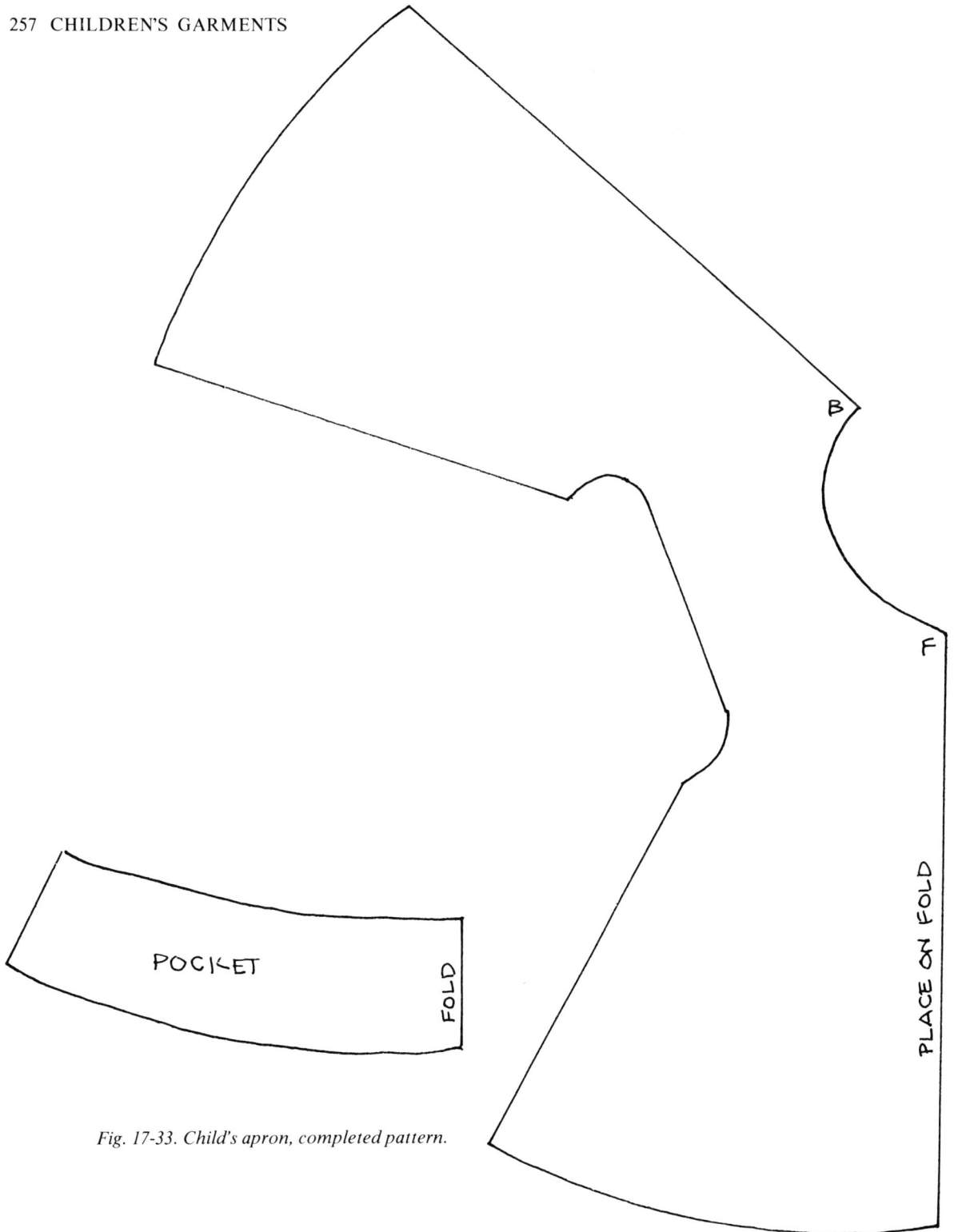

Fig. 17-33. Child's apron, completed pattern.

Child's Coat

The child's coat should have enough flare to make it comfortable to wear over other clothing. Ease must first be added and then the sloper altered for the desired coat design (see Fig. 17-34).

STEP 1: Trace sloper (bodice front and back; sleeve).

STEP 2: Increase sloper size as following manner (see Fig. 17-35):

Add ½" to center front, ¼" to side seams, ⅛" to shoulder width.

Lower ¼" armhole, ¼" neck in front.

STEP 3: Flare coat sides; cut from lower edge to side seam and flare; flare front and back side seams the same amount (see Fig. 17-35).

STEP 4: Add pleat extension in coat back; add 1½" in width, and 6" in length as shown (see Fig. 17-35).

STEP 5: Add 2" extension to center front for button closure; put buttons and buttonholes where desired (see Fig. 17-35).

Fig. 17-34. Child's coat.

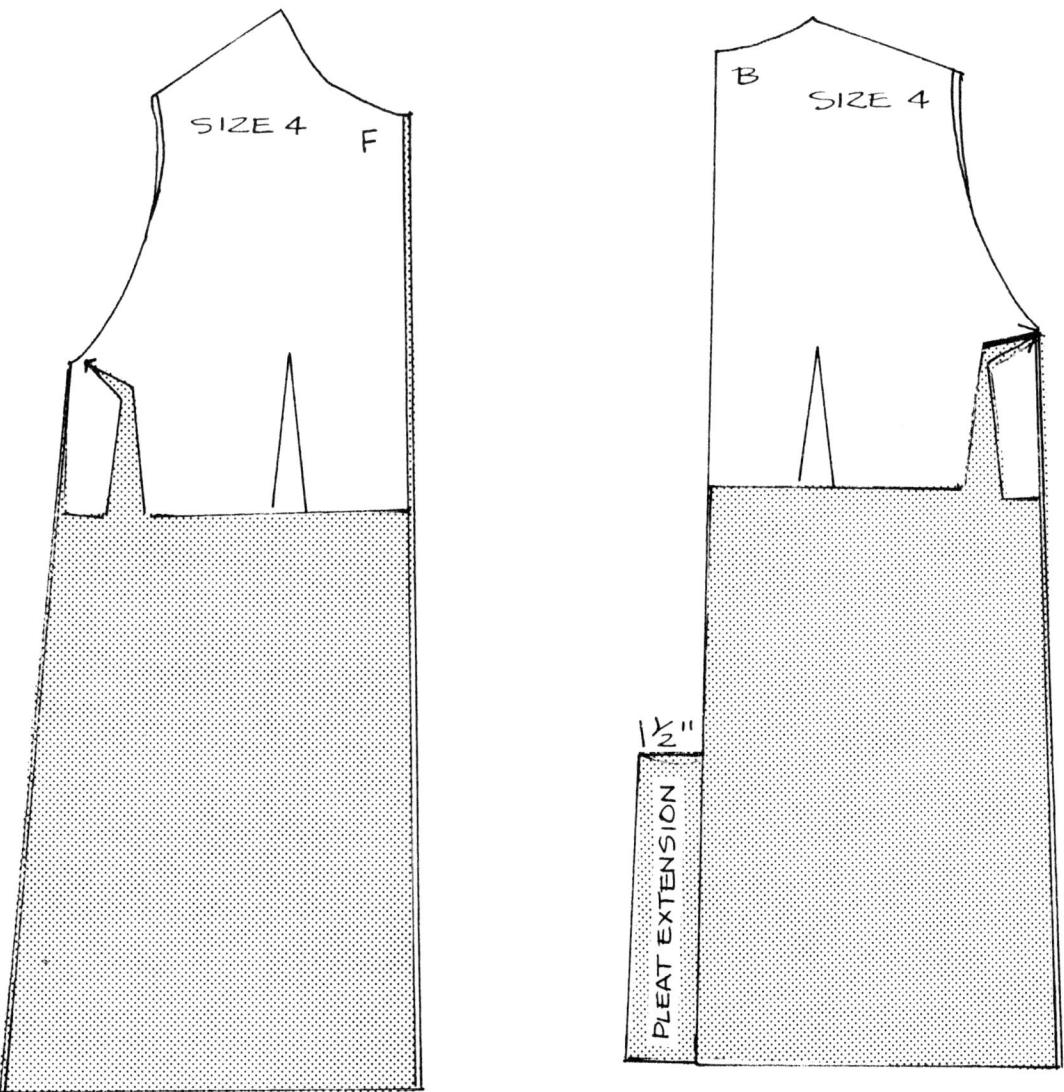

Fig. 17-35. Child's coat, Steps 1, 2, 3, 4, 5.

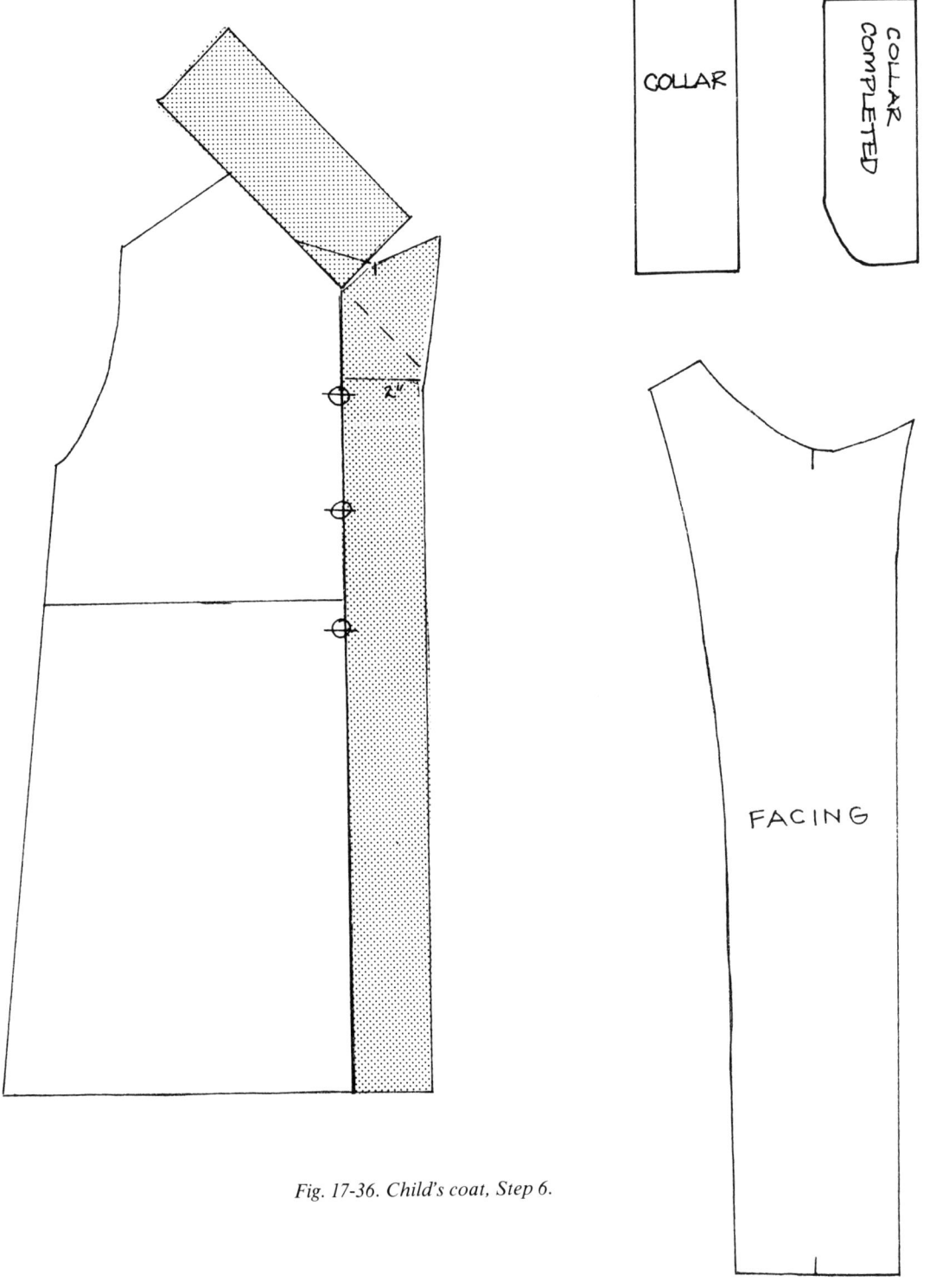

Fig. 17-36. Child's coat, Step 6.

261 CHILDREN'S GARMENTS

STEP 6: Develop shawl collar; follow procedures learned in section on collars; completed collar sections and facing patterns are shown (see Fig. 17-36).

STEP 7: Develop either a one-piece or two-piece sleeve following procedures previously presented (see Fig. 17-37).

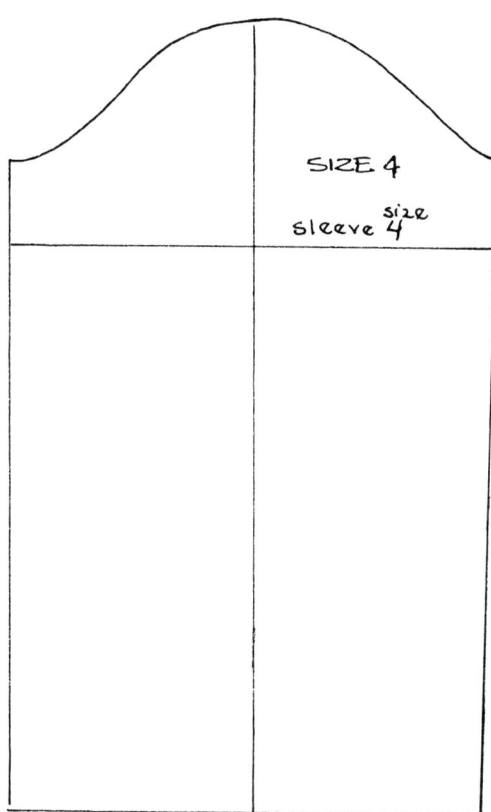

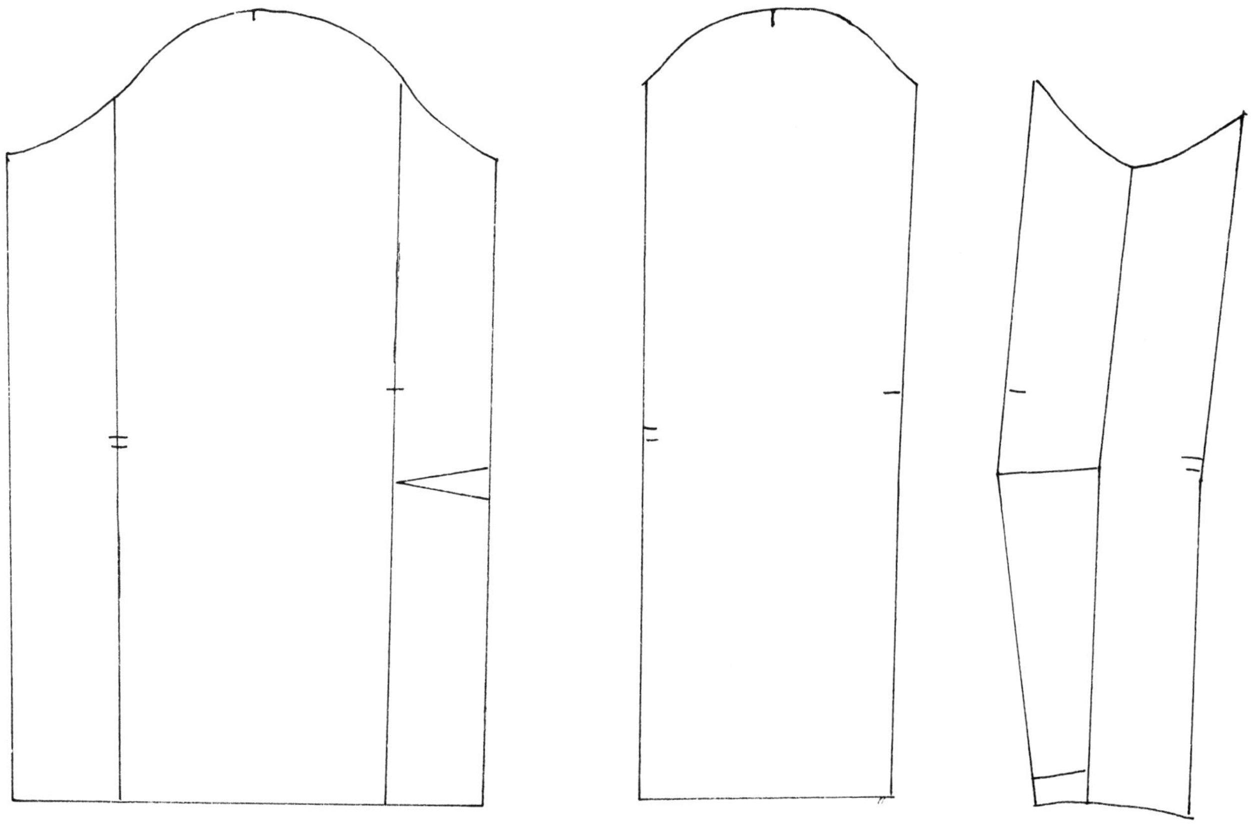

Fig. 17-37. Child's coat, Step 7.

2 PIECE SLEEVE

Child's Trousers

The variations developed for women's trousers can likewise be made for children's trousers. This chart shows the relationship of common trouser lengths. Slopers for various children's sizes follow on the graph paper (see Fig. 17-38).

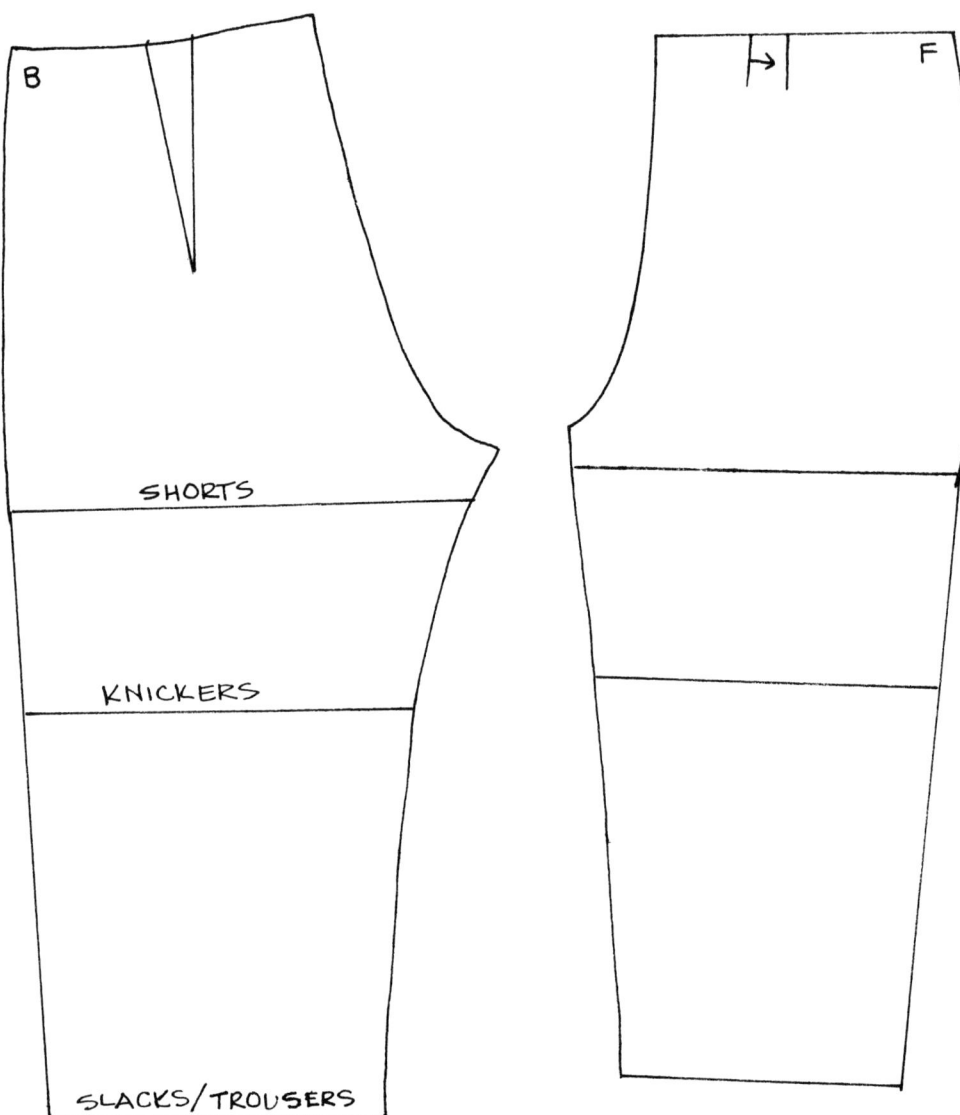

Fig. 17-38. Child's trouser length chart.

APPENDIX I

WOMEN'S SLOPERS QUARTER-SCALE

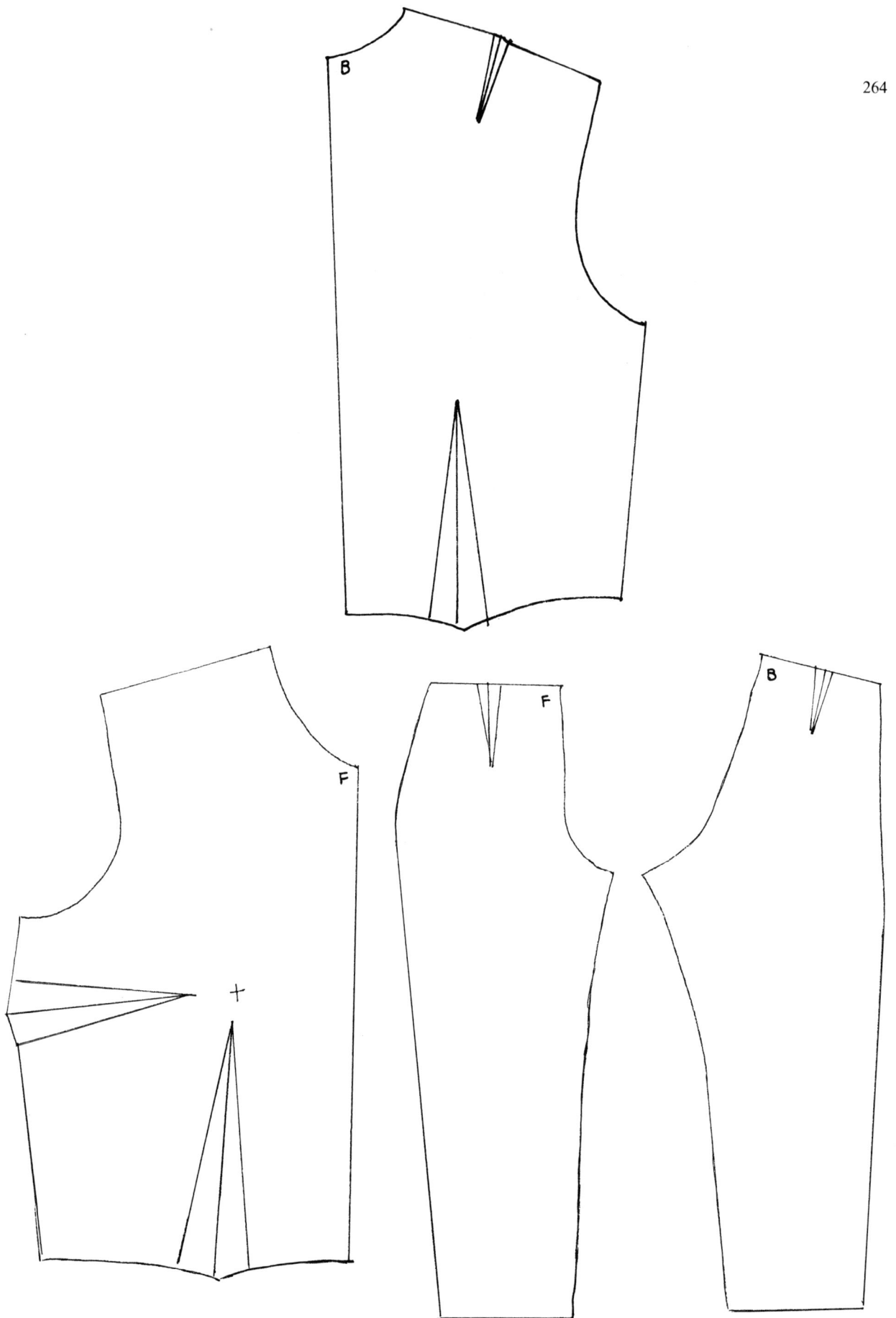

265 WOMEN'S SLOPERS—QUARTER-SCALE

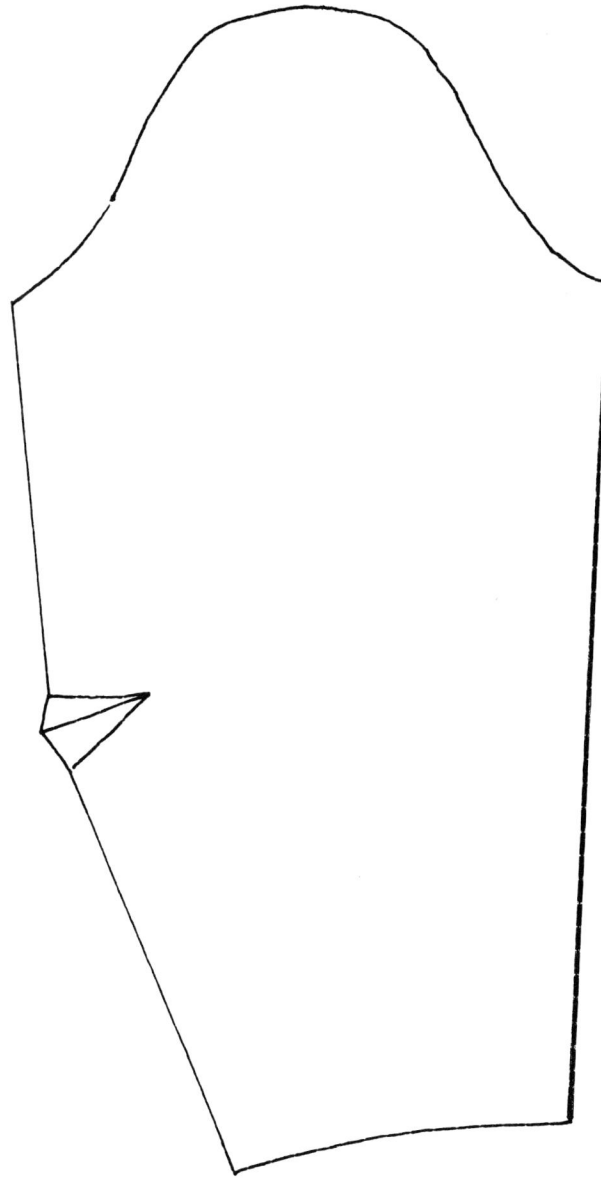

APPENDIX **II**

WOMEN'S SLOPERS HALF-SCALE

268

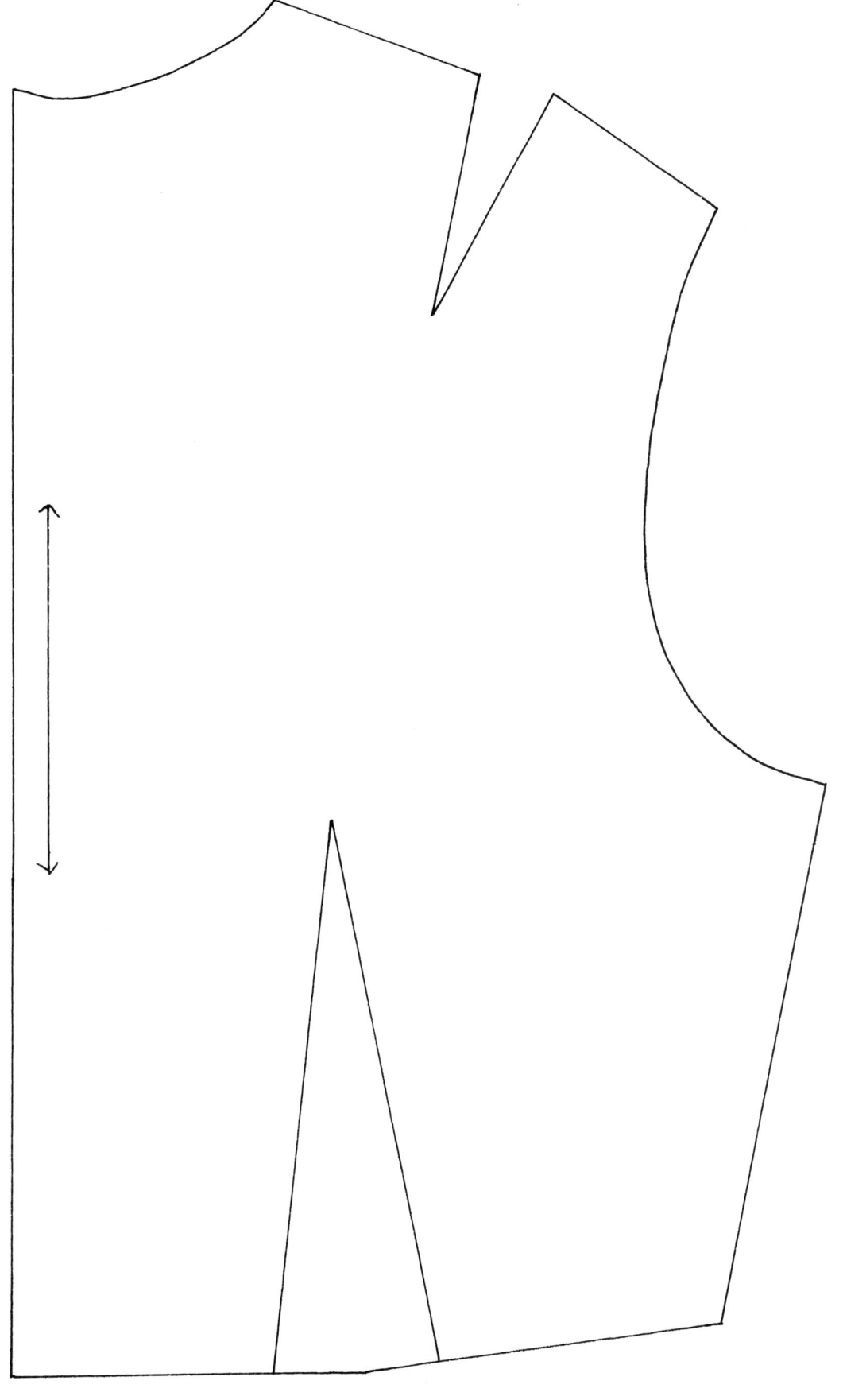

B

271

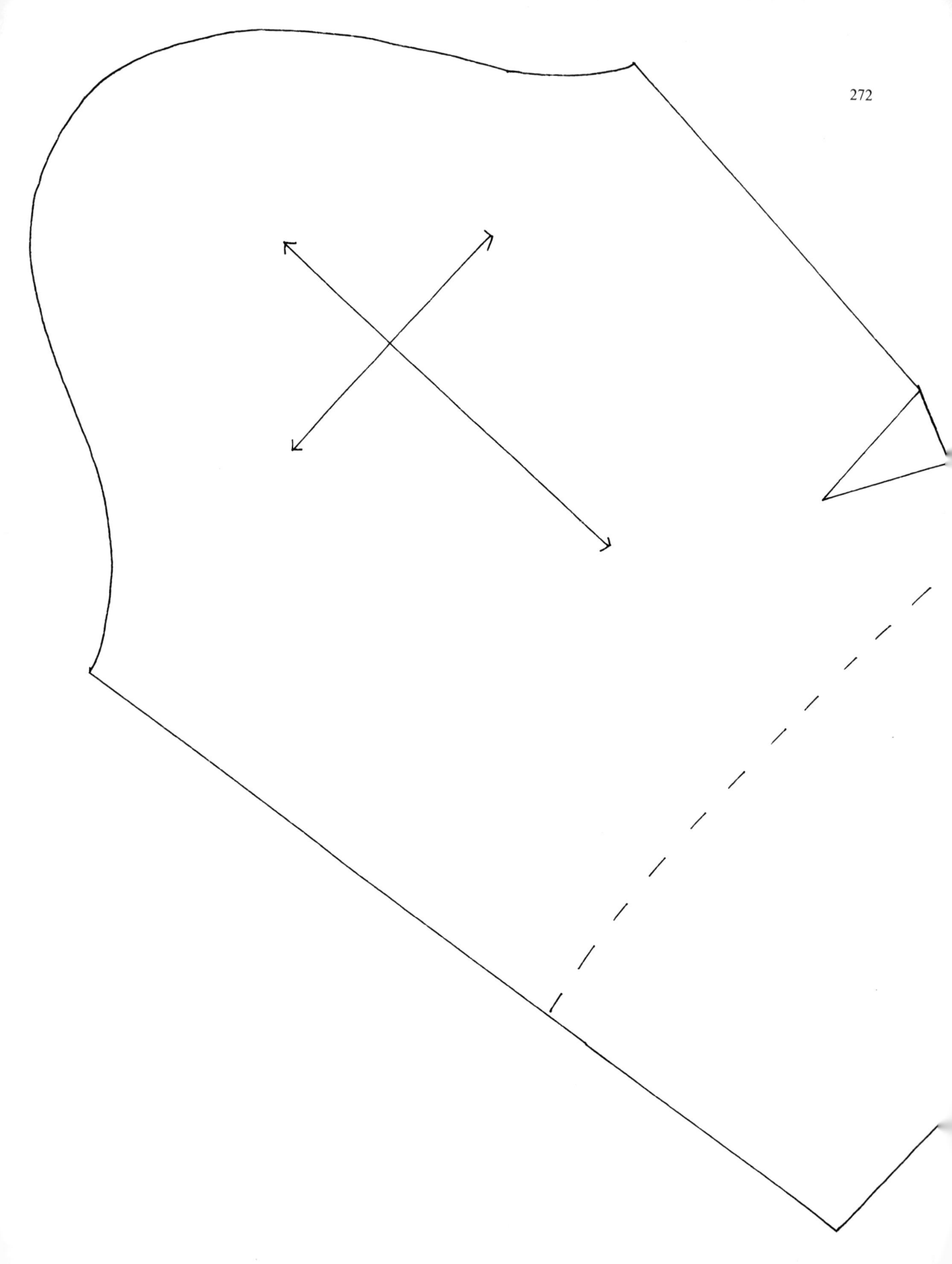

APPENDIX **III**

CHILDREN'S SLOPERS FULL-SCALE

Bodice Front
Bodice Back
Sleeve

Key

— ·· — ·· — Size 1

· · · · · · · · · Size 2

— — — — — Size 3

— · — · — · Size 4

— — — — Size 5

—————— Size 6

THE COMPLETE GUIDE TO PATTERN-MAKING 274

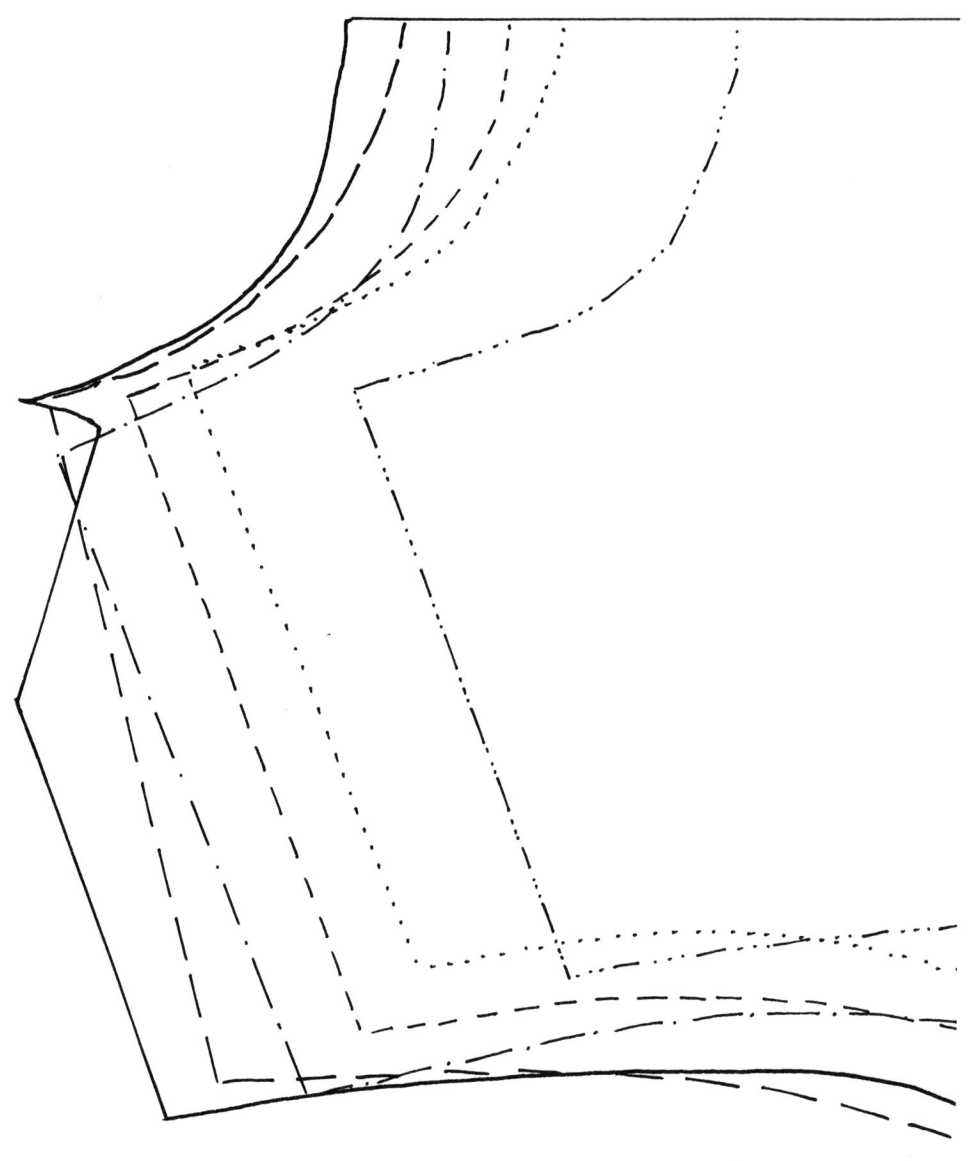

275 CHILDREN'S SLOPERS—FULL-SCALE

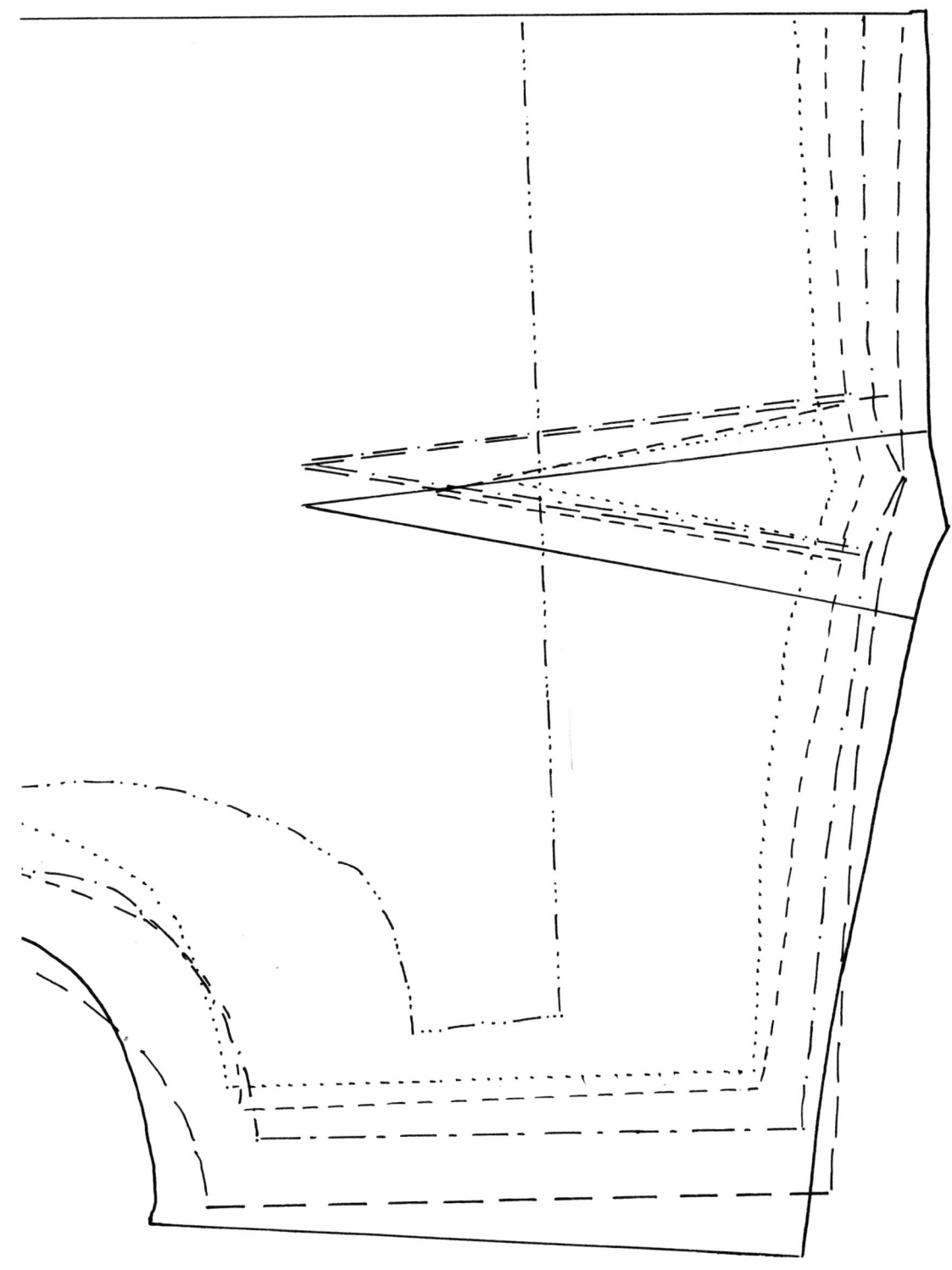

THE COMPLETE GUIDE TO PATTERN-MAKING 276

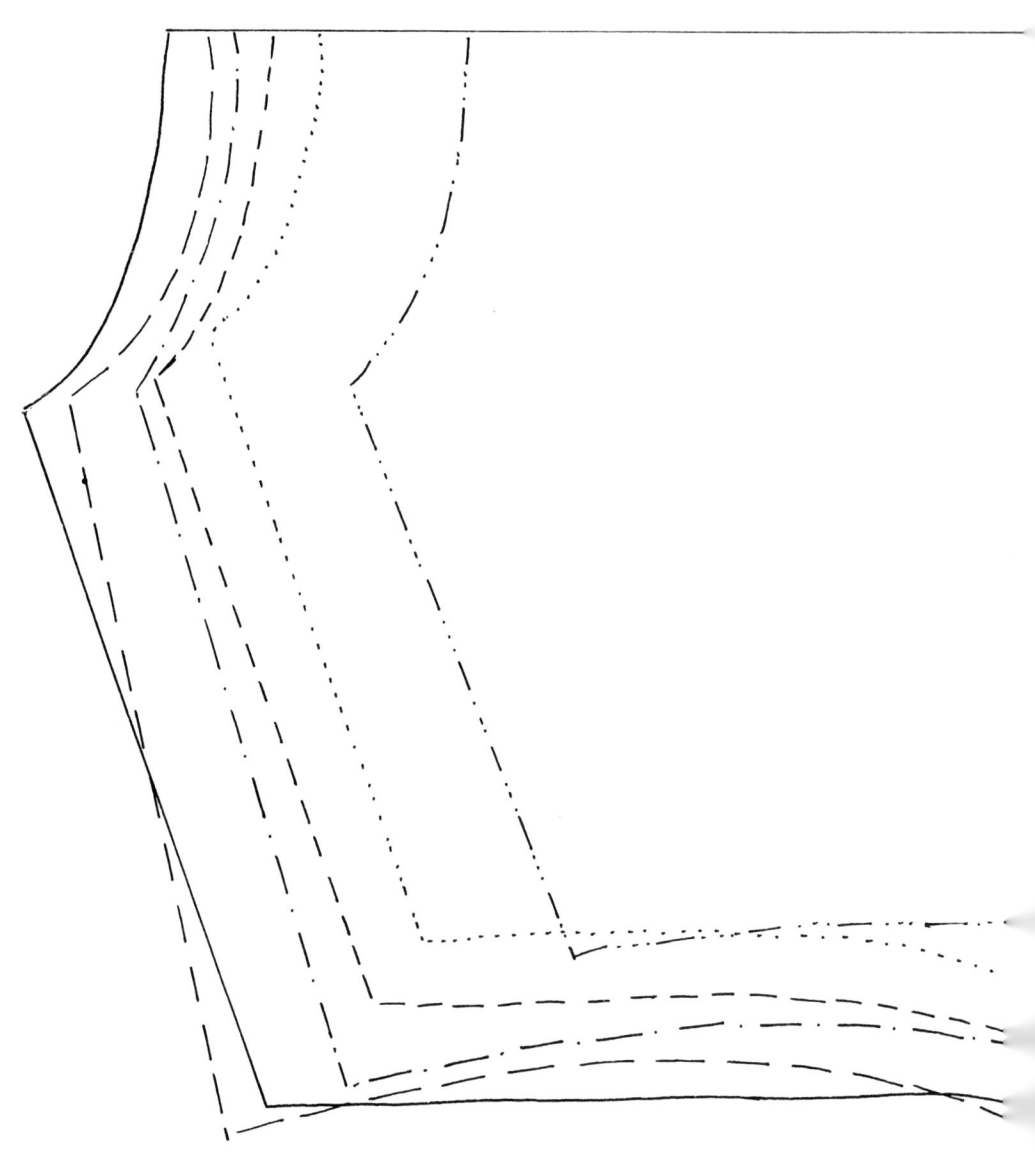

277 CHILDREN'S SLOPERS—FULL-SCALE

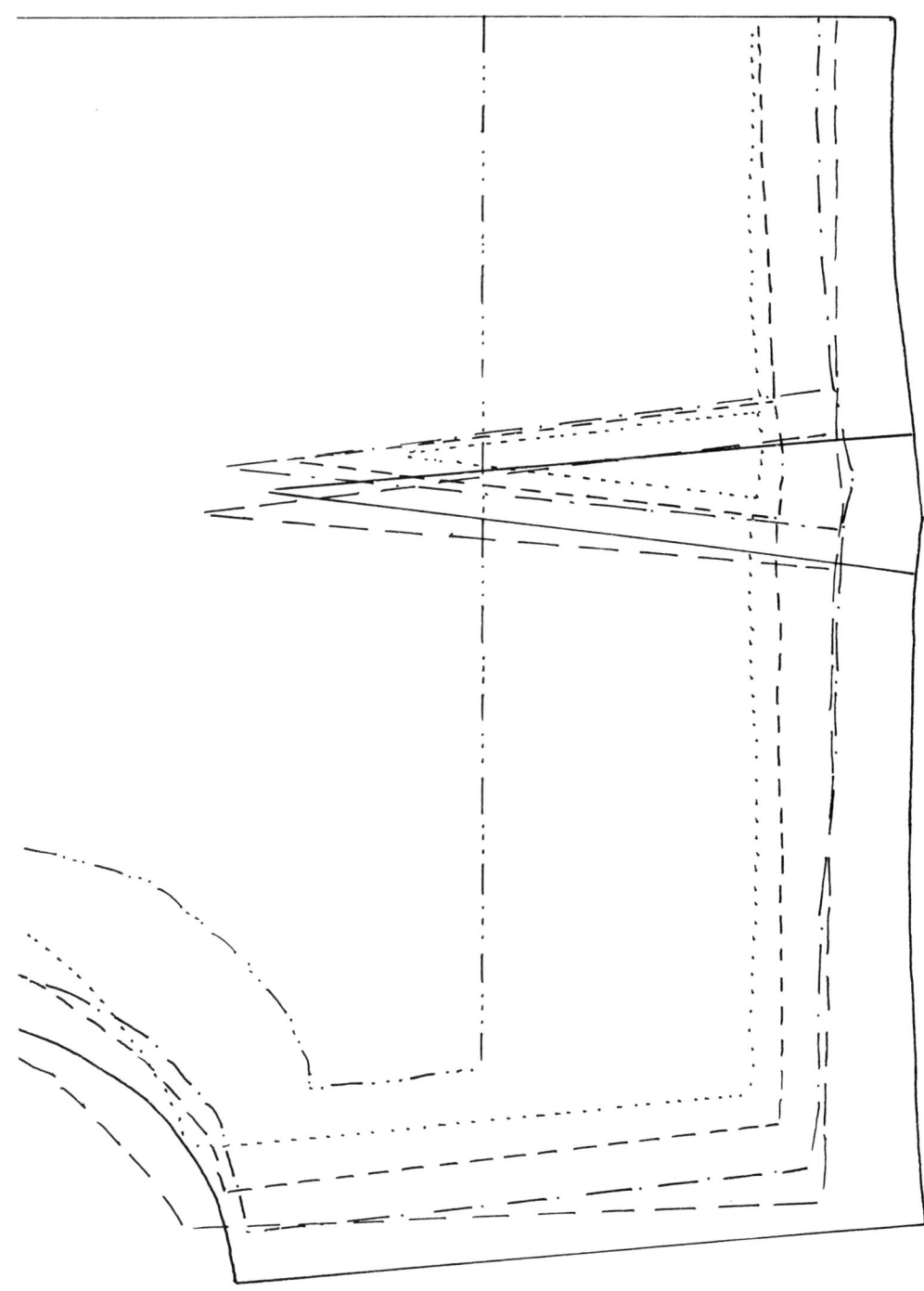

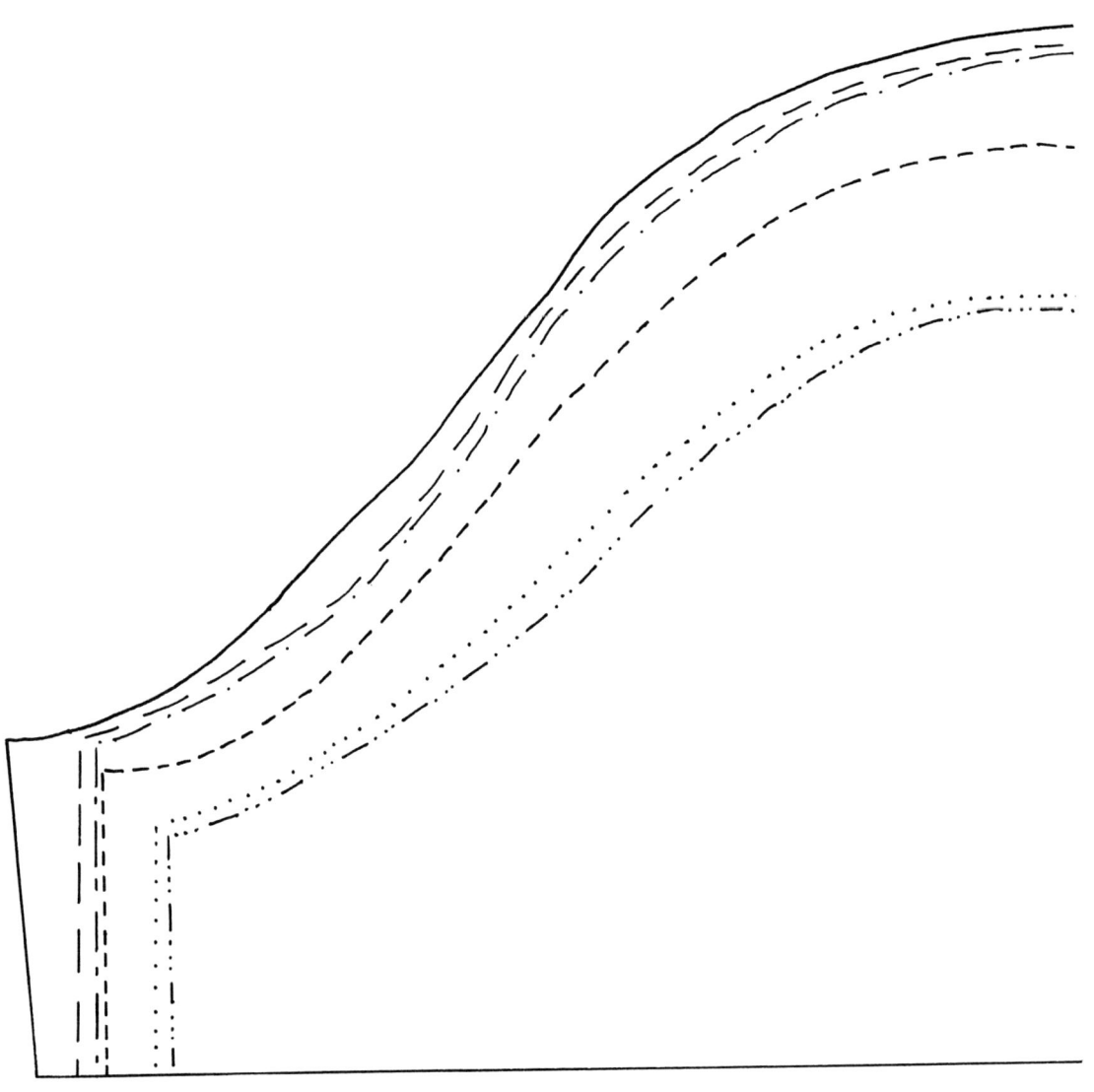

279 CHILDREN'S SLOPERS—FULL-SCALE

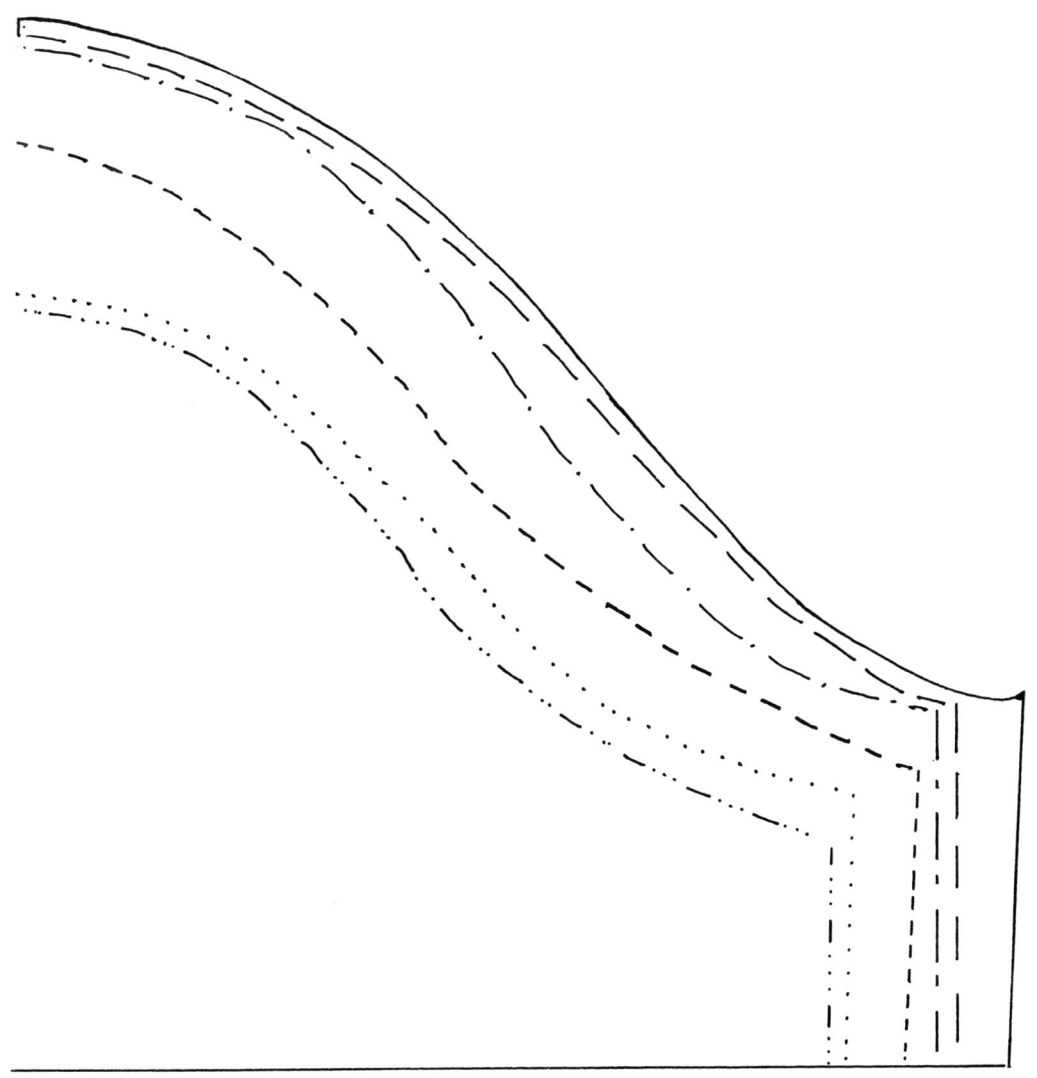